This effort is dedicated to The One:
the Giver of energy, passion, and understanding;
Who makes life worth living and endeavors worth pursuing
and accomplishing;
the Teacher of love and forgiveness.

PREFACE

The preparation of professional school counselors has become increasingly more specialized over the past decade, stemming primarily from systemic changes in the nature of what professional school counselors do. These changes were brought about by several professional and societal changes, including school reform movements and the American School Counselor Association's National Standards and National Model. In addition, professional school counselors now make up close to one-half of the counselors graduating from master's-level training programs, and group work in schools is very different from group work in clinics. School students are often referred by teachers, parents, and administrators for group counseling; professional school counselors are frequently in the classroom conducting large-group guidance and psychoeducational group work on topics of importance to the entire class or grade; professional school counselors are members of important school committees that must function efficiently to serve the needs of all students.

Interestingly, professional school counselors are often the only employees in the school with any formalized training in group work, but ordinarily that training is a generic course in how to run counseling or psychotherapy groups. Few professional school counselors have received any formal instruction on how to run task groups or psychoeducational groups or even how to conduct group counseling within the specialized school context. *Group Work in the Schools* is specifically designed to address this burgeoning and increasingly specialized population of school counselors-in-training with a text suited to their individualized needs. School counselors-in-training need a book that addresses how to run all types of groups in schools.

Using a systemic perspective, *Group Work in the Schools* focuses on the specialized group work that professional school counselors perform in a multicultural context. A number of group counseling and psychotherapy texts focus on conducting counseling or psychotherapy with small groups of clients, usually adults. Professional school counselors rarely conduct psychotherapy groups in schools and conduct counseling groups less frequently today than a decade ago due to the changing needs of students and the changing role of the counselor as a systems change specialist. Today, professional school counselors are more likely to run psychoeducational groups and task groups to address the developmental needs of students and systems.

Just as importantly, professional school counselors still frequently run small groups with a counseling focus, but the counselors running these groups have a marked tendency to use an integrated counseling approach, rather than a specific theoretical orientation, such as a humanistic, rational emotive behavior therapy (REBT), Adlerian, or Gestalt approach. Many group psychotherapy texts make these theoretical approaches the core of the student learning experience, an approach that does not prepare school counseling trainees for the reality of group work in the schools. *Group Work in the Schools* briefly covers these traditional theoretical approaches, but the core of the text involves the systemic approach to group work—that is, preparing school counseling students to facilitate the systemic group process in the school context, from planning the group through the four stages of group work: forming and orienting, transition, working, and termination. Mastering the facilitation of these stages of group work allows professional school counselors to effectively work with students in all types of school-based group contexts.

GROUP WORK IN THE SCHOOLS

Bradley T. Erford
Loyola University Maryland

Boston   Columbus   Indianapolis   New York   San Francisco   Upper Saddle River
Amsterdam   Cape Town   Dubai   London   Madrid   Milan   Munich   Paris   Montreal   Toronto
Delhi   Mexico City   Sao Paulo   Sydney   Hong Kong   Seoul   Singapore   Taipei   Tokyo

Vice President and Executive Publisher: Jeffery W. Johnston
Acquisitions Editor: Meredith D. Fossel
Editorial Assistant: Nancy Holstein
Director of Marketing: Quinn Perkson
Marketing Manager: Amanda L. Stedke
Operations Specialist: Renata Butera
Cover Design: Diane C. Lorenzo
Creative Art Director: Jayne Conte
Cover Art: © Ferrell McCollough / SuperStock
Full-Service Project Management: Suganya Karuppasamy
Composition: GGS Higher Education Resources, PMG
Printer/Binder: R.R. Donnelley/Harrisonburg
Cover Printer: R.R. Donnelley/Harrisonburg
Text Font: 10/12 Garamond

10 9 8 7 6 5 4 3 2 1

Library of Congress Cataloging-in-Publication Data

Group work in the schools/edited by Bradley T. Erford.
   p. cm.
Includes bibliographical references and index.
ISBN-13: 978-0-13-503482-8 (alk. paper)
ISBN-10: 0-13-503482-5 (alk. paper)
1. School psychology. 2. Group counseling. I. Erford, Bradley T.

LB1027.55.G76 2010
371.4'6—dc22

2009004886

www.pearsonhighered.com

ISBN 13: 978-0-13-503482-8
ISBN 10:   0-13-503482-5

As such, *Group Work in the Schools* is the first textbook of its kind to focus totally on the group work needs of children and adolescents within the school context. The content of *Group Work in the Schools* is precisely aligned with the 2009 standards of the Council for Accreditation of Counseling and Related Educational Programs (CACREP) because CACREP defines the standard of quality in the counselor preparation field. Thus, this text helps CACREP-accredited programs meet the CACREP standards, and helps non-CACREP programs provide counselors-in-training with instruction that meets the most current, highest-level professional standards.

The text is structured in three sections: Section One: Foundations of Group Work; Section Two: Systemic Group Work; and Section Three: Group Work in Action. Importantly, students will appreciate the integration throughout the book of numerous specific group work techniques, including drawing out, giving feedback, I-statements, pairing, paradox, reframing, self-disclosure, active listening, blocking, clarifying, confrontation, empathy, evaluating skills, initiating skills, instructing skills, linking, modeling, questioning, summarizing, using enthusiasm, holding the focus, shifting focus, cutting off, journal writing, rounds, dyads, sentence completion, scaling, values contract, journaling, reunions, scrapbooks, comfort zone, and personal growth charts—among others.

Section One: Foundations of Group Work (Chapters 1–5) provides counseling students with a basic knowledge of group work. In Chapter 1: The Value of Group Work: Functional Group Models and Historical Perspectives by Julia A. Southern, Bradley T. Erford, Ann Vernon, and Darcie Davis-Gage, students explore the historical forces that shaped group work in schools today, the therapeutic factors that underlie effective group approaches, and the advantages and disadvantages of group work in the schools. This initial chapter leads readers to appreciate the value of group work approaches. To understand group work models, leaders need to consider model characteristics, subtypes, stages, and the classic role and function of the leader. To accomplish this objective, Chapter 1 presents an overview of the four main types of functional group models categorized by the Association for Specialists in Group Work (ASGW): task groups, psychoeducational groups, counseling groups and psychotherapy groups.

In Chapter 2: Ethical and Legal Foundations of Group Work in the Schools by Lynn E. Linde, Bradley T. Erford, Danica G. Hays, and F. Robert Wilson, readers encounter the essential ethical and legal issues related to group work in the schools. These include confidentiality, informed consent, relationships among group members, termination issues, group participation, diversity issues, and the Family Educational Rights and Privacy Act.

In Chapter 3: Multicultural Issues in Group Work by Cheryl Holcomb-McCoy and Cheryl Moore-Thomas, students will build a foundation of multicultural group work attitudes, knowledge, and skills. Chapter 3 addresses group work with diverse students, using oppression and marginalization as the frameworks from which group leaders can conceptualize group members' problems, behaviors, and actions. Because research indicates that people from oppressed backgrounds (e.g., ethnic minorities, persons with disabilities, the materially poor, gay and lesbian persons) are more likely to avoid counseling experiences, to drop out prematurely from counseling, and to report less beneficial outcomes, it is important that group leaders become more responsive to members' experiences of discrimination, prejudice, and inequities. Leaders can and should act to prevent or address these issues in the group. Also, because oppressed and marginalized students are accustomed to being silenced, being made to feel inferior, and "having no voice," leaders must be skilled in working with students who are quiet, suspicious, pessimistic, cynical, and even angry. The authors also address how issues of oppression and marginalization may influence each stage of the systemic group process and provide a discussion of dilemmas that may arise when implementing groups with culturally diverse members.

While so many texts portray group member roles from a negative or destructive perspective, this text looks at the pro-developmental needs of group members with a focus on helping members to appropriately self-disclose and give and receive feedback so as to enhance the therapeutic value of the group experience. Thus, Chapter 4: Distinguishing Group Member Roles by George R. Leddick provides a discussion of what students should both do and not do. Chapter 4 begins by describing essential tasks for group members (i.e., self-disclosure and feedback) and later identifies ways student behavior might prove challenging for leaders. This approach does not pathologize students. It helps leaders to understand effective leader techniques and strategies to move the group forward, while emphasizing that members also have responsibilities to the group and that those members who fill specific roles can be handled in pro-developmental ways that help to promote the group process.

Leader skills are emphasized early in the text to help students understand and master the role of the leader as a facilitator of group process. Techniques are provided that help group leaders to keep groups moving in a positive direction. Chapter 5: Leading Groups in the Schools by Amy Milsom addresses the common concern that leading a group can feel overwhelming for many school counselors-in-training. Dr. Milsom acknowledges that effectively attending to and facilitating interaction among many students might seem nearly impossible to students who just may be starting to feel comfortable conducting counseling sessions with one student. Basic knowledge of important group leadership styles, characteristics, and skills for effective group leadership is provided in Chapter 5 to help ease the transition to effective group work.

Professional school counselors almost always use a systemic process orientation when planning and running groups (i.e., planning, forming and orienting, transition, working, termination), rather than a strictly theoretical orientation (e.g., REBT, Gestalt). Section Two: Systemic Group Work: Planning and Process (Chapters 6–10) addresses this systemic approach to group work in schools and gives professional school counselors real-life examples of leader and member responses within the context of the group process being covered. In Chapter 6: Planning for Group Work in the Schools by F. Robert Wilson, planning is proposed as an essential component of successful school-based group work. Key elements of planning, drawn from group work best practices and group work training standards, are identified and discussed within this chapter, including screening, selecting, and preparing members; selecting methods for deriving meaning and transferring learning; determining needed resources; measuring outcomes; and using closed or open groups.

Chapter 7: Forming and Orienting Groups by Nathaniel N. Ivers and Debbie W. Newsome provides an overview of the forming and orienting stage of group work in schools, including descriptions of primary tasks that are accomplished during the forming and orienting stage, a discussion of responsibilities of group leaders during this stage, and a case example that illustrates what might occur during an initial group session.

The theory behind the developmental and systemic tasks of the transition stage in groups is explored in Chapter 8: The Transition Stage in Group Work by D. Paige Bentley Greason. Topics covered include the internal and external determinants of transition dynamics, how these dynamics manifest in the group, and what leaders can do to effectively work with the sometimes intense emotions and behaviors of this transition stage.

For as long as groups have been studied, researchers have noted that part in the life of the group where members actively and freely work on group and personal goals, honestly share aspects of self, courageously give feedback, and feel a sense of "we-ness" that enables them to truly believe in the process of group like never before. Chapter 9: The Working Stage by Kevin A. Fall, H. George McMahon, and Danica G. Hays provides an overview of the working stage of group work with emphasis on student and leader functions within this important part of the group process. Additionally, components of this stage related to group foundations and design are discussed to illustrate indicators for optimal working stage process.

Finally, Chapter 10: Termination in the School Setting by Danica G. Hays, Tammi F. Milliken, and Catherine Y. Chang provides an overview of the termination stage, including a general description of termination characteristics, goals, and benefits and challenges. Following these general descriptions, three types of termination for elementary, middle, and high school levels are discussed: premature termination, termination of group sessions, and termination of the group.

Section Three, the final section of the text, is entitled Group Work in Action: Models and Special Issues (Chapters 11–17). This section includes entire chapters on using task groups, psychoeducational groups, and theoretically based models for counseling and psychotherapy groups. Each of these chapters goes into depth to describe for school counselors how to effectively facilitate task, psychoeducational, and counseling groups in the schools—with numerous real-life examples that help expose students to and ground them in the true-to-life context of school counseling. Task and psychoeducational groups require different skills and approaches than do counseling and psychotherapy groups. Including all four approaches to group work recognizes that the role of the professional school counselor is shifting more from small-group work to large-group guidance and that the professional school counselor is becoming a systemic change agent.

Chapter 11: Leading Task Groups in Schools by Janice L. DeLucia-Waack and Amy Nitza starts with the observation that, if you look hard enough, task groups are everywhere in schools. Clubs, classrooms, and most meetings can be defined as task groups because task groups are groups of people who come together to accomplish a common goal. Chapter 11 provides strategies for using group dynamics, group process, and leadership skills to create successful task groups. Guidelines for leading effective task groups are included, focusing on task groups of students (e.g., groups having classroom guidance lessons, clubs, groups participating in community service projects, student government) and task groups of staff (e.g., departments or teams, curriculum committees, child study teams). Case examples are included to illustrate successful strategies and leadership styles.

Chapter 12: Psychoeducational Groups in Schools by Julia Bryan, Sam Steen, and Norma L. Day-Vines acknowledges that psychoeducational groups for students provide unique learning experiences that support the traditional learning that occurs in school settings. Chapter 12 provides information about psychoeducational groups with a focus on both small-group and large-group formats and strategies for enhancing the delivery of classroom or large-group guidance. A group model developed by Dr. Steen, Achieving Success Everyday (ASE), and strategies for incorporating culturally relevant bibliotherapy into group work, pioneered by Dr. Day-Vines, are provided to promote students' academic success.

Today's reality is that few professional school counselors conduct group psychotherapy in schools, so in-depth training in group psychotherapy is unnecessary, and perhaps misleading to trainees. Some texts go into theoretical models (e.g., REBT, Gestalt) in tremendous depth, often taking up one-half of the book or more. When running counseling groups, nearly all professional school counselors use a focused, integrated approach, aimed at achieving group goals. Chapter 13: Theoretically Based Group Models Used in Counseling and Psychotherapy Groups by Ann Vernon and Darcie Davis-Gage presents information about numerous theoretically based treatment approaches commonly used in counseling and psychotherapy groups in schools, including Adlerian, behavioral, Gestalt, rational emotive behavior therapy, and choice theory/reality therapy approaches.

A special chapter on group work with children and adolescents is included to highlight the special developmental issues of school-age students. The chapter also introduces the major group counseling student-centered themes that professional school counselors encounter in the schools, giving counselors-in-training valuable information about how to address these issues with members of psychoeducational and counseling groups. Chapter 14: Special Issues in Group Work in Schools by Susan H. Eaves and Carl J. Sheperis covers a number of special issues in group work with children and adolescents, including the basic principles of group work with children of alcoholics, children of divorce, sexual abuse victims, adolescents struggling with addictions, and children in need of social skills training.

Chapter 15: Using Activities and Expressive Arts in Group Work by Bradley T. Erford, Debbie W. Newsome, and Mary Keene is tailor-made for professional school counselors who try to engage students in the learning process by implementing planned activities that keep students active and focused on group topics through less formal and more expressive means. Chapter 15 also gives professional school counselors insights into how to transfer group work activities, expressive arts, skills, and process into specific topical areas (e.g., substance abuse, grief, children of alcoholics, divorce). Expressive arts and group activities are powerful additions to the professional school counselor's toolbox. While these techniques and strategies work well under normal circumstances and with individual students, expressive arts also enable group leaders to reach resistant, creative, and sensitive members, allowing them to use the many gifts each possesses. Expressive arts and activities challenge members to use their creativity and talents to overcome adversity. Likewise, counseling and therapeutic games have been used for years with small groups of children to help them achieve developmental and therapeutic goals when dealing with such issues as social skills, study skills, anger management, and changing families. In addition, the use of creative arts (e.g., drawing, journaling, music therapy) is on the rise in group work, particularly with school-age youth. This chapter surveys the use of each of these procedures within the context of group work to help motivate group members and facilitate the group work. Chapter 15 also explores ways that leaders can expand introductory activities, games, and the creative arts in order to increase the comfort level of students and to add a new dimension to groups.

Finally, accountability practices and procedures and outcome research in group work are presented to help leaders understand what works in group work and how to document members' outcomes in order to determine the effectiveness of group interventions. Chapter 16: Accountability in Group Work and School Counseling by Bradley T. Erford addresses the following facets of accountability: needs assessment, program evaluation, process evaluation, and outcome studies. Each facet contributes to a cycle of quality improvement for group work practice. In addition, Chapter 17: Outcome Research in Group Work by Bradley T. Erford reminds readers that group work leaders have an ethical responsibility to "use techniques/procedures/modalities that are grounded in theory and/or have an empirical or scientific foundation" (Herlihy & Corey, 2006, p. 39). Research has concluded that group work can affect members in powerful ways, and this chapter reviews research on the effectiveness of group work with children and adolescents in schools.

As one can see, *Group Work in the Schools* provides a wealth of information on the foundations, systemic perspectives, and current critical topics and issues of school-based group work practice. *Group Work in the Schools* is specifically designed to enhance the knowledge, skills, and attitudes of school counselors-in-training with regard to the specialty area of group work (i.e., task groups, psychoeducational groups, counseling groups, and psychotherapy groups), an approach shown to be very effective in addressing the academic, career, and personal-social needs of school-age children, a population we have all dedicated our careers and lives to serving.

SUPPLEMENTAL INSTRUCTIONAL FEATURES

Supplemental to this book are pedagogical tools helpful to counselor educators choosing to use this book as a course textbook. The companion *Instructor's Manual* contains at least 25 multiple-choice questions, 10 essay questions, and 10 suggested in-class or out-of-class activities per chapter. Numerous case studies and activities included in the text also can stimulate lively classroom discussions.

ACKNOWLEDGMENTS

I thank Megan Earl, Lacey Wallace, and Emily Miller, graduate assistants extraordinaire, for their tireless assistance in the preparation of the original manuscript. All of the contributing authors are to be commended for lending their expertise in the various topical areas. As always, Meredith Fossel, Nancy Holstein, and Renata Butera of Pearson have been wonderfully responsive and supportive. Finally, special thanks go to the outside reviewers whose comments helped to provide substantive improvement to the original manuscript: Deryl F. Bailey, University of Georgia; Michael Moyer, University of Texas, San Antonio; Glenda P. Reynolds, Auburn University; and Adria Shipp, University of North Carolina, Greensboro.

BRIEF CONTENTS

CONTENTS

ABOUT THE EDITOR

Bradley T. Erford, Ph.D., NCC, LCPC, LPC, LP, is a professor in the School Counseling Program of the Educational Specialties Department in the School of Education at Loyola University Maryland. He is the recipient of the American Counseling Association (ACA) Research Award, ACA Hitchcock Distinguished Professional Service Award, ACA Professional Development Award, and ACA Carl D. Perkins Government Relations Award. He has also been inducted as an ACA Fellow. In addition, he has received the Association for Assessment in Counseling and Education (AACE)/Measurement and Evaluation in Counseling and Development Research Award, the AACE Exemplary Practices Award, the AACE President's Special Merit Award, the Association for Counselor Education and Supervision's Robert O. Stripling Award for Excellence in Standards, Maryland Association for Counseling and Development (MACD) Maryland Counselor of the Year, the MACD Counselor Advocacy Award, the MACD Professional Development Award, the MACD Professional Service Award, the MACD Outstanding Programming Award, and the MACD Counselor Visibility Award. He has co-authored and edited a number of texts, including *The American Counseling Association Encyclopedia of Counseling* (ACA, 2009); *Transforming the School Counseling Profession* (Pearson/Merrill, 2002, 2006, 2010); *Professional School Counseling: A Handbook of Principles, Programs and Practices* (Pro-Ed, 2004, 2009); *35 Techniques Every Counselor Should Know* (Pearson/Merrill, 2010); *Orientation to the Counseling Profession* (Pearson/Merrill, 2010); *Developing Multicultural Competence: A Systems Approach* (Pearson/Merrill, 2010); *Group Work: Processes and Applications* (Pearson/Merrill, 2010); *Crisis Intervention and Prevention* (Pearson/Merrill, 2010); *Assessment for Counselors* (Houghton Mifflin/Lahaska Press, 2007); *Research and Evaluation in Counseling* (Houghton Mifflin/Lahaska Press, 2008); and *The Counselor's Guide to Clinical, Personality and Behavioral Assessment* (Houghton Mifflin/Lahaska Press, 2006). His research specialization falls primarily in development and technical analysis of psychoeducational tests and has resulted in the publication of numerous refereed journal articles, book chapters, and published tests. He is an ACA Governing Council Representative; Past President of the AACE; Past Chair and Parliamentarian of the ACA—Southern Region; Past President of the MACD; Past Chair of the ACA's Task Force on High Stakes Testing, Standards for Test Users Task Force, Interprofessional Committee, and Public Awareness and Support Committee; Chair of the Convention Committee and Past Chair of the Screening Assessment Instruments Committee for the AACE; Past President of Maryland Association for Counselor Education and Supervision; Past President of Maryland Association for Measurement and Evaluation; and Past President of the Maryland Association for Mental Health Counselors. Dr. Erford has been a faculty member at Loyola since 1993 and is a Licensed Clinical Professional Counselor, Licensed Professional Counselor, Nationally Certified Counselor, Licensed Psychologist, and Licensed School Psychologist. Prior to arriving at Loyola, Dr. Erford was a school psychologist/counselor in the Chesterfield County (VA) Public Schools. He maintains a private practice specializing in assessment and treatment of children and adolescents. He holds a Ph.D. in counselor education from The University of Virginia, an M.A. in school psychology from Bucknell University, and a B.S. in biology/ psychology from Grove City College (PA). He teaches courses in testing and measurement, psychoeducational assessment, lifespan development, research and evaluation in counseling, school counseling, counseling techniques, and stress management (not that he needs it).

ABOUT THE AUTHORS

D. Paige Bentley Greason, MA.Ed., LPC, NCC, is a doctoral candidate in the Department of Counseling and Counselor Education at the University of North Carolina at Greensboro and a professional counselor in private practice in Winston-Salem, NC. She has extensive experience leading therapy and psychoeducational groups in both her private practice and her previous work as a counselor at a local mental health agency. She earned her bachelor's and master's degrees at Wake Forest University.

Julia Bryan, Ph.D., received her doctorate in counselor education from the University of Maryland. She is currently an assistant professor of education and Director of the School Counseling Program at The College of William and Mary. Her research interests focus on school–family–community partnerships in school counseling, the impact of school counselor contact on student outcomes, group work with children and adolescents, and experiences of Caribbean immigrant students.

Catherine Y. Chang, Ph.D., is an associate professor and Program Coordinator of the Counselor Education and Practice Doctoral Program in the Department of Counseling and Psychological Services at Georgia State University. She received her doctorate in counselor education from the University of North Carolina at Greensboro. Her areas of research interest include multicultural counseling and supervision, Asian and Korean concerns, and multicultural issues in assessment.

Darcie Davis-Gage, Ph.D., LPC, received her master's and specialist degrees from Pittsburg State University and her doctorate from the University of Iowa. She currently is an assistant professor at the University of Northern Iowa. She has presented and published in the areas of group counseling, supervision, and ethics.

Norma L. Day-Vines, Ph.D., is an associate professor in the Counselor Education Program at Virginia Polytechnic Institute and State University. She writes extensively about culturally responsive strategies for working more effectively with ethnic minority students in general and African American students in particular.

Janice L. DeLucia-Waack, Ph.D., is an associate professor in the Department of Counseling, School, and Educational Psychology at the University at Buffalo, State University of New York. She is the former editor of the *Journal for Specialists in Group Work* and is a Fellow in the Association for Specialists in Group Work (ASGW) and American Psychological Association (APA) Division 49: Group Psychology and Group Psychotherapy. She is the author or co-author of six books, Past Secretary of APA Division 49, and Past President of the ASGW. She is also a group co-facilitator in *Leading Groups for Adolescents*, a DVD available from the American Counseling Association.

Susan H. Eaves, Ph.D., NCC, LPC, received her doctorate in counselor education from Mississippi State University. She has worked with children, adolescents, and adults, with emphasized experience conducting group therapy and commitment screenings. Dr. Eaves's research interests include marital infidelity, sexually risky behaviors, assessment, and Borderline Personality Disorder.

Kevin A. Fall, Ph.D., is the Chair of and an associate professor in the Department of Counseling, Loyola University New Orleans. Dr. Fall is the author of several books, including *Group Counseling: Concepts and Procedures* (with Robert Berg and Garry Landreth) and *Theoretical Models of Counseling and Psychotherapy* (with Jan Miner Holden and Andre

Marquis). He has published articles and presented at conferences on the topics of group work, ethics, and Adlerian theory. He also maintains a private practice focusing on adolescents and their families.

Danica G. Hays, Ph.D., LPC, NCC, is an assistant professor in the Department of Educational Leadership and Counseling at Old Dominion University. She has conducted individual and group counseling in community mental health, university, and hospital settings. Her research interests include qualitative methodology, assessment and diagnosis, domestic violence intervention, and multicultural and social justice issues in counselor preparation and community mental health.

Cheryl Holcomb-McCoy, Ph.D., received her doctorate in counseling and educational development from the University of North Carolina at Greensboro. She is an associate professor in the Department of Counseling and Personnel Services at the University of Maryland, College Park, and is the former Director of the School Counseling Program at Brooklyn College, City University of New York. Her areas of research specialization include multicultural school counseling, school counselor multicultural self-efficacy, and urban school counselor preparation. She has written over 40 book chapters and refereed articles on issues pertaining to diversity in school counselor education. Dr. Holcomb-McCoy is a former elementary school counselor and kindergarten teacher.

Nathaniel N. Ivers, MA, is a doctoral student in the Counseling and Educational Development Program at the University of North Carolina at Greensboro. He received his master's in counseling from Wake Forest University. Mr. Ivers has practiced counseling primarily with the Latino/a Spanish-speaking population.

Mary Keene, M.Ed., received her master's in school counseling from Johns Hopkins University. She is an experienced professional school counselor and former teacher who worked in the Baltimore County Public Schools for more than 25 years. Now retired, she is an affiliate faculty member in the School Counseling Program at Loyola College in Maryland. She is a Past President of the Maryland Association for Counseling and Development and the Maryland School Counseling Association. Ms. Keene is an experienced and energetic workshop and leadership development facilitator.

George R. Leddick, Ph.D., earned his doctorate at Purdue University and was influenced by group work pioneers Allan Dye, Allen Segrist, John Sherwood, and Rex Stockton. For the past 25 years, he has conducted both beginning and advanced group work practica in graduate schools in Indiana, South Carolina, New York, and Texas. He also taught organizational development consulting courses and maintained a private consulting practice. He served on the editorial board of the *Journal for Specialists in Group Work* and was elected both President and a Fellow of the Association for Specialists in Group Work (ASGW). He currently represents the ASGW on the Governing Council of the American Counseling Association.

Lynn E. Linde, Ed.D., is Coordinator of Clinical Experiences in the School Counseling program at Loyola College in Maryland. She received her doctorate in counseling from George Washington University. She is a former Branch Chief for Pupil Services at the Maryland State Department of Education and representative to the American Counseling Association (ACA) Governing Council. She is an ACA Fellow, Past Chair of the ACA—Southern Region, and Past President of the Maryland Association for Counseling and Development.

H. George McMahon, Ph.D., is an assistant professor in the Counseling and Psychological Services Department at Georgia State University in Atlanta. He is a former middle and elementary school counselor who received his doctorate in counseling psychology from The University of Georgia and his M.Ed. in school counseling from The University of Virginia. Dr. McMahon has led groups in schools, psychiatric hospitals, residential treatment centers, and substance abuse programs. He has co-authored journal articles and book chapters and has presented at state, regional, and national conferences on various topics related to group work. His professional interests include school counselor preparation, group work in school settings, and the role of counselors of privilege in multiculturalism.

Tammi F. Milliken, Ph.D., NCC, is assistant professor of human services in the Department of Educational Leadership and Counseling at Old Dominion University. She received her doctorate in counselor education with an emphasis in family-school collaboration from the College of William and Mary, and her M.S. in education from Old Dominion University. Her work experience includes serving as Director of Project EMPOWER, a school-based prevention program, as an elementary school counselor in Norfolk Public Schools in Virginia, and as a family counselor for New Horizons at the College of William and Mary. She is an endorsed Harvard Mind/Body Stress Management Education Initiative facilitator and trainer. Dr. Milliken's research interests include critical issues in human services, developmental theory and application, adult development and learning, ethics, and multicultural competence in human services.

Amy Milsom, Ph.D., NCC, LPC, is an assistant professor at the University of North Carolina at Greensboro. She earned her doctorate from Penn State University and is a former middle and high school counselor. Her primary research interests are in the areas of students with disabilities, school counselor preparation and professionalism, and group work.

Cheryl Moore-Thomas, Ph.D., NCC, is an associate professor of education in the School Counseling Program at Loyola College in Maryland, where she teaches courses in group and multicultural counseling. She has published and presented in the areas of multicultural counseling competence, racial identity development, spiritual identity development in African American children and adolescents, and accountability in school counseling programs. Additionally, Dr. Moore-Thomas consults with public school systems on issues of diversity and academic achievement.

Debbie Newsome, Ph.D., LPC, NCC, is an associate professor of counselor education at Wake Forest University, where she teaches courses in career counseling and in appraisal procedures and statistics and supervises master's students in their ?eld experiences. She also serves as an adjunct clinician at a nonpro?t mental health organization, where she counsels children, adolescents, and families.

Amy Nitza, Ph.D., is an assistant professor of counseling and counselor education in the School of Education at Indiana University–Purdue University Fort Wayne. She is the producer of a group training DVD titled *Leading Groups for Adolescents,* co-author of a group work book, editor of the newsletter of the Association for Specialist in Group Work, and author of several journal articles on group topics. Her research interests include the use of psychoeducational groups for prevention and therapeutic factors in groups for children and adolescents.

Carl J. Sheperis, Ph.D., NCC, LPC, is an associate professor in the Department of Counseling, Educational Psychology, and Special Education at Mississippi State University. His research interests include Reactive Attachment Disorder, parent–child relationships, and peer con?ict.

Julia A. Southern, M.Ed., received her master's in school counseling from Loyola College in Maryland and her bachelor's in communication arts and psychology from

Salisbury University. She is a professional school counselor in the Howard County Public Schools in Maryland. She is also an experienced public relations and events professional.

Sam Steen, Ph.D., is an assistant professor of school counseling at The College of William and Mary, where he teaches courses in school counseling and counseling children and adolescents. He conducts research in the areas of group counseling for school counselors. His publications cover cross-cultural group counseling and using literacy to promote achievement in group counseling as well as integrating academics and personal-social topics in group counseling targeting students having difficulty in the classroom. Prior to working in academia, Dr. Steen was employed as a professional school counselor for approximately 10 years in Northern Virginia.

Ann Vernon, Ph.D., NCC, LMHC, is professor emeritus and former Coordinator of Counseling at the University of Northern Iowa and a therapist in private practice, where she works extensively with children, adolescents, and their parents. Dr. Vernon is the former Director of the Midwest Center for REBT and Vice-President of the Albert Ellis Board of Trustees. She is the author of numerous books, chapters, and articles, including *Thinking, Feeling, Behaving* and *What Works When with Children and Adolescents*.

F. Robert Wilson, Ph.D., has been a member of the University of Cincinnati counseling faculty for nearly 30 years, where he coordinates the master's program in mental health counseling. In addition to teaching courses in clinical mental health counseling, group work, and the foundations of counseling, he supervises beginning and advanced master's counseling interns. His research and clinical interests include service to indigent and homeless people with mental illnesses; assessment, problem identification, and diagnosis; and individual and group treatment modalities with emphasis on ecological psychotherapy and evidence-based clinical practices. Dr. Wilson received his doctorate from Michigan State University and completed postdoctoral training in Gestalt Therapy at the Cincinnati Gestalt Institute. He is a Nationally Certified Counselor and an Approved Clinical Supervisor. He is a Fellow of the Association for Specialists in Group Work and was recently recognized as the Susan J. Sears "Counselor of the Year" by the Ohio Counseling Association. An active professional leader, he has served as President of the Association for Assessment in Counseling and Education, Vice Chair of Council for Accreditation of Counseling and Related Educational Programs, member of the Governing Council of the American Counseling Association, and member of the governing board of the Ohio Mental Health Counseling Association.

Foundations of Group Work

CHAPTER 1

The Value of Group Work: Functional Group Models and Historical Perspectives

JULIA A. SOUTHERN, BRADLEY T. ERFORD, ANN VERNON, AND DARCIE DAVIS-GAGE

PREVIEW

This initial chapter provides a tour through the essential historical and foundational issues of group work, leading the reader to appreciate the value of the group approach. To understand group work models, leaders need to consider each model's characteristics, subtypes, and stages and the classic role and function of its leader. This chapter presents an overview of the four main group formats categorized by the Association for Specialists in Group Work: task groups, psychoeducational groups, counseling groups, and psychotherapy groups.

DEFINING GROUP WORK

Throughout time, humans have naturally gathered together in groups for the purpose of ensuring their survival and development. Most individuals spend a considerable amount of time in groups for social, professional, religious, and other purposes. But what exactly defines a group? Do specific parameters exist? Researchers in the field have proposed varying descriptions to categorize a group's unique characteristics. Charles Cooley defined the primary group concept as a face-to-face encounter between individuals that involves intimate cooperation. Gladding (2008) expanded on this concept by defining a group as two or more individuals who meet interdependently, with the awareness that each belongs for the purpose of achieving mutually set goals.

Gladding's (2008) depiction of groups as functional organisms led to his description of group work, characterized as the application of knowledge and skill in group facilitation to assist members in reaching their mutual goals. These goals include work- or education-related tasks, personal development, problem solving, and the remediation of disorders. These goals can be accomplished through different procedures, processes, and approaches. The Association for Specialists in Group Work (ASGW; 2007) categorized group work into four functional approaches: task groups, psychoeducational groups, counseling groups, and psychotherapy groups. This book adheres to this categorization scheme.

FUNCTIONAL GROUP MODELS

The ASGW (2007) categorized the various functional types of group work experiences as task groups, psychoeducational groups, counseling groups, and psychotherapy groups. Each of these group models will be discussed in relation to its characteristics, subtypes, and stages and the role and function of its leader, and each of these group work types will be discussed in greater depth within the school context in Chapters 11–13.

But how does a group leader know which type of group model to use? Professional school counselors determine which type of group model to implement based on the structure and goals of the group. For example, task groups ordinarily are formed with the goal of accomplishing some task or solving some problem. Once the task is completed or the problem is addressed, the group terminates. An example of a task group is a student assistance team.

Psychoeducational groups ordinarily are formed with the primary goal of conveying knowledge and skills to students through psychoeducational techniques, either in small groups or through classroom guidance. Examples of psychoeducational groups include a teacher/student training on implementing a peer mediation program and a study skills group meant to help students who are having academic difficulties to develop the knowledge, skills, and attitudes needed to increase academic successes in the classroom.

Group counseling may also address student knowledge and skills, but it does so through the application of a theoretically based counseling approach (e.g., humanistic, rational-emotive behavior therapy; reality therapy; integrative approach). Goals for counseling group members ordinarily are written to address cognitive, affective, and behavioral changes agreed to by the leader and members. Counseling groups in schools are usually time-limited (e.g., 6–12 sessions) and may deal with issues such as "changing families" or grief and loss in order to help small groups of students adjust to the developmental changes required by life changes and loss.

Psychotherapy groups are seldom run by professional school counselors because these groups involve in-depth, long-term commitments (i.e., 12–50+ sessions) and usually require leaders with advanced levels of training and expertise. Examples of psychotherapy group topics include coping with long-term, traumatic physical or sexual abuse or with personality disorders, with the goals of personality restructuring and reintegration. School counselors rarely have the luxury of dedicating the time required to successfully complete these types of psychotherapy groups and ordinarily refer students in need of group psychotherapy to private or community service providers. For each of these group models (i.e., task, psychoeducational, counseling, and psychotherapy), the characteristics, types, and stages and the role and function of its leader will be reviewed in the following pages.

Task Groups

Task groups are used in a variety of settings from schools and mental health agencies to large businesses and corporations. They are designed around accomplishing a specific goal, use principles of group dynamics, and incorporate such methods as collaboration, problem-solving, and team-building exercises to reach their goal. The focus is not on changing people but on completing the task at hand in an efficient and effective manner. For example, if a principal wanted to address the complex problems of students at risk of academic failure from a systemic, multidisciplinary perspective, the principal might appoint members of a task group to identify and then establish authentic partnerships with community and government organizations.

Hulse-Killacky, Killacky, and Donigian (2001) identified the elements of successful task groups, including having well-defined goals and purposes, addressing and processing conflicts between members, blending content and process, and encouraging members to give and receive feedback as well as to reflect on their work as a group. Leaders of task groups should have a clear purpose, take time to build rapport, encourage members to be reflective and active, and pay attention to the here and now.

CHARACTERISTICS OF TASK GROUPS   Task groups can vary greatly in size but often function more effectively if there are fewer than 12 people to avoid problems with subgrouping. With younger school-aged children, task groups of 6–8 students often work best. Task groups also vary in duration and the number of sessions, which are usually dependent on the time needed to accomplish the identified goal. Once the goal is accomplished, the group generally disbands unless another task is identified. Task group members also tend to have contact with each other outside the group, which is one of the unique characteristics of task groups not often encountered in counseling or psychotherapy groups.

TYPES OF TASK GROUPS   There are as many different types of task groups as there are tasks. Examples of tasks completed by groups in schools include choosing officers for a club or organization, planning a fund-raising event or social function, and completing school tasks. ASGW standards identify committees, task forces, and learning groups as types of task groups. For example, elementary students can form task groups to work on a social studies project. Upon completion, these students can be taught to evaluate how well they worked together, reflecting on the roles each student played and what, if anything, interfered with their functioning well as a group. Age-appropriate formats can be devised using typical process observer criteria such as these:

1. What role did you play in the group? Were you a leader or a follower?
2. How successful was the group in completing the task?
3. If you did not complete the task, what prevented you from completing it?
4. If you worked as a group again, how could you work more effectively?

Questions such as these can be adapted and expanded on, depending on the age of the group members. At times, it is also effective to assign one or two students to be process observers and give feedback to the rest of the group members.

ROLE AND FUNCTION OF THE LEADER IN TASK GROUPS   The leaders of task groups tend to take on the role of process consultant (Kottler, 2001). A task group leader's main goal is to help the group complete a task or reach a goal. This is best facilitated when the leader is able to strike a balance between content and process, while still accomplishing the task at hand in a timely manner. Leaders of task groups need to be able to facilitate communication and keep the group focused on the goals of the group. When a student is the leader of the task group, he or she may struggle with the content/process facilitation and may need more assistance from a teacher or professional school counselor.

STAGES OF TASK GROUPS   Hulse-Killacky, Kraus, and Schumacher (1999) described a conceptual framework that a group leader can use when conducting task groups. Within this framework, the authors identified three stages: a warming-up period, followed by a working stage, and ending with the termination of the group. Although these phases may be present in the other types of groups such as psychoeducational or counseling groups, they seem to be particularly applicable to task or work groups. Using these stages allows trust and cohesion to form, which will in turn facilitate a more productive task group.

During the first stage, Hulse-Killacky et al. (1999) stressed that members should introduce themselves to one another and identify the task and purpose of the group. The second stage includes working on accomplishing the identified task, while also developing an understanding of how members will work together. During this phase, it is important for the leader to work within the here-and-now context, while emphasizing direct communication and feedback between members. In order to achieve a balance between content and process, it may also be helpful for the leader to pay attention to how members are interacting and not overemphasize the completion of the task. The final stage involves bringing the group to completion, which is best accomplished by having members reflect on the progress as well as the process of the group. Hulse-Killacky et al. (1999) emphasized that leaders should maintain a balance of content and process throughout all stages because, without this balance, groups risk becoming stagnant and unproductive.

When using task groups with students in a school setting, there may be some variation in these stages. For example, the teacher or professional school counselor will most likely structure some rapport building during the warming-up stage and may identify the task and give specific instructions for the working stage. If multiple task groups are operating within a classroom, the degree to which the teacher or counselor will be a more active facilitator will depend on the age of the students and/or the nature of the task. Experience has shown that children as young as seven years old can be taught about group roles and factors that facilitate and impede group process and can learn to give and receive feedback about the group experience.

SOME FINAL COMMENTS ON TASK GROUPS   Task groups are designed around the accomplishment of a certain task and are an effective way of accomplishing that task because the group members bring various perspectives and multiple sources of energy and expertise together to accomplish their goal. By employing various group principles, leaders can help task groups be more productive and complete their goals in a timely manner. Personal change and growth usually do not occur in task groups; however, if a task group is properly facilitated, members may leave the group with a better understanding of group dynamics as well as possibly gaining insight into their individual interpersonal skills. In the school setting, task groups are an exceptionally good way to educate young people about group roles and group dynamics that will facilitate their group participation in the present as well as in the future. Task groups are covered in much greater detail in Chapter 11.

Psychoeducational Groups

Psychoeducational groups were originally developed for use in schools but are also increasingly used in mental health agencies, hospitals, social service agencies, and universities (Aasheim & Niemann, 2006). These groups, which are more structured than counseling or psychotherapy groups, emphasize skill development through various nonthreatening skill-building exercises, while at the same time encouraging discussion, sharing, and feedback among members (Corey, Corey, Callahan, & Russell, 2004). The goal of psychoeducational group work is to prevent psychological disturbance by increasing self-awareness, knowledge, and skills about specific developmentally relevant issues. The fact that psychoeducational groups can be preventive, growth oriented, or remedial makes this a very versatile type of group model. The psychoeducational group model is commonly used in preK–12 comprehensive, developmental school counseling programs, whether in small groups to address study or social skills or in classroom guidance to address educational planning or career developmental goals.

CHARACTERISTICS OF PSYCHOEDUCATIONAL GROUPS   Psychoeducational groups are appropriate for all age groups and can be adapted to the specific needs of group members. In the school setting, they may be called guidance groups and are "more structured, issue specific, and leader directed" (Aasheim & Niemann, 2006, p. 269). Psychoeducational groups serve several purposes, including giving members information, encouraging them to share common experiences, teaching them problem-solving skills, and helping them to create their own support systems outside of the group setting. The focus is both educational and therapeutic in that information about the specific topic is shared and self-development is emphasized (Ivey, Pedersen, & Ivey, 2001).

TYPES OF PSYCHOEDUCATIONAL GROUPS   Aasheim and Niemann (2006) identified three types of psychoeducational groups: (1) education groups that focus on presenting new information and concepts, (2) skills-training groups that are generally experiential and emphasize skill acquisition, and (3) self-understanding groups that are similar to counseling groups but focus less on self-disclosure and more on building self-confidence by giving feedback about members' behavior and how it affects others. This latter type of group is more appropriate for adolescents than for children, although it could be beneficial with elementary-aged children, depending on their maturity and the group composition.

   Psychoeducational groups are typically centered around a particular topic and have been widely used to address broad-ranging issues such as stress management, assertion, interpersonal skills, substance abuse, eating disorders, anger, loss, self-esteem, domestic violence, responsible sexual behavior, healthy choices, and diversity awareness. Other topics applicable in a school setting include improving study skills, getting along with friends, making career decisions, and dealing with family changes. Regardless of the focus of a group, growth is acquired through knowledge. Group members obtain this knowledge through discussions, presentations, videos, computer-assisted programs, or activities/exercises. Depending on the age level, games, simulations, role playing, and worksheets designed to convey information and stimulate discussion may also be used.

ROLE AND FUNCTION OF THE LEADER IN PSYCHOEDUCATIONAL GROUPS   Because this type of group is focused on presenting knowledge and helping members change perceptions, the leader needs to have expertise in the content area as well as group facilitation skills. It is also imperative that the group leader create a safe environment so that students will feel comfortable sharing feelings and engaging in self-disclosure. Because this type of group is more structured than counseling or psychotherapy groups, the leader must engage in careful planning that includes having a well-designed curriculum that will allow sufficient time for group members to process and discuss the information presented.

   The leader needs to be adept at juggling content as well as process and, at the same time, to be sensitive to the readiness of group members to address various issues and engage in certain activities. Planning is essential in psychoeducational groups and includes planning for session length, frequency, number of sessions, content, and follow-up sessions. Although these factors may vary due to member age and setting, typically high school groups meet once a week for 45–60 minutes, whereas with elementary students, 30–45 minutes is sufficient. The number of sessions varies widely, depending on the topic and the depth of coverage, but the average is 6–12 sessions. The optimal number of members in a psychoeducational group also varies widely, but with children and adolescents, 6–10 members is the ideal composition in order to facilitate discussion and feedback. Classroom guidance lessons are frequently conducted with 20–30 students, but such large groups allow for less discussion, feedback, and individualized attention.

It is also helpful for the leader of a psychoeducational group to help members clarify what they want from the group and translate these vague goals into specific, measurable objectives. Asking students to write down their goals or a description of what they hope to get from the group experience can help. Having members complete contracts that identify specific, realistic, and attainable goals is also a helpful strategy.

STAGES OF A PSYCHOEDUCATIONAL GROUP   The beginning and closing stages are often shorter in psychoeducational groups than in counseling or psychotherapy groups, but the leader nevertheless has to plan for these stages. The middle stage includes delivery of content, which may be through a short lecture or a variety of experientially based activities that introduce the topic and engage members in learning more about it. In this stage, the leader's job is to shift between giving information and facilitating discussion, which helps members learn the information and apply it to their own lives. All too often inexperienced leaders focus too much on providing information and lose sight of the group process, or they allow too much sharing and don't provide enough information. A good balance of information and interaction is essential.

Some Final Comments on Psychoeducational Groups

The *ASGW Best Practices Guidelines* (2007) state that psychoeducational groups stress growth through knowledge. Using this approach, students of all ages can benefit from the learning and support that this type of group offers and apply what they have learned to their real-life situations. Psychoeducational groups have extensive applicability in schools because of the variety of topics that can be introduced to help students acquire knowledge and skills that will enhance their development. Group leaders can structure age-appropriate activities that stimulate the discussion and application of concepts, thus increasing children's and adolescents' ability to deal with present and future concerns. Leaders of psychoeducational groups walk a fine line between presenting information and facilitating the group process that encourages sharing and self-disclosure, both of which are essential to an effective group. Psychoeducational group approaches are covered in much greater detail in Chapter 12.

Counseling Groups

Counseling groups are designed to help students work on interpersonal problems and to promote behavioral changes related to these problems. However, while counseling groups are typically problem oriented, helping members explore their problems and seek resolution, they can also be preventive, growth oriented, or remedial.

Kottler (2001) described counseling groups as relatively short in duration and focused on adjustment issues for individuals who function relatively normally. People usually come to group counseling because they are experiencing some sort of problem, such as dealing with family issues, difficult relationships, or stress-related problems.

CHARACTERISTICS OF COUNSELING GROUPS   Various goals of students can be addressed in counseling groups. For example, counseling groups help students to explore issues affecting their development, experience acceptance and support from their peers while exploring various problems, and increase coping skills. As a result of attending counseling groups, students may also improve their abilities to build and maintain healthy relationships. Counseling groups can help students to develop more positive attitudes about interpersonal functioning. The fact that students can practice these skills in a group forum may increase their interpersonal effectiveness. Once these behavior changes occur in the group setting, students will hopefully transfer the skills into their everyday living.

In order to maintain the personal focus, counseling groups for children (preK–5) ordinarily range in size from four to six individuals. Leaders might consider having three to four students in a group if they are working with children with attentional difficulties or severe behavioral problems. In adolescent counseling groups, numbers can range from six to eight students. Typically, the number of sessions for children and adolescents can range from 6 to 12, depending on the issues being addressed and the age of the members. Group sessions ideally run for 30–60 minutes, again depending on the age of the students and the amount of time available according to the school's class schedule.

TYPES OF COUNSELING GROUPS   Various types of counseling groups may be offered in school settings, and participation can have multiple benefits for children and adolescents. Counseling groups for children may focus on adjusting to parents' divorce or dealing with other types of loss. The goal is to help children develop coping skills, share feelings about their situations, and gain support from others who are experiencing similar circumstances. Counseling groups may prevent more serious problems from occurring.

Counseling groups are also helpful for adolescents. Groups appropriate for adolescents include those addressing sexual orientation issues, teenage pregnancy and parenting, and relationship skills, among numerous other potential topics. By attending group sessions, students are given a chance to process their problems, receive constructive feedback, and work on interpersonal relationship skills.

ROLE AND FUNCTION OF THE LEADER IN COUNSELING GROUPS   Group leaders tend to be less directive in counseling groups than in psychoeducational groups. When working with children and adolescents, leaders must also be aware of students' developmental levels and choose topics and activities that are age appropriate. When forming counseling groups, leaders should try to make them as diverse as possible in regard to race, ethnicity, socioeconomic status, sexual orientation, and other groups so that members can experience a wide variety of interactions that mirror the pluralistic society.

Leaders have various functions when facilitating counseling groups. First, they build an atmosphere that is conducive to students openly sharing their problems without fear of rejection or ridicule. Second, leaders facilitate communication and protect members if necessary. Finally, group leaders need to help students apply the insight they gain in the group to their lives outside the group.

STAGES OF COUNSELING GROUPS   The development of a counseling group is dependent on effective leadership and knowledge about how groups transition through various stages. In the beginning of the counseling group experience, students spend time getting acquainted and sharing information about themselves. This phase can last from one to three sessions. Some groups may cycle through a transition period during this beginning phase if the group members challenge the leader or share only superficial information about themselves and their issues.

Next, students enter the working stage, where they begin to work on the issues that brought them to the group. Leaders need to be skilled in helping to link students as they share similar problems in order to help build cohesion and universality. The ending phase usually lasts one to two sessions and focuses on processing feelings related to the termination of the group. These stages of group process are expanded on in Chapters 6–10.

SOME FINAL COMMENTS ON COUNSELING GROUPS   Counseling groups can prevent problems and help improve students' interpersonal skills. They are most helpful for children and adolescents who are having difficulties adjusting to a variety of life circumstances and who could benefit from a growth-producing experience. Counseling groups are often provided for children and adolescents as part of a comprehensive school counseling program. Counseling groups outside of the school system may be more difficult to access if children or adolescents do not have adequate health insurance coverage or if their families do not have the means to pay for the services, since counseling groups are usually offered by trained professionals and may be rather expensive. Regardless of the cost, group counseling may be more beneficial than individual counseling for certain types of problems (see Chapter 17). Counseling groups are covered in much greater detail in Chapter 13.

Psychotherapy Groups

Psychotherapy groups can be used with children and adolescents with most types of mental illness (Carrier & Haley, 2006) and are designed to treat those who may be experiencing severe or chronic problems in their lives. Ordinarily, members in psychotherapy groups display more dysfunctional behavior and typically carry a psychiatric diagnosis (i.e., one from the *Diagnostic and Statistical Manual of Mental Disorders or* DSM). Psychotherapy groups for children and adolescents are typically offered by agencies and in residential treatment settings but are increasingly being offered in alternative schools and in full-service schools that offer school-based mental health services. Psychotherapy groups are rarely conducted in comprehensive developmental school counseling programs because a time-intensive commitment is involved and because psychotherapy groups sometimes require a leader to possess advanced training and knowledge of the group topic. Still, professional school counselors should understand what is involved in psychotherapy groups so that appropriate referrals can be made to practitioners outside the school setting.

Members of psychotherapy groups are usually identified through a screening process, and although some individuals who participate in psychotherapy groups may have problems similar to those of members in counseling groups, psychotherapy groups are more appropriate for individuals whose symptoms are more severe or pervasive. The goal of a psychotherapy group is to change people on a deeper level as compared to the other types of groups (Carrier & Haley, 2006) by engaging in a process of personality reconstruction. This makes changing personality traits, cognitive distortions, and behavioral patterns that interfere with a member's functioning a major focus.

CHARACTERISTICS OF PSYCHOTHERAPY GROUPS   Psychotherapy groups for children and adolescents tend to be smaller than task or psychoeducational groups and may be similar in size to counseling groups. Psychotherapy groups typically have four to six members but can range from as few as two to three members up to perhaps eight members. Co-leadership may be helpful for psychotherapy groups with children and adolescents.

Typically, psychotherapy groups meet for 30–60 minutes one or more times a week, depending on the setting. Spitz and Spitz (1999) found that psychotherapy groups vary in duration from a small number of sessions (e.g., 8–15) to a longer-term treatment (e.g., years). When conducting school-based group psychotherapy, leaders must be conscious of the academic schedule, so groups may be offered twice a week but for shorter periods of time.

Spitz and Spitz (1999) emphasized that the goals of the individual members and the group should drive the decision regarding the length of treatment. Brief psychotherapy groups are appropriate when member goals focus on reducing mild symptoms or on increasing social skills. Shorter-term groups also tend to be more effective if the members have similar psychological problems or disorders. Longer-term groups tend to focus on building insight and self-awareness, examining the past, and working on the relationship with one's family.

TYPES OF PSYCHOTHERAPY GROUPS   Psychotherapy groups are usually reserved for people who have a clinical diagnosis or who have serious problems of adjustment (Spitz & Spitz, 1999). Psychotherapy groups for children and adolescents offered in the school setting are usually led by practitioners from local mental health agencies. These types of groups are typically provided to children and adolescents with problems such as depression, substance abuse, and disruptive behavioral disorders. For these types of groups to be successful in the schools, group leaders should establish therapeutic and educational goals as part of their groups. For example, educational goals could include improving school attendance, increasing individual grade point averages, or reducing the number of detentions. Psychotherapy groups in the schools are usually most successful if the leader carefully considers and respects the context, culture, and rules of the school.

ROLE AND FUNCTION OF THE LEADER IN PSYCHOTHERAPY GROUPS   Spitz and Spitz (1999) stressed that psychotherapy groups should be led by a professionally trained group facilitator who is familiar with and has experience serving individuals with severe and pervasive problems. In addition, the psychotherapy group leader must be an active facilitator who screens members and carefully selects appropriate interventions based on the composition and goals of the group. Since members of psychotherapy groups tend to have more serious problems, it is especially important that the leader should have training in abnormal psychology, psychopathology, and diagnosis (ASGW, 2000).

Leaders of psychotherapy groups usually operate from a theoretical framework as well (see Chapter 13). While working with members of psychotherapy groups, leaders must have knowledge of Yalom's therapeutic factors (Yalom & Leszcz, 2005), which are reviewed later in this chapter, and be able to use them to promote and facilitate change among group members.

STAGES OF PSYCHOTHERAPY GROUPS   Although the stages of psychotherapy groups can be dependent on the duration of the group and the theoretical orientation of the group leader, some general commonalities exist. As mentioned above, the planning phase is critical to the success of a psychotherapy group because of the importance of screening and selecting members. Spitz and Spitz (1999) emphasized that psychotherapy groups begin with a warm-up stage where members introduce themselves and learn about each other. This is followed by a period of vying for power and control in the group (i.e., transition), after which time the group rules and norms are often formed. Once those issues are resolved, the group will move into a working stage where members address issues with intimacy, dependency, and independence. The group then concludes with a termination phase where group members are able to reflect on their accomplishments, while also dealing with issues of grief and loss. These stages are expanded on in Chapters 6–10.

SOME FINAL COMMENTS ON PSYCHOTHERAPY GROUPS   Psychotherapy groups can be beneficial for a variety of children and adolescents with many different problems, but they are particularly beneficial for those with serious problems who may need the support of a group. Psychotherapy groups can be very cost-effective, and treatment not only offers a level of support to individuals but also provides an opportunity for members to experience caring relationships. Psychotherapy groups are typically reserved for people with the most severe problems; it is an approach that allows members to reconstruct parts of their personalities in a safe environment where they can receive constructive feedback and the space to practice new skills in living. Psychotherapy groups are covered in much greater detail in Chapter 13.

AN INTRODUCTION TO THE STAGES OF GROUP WORK PROCESS

During the introduction of functional group models provided above, it was hard not to notice that different researchers conceptualized the stages of different group models differently. Some suggested a three-stage, four-stage, five-stage, or even-more-stage model. The identification of stages in group work is oftentimes helpful when teaching counselors-in-training about group process and development as well as when helping leaders evaluate the progress that groups and students are making from session to session. For the purpose of this book, we have chosen to identify the stages of group work as (1) the forming and orienting stage, (2) the transition stage, (3) the working stage, and (4) the termination stage. The precursor to these four stages is known as the planning phase. These phases and stages will be expanded on substantially in Chapters 6–10, but for now, a very brief explanation of each is necessary for general knowledge and identification purposes.

The planning phase occurs well before the first group meeting. Planning involves identifying potential group members and screening these students to determine their appropriateness for the group (e.g., willingness to participate, consistency of personal goals with group goals). The planning phase also allows the leader to discuss confidentiality, limits of confidentiality, informed consent, and myriad other details related to setting up and running groups in schools. Planning also infers that the leader has researched and selected essential content to be conveyed (in the case of psychoeducational or counseling groups) and any experiential activities that will be implemented and, in general, is ready to lead the group and infuse relevant content. Once the potential students have been screened and the members selected, the group sessions are ready to commence.

Forming and orienting, the initial stage of group process, is an interesting and sometimes anxiety-producing time for students and the leader. During the first couple of sessions, the leader seeks to collaboratively determine goals, orient the students to the goals of the group, collaboratively set ground rules with members, and structure the sessions to help students communicate and give feedback to each other. The leader's style of interaction is very important during this stage, as it sets the tone for student interactions. At this point, many task and psychoeducational groups are structured and led in such a way that they are ready to begin the working stage. This is because the leader is usually using an active and directive approach, the group's goals are well defined, and the group is time-limited. However, leaders of counseling and psychotherapy groups ordinarily are less directive and attempt to harness the experiences and power of group process, transferring responsibility for group and member successes to the students themselves. This transfer of responsibility is accomplished through the stage known as transition, which is frequently anxiety-producing for both students and leaders. As students take responsibility for the group, become familiar with each other, and become serious about making progress toward meeting their goals, the group is poised to enter the working stage. Navigating the transition stage takes a great deal of skill on the part of the group leader.

Ordinarily, most of the group meeting time is spent in the working stage, accomplishing the goals the students are committed to achieving during the planning phase and as the group experience commenced. During this stage, leaders must skillfully facilitate group process, while empowering students to take control and to pursue and accomplish individual and group goals. As goals are accomplished and the time approaches for the group experience to end, the termination stage arrives. While evaluation of group content and process is conducted throughout the group experience, assessment of group and individual goals becomes particularly important in this final stage. The termination stage also gives students and leaders an opportunity to debrief, resolve unfinished business, and process the interpersonal and intrapersonal progress each member made.

Usually, the stages of a group experience unfold in a predictable manner. However, there is one important caution to be aware of when identifying the stage a group may be displaying: It can change at any time. The dynamics of group interaction are fluid and changeable, members may arrive at sessions with pressing issues (e.g., life crises, breaches in confidentiality) that the group is forced to deal with, and skillful group leaders will need to adjust and adapt to harness the power of the group to deal with pressing issues, while still suavely segueing back to the primary goals of the group. Thus, while stages give the impression of proceeding progressively from one step to the next, complex group processes frequently lead groups in more of a spiraling path. Part of becoming a skillful group leader is becoming flexible and adept at recognizing these subtle shifts and turns and then skillfully facilitating the process of the group so that the students continue to make progress. With this brief introduction to the stages of group work as context, we are now ready to proceed with a review of the historical foundations of group work, with specific reference to its development within the schools.

THE HISTORY OF GROUP WORK

Each era in the history of group counseling has reflected the national, regional, and local climate of that time period. Sociologists and social psychologists began researching collective group behavior in the 19th century, although not necessarily in direct relation to therapeutic possibilities. Early research topics focused on exploring the impact of social experiences on behavior—specifically, the effects of working in groups on childhood performance in school, group influences on thought processes, and the effect of competition on performance. Today, group work is known to be an effective methodology for meeting various human needs and finding solutions to a multitude of problems. School counselors are increasingly called on to address problems that are interpersonally based, and they have discovered that the social connections provided by counseling groups are often the most effective forms of treatment.

The Late 1800s and Early 1900s

The development of groups in the late 1800s emerged from the fledgling disciplines of psychology, sociology, and philosophy as a result of the need for social reform and education. Those who received treatment in group settings at that time were generally immigrants, poor, or mentally ill. Joseph Pratt, a Boston internist, is credited with establishing the first group experience that was not intended specifically for psychoeducational or occupational purposes. He used groups to save time in educating and supporting patients and discovered therapeutic value in the format. Pratt was treating patients with tuberculosis and began seeing them in groups for the sake of efficiency. The patients shared the commonality of having tuberculosis, and over time, they became concerned with one another's well-being. This sense of caring had a positive effect, and the patients' spirits seemed to be lifted as they gathered together for weekly meetings (Posthuma, 2002). Startlingly, 75% of Pratt's patients eventually recovered from the disease, despite the fact that they were given no hope of survival upon their initial diagnosis. Pratt provided the first known description of group counseling and the curative effect of group interactions on group members. It is widely believed that his work paved the way for present-day psychotherapy.

Building on Pratt's initial findings, two pioneers of the school counseling profession began to apply group work within the school context just after the turn of the century. Jesse Davis, a school principal in Grand Rapids, Michigan, introduced group work in a school setting in 1907. Davis's groups were intended to provide students with effective tools for making educational, vocational, and moral decisions (Herr & Erford, 2007). Davis emphasized the use of the group as an effective environment for teaching life skills and values. Frank Parsons, often cited as the founder of the vocational guidance or school counseling profession, also used groups to facilitate career and vocational development. However, despite their groundbreaking efforts in the field, neither Davis nor Parsons conducted evaluations to empirically test the effectiveness of group work for students.

During World War I (and later in World War II), the importance of group work greatly increased, as soldiers were tested and instructed in groups and teamwork was emphasized. Groups were also used on occasion to treat combat fatigue, known today as Posttraumatic Stress Disorder (PTSD). It is fair to say that throughout the history of counseling, the cost-effectiveness and time-effectiveness of group work have been demonstrated time and time again during wars and natural disasters—indeed, during any circumstance in which a large number of people required psychoeducational or counseling services.

The 1920s and 1930s

The use of group therapy increased between 1920 and 1930, as did efforts to measure its effectiveness. One of the first outcome studies was noted for individuals with schizophrenia who had previously been considered "untreatable." When Edward Lazell, using a psychoeducational group model, presented lectures on Freudian psychology to groups of these patients with schizophrenia, the medical staff reported that the patients consequently exhibited positive behavioral changes and a reduction in the use of sedatives. These findings led other practitioners who had reported success with group work to supplement their anecdotal documentation with observations from additional medical staff, patients' family members, and patients' self-reports. Today, it is still considered an excellent practice to gather information from multiple respondents when measuring the effectiveness of group interventions or counseling outcomes.

During the 1920s and 1930s, several early theorists of group work emerged. Alfred Adler emphasized the innate social nature of human beings to support a group treatment model and conducted groups in the 1920s that investigated the relationship between children's problems and family experiences (Gazda, Ginter, & Horne, 2008). Adler and his associates developed group family meetings, or family councils, to obtain input from each member about how to best approach disputes and improve family relations. This new, systematic form of group guidance became known as collective counseling. However, Adler did not seek external validation to demonstrate the effectiveness of his techniques, as he claimed that effectiveness should be clearly evident to the group leader.

In the late 1920s, Trigant Burrow developed an interest in how individuals were affected by loneliness and how relationships affected psychiatric issues. He witnessed individuals interacting in groups and determined that individual relationships in one's community have a tremendous impact on the development of psychopathology.

Another major development of the 1920s was J. L. Moreno's creation of the Theater of Spontaneity, the earliest form of psychodrama. Psychodrama was a technique developed to bring about mental and emotional catharsis for the purpose of tension relief. Techniques that arose from this early group work—including role play, catharsis, and a focus on empathy and the encouragement of group members—are still frequently used today.

Also during the 1920s, some early pioneers began to look at the process variables that underlay group work effectiveness. For example, Lewis Wender articulated the first guidelines for group therapeutic factors (e.g., factors that promote the effectiveness of group work with members) after examining the many difficulties associated with conducting successful psychotherapeutic interventions with inpatient populations (i.e., patients hospitalized with severe mental disorders). Individual transference relations (e.g., individual clients reacting to therapists as they would toward a parent or sibling) were hard to accomplish with inpatients, and the associated time and cost were often prohibitive. After determining that analytic procedures were ineffective, Wender discovered that group therapy produced such desired qualities as intellectualization, patient-to-patient transference, and catharsis in the family, all of which promoted therapeutic progress.

What is known as the Developmental Period in group counseling began in the 1930s and continued into the 1960s. During this time, group work in the schools underwent a transformation from predominantly a psychoeducational usage to a more balanced use of classroom guidance (psychoeducational group work) and group counseling, in both elementary and secondary settings. From 1930 to 1945, substantial laboratory research was conducted to quantify the influence of social interactions on behavior and to determine how different methods of group persuasion and peer pressure changed people's convictions and beliefs. Throughout this time period, research was focused primarily on identifying individual changes in a group setting, rather than on studying the dynamics within the group itself. The work of two leading figures led to considerable expansion of the interest in group work and high-quality group research. Moreno's prominence as a pioneer in the group counseling field continued to grow during the 1930s. He wrote prolifically; organized the first society of group therapists, called the American Society for Group Psychotherapy and Psychodrama; and first coined the term *group psychotherapy*. He also introduced the first professional journal on group therapy: *Sociometry: A Journal of Interpersonal Relations.*

S. R. Slavson, an educator and self-taught therapist, founded the American Group Psychotherapy Association (AGPA) in 1942, along with its accompanying publication, the *International Journal for Group Psychotherapy*. The AGPA was an interdisciplinary organization for group psychotherapists dedicated to improving the practice, research, and theory of group psychotherapy. Today, the AGPA has standards for ethical practice and clinical membership and a voluntary Clinical Registry of Certified Group Psychotherapists. As part of his research, Slavson offered activity therapy groups for children and reported that group activity sessions were equally as effective as individual counseling for stimulating change. His work was a catalyst for significant increases in the use of group treatment procedures for children and adolescents, and it became an impetus for the introduction of group counseling in the schools.

As research provided more evidence of the effectiveness of group therapy, widening patient populations began to seek out this means of treatment for personal growth. Another significant event of the 1930s was the founding of the first major self-help group in America, Alcoholics Anonymous. The originators of this group model recognized the power of bringing together individuals in a supportive way to produce change. Listening, empathizing, and teaching were hallmark characteristics.

The 1940s and 1950s

In the 1940s, more and more practitioners began to realize the powerful dynamics created in group therapy settings. The use of this therapeutic medium expanded tremendously during this time due to the needs of military personnel after World War II. Specifically, the war increased interest and innovations in the use of groups due to a shortage of therapists and a need to treat large numbers of veterans through rehabilitation counseling and psychotherapy as well as through the use of psychoeducational approaches for vocational planning and career development. Interestingly, much of the emphasis in vocational approaches with returning veterans was patterned after psychoeducational group work approaches that had been used with school-aged adolescents for several decades in schools.

Kurt Lewin, a major figure of this era, is known as the founder of the study of modern group dynamics. In 1940, Lewin began the study of intragroup relations. He viewed groups as agents for change and has been credited with the invention of training groups (or T-groups), which blossomed into the encounter and sensitivity groups of the 1960s and 1970s and which were commonly used in schools at that time. His approach, known as field theory, emphasized the interaction between individuals and their environments, and he was heavily influenced by the ideas of Gestalt psychology, which emphasized the relationship of the part to the whole. Lewin's research on T-groups was conducted at the National Training Laboratories in Bethel, Maine, and resulted in the finding that people's ideas and behaviors were more susceptible to change in group settings than in individual interactions. Lewin also studied the characteristics of group leaders and noted the ways in which leaders facilitated growth and change in group members. His research resulted in the identification of the predictable stages of group work and specific change markers for individual clients.

In the late 1940s, Wilfred Bion, a member of the Tavistock Institute of Human Relations in Great Britain, studied group cohesiveness and stated that group dynamics often differ greatly from the dynamics of a family unit (Gladding, 2008). The trend toward structured group counseling investigations continued in the 1950s, as additional research was conducted on group structure, climate, leadership, and settings (Gazda et al., 2008). Many therapists recognized that group work was more effective and advantageous than individual counseling, but individual therapists argued that changes made in group therapy were only superficial in nature because proper transference with the therapist could not be achieved. This argument was quelled, however, when evidence was consistently presented to demonstrate that transference was not only achieved but also enhanced in group therapy settings.

The American School Counselor Association (ASCA) was founded in 1952 and became a division of the American Counseling Association (ACA) the following year. While educational institutions continued to implement career guidance, a new emphasis was placed on group and individual counseling to increase academic achievement and enhance the school climate. The 1957 launching of the Soviet satellite *Sputnik I* created an urgency in the United States. Many leaders believed the United States had fallen behind in the "space race" because public K–12 schools and colleges were not producing students competent enough in math and the sciences to compete in the increasingly technological world. In 1958, the National Defense Education Act (NDEA) was signed into law, targeting money for the training and employment of school counselors in U.S. public high schools. Primarily, these school counselors were tasked with identifying and encouraging students with high math and science aptitudes to pursue college degrees in the sciences. Of course, the role of the professional school counselor over time evolved beyond the emphasis on "test and place" to encompass a developmental approach involving group work and individual counseling (Herr & Erford, 2007). By the end of the 1950s, classroom guidance, a psychoeducational group work approach, while still used quite often to achieve educational and career development goals, was largely replaced by group counseling when the goal was to bring about behaviorally based changes in educational environments.

The 1960s and 1970s

The popularity of groups flourished during the 1960s, largely due to the social climate of that era. The power of groups to create change became evident in the light of such historical events as the Vietnam War and the "hippie movement." Interestingly, group therapy research decreased from 1960 to 1980 (Gazda et al., 2008). Although group treatment was used extensively in societal settings, there was a greater emphasis on experiential rather than empirical validation of its effectiveness. Many have speculated that this shift in research practice was fueled by the general disdain for authority that was prevalent during that time period.

Advances in psychoanalytic theory and object relations theory for group therapy were made in the 1960s and 1970s. Several humanistic-existential therapists also aided in the development of group therapy and practice during this time. Fritz Perls developed Gestalt therapy, based on Gestalt psychology, and demonstrated its use in a group setting through workshops conducted at the Esalen Institute in California.

During the 1960s and 1970s, Carl Rogers initiated encounter groups, also known as sensitivity training groups, to encourage and assist in the pursuit of individual growth and development. These groups emphasized an increased awareness of the group member's emotions and the behaviors of other members, and members were encouraged to explore interpersonal issues within a connected and caring community. Rogers's person-centered approach was very applicable to school settings and helped group counseling to flourish there.

An unfortunate side effect of the tremendous popularity of group work was an increase in the incidences of misuse by untrained practitioners seeking to ride the wave of the movement. The exploitation of group therapy was sensationalized by journalists during the 1960s and beyond, especially because many participants with emotional disturbances were harmed by membership in groups that functioned without adequate prescreening. Leaders who abused and distorted the group process set the field back considerably by garnering bad press and ill-will among members of the public. Unfortunately, some of this public backlash also tarnished the use of groups in schools.

Group work in the 1970s continued to reveal an awareness of the potential hazards of this treatment modality. The term *groupthink* was coined to describe the power that members had over one another to compel conformity. This was seen as a hindrance to individual growth and problem-solving abilities. The classic example of groupthink involved the performance of high-level government officials in President Kennedy's administration during the Cuban Missile Crisis. In this example, those officials with less close relationships to the President chose not to share concerns or interpretations that varied from or did not conform to the concerns or perspectives voiced by more powerful and closely related officials. The power of the group process has both positive and hazardous consequences; skilled leaders know this and address harmful issues when they occur within the group.

Carl Rogers, the leading pioneer of person-centered therapy, bore witness to the powerful changes in attitudes and beliefs that could be achieved in group settings. While many practitioners shared Rogers's enthusiasm for the medium, others came to doubt its validity in the face of overzealous and undertrained therapists, whose practices were controversial and occasionally harmful to clients. For this reason, the need for increasing the professionalization of group work was recognized.

In response to this call for the advancement of professionalism in group work, the ASGW was founded as a division of the ACA in 1973. Its purpose was to "establish standards for professional and ethical practice; to support research and the dissemination of knowledge; and to provide professional leadership in the field of group work" (ASGW, 2006), and it has continued that mission through the present day. In 2000, the ASGW revised the *ASGW Professional Standards for the Training of Group Workers* (ASGW, 2000). This important document provides core training standards for all master's- and doctoral-level counselor education programs and specialization guidelines for counselor education programs that provide advanced and specific group work training to professional counselors. An even more important document, and one referenced throughout numerous chapters in this book, is the *ASGW Best Practice Guidelines* (ASGW, 2007). The ASGW (see www.asgw.org) continues to be an association dedicated to the effective practice of group work by providing consultation, sponsoring continuing education, and contributing to the extant literature through its flagship journal, *The Journal for Specialists in Group Work.* Likewise, the ASCA helped professionalize the practice of group counseling in the schools by publishing its first position statement on group counseling in 1989.

The percentage of research articles on groups in counseling journals rose from 5% in the 1950s to 20% in the 1970s. Particularly important research was conducted by Irvin Yalom, who analyzed group methods and processes and described therapeutic factors within groups that had positive, curative effects on members. In particular, group leaders' styles and methodologies were found to have an especially strong impact on group success or failure. Yalom's research was published as the definitive resource on the therapeutic factors in group counseling and has retained its prominence into the 21st century. See Table 1.1 for a

TABLE 1.1 Therapeutic Factors in Group Work

In group work, a therapeutic factor is an element, generally created by the group leader or by relationships with other members, that improves a member's overall condition. Building on the work of several researchers (e.g., Corsini and Rosenberg; Hill; Berzon, Pious, and Farson), Irvin Yalom developed in the 1970s what is now considered the landmark classification of curative or therapeutic factors (Yalom & Leszcz, 2005):

1. *Instillation of hope* provides clients with a sense of assurance that the treatment will work.
2. *Universality* is the awareness of the similar concerns of others. As students interact with other group members, they come to realize that other members are going through similar situations and so feel much less alone and isolated, creating a sense of unity.
3. *Imparting of information* about healthy living is important to the growth of members and their ability to function more effectively. Leaders may provide information about helpful techniques such as those that aid in socialization, while students learn how to deal with academic, career, personal/social, mental health, mental illness, and other real-life problems.
4. *Altruism* is exemplified by students giving of themselves and working for the common good.
5. *Family reenactment* helps re-create early childhood dynamics so that members are able to relive early family conflicts and effectively resolve them. Psychotherapy (and sometimes counseling) groups can create a caring family environment in which issues of trauma can be safely aired and confronted.
6. *Development of socialization techniques* is necessary for students to function successfully in their everyday lives. Group work allows members to give and receive personal feedback that facilitates learning about the desirability of one's behaviors.
7. *Imitative behavior* occurs when students have an opportunity to observe the behaviors of other members and witness the positive or negative responses elicited by their actions.
8. *Interpersonal learning* occurs through student interactions with others. Each member affects the others in much the same way that they affect the people they interact with in their everyday lives, and members can receive feedback on their conduct that helps them to learn new ways of being, while feeling safe and supported.
9. *Group cohesiveness* is similar to a feeling of unity and a sense of being bonded together. Cohesiveness indicates that effective therapy is occurring because it facilitates trust and a willingness to take risks. Groups provide acceptance, belonging, and an outlet to express previously unexplored emotions.
10. *Catharsis* is the expression of strong and often hidden emotions by an individual. Catharsis is characterized primarily by a sense of freeing oneself. Instead of masking one's true feelings, group work provides a forum for releasing tension and venting about whatever a member has kept inside.
11. *Existential factors* are realized when students are encouraged to consider important and sometimes painful truths about life, including an awareness of their own mortality and the unpredictability of existence.

brief introduction to these therapeutic or curative factors. These factors will be expanded on in the later chapters when contextually relevant.

   During the 1970s, group work received another strong push when soldiers returning from the Vietnam War received rehabilitation counseling and group counseling and psychotherapy to help readjust to society. Professional counselors relied on group work as a cost- and time-effective method for addressing the complex issues of numerous soldiers.

This trend continued even more recently as soldiers from the first and second wars in Iraq experienced similar war-related trauma and physical or emotional disabilities.

The 1980s and Beyond

In the 1980s, group counseling continued to increase in popularity and professionalism. The AGPA worked to refine group theory and practice through the publication of scholarly articles on group counseling innovations, and in 1980, the ASGW published a professional code of ethics for group workers to address increasing concerns over unprofessional behaviors demonstrated by unqualified or poorly trained individuals. The quest for personal growth and the expansion of counseling theory led to a proliferation in the different types of groups available to clients. Self-help groups, frequently led by group members rather than professionals, but still falling under the group counseling functional model, became particularly prevalent, with between 2,000 and 3,000 self-help groups in existence during the 1980s (Gladding, 2008), some hosted by schools and school-community partnerships. Psychoeducational groups and classroom guidance were also popular, particularly in schools, where they were used to address the developmental personal/social, academic, and career needs of children and adolescents. Leaders in the field, such as George Gazda, advocated for the use of developmental group counseling for teaching basic life skills. By the close of the 1980s, group work was widely recognized as a viable option for helping students and was readily available to the public.

Division 49 of the American Psychological Association, called the Group Psychology and Group Psychotherapy Division, was founded in 1991 to provide a forum for the practice, research, and teaching of group work in psychology. Division 49 publishes the journal *Group Dynamics: Theory, Research, and Practice.*

The Council for the Accreditation of Counseling and Related Educational Programs (CACREP) revised its standards in 1994 (and again in 2001 and 2009) to include specific group work specialist preparation guidelines for the graduate-level degrees. The importance of group work was reemphasized by these revisions, which identified specific principles for group dynamics, leadership styles, and group counseling theories, methods, and ethical considerations.

Group work proliferated in schools during the 1990s as an effective means for improving student academics and social skills. It was also used extensively with special populations, from those with disabilities to individuals experiencing major life changes. Greater specialization and segmenting in group work occurred during this time period, with practitioners seeking proficiency in such areas as occupational, psychoeducational, and psychotherapy groups (Gladding, 2008). While self-help groups continued to be a dominant force in the field, task groups in schools and work settings experienced the most remarkable growth in North America. Additional branches such as parenting groups, cooperative learning groups, and focus groups also emerged. It was during this time that the ASGW converged on a preferred language, featuring the term *group work*, and specified four types of group work: task groups, psychoeducational groups, counseling groups, and psychotherapy groups. These four different types of group work will be referred to throughout this book.

The ASCA has emerged as a positive force for school counseling and group work in the schools. Its *National Model* (ASCA, 2005) features systemic and data-driven approaches to school counseling delivered through a comprehensive, developmental school counseling program model. Classroom guidance, psychoeducational group work, and group counseling are primary methods for achieving the goals of the school counseling program. The ASCA

(2007) has revised its position statement on group counseling, adding the emerging evidence of the effectiveness of group counseling in achieving positive outcomes for students. Also, the 2004 ASCA *Ethical Standards for School Counselors* (see Chapter 2) include language that addresses issues specific to group work in the schools, including confidentiality, informed consent, and relationships among group members.

Group work has continued to develop and evolve at a rapid pace to meet the needs of the current generation. In the 21st century, group work has become an elemental part of the professional lives of school counselors. Group work's effectiveness has encouraged its ongoing refinement and use. Importantly, the evolution in the research and practice of group work from its roots in the early 20th century to its current practice in schools has produced reliable evidence of its advantages over other approaches to changing thoughts, feelings, and behaviors. Various group work approaches possess particular strengths, depending on the specific therapeutic context and process. Likewise, despite the many benefits that can be derived from group work, group work is not appropriate for all students or in all cases. Indeed, there can be both challenges and dangers associated with group work. As a conclusion to this chapter, some of these strengths and challenges are outlined in Table 1.2.

TABLE 1.2   Strengths and Challenges of Group Work

Strengths of Group Work

---

1. *Time Efficiency for the Leader.* Meeting with several students simultaneously for a common purpose (e.g., advising, solving problems, strengthening social support, aiding in personal development) can save substantial time and effort, especially when a counselor's caseload is quite large, as is the case in many schools.

2. *Less Costly per Individual.* There is generally a lower cost associated with group work as compared with individual counseling; all other things being equal, a school counselor seeing 5 to 10 students at a time is 5 to 10 times more time- and cost-efficient.

3. *Greater Resources.* Group members often have access to a greater variety of resources (e.g., concrete information, problem-solving tools, abstract viewpoints, values) from multiple members within a group than does a student in a one-on-one counseling relationship.

4. *Feeling of Safety.* Interpersonal safety can be achieved in groups. Member relationships are developed with a controlled intimacy, which makes it possible for individuals to open up and share their true emotions without the contingent obligations that often arise with this type of self-disclosure in personal relationships.

5. *Experiencing a Sense of Belonging.* Most humans have a powerful need to belong. Working with a group of individuals in a therapeutic setting allows members to exchange ideas and feel greater self-confidence as well as a sense of belonging. Students often perceive that their feelings are not shared by others, but in a group setting, they come to realize that others are experiencing similar struggles. Children and teenagers have reported that the acceptance they felt by other members during group counseling was one of the most important aspects of their counseling experience.

6. *Replication of the Everyday World.* The group is essentially a microcosm of society. Conflicts that arise in group settings are often similar in nature to those that are experienced in the outside world, especially if the group's membership is diverse and true-to-life issues are addressed.

(continued)

TABLE 1.2   Strengths and Challenges of Group Work *(continued)*

---

7. *Safe Setting in Which to Practice New Skills and Receive Feedback.* Students can use the group as a sounding board for trying out alternative problem-solving techniques and consequently assess the likelihood that they will be successful when using those techniques in their everyday lives. Groups provide an atmosphere of empathy and trust in which students can build on their existing skills and develop new interaction patterns to facilitate greater interpersonal success in their lives.

8. *Commitment.* Group settings often enhance students' motivation to follow through with commitments that are made during group sessions. The support that students feel from others and the desire to live up to their expectations so as not to let anyone down are powerful forces that effect individual change.

9. *Power of the Peer Group.* The influence of various groups on an individual's life is almost inevitable and can affect member development in diverse ways, especially in terms of conformity, identity, reward and punishment, and social controls. When all group members are from the same generation, the impact of group dynamics is generally the most significant. This is particularly true during adolescence.

10. *Interpersonal Power.* In group settings, members not only have the opportunity to receive help but also are empowered to help others. As students witness the positive influence that their interventions have on others, they may become more willing to accept the influence of other members and grow in positive ways.

Challenges of Group Work

---

1. *Pressure to Conform.* The power of the group can be problematic if it leads students to actively pursue unrealistic goals, take actions that are detrimental to their well-being, or conform to behaviors that go against their beliefs in order to be accepted by other members.

2. *Reality Distortion.* Reality distortion (Trotzer, 1999) occurs when the group provides an example of social reality that is not achievable in the outside world. This can be devastating to an individual if the other members or the group leader fails to consider reality factors when helping to formulate workable solutions to his or her problems.

3. *Avoidance.* Certain group members may not reap adequate benefits from group work if they are less comfortable participating openly or are not given enough attention. Individual members are sometimes able to avoid confronting their problems if they blend in with the group (e.g., camouflage) or if the group setting becomes so safe and accepting that the individual members do not feel compelled to take risks or action toward addressing the issues for which they sought counseling in the first place.

4. *Confidentiality.* Confidentiality cannot be guaranteed in group settings. Since there are numerous individuals participating in each session, there is a greater risk of information being shared with others outside of the group. During prescreening and in the first session, it is critical for group leaders to convey the importance of maintaining confidentiality as well as the conditions under which content that is disclosed might have to be revealed.

5. *Unhealthy Attachments.* The counseling group is transitional, not a permanent social outlet. Students who lack a feeling of acceptance from others in their everyday lives can rely too heavily on relationships formed in groups. Experiencing a sense of belonging is only valuable if it facilitates the achievement of a better life outside of the group.

6. *Institutional Barriers.* Some schools have systemic barriers in place that inhibit effective group work (e.g., parental permission, personnel not realizing the value of group work versus missing class time, scheduling challenges, finding space in school buildings to run groups). Leaders must realize that these barriers may exist and persevere. In schools, counselor initiative often determines the prevalence and promise of group work.

Summary

This chapter highlighted several different types of functional group models: task groups, psychoeducational groups, counseling groups, and psychotherapy groups. The various types of groups provide different ways to meet the needs of students. With regard to leadership, leaders of some groups (i.e., counseling and psychotherapy groups) may take on a more facilitative, less active role. With the other types of groups (i.e., task and psychoeducational groups), leaders may be more directive and active in the group process. These functional group models will be described in much greater depth in Chapters 11–13.

Throughout recorded history, human beings have gathered in groups for common benefit. Group work is the field of counseling intervention that applies knowledge and skill to help group members to meet their goals. Numerous influential pioneers have contributed to the development of group work practices commonly used in schools today, including Joseph Pratt, Jesse Davis, Frank Parsons, J. L. Moreno, S. R. Slavson, and Irvin Yalom. Kurt Lewin was particularly influential during the 1940s, inventing T-groups and field theory approaches to group work. During the 1960s and 1970s, the leaders of various approaches to individual counseling, including Fritz Perls (Gestalt therapy) and Carl Rogers (person-centered counseling), applied their theoretical approaches to working with group members. Group work, especially psychoeducational and counseling groups, is particularly popular in schools.

Several strengths of group work were discussed, including time efficiency, cost efficiency, greater resource contributions by more members, a feeling of safety, a sense of belonging, replication of the everyday world, a safe place to practice new skills and receive feedback, increased member commitment, peer group power, and interpersonal power. Noted challenges of group work include pressure to conform, reality distortion, avoidance, potential lack of confidentiality, unhealthy attachments, and institutional barriers.

Finally, Yalom has described a number of curative or therapeutic factors leading to student progress, including the instillation of hope, universality, the imparting of information, altruism, family reenactment, the development of socialization techniques, imitative behavior, interpersonal learning, group cohesiveness, catharsis, and existential factors.

CHAPTER 2

Ethical and Legal Foundations of Group Work in the Schools

Lynn E. Linde, Bradley T. Erford,
Danica G. Hays, and F. Robert Wilson

PREVIEW

This chapter highlights essential ethical and legal issues in group work in the schools, including confidentiality, informed consent, relationships among group members, termination issues, group participation, diversity issues, and the Family Educational Rights and Privacy Act.

ETHICAL ISSUES IN GROUP WORK

One of the attributes of sound group work practice in the schools is the continuous assessment of and reflection on the way in which a leader interacts with students. This reflective process is necessary to ensure that the leader provides the most appropriate ethical and legal group work services to students and is particularly important given the myriad issues with which group leaders deal on a daily basis. Some issues are clearly governed by either legal or ethical mandates; other issues are not as clear and challenge leaders to determine the appropriate course of action. When challenges arise, it is wise to begin with an examination of the ethical standards and legal issues. This process is particularly important when conducting groups, as the issues are often more complex than when dealing with one student at a time.

Both laws and ethical standards are based on generally accepted societal norms, beliefs, customs, and values. However, laws are more prescriptive, have been codified, and carry penalties for failure to comply. Another difference is that laws "dictate the *minimum* standards of behavior that society will tolerate, whereas ethics represent the *ideal* standards expected by the profession" (Remley & Herlihy, 2005, p. 3). Ethical standards are generally developed by professional associations to guide members in the practice of their profession.

Ethical standards can be further delineated into two categories: mandatory ethics and aspirational ethics. Mandatory ethics describe minimal adherence to the professional standards; they are the "musts" of counseling practice, and group leaders must comply with them. Aspirational ethics are the "oughts" of counseling, wherein group leaders try to aspire to the highest standards and think about the impact of their behavior. According to Herlihy and Corey (2006), in order to practice aspirational ethics, leaders must go beyond compliance with ethical standards and understand the underlying principles or intent, sometimes referred to as meta-ethical principles.

META-ETHICAL PRINCIPLES

Forester-Miller and Davis (2002) delineated five moral principles that undergird counseling ethical standards and that are important to understand in order to move toward aspirational ethics: autonomy, beneficence, nonmaleficence, fidelity, and justice. Ethical dilemmas occur when meta-ethical principles conflict with one another. While these principles often overlap and are congruent within group work, there are instances when group leaders may be unsure which principle is most beneficial to promote. Dilemmas may also ensue when ethical principles applied to both individual group members and the group as a whole conflict.

Autonomy refers to independence and the right of the student to make his or her own decisions. Leaders need to respect the right of students to make sound and rational decisions based on the students' values and beliefs, rather than on what the school counselor may view as best for students. Leaders do this by addressing and supporting individual group members' goals. Goal setting, a task of early group stages, is conducted both by individuals and by the group as a whole and is related to autonomy. For example, individual and group goals may not be congruent—and at times may even appear to be at cross-purposes. It is imperative that group leaders select students who will not impede or whose well-being will not be harmed by the group process. Students should be encouraged to set goals that can be addressed in the time allotted for the group.

Beneficence refers to doing what is in the best interests of students and promoting well-being, growth, and an optimal group experience. For example, group leaders promote the greater good for students by providing adequate time for processing group dynamics and content and for evaluating the group experience. An optimal group experience for students may begin with informed consent in the planning phase of the group. Leaders may prepare students from the onset of the group for how and when termination will take place, alternatives to the group experience, follow-up procedures, and potential referrals for continued group work. In addition, group leaders create an optimal group experience by adapting the group content and process as needed and by respecting diverse perspectives and cultural identities present within the group.

Nonmaleficence is often referred to as "doing no harm", that is, leaders avoid doing anything that may harm students. This includes preventing psychological or emotional harm potentially resulting from group member–leader interactions, group leader incompetence, inadequate treatment procedures, student abandonment, or premature termination.

Fidelity refers to honoring commitments and establishing a relationship based on trust. Group leaders promote open communication with students while fostering group relationships. Communication in the form of honest expression of emotions by both group leaders and students can create ethical dilemmas. Along with the challenges of the group process itself, students may experience additional stress if they feel pressured to conform to member functions (e.g., providing feedback to others, evaluating the group experience).

Justice involves the fair treatment and consideration of each student—that is, doing what is best for each student according to the needs of each student by facilitating equitable and culturally relevant treatment. Equitable treatment may refer to equal access to group resources (e.g., "individual" time, content relevant to students' needs). Students may feel that their access is compromised by other group members, as in the case of members who monopolize group time, interrupt others, give inappropriate advice, or ask too many questions during group sessions. Unequal access to group resources may cause some students to feel slighted and lead to premature termination.

Group leaders have a responsibility to students that extends from the screening of members during the group planning phase to the follow-up sessions after termination. This responsibility is guided by ethical behavior and a consideration of the cultural diversity of all students. Thus, group leaders are expected to foster and respect individual development within the context of group learning, facilitate a group in a manner that promotes the group's purpose, avoid and minimize potentially harmful content and process, and be truthful and just with students.

GROUNDING ONESELF IN THE ETHICS OF GROUP WORK

Group leaders are governed by the ethical codes of their professional organizations and certifying bodies. Members of the American Counseling Association (ACA) are bound by the *ACA Code of Ethics* (ACA, 2005) and are encouraged to adhere to the *Cross-cultural Competencies and Objectives* (ACA Professional Standards Committee, 1991). Likewise, members of American School Counselor Association (ASCA) are bound by the *Ethical Standards for School Counselors* (ASCA, 2004). Counselors certified by the National Board for Certified Counselors (NBCC) are expected to adhere to its *Code of Ethics* (NBCC, 2005). Members of the Association for Specialists in Group Work (ASGW) are expected to follow the *ASGW Best Practices Guidelines* (ASGW, 2007) and demonstrate mastery of the *ASGW Principles for Diversity-Competent Group Workers* (ASGW, 1998; see www.asgw.org/PDF/Principles_for_Diversity. pdf). Graduate counselor training programs are encouraged to design their group work training programs to be consistent with the *ASGW Professional Standards for the Training of Group Workers* (ASGW, 2000) and the national accreditation standards of the Council for Accreditation of Counseling and Related Educational Programs (CACREP; 2009).

The ACA is the professional association for all professional counselors. One of the functions of professional associations is to promulgate ethical standards and thereby provide direction and information to the members and their clients about appropriate and ethical behavior. The *ACA Code of Ethics* (ACA, 2005) addresses the responsibilities of leaders toward their clients, colleagues, workplace, and themselves by delineating the ideal standards for conducting one's behavior. All ACA members are required to abide by the *ACA Code of Ethics*, and action will be taken against any member who fails to do so. In effect, as these are the standards of the profession, all leaders, including those counselors who lead groups in schools, are held to the *ACA Code of Ethics* by the mental health community, regardless of whether they are members of the ACA (Linde, 2007).

The *ACA Code of Ethics* is applicable to counseling in all settings and with all populations. However, more to the purpose of this book, two sections address issues specific to groups and especially the use of group work in schools:

A.8.A. SCREENING

Counselors screen prospective group counseling/therapy participants. To the extent possible, counselors select members whose needs and goals are compatible with the goals of the group, who will not impede group process, and whose well-being will not be jeopardized by the group experience.

A.8.B. PROTECTING CLIENTS

In a group setting, counselors take reasonable precautions to protect clients from physical, emotional, or psychological trauma.

Thus, Section A.8 outlines, in broad terms, the responsibilities of the group leader when creating a group to screen potential members, ensure the appropriateness of the students chosen, and do what is in the best interest of the other students in the group.

Several divisions of the ACA and other counseling organizations have created their own codes of ethics or guidelines for ethical behavior that pertain more specifically to their work setting or specialty area. For professional school counselors, whether or not you are a member of the ASCA, the *Ethical Standards for School Counselors* (ASCA, 2004) provide the guidelines that are most relevant to group counseling in schools. Section A.6. Group Work states:

The professional school counselor:

a. Screens prospective group members and maintains an awareness of participants' needs and goals in relation to the goals of the group. The counselor takes reasonable precautions to protect members from physical and psychological harm resulting from interaction within the group.
b. Notifies parents/guardians and staff of group participation if the counselor deems it appropriate and if consistent with school board policy or practice.
c. Establishes clear expectations in the group setting and clearly states that confidentiality in group counseling cannot be guaranteed. Given the developmental and chronological ages of minors in schools, the counselor recognizes that the tenuous nature of confidentiality for minors renders some topics inappropriate for group work in a school setting.
d. Follows up with group members and documents proceedings as appropriate. (p. 2)

In summary, the *Ethical Standards for School Counselors* describe the safeguards a professional school counselor must address in the development and implementation of a school counseling group. The application of these issues will be addressed more concretely later in this chapter.

The ASGW, a division of the ACA, developed the *ASGW Best Practice Guidelines* (ASGW, 2007; see www.asgw.org/PDF/Best_Practices.pdf at this point and review these guidelines in detail) and the *ASGW Professional Standards for the Training of Group Workers* (ASGW, 2000; see www.asgw.org/PDF/training_standards.pdf at this point and review these training standards in detail). The *ASGW Best Practice Guidelines* identify sound practices when planning a group, selecting members for that group, conducting group sessions, and processing the workings of the group. These guidelines are consistent with the *ACA Code of Ethics* (ACA, 2005) but contain more detail that is useful when conducting groups.

In 2000, the ASGW revised the *ASGW Professional Standards for the Training of Group Workers* to use the more inclusive term *group work* to describe what leaders do, and delineated the levels of training: core training and four specializations. The standards continue to provide guidance to counselor education programs regarding curriculum and delineate the coursework and experiential requirements, knowledge and skill objectives, and assessment and planning skills for the core training on each of the specialty areas. Readers are strongly encouraged to review the *ASGW Best Practices Guidelines* and *ASGW Professional Standards for the Training of Group Workers* to become thoroughly familiar with these critical group work documents.

Finally, group work takes place within a school community and is subject to that school community's culture, norms, and standards of conduct. Whether one is participating in a school-based task group, providing classroom guidance experiences in a school, conducting a group counseling experience for young children with perfectionistic tendencies and concomitant anxiety, or providing group psychotherapy for students who have been sexually traumatized, the leader and students are influenced by the cultural matrix in which they are embedded. The group work truism "all group work is multicultural" provides a helpful reminder. To successfully practice in the multicultural context of group work, leaders must be aware of different worldviews and these worldviews' effect on group work interventions; be aware of personal beliefs and attitudes related to relationships, healing, and health; and learn and provide culturally relevant group work interventions (DeLucia-Waack & Donigian, 2003).

MAJOR ETHICAL ISSUES IN GROUP WORK IN THE SCHOOLS

Leaders conducting group work in the schools will be faced with myriad challenges. Group leaders recognize that conducting groups in any setting is challenging, but conducting groups in school settings involves additional challenges due to the varied and nuanced cultures of different schools, the minor age status of group members, and school policies and procedures that may influence the way in which groups are conducted. This is not to say that running groups in schools is difficult; ordinarily, it is not. But the nuances of school culture, the demands for increased achievement, and the fact that the vast majority of students are minors and may not hold their own privilege and confidence make for special challenges to group work in schools that leaders must attend to. This section provides a brief analyses of and instructions for dealing with confidentiality, informed consent, relationships among group members, participation and termination issues, counselor competence, and diversity issues.

Confidentiality

Confidentiality is the cornerstone of counseling and helps create the atmosphere in which the student feels able to trust and share with the leader and other group members. Students must feel that whatever they tell the group members will not be shared outside of the group except in instances in which the leader recognizes a duty to warn or the member consents. Group work presents special challenges for confidentiality, as the session is not like individual counseling with just one student and one counselor. If a group is going to be productive, members must trust each other. In groups, there is no guaranteed confidentiality between members because there are multiple students in the session. However, there is an ethical obligation for confidentiality that leaders must uphold. Section A.7.d of the *ASGW Best Practice Guidelines* (ASGW, 2007) states:

> Group Workers define confidentiality and its limits (for example, legal and ethical exceptions and expectations; waivers implicit with treatment plans, documentation and insurance usage). Group Workers have the responsibility to inform all group participants of the need for confidentiality, and the potential consequences of breaching confidentiality, and that legal privilege does not apply to group discussions (unless provided by the state statute). (p. 5)

Section A.6.c of the *Ethical Standards for School Counselors* (ASCA, 2004) indicates that the professional school counselor

> Establishes clear expectations in the group setting and clearly states that confidentiality in group counseling cannot be guaranteed. Given the developmental and chronological age of minors in schools, the counselor recognizes the tenuous nature of confidentiality for minors renders some topics inappropriate for group work in a school setting.

Conducting groups with minor children places an extra responsibility on school counselors to collaborate with parents/guardians and provide them with accurate and comprehensive information, while still maintaining ethical responsibilities to the students.

It is the responsibility of the group leader to emphasize the importance of confidentiality and to establish this as the norm (Cottone & Tarvydas, 2007). A discussion of confidentiality should be a part of the screening interview and the first session and should be repeated throughout the group experience as appropriate. However, the group leader must also be honest that confidentiality cannot be guaranteed. If confidentiality is broken during the group experience, the group leader must address the issue with the students and reinforce the norm of confidentiality.

There are additional issues involved when counseling minors. Legally, the confidentiality rights of minor children belong to the parent/guardian, but the ethical rights belong to the child. Balancing the rights of the parents/guardians against the needs of the child is a continuous process and involves many factors (Linde, 2007). Professional school counselors must try to maintain confidentiality within the group but must disclose to parents/guardians when necessary. Leaders should help parents/guardians understand the importance that confidentiality plays in school counseling and in groups and engage the trust of the parents/guardians as well as the group members. Should a parent/guardian desire to know what is going on in a group, the leader may divulge information only about that parent's/guardian's child as appropriate and may not share information about other students in the group. Leaders should be aware of state statutes or school policies affecting the counseling of minor children. Professional school counselors may want to obtain passive consent (commonly called assent), if not informed consent, from parents/guardians to ensure their support of their child's participation in the group and their willingness to respect the confidential nature of counseling. (See the next section on informed consent.)

The ACA (2005) and ASCA (2004) discuss the limitations of confidentiality. The major exception to confidentiality is the duty to warn. Should it become apparent that a group member is being harmed (such as by abuse), is harming or threatening someone else, or is threatening to harm him- or herself, the leader has a duty to warn the appropriate entity.

Finally, group leaders should encourage students to honor other group members' right to privacy even after termination of the group experience. A group leader should disseminate information about a group member to a clinician to whom the leader refers that student only when the student/parent/guardian consents, when it is beneficial to the counseling process, when there is an imminent risk of harm to the group member or others, or when there is a court-ordered requirement to disclose information about a group member. In short, confidentiality is for all time unless legal or ethical circumstances require leaders to divulge confidential information.

Informed Consent

As part of the screening interview process, professional school counselors should obtain informed consent from potential group members, or in the case of minor children, they may want or be required to obtain informed consent from the parents. The ASCA ethical standards (2004, Section A.6.b) state that the professional school counselor "Notifies parents/guardians and staff of group participation if the counselor deems it appropriate and if consistent with school board policy or practice." In school settings, professional school counselors must follow the policies and procedures established by the system regarding parent/guardian consent for participation in group. If the system requires parent/guardian consent, it must be obtained prior to beginning the group. If the system either does not require consent or has no policies regarding consent, the professional school counselor must weigh the merits of the situation. While a professional school counselor may have the legal right to conduct groups without parent/guardian consent, in some systems it may be unwise politically to do so. Having a parent/guardian make a complaint to a building administrator or school system official is rarely a pleasant experience, even if the professional school counselor is in the right. In such cases, the professional school counselor may wish to use passive consent (assent), which ordinarily involves a written notification, or to touch base informally with the parents/guardians, ordinarily through a verbal communication, to let them know that the child is going to be included in a group.

Regardless of the consent requirement, it is essential that students understand their rights as group members (ASCA, 2004), the purpose of the group, generally what to expect from the group including the possible outcomes, the limits of confidentiality, and whether participation is voluntary. Cottone and Tarvydas (2007) emphasized that informed consent also addresses the issue of the match between the member and the group. The screening must be sufficient to ensure that the student is being placed in a group that is consistent with the student's goals and that the student is compatible with the group. Group members must also understand (1) the ground rules, the role of the group leader, and the expectations for group members; (2) the limits of and exceptions to confidentiality; (3) the logistics of the group, such as the duration and number of sessions, the expectations for attendance, and the follow-up to the group; and (4) the potential impact of group participation.

If the professional school counselor sends a consent form home with the student, it should contain sufficient information for the parent/guardian to make a determination regarding participation. The form should cover the topic/goal of the group, the number and length of sessions and when sessions will be held, the name and position of the person(s) conducting the group, the expected outcomes, and the contact information of the group leader. If informed consent is required, the form should include a line for the parent's/guardian's signature and the date. Passive consent (assent) would not require the parent/guardian to return a signed form to the school. A sample form can be found in Figure 2.1.

Relationships Among Group Members

The issue of personal relationships among group members sometimes is an ethically gray area. In private practice or mental health center groups, it is unlikely that group members will see each other outside of the group, depending on the size of the community, of course. In school settings, students may often interact outside of the group. It is very common in schools for students to know each other and perhaps even to be in the same class or extracurricular activity. There are times in schools when leaders plan a group on a specific topic, such as loss and grief or changing families, and must decide whether to include siblings/relatives in the same

---

SCHOOL LETTERHEAD

SCHOOL COUNSELING DEPARTMENT

Date
Dear Parent/Guardian:

One of the services our school counseling program provides is to work with students in small groups on a variety of topics throughout the school year. Participation in these groups is voluntary. Group sessions are usually scheduled once a week for eight weeks during the school day. The groups are scheduled to minimize the amount of time that students miss from their classes, and students are expected to make up any work they may miss. Confidentiality of what students share will be respected but cannot be guaranteed.

Your child, _____, has been invited to participate in a group on
_____. The group should begin _____
and should end _____. The purpose of the group is _____
_____, and it is expected that participation in the group will lead to
_____.
Please sign the form at the bottom of this letter and return it to me to allow your child to participate by (date) _____.

Please feel free to contact me if you have any questions. I can be reached by telephone at
_____ or by email at _____.

Sincerely,

Professional School Counselor

Group Counseling Consent Form

I give permission for my child, _____, to participate in group counseling with the school counselor. I understand this group will focus on _____.

_____   _____

Parent/Guardian Signature   Date _____

FIGURE 2.1 A sample informed consent letter to parents/guardians.

group. Which is ethically more appropriate: to provide the service for all members needing the help and to deal with any relationship issues that arise or to deny group membership to some students because they have a relative in the group? Professional school counselors sometimes are faced with this and other dilemmas. So long as care is taken to minimize problems and maximize participation, either course of action may be ethically appropriate.

When Should a Group Terminate?

The *ACA Code of Ethics* (ACA, 2005) states that group leaders should terminate groups when services are no longer effective or required. Services may be considered ineffective when group content and process are not appropriate for students or when leaders lack competence regarding group leadership or content. In addition, group leaders should be cognizant that not all students will be ready to end the group at the same time, creating a dilemma between individual group member and group development. Students develop differently throughout the group as they set goals, overcome resistance, develop and apply new skills, and say good-bye to each other. A number of issues specifically related to a student's readiness for termination can present the group leader with ethical dilemmas. Group leaders help students meet individual goals (e.g., applied learning, minimization of unfinished business), but in reality, how responsible are group leaders for ensuring applied learning? How much unfinished business is allowed at the end of a group experience to still have successful termination? What professional and ethical obligation do group leaders have to follow up with students after termination? These are all questions group leaders will face.

In school settings, classroom guidance and counseling groups are generally planned for a finite number of sessions and terminate at the designated date. Professional school counselors must be sensitive to the progress made by individual students during the sessions and provide appropriate follow-up—and, if appropriate, referrals—for those students in need of continuing assistance.

Group Participation

Group leaders should encourage silent members to participate, acknowledge nonverbal communication, and discourage students from monopolizing the time or content of the group session. Because a key assumption in group work involves verbal expression for group member growth, group leaders should also respect individual differences related to communication patterns. For instance, some students may value nonverbal communication, view group leaders as expert, and thus be less inclined to challenge others. It is good practice to get all members active in the group process early on in group sessions to facilitate participation, trust, and cohesion.

The Right to Terminate Prematurely

Premature termination may be beneficial to individual group members, particularly if they perceive that the group is not meeting their needs in some way. In addition, students may choose to terminate prematurely as a result of an improper placement in the group. For closed groups (i.e., groups that will not accept new members once the group sessions have begun), group leaders should encourage students who wish to leave the group early to discuss why they want to leave the group with other group members within a session. Such actions help bring some degree of closure for the student who wants to leave and those students who will remain. The discussion also frequently creates interesting content and process related to individual and group goals.

Ethical standards (ACA, 2005) and best practice guidelines (ASGW, 2007) require that leaders not abandon or neglect members and that they monitor their services to ensure that students who are not benefiting from a particular group experience are referred for a more appropriate form of therapy or to a different type of group.

Counselor Competence

The *ACA Code of Ethics* (ACA, 2005) cautions professional counselors to practice only within the scope of their education, training, and experience. Section A of the *ASGW Best Practices Guidelines* (ASGW, 2007) discusses the issues involved in counselor competence when conducting groups and states that group workers should be aware of their strengths and weaknesses when leading groups, practice in those areas for which they meet the training criteria, and assess their knowledge and skill in the type of group they lead. Developing competence in the core areas delineated by the ASGW training standards is the foundation for conducting groups. It is essential that professional school counselors continuously monitor their own competence, as different groups and clients require different skills (Remley & Herlihy, 2005).

Additionally, leaders must be aware of how their personality and character influence the way in which the group functions and ultimately affect the success of the group. Group workers must go through the self-reflective process to examine their positions on issues. This is particularly important because value-laden issues often arise in counseling sessions. The group leader's values and beliefs will come out during the group sessions. Gladding (2008) believed that group leaders who try to hide or are unaware of their values may actually do more harm than good, and encouraged leaders to model openness by displaying a willingness to explore and accept diverse viewpoints, values, and beliefs.

Competence in group counseling involves group leaders employing interventions that are congruent with group purpose and that are culturally relevant. Group leaders should continually monitor their effectiveness by formal and informal methods to avoid group member harm. In addition, group leaders should seek continuing education in group leadership, including culturally sensitive and culturally relevant group practice (ACA, 2005; ASGW, 2007).

While it is typically viewed as unethical for a group leader to prematurely terminate a group, it may be ethically imperative to do so if a group leader does not possess group leadership skills or have specialized knowledge needed to facilitate a group. Ethical standards (ACA, 2005) and best practice guidelines (ASGW, 2007) state that counselors in a group setting should discontinue services and provide appropriate referrals to avoid client abandonment.

Diversity Issues

Chapter 3 will review diversity issues in group work in greater depth. The major point of this section is to reinforce the concept that when group leaders are knowledgeable of diversity issues and skilled in the implementation of approaches to meet diverse student needs, they are behaving ethically. The group leader must be culturally competent and sensitive to personal and group member behaviors for the group to be successful (Cottone & Tarvydas, 2007). The *ASGW Principles for Diversity-Competent Group Workers* (ASGW, 1998) stress the need for group leaders to be culturally sensitive to and to understand how their cultural and diversity issues affect the group process and dynamics. Group leaders must also be aware of how the backgrounds of the students may influence their acceptance into the group and their behavior once in the group.

As part of their training, leaders should be able to identify, describe, and demonstrate skill in "use of personal contextual factors (e.g., family-of-origin, neighborhood-of-residence, organizational membership, cultural membership) in interpreting the behavior of members in a group" (ASGW, 2000, p. 6). Group workers who gain these skills and self-awareness are able to lead groups that are responsive to issues of diversity.

LEGAL ISSUES IN GROUP WORK

The previous discussion centered on the codes of ethics and ethical behavior. Group leaders must also comply with those laws that apply to counseling practice. Laws are most often based on the same, generally accepted norms, beliefs, customs, and values as ethical standards. However, laws are more prescriptive, have been incorporated into a legal code, and carry greater sanctions or penalties for failure to comply. Both laws and ethical standards exist to ensure appropriate behavior by professionals within a particular context—in this case, to ensure that the best interests of the members of a group are met. When laws and ethics appear to be in conflict with each other, the professional must attempt to resolve the conflict in a responsible manner (Cottone & Tarvydas, 2007). Remley and Herlihy (2005) suggested that there are few conflicts between laws and ethics in professional counseling. If a conflict does occur, group leaders must make their members aware of the conflict and their ethical standards. But because there are greater penalties associated with laws, group leaders will often follow the legal course of action if there is no harm to the students. Many ethical standards recognize that other mandates must be followed and suggest that leaders work to change mandates that are not in the best interests of their students (Linde, 2007).

First and foremost, group leaders are governed by law. Before engaging in any form of counseling practice, a leader should become thoroughly grounded in the state statutes that regulate the practice of their profession. These include the specific statute that establishes and regulates the practice of counseling, the statutes that regulate a mental health care professional's duty to warn or protect third parties from harm threatened by a client, the statutes that limit the conditions under which a client or student may claim privileged communication rights, and the statutes that limit liability should a professional counselor breach confidentiality by reporting student communications to potential victims or to authorities. For counselors who conduct groups in schools, the most important law to be aware of is the Family Educational Rights and Privacy Act of 1974, which governs student records, including the records of counseling sessions, but not personal notes.

The Family Educational Rights and Privacy Act of 1974

The Family Educational Rights and Privacy Act of 1974 (FERPA; 20 U.S.C. § 1232g; 34 C.F.R. Part 99) is the federal law that protects the privacy of all student records in all preK–12 schools, colleges, and universities that accept funding from programs administered by the U.S. Department of Education. It is often referred to as the Buckley Amendment. FERPA defines education records as all information collected by a school for attendance, achievement, group and individual testing and assessment, behavior, and school activities. It gives parents/guardians and non-minor students specific rights regarding this information, including the right to inspect and review the student's records and an appeals process if they disagree with anything in the record. The law also limits who may access records. Under FERPA, only those persons with a "legitimate educational interest" can access a student's records. Some personally identifiable information, usually referred to as directory or public information, may be released without parent/guardian consent and generally includes such information as the student's name, address, telephone number, date and place of birth, honors and awards, and attendance information. The major exception to the confidentiality of student records relates to law enforcement issues: The school must comply with a judicial order or lawfully executed subpoena. In cases of emergency, information about the student relevant to the emergency can be released without parent/guardian consent. (See www.ed.gov/print/policy/gen/guid/fpco/ferpa/index.html for an electronic copy of the law.) All states and local jurisdictions have incorporated FERPA's requirements into state statutes and local policies that schools must follow.

The right of consent transfers to students upon their 18th birthday, although the law does not specifically limit the rights of parents whose children are over the age of 18 years but who continue to attend a secondary school or to a student who attends a postsecondary institution at any age, that is, parents/guardians may be entitled to their non-minor child's confidential information under some circumstances, unless a court prohibits the information's release. In addition, noncustodial parents have the same rights as custodial parents/guardians unless a court order has limited or terminated the rights of one or both parents/guardians. Without court-appointed authority, stepparents and other family members who do not have legal custody of the child have no rights under FERPA.

FERPA requirements affect group work in public schools. Leaders conducting groups in schools must be aware of the limitations that FERPA may impose on any curriculum materials they use in groups, on any assessments used to identify or evaluate students in the group process, and on the types of information that should be kept in counseling notes. While some schools do not require informed consent for participation in groups, professional school counselors may want to consider using informed consent or assent forms to avoid problems, particularly if they are touching on sensitive areas.

Additionally, leaders need to remember that parents/guardians have the right to access their children's records. FERPA distinguishes personal notes as separate from the educational record and therefore as not subject to its provisions. However, counseling notes constructed by the school counselor may be construed as part of the educational record and therefore as subject to review by or sharing with others if the counselor reads from the notes or shares summary findings from the notes with colleagues in the school. Group leaders need to remember this when writing counseling notes. Once the personal notes are shared, the notes are no longer personal notes; they belong to the student's educational record.

Summary

Ethical and legal issues are of particular import in counseling. Group work, like other forms of counseling, presents a variety of ethical issues, and it is critically important to be aware of the codes of ethics, the best practice guidelines, laws, and other resources that may help the leader determine the most appropriate course of action when conducting groups. FERPA governs the sharing of student information in preK–12 schools, colleges, and universities that accept public funding from the U.S. Department of Education.

The *ACA Code of Ethics*, FERPA, the *ASGW Best Practice Guidelines*, and the *ASGW Professional Standards for the Training of Group Workers* are critically important documents with which all professional counselors conducting group work should be thoroughly familiar. Issues that will continue to challenge leaders striving for ethical counseling practice include confidentiality, informed consent, relationships among group members, counselor competence, diversity issues, and record keeping. As a final activity, test your understanding of ethical and legal issues in group work by reading and responding to the brief case scenarios presented in Case Dilemmas 2.1.

Case Dilemmas 2.1   How will you handle the following ethical/legal scenarios?

1. Jonathan comes to groups very angry. He accuses Sam of divulging private information about him to other students in the school—information Sam could have known only because Jonathan shared the information two sessions ago.
2. Sam's mother calls and tells you she is concerned about some information Sam divulged to her about another student in the group named Jonathan.
3. Susan's guardian called and wants an update on Susan's progress in the grief and loss group.
4. The mother of twins Rowdy and Serenity called to ask if they could be included in the group counseling experience on grief and loss that you intend to begin shortly. She indicated that her husband died less than six months ago and the twins are not adjusting as she had hoped.
5. You are beginning a counseling group on substance abuse for current users and are wondering whether you should obtain parent/guardian consent.
6. You are now in the sixth session of an eight-session group experience for children of alcoholics, and Leroy has not said a word since the introductions during session one. On several occasions, he has opted to "take a pass." Several other group members have exchanged looks and seem uncomfortable with his lack of sharing.
7. The day after the sixth session of an eight-session group for children of alcoholics you receive an e-mail from Leroy telling you he is dropping out of group because other group members are giving him and each other "looks"; he feels uncomfortable sharing anything with them.
8. Juan's mother has asked you to testify in a child custody case on her behalf. Juan has been attending "changing family" group counseling sessions for the past two months. Her lawyer told her that your testimony and personal notes about how Juan feels about his father would help her to gain sole custody.

CHAPTER 3

Multicultural Issues in Group Work

CHERYL HOLCOMB-MCCOY AND
CHERYL MOORE-THOMAS

PREVIEW

Group work with diverse students is addressed in this chapter, using oppression and marginalization as the frameworks from which group leaders can conceptualize group members' problems, behaviors, and actions. Because research indicates that people from oppressed backgrounds (e.g., ethnic minorities, disabled persons, the materially poor, gay and lesbian persons) are more likely to avoid counseling experiences, to drop out prematurely from counseling, and to report lower outcomes, it is important that group leaders become more responsive to member experiences of discrimination, prejudice, and inequities. Leaders can act to prevent or address these issues in the group. Also, because oppressed and marginalized students are accustomed to being silenced, being made to feel inferior, and "having no voice," leaders must be skilled in working with students who are quiet, suspicious, pessimistic, cynical, and even angry. In addition, the influence of issues of oppression and marginalization on each stage of the group process is introduced. Finally, the chapter ends with a discussion of dilemmas that may arise when implementing groups with culturally diverse members.

MULTICULTURAL ISSUES IN GROUP WORK

Whether through varying communication styles, languages, sexual orientations, abilities, ethnicities/races, beliefs, behaviors, or perceptions, every group will be influenced by the cultural backgrounds of its members. In essence, a group becomes a social microcosm whereby the group members' values, beliefs, prejudices, cultural biases, and past experiences are played out in the group setting. With the increasing diversity of today's society, the need for more culturally competent work among group leaders is critical and has received much attention in recent literature (Chen & Han, 2001; Conyne, Wilson, & Tang, 2000; DeLucia-Waack, 2000; DeLucia-Waack & Donigian, 2003). This is particularly relevant for today's public schools, where more than one-third of the population is comprised of students of color. In support of the need for more culturally competent group workers, many scholars have cited the positive impact of multicultural group work on interethnic group relations (Gloria, 1999; Merta, 1995).

From a multicultural perspective, there are several goals or frameworks that are important to consider when working with multicultural groups. According to DeLucia-Waack (1996b), three common goals of multicultural groups are (1) to understand the situations that brought the students to the group from a cultural perspective, (2) to approach all events and behaviors in the group from a functional perspective, and (3) to help members make sense of "new behaviors, beliefs, and skills within a cultural context" (p. 171). Bemak and Chung (2004) believed that group leaders should have two additional goals when working with culturally heterogeneous group members: (1) to foster the acceptance of and respect for diversity within and between group members and (2) to promote social justice and social change among members and the communities the leaders represent.

Historically, group work has been predominately based on the Eurocentric models of therapy and counseling, with very little attention to working across cultures. For instance, it was only in 1998 that the Association for Specialists in Group Work (ASGW) adopted the *ASGW Principles for Diversity-Competent Group Workers*. These principles serve as a guide for multicultural training, practice, and research and marked the beginning of a movement to address multicultural and diversity issues in group work. Gladding (2008) cited three reasons for the delay in addressing culture and diversity in groups. First, he contended that the death of Kurt Lewin in 1947 marked the end of the first movement to include cultural aspects of group work. In the 1940s, Lewin and his associates began a movement to train community leaders to use group work as a means to reduce tensions among interracial groups and to facilitate changes in racially biased attitudes. Gladding believed that the emphasis on reducing racial tension among groups and through group work ended when Lewin died.

Second, Gladding (2008) attributed the delay in addressing cultural issues in group work to the fact that culturally different group members were not considered to be significantly different from dominant group members. In other words, professional counselors believed that it would be best to be "color-blind" or that issues of race and culture did not have an influence on one's presenting problems. As a result of the multicultural movement in counseling, however, the color-blind approach was deemed inappropriate and unethical (Pack-Brown & Braun, 2003).

Finally, Gladding stated that many counseling professionals did not believe that cultural minority group members' behaviors and attitudes had a significant effect on group dynamics. However, recent thinking has indicated that culture can become the foundation from which a group functions (Baca & Koss-Chioino, 1997; Brinson & Lee, 1997; Johnson, Torres, Coleman, & Smith, 1995). For instance, ethnically or racially diverse students may bring their negative and faulty stereotypical beliefs about one another to a group, creating disharmony and distrust among members.

There are various definitions of multiculturalism found in the counseling literature. The multicultural movement has defined culture in a narrower manner, including only ethnic and racial differences. However, culture can and should be defined broadly to include demographic factors (e.g., age, gender, sexual orientation) and status factors (e.g., economic, social, disability). For the sake of clarity, this chapter applies the broadest definition of culture because all of these groups can experience oppression and marginalization. Also, the use of this broad definition is in keeping with the fact that all group work is multicultural. In addition, definitions of the terms *diverse persons, minorities,* and *non-dominant* will be the same as delineated in the *ASGW Principles for Diversity-Competent Group Workers* (ASGW, 1998). The *Principles* state that "non-dominant" and "target populations" are

> groups of persons who historically, in the United States, do not have equal access to power, money, certain privileges (such as access to mental health services because of financial constraints, or the legal right to marry, in the case of a gay or lesbian couple) and/or the ability to influence or initiate social policy because of unequal representation in government and politics. (p. 7)

OPPRESSION AND MARGINALIZATION

Oppression manifests differently in varying contexts (Bernardez, 1996). For that reason, it is impossible to identify a single set of criteria that describe oppression. Generally, oppression refers to the unjust use of authority, force, or societal norms and laws to exert control over individuals, a people, or a group. More specifically and contextually important, oppression includes situations of exploitation, marginalization, powerlessness, cultural imperialism, and violence (Zutlevics, 2002). As oppression intensifies and progresses through individualized and systemic manifestations, it may lead to denigration, dehumanization, and scapegoating (i.e., blaming the oppressed for societal problems). Underlying this progression is the faulty belief that the target of oppression is less than or inferior to those of the dominant culture. For instance, a long history of oppression in American schools has led many educators to believe that students of color, particularly African American and Latino/a students, are less intelligent or are intellectually inferior to White and Asian students. In turn, this faulty belief has led to the achievement gap and lower expectations for many students of color.

Marginalization, one of the specific contexts of oppression, must be seen in reference to the dominant group. Marginalization is the social process of becoming excluded from or existing outside of mainstream society or a given group. Given this dominant group reference, marginalization oddly places individuals of the target group on the outside or fringes of the dominant culture, while simultaneously placing them inside the dominant culture (Cuadraz, 1996). This outside/inside orientation has social, psychological, political, and economic consequences. Persons from marginalized and oppressed backgrounds often feel as if they will not receive equality, justice, or fair treatment. These beliefs stem from their experiences with discrimination, racism, sexism, injustice, and other types of oppression.

Another important consideration for leaders is the concept of invisible diversity. Even if all of the members have the same skin color or gender, differences in socioeconomic levels, disability, beliefs, and values prevail. The multiculturally competent group leader in the schools is aware of potential invisible diversity among members and addresses the issues of oppression and marginalization that stem from it.

Stages of Group Development

Oppression and its specific structure of marginalization have specific implications for group development.

During the pregroup process or planning phase, leaders are primarily concerned with determining group needs and member characteristics. These issues, although simply stated, are actually quite complex. In particular, determining who may benefit most from a specific group experience requires a series of leader decisions and selections. Each of these leader decisions has implications for culture and for the potential manifestation of the related issues of oppression and marginalization.

Heterogeneous groups by definition involve members of diverse cultural identities (e.g., race, ethnicity, sexual orientation, disability, gender). Due to historical, social, and economic factors, there are often power differentials between members of these various groups. Consequently, some members of these cultural groups experience levels of oppression and marginalization that will undoubtedly emerge as the group social microcosm struggles to develop a sense of cohesion. While the emergence and discussion of these issues may lead to some anxiety, they should not be ignored. DeLucia-Waack (1996a) suggested that the discussion of such issues increases group cohesion. Group cohesion is significant for the effective movement through all aspects of group work, including matters of commitment and attendance, goal and norm establishment, and process factors. Although the issues of oppression and marginalization may be more visible in heterogeneous groups (e.g., groups with male and female members, groups with African American and Asian American members), these issues may also emerge in seemingly homogeneous groups. For example, students in a teenage, female-only group on stress management may need to address marginalization if the subculture dynamics of females in Advanced Placement courses, female athletes, and teen mothers emerge. Ideally, group leaders should explore these issues during the pregroup selection interviews and the planning phase.

As group work begins in the forming and orienting stage, students struggle to find their place. Trust, safety, and avoidance of rejection are central to this stage of group development. Effective leaders use a variety of skills to assist students in developing a strong sense of security. However, effective leaders must move beyond traditional counseling skills and techniques to address these same issues for group members who may be oppressed or marginalized. In particular, in the forming and orienting stage, group leaders must recognize that the effective development of trust occurs not only between the actual group members but also between the sociopolitical identities that are often played out and stereotyped in society at large. Although this task can be overwhelming, it may be necessary to recognize in verbal and nonverbal ways the dehumanizing and weighty baggage that society places on marginalized people. For example, in schools, bullying is a form of discrimination, usually against marginalized students. Until this often unspoken and disregarded reality is acknowledged, trust, safety, and avoidance of rejection may not be possible. If trust, safety, and avoidance of rejection are not established, the public image that is characteristic of group members' interactions at this early stage of group development may be maintained and prohibit deeper, more authentic levels of member growth and exploration.

Different leaders use differing strategies to address these issues, but most leaders raise these issues in the group to allow members to openly discuss and deal with them in a supportive environment. Growth, understanding, and trust seldom occur when issues of oppression or marginalization are glossed over or treated as taboo topics. As will be discussed in the chapter on group planning (Chapter 6), recruiting and screening group members prior to initiating group work are critical. It is essential that leaders become aware of the cultural/ethnic identities of potential members in order to plan for or at least anticipate issues that may arise later in the group.

The transition stage of group development, characterized by struggles for power and control and the building of group cohesiveness, also requires specific group leader functions. The culturally competent group leader recognizes that building awareness, providing support, and modeling must include the potential needs of marginalized students. While recognizing and dealing with potential conflicts and resistance is a leader's primary task when facilitating a group's movement through the transition stage, it would be negligent and unethical to fail to address social and political issues that may underlie the emerging group conflicts or resistance.

For example, a transition stage conflict that emerges in a male and female middle school group on conflict resolution and social skills may be fueled not only by the students' anxiety about the group experience but also by concerns tied to societal power differentials between boys and girls. To ensure that such a group moves effectively through this stage of development, a skilled group leader must assist the group in effectively managing the surface-level conflicts, while simultaneously addressing the underlying social and political issues of gender as appropriate. In the given case, this could include imparting information on the history and politics of gender and issues of gender socialization to the group members in developmentally appropriate ways. For middle school students, this may involve sharing school- and grade-level behavioral data. Disclosed in appropriate and sensitive ways, these data may inform and inspire creative and effective solutions for students and their individual behavioral situations and needs. Additionally, the group leader could continue to explore and develop his or her own awareness of knowledge and skills concerning gender preferences in counseling and the relation of gender and value structure. These topics are discussed elsewhere in this chapter. The extent to which these knowledge and skills sets should be introduced into group work depends on a number of factors, including the developmental level of the group members and the degree to which the particular cultural factor is salient for the individual group members and for the group as a unit.

Oppression and marginalization must be vigorously addressed during the working and termination stages of group work. Typically, during these stages, students begin to acquire new insights, behaviors, and skills that are first practiced in the group and then integrated into the students' lives beyond the group. Group leaders should safeguard the group environment so that individualized and systemic applications of oppression do not form barriers for members during this significant time of growth and exploration. While this practice may unfortunately be impossible beyond the group setting, group members can explore the realities of social injustice and come to understand and adapt newly acquired behaviors and skills in ways that are culturally relevant and personally empowering. For example, a leader working with a group of African American students of any age on academic achievement can help the members discover growth-engendering strategies that promote school success. While the strategies may in no measurable way affect the societal injustices of oppression, the acknowledgment and discussion of the dynamic—particularly as it relates to the academic achievement gap, educational opportunities, and learning outcomes—could provide the group members with valuable information and insight that could acknowledge and validate their personal experiences and ultimately fuel their commitment to maximized academic performance. In contrast, denying or ignoring the existence of oppression and its affects on the African American population could prove detrimental. Failing to address, discuss, and act on oppression perpetuates oppression.

Leaders must consider the relevance and the developmental levels of students in order to accurately assess the extent to which, as well as the manner in which, these should be introduced into group work. For example, the manner in which a leader facilitates group exploration of oppression and achievement with 2nd-grade children or 7th-grade students may differ from the way the leader could appropriately address the same issue with 11th-grade adolescents.

GROUP LEADERSHIP AND OPPRESSION

In order to combat oppression and marginalization, group leaders must first engage in a process of self-exploration. By exploring their feelings about their own cultural and political identities, group leaders can become more culturally sensitive to others' differences. This process of developing a sense of cultural awareness also causes group leaders to take into account how they experience their own cultural differences and how their experiences and beliefs may affect their interactions with students from other backgrounds. Leaders should become very familiar with the *AMCD Multicultural Counseling Competencies* (available from the Association for Multicultural Counseling and Development at www.amcdaca.org/amcd/competencies.pdf) and explore their own attitudes, beliefs, and values regarding diversity and marginalization.

Before implementing groups with diverse students, it is also important for group leaders to explore and understand the complexities of oppression and how members from historically oppressed cultural groups may view the group process and the group leader. When group leaders recognize that group members come to the group with various perspectives based on their experiences with oppression, they are better equipped to help group members process their thoughts and feelings and to overcome any cultural conflict in the group. The reality of ethnic and racial superiority themes in our society, as well as classism, sexism, and the history of depriving certain groups of rights and resources, should be considered when exploring one's cultural self-awareness.

Group leaders should also be open to the differences exhibited by diverse people. It is important for group leaders to be accepting and nonjudgmental about the values, lifestyles, beliefs, and behaviors of others and to appreciate difference and diversity (Toseland & Rivas, 2001). Because group work tends to be based on Eurocentric values, leaders must be cognizant of the fact that students with culturally diverse backgrounds may have values that conflict with the norms of many group members and leaders. For instance, being on time and taking turns to speak are two societal norms for Eurocentric persons that may not be the expectation of other cultural groups.

It is also important for a group leader to gain knowledge of the backgrounds of client groups. Leaders can gain cultural knowledge through researching literature pertaining to a particular cultural group, consulting with members of a particular cultural group, or visiting a cultural community and becoming a participant observer. Living or spending a period of time in a cultural community (i.e., immersion), with all of its contextual richness and without the overlay of stereotyping, can help a group leader better understand the common values, norms of behavior, and worldviews held by students of that particular culture.

If immersion is not possible, a group leader might go through the process of social mapping, which consists of observing and analyzing formal and informal relationships among members of a community. For instance, a school counselor conducting a group for adolescent boys at a school where a majority of its students are African American and Latino could observe classrooms, special school activities, and after-school programs as well as meet with parents and other community members to get their perspective on the needs of boys in the community.

Group leaders must also attempt to learn how students identify themselves. It is important for leaders to be aware of the politically correct reference to groups and, most importantly, to be sensitive to how group members want to be identified. If a leader is in doubt as to a group member's cultural or racial identification, the group leader should ask and spend time discussing the issue openly. For instance, a group leader may ask a group member, "Carlos, I notice that you refer to yourself as a Chicano, rather than Hispanic or Latino. Would you mind telling us more about what that label means to you?" It is important for the group leader to demonstrate respect for the group member as well as interest in knowing more about the group member's cultural background. If the group member appears uncomfortable with the request for more cultural information, the group leader should then accept the student's feelings and decision to not discuss his or her cultural identification. A student should never feel pressured to self-disclose about cultural issues.

Developing culturally sensitive group strategies is another important task for culturally competent group leaders. Although there is very little research regarding the effectiveness of specific group strategies for diverse populations, there is some promising literature related to culturally sensitive group formats. For instance, Pearson (1991) suggested that group leadership should be more structured for Asian and Asian American people. Using a traditional style with less structure and with reliance on members to take responsibility for group interactions would cause discomfort and contradict the cultural expectations of some Asian group members. On the other hand, Rittenhouse (1997) suggested that feminist group work should use an unstructured format to minimize the power distance between members and the leader. Other culturally sensitive formats suggested in the literature include empowerment groups for urban African American girls (Bemak, Chung, & Siroskey-Sabdo, 2005), structured task groups for Latino youth (Lopez, 1991), psychoeducational groups that use poetry for immigrants (Asner-Self & Feyissa, 2002), survival skill training groups for African American adolescent males (Bradley, 2001), and culturally consonant groups that use a Native Hawaiian healing method for Native American adolescent groups (Kim, Omizo, & D'Andrea, 1998).

Finally, leaders should have information about the group process in "naturally occurring groups" (Lee, 1995). Naturally occurring groups include groups where culturally different persons come together for some type of ritual, ceremony, or entertainment. Typically, these groups include persons with similar or shared cultural experiences. Some examples of naturally occurring groups are African American church congregations, Latino youth clubs, gay families, and Native American tribal councils. Group leaders, if given the opportunity to observe naturally occurring groups, should note the nonverbal behaviors of individuals in those groups. For instance, eye contact and conversational distance will vary across cultures. However, through the observation of naturally occurring groups, a group leader can acquire knowledge about how students may react in the group.

GENDER AND GROUP WORK

Group experiences provide opportunities for members to explore their personal narratives and challenges within the context of gender and its associated social roles and stereotypes (Lazerson & Zilbach, 1993; Schoenholtz-Read, 1996). Consequently, group leaders work in ways that either support or disempower members as they explore and confront important issues of gender and gender bias. Taking steps to evaluate personal beliefs, feelings, and assumptions regarding gender and gender-based sociopolitical issues (e.g., socioeconomic status, employment opportunities, child rearing, thinking and communication patterns) and to consider how those factors may affect the group and group processes is critical to working toward positive group outcomes and experiences for all group members. Furthermore, group leaders should familiarize themselves with relevant theory and perspectives. Feminist theory, for example, may provide group leaders with meaningful conceptualizations of the interaction of gender and culture (Lazerson & Zilbach, 1993).

Research and theory regarding the merits of single-gender and mixed-gender groups is extensive (Bernardez, 1996; Lazerson & Zilbach, 1993; Schoenholtz-Read, 1996). Group leaders must consider the purpose of the group and the needs of the students in order to determine which composition is most appropriate. Homogeneous groups may provide members with a level of security, acceptance, and shared experience, while simultaneously limiting the barriers of gender-based oppression, unintentional miscommunication, and other gender-related challenges within the group context. However, mixed-gender groups allow students to explore problems and concerns within a cultural context that more closely matches society. Regardless of group composition, group leaders must keep in mind that both girls and boys are affected by a host of gender-influenced factors, including, but not restricted to, developmental processes, value structures, belief systems, behavioral repertoires, sex-role stereotypes and expectations, power dynamics, and gender-related oppression and marginalization. Racial and ethnic diversity may add dimensions of complexity to all aspects of gender and gender interaction. This may be particularly true for cultures that have extremely differentiated roles and expectations for males and females. The following case study explores the issues of gender and group work.

CASE STUDY 3.1

Gender

Ms. Harmon, a European American, is a professional school counselor working in a large, East Coast high school. She is running a group on grief and loss for eight students who have lost parents/guardians or siblings in the last year. Each group member was referred to the school counseling group by a classroom teacher, and each had previously received varying levels of encouragement from family and friends to seek counseling. The group is comprised of five females and three males. Two of the females are African American. All other students are European American.

The group has met for four sessions. Although students report that the group is helpful, Ms. Harmon is concerned about several issues of early group development, including universality and cohesion. Although all members are beginning to interact in productive ways, Ms. Harmon cannot help thinking that the students are not really "hearing" each other. She realizes trust will develop and authentic, meaningful disclosures will emerge over time, but she wonders what she can do to facilitate the process.

After consulting with her school counseling colleagues, Ms. Harmon realizes that her group members' lack of "hearing" may be related to gender-based factors. In addition to more obvious differences in gender-based communication patterns, Ms. Harmon considers gender-based roles and expectations regarding responses to grief. Ms. Harmon challenges herself to consider her own stereotyped views of men's and women's experiences of grief. She also reflects on the societal role expectations of surviving individuals. She wonders, for example, if society expects men who have lost a loved one to take on different roles than women who have lost a loved one. Ms. Harmon is also aware of the possible implications of race and ethnicity for the grief-and-loss process. Being careful not to inappropriately attribute these issues to the group and its process, Ms. Harmon decides to encourage the group to explore gender and race in the next session. Ms. Harmon believes the students can best determine the salience of these issues for themselves within and outside of the group context.

During the fifth session, Ms. Harmon poses a series of interpersonal and intrapersonal processing questions to encourage the students to self-determine the meaningfulness of gender in their personal and collective experiences of grief and loss. Although they initially resist Ms. Harmon's questions, the students slowly begin to express a range of emotions regarding their views of society's gender-based expectations. In particular, one of the male students states that he was angry that people expected him to "get over my brother's death and focus on school." He reported that many of his friends wanted him to "get on with life—go to the movies and hang out, as if my brother never died." A female member shares that she is sure her family and friends saw her as "a weak, helpless little girl who could not handle the truth of her mother's illness and death." The students agree that perhaps they have been unintentionally interacting with each other based on gender-based stereotypes and expectations.

Ms. Harmon and the group members are pleased with the group session. Ms. Harmon is happy to see the students' willingness to address the here and now of the group by examining the person-to-person interactions. Overall, Ms. Harmon believes broaching the issues of gender has enabled the students to gain significant insight into their emotions and experiences and achieve deeper levels of trust.

SEXUAL ORIENTATION AND GROUP WORK

Gays, lesbians, and bisexuals (GLBs) are a diverse population with diverse perspectives, needs, and concerns. Due to these varying needs and perspectives, GLBs, like their non–sexual minority peers, are well served in a variety of group counseling structures: homogeneous groups, heterogeneous or mixed groups, and special groups (e.g., issue-centered groups that may have particular relevance for GLBs) (Hawkins, 1993). In determining which group setting is most appropriate, the group leader should use, in part, the pregroup selection process during the planning stage to assess the degree to which sexual orientation and the presenting problem overlap and to determine the current, self-identified reference group of the client. For example, a female student in her senior year who is questioning her sexual identity, while struggling with her approaching transition to college and life away from home, may not be comfortable in a transitions lesbian group run by her high school counselor, whereas a young woman of a similar demographic who came out earlier in high school and has accepted her sexual identity as lesbian may appreciate and benefit from group counseling support in the described context (see Chojnacki & Gelberg, 1995).

Although many in American society have made some gains in appreciating and accepting the diversity of the GLB population, the GLB community still experiences a good deal of oppression, prejudice, and harassment. Group leaders working with this population must be keenly aware of the extreme levels of oppression experienced by this population and the resulting manifestations, which include substance abuse, family conflicts, academic and career concerns, emotional turmoil, and suicide attempts (Hawkins, 1993; Robinson, 1994; Sears, 1991; Teague, 1992). Furthermore, group leaders must be extraordinarily committed to maintaining confidentiality, establishing trust and an environment that promotes emotional security, examining their personal perspectives and assumptions regarding sexual minorities, and developing awareness of cultural and intrapsychic issues of the GLB population (Hawkins, 1993). The following case study further explores many of these issues.

CASE STUDY 3.2
Sexual Orientation

Mr. Greer is a middle school counselor in a small southern town. He is running a time-limited career exploration group for four female and two male students. The work of the group has progressed well during the previous six sessions. With only two more sessions left, the group members are beginning to process significant learning from the group experience that they will be able to transfer to their four-year plans for high school. Douglas, one of the group members, discloses that he has learned a lot about who is and the relation of true self and satisfaction in work through the many group experiences. He says that he now realizes how important it is to be happy with yourself and your career. He further shares that during the group process he has come to accept that he is gay and wants to be true to himself. Tamara, another group member, obviously shocked and troubled by Douglas's disclosure, shares that she believes the disclosure has nothing to do with the group and is totally "disgusting and unnecessary." Mr. Greer recognizes the importance of both disclosures and encourages the group members to work through the current tension. Using advanced empathy and processing skills, Mr. Greer is able to help the group move forward and, in particular, to provide Douglas with the supportive and affirming environment that he needs at that particular moment. In "coming out," Douglas has self-identified as a sexual minority who could, unfortunately, be subjected to oppression, prejudice, and harassment. In order to safeguard Douglas's well-being and the validity of the process, Mr. Greer ends the session with a review of confidentiality and its importance in group work and an affirmation of each member as an individual who has fully participated in the meaningful group process. The members agree with Mr. Greer and state that out of respect for each other and the work they have done over the past several weeks, confidentiality must be maintained.

Mr. Greer also believes the additional aspects of Douglas's situation may need to be considered in order to protect Douglas in the school environment. He consults administration and his department head to discuss and implement these safeguards. As he discusses these safeguards with Douglas, Mr. Greer also broaches the subject of how Douglas intends to break the news to his parents, as informing parents of one's homosexual orientation frequently leads to emotional distress, even estrangement.

DISABILITIES AND GROUP WORK

The interactive nature, high levels of peer support and encouragement, group sense of belonging and cohesion, opportunities for interpersonal and intrapersonal learning, and opportunities to develop and practice new skills may make counseling groups ideal delivery interventions for individuals with physical and mild disabilities, including learning disabilities, emotional disorders, and mild mental retardation (Arman, 2002; Deck, Scarborough, Sferrazza, & Estill, 1999; Livneh, Wilson, & Pullo, 2004). Of course, individuals with disabilities represent a very diverse community and are entitled to appropriate counseling services. This significant population, about 9% of school-age students, may receive the most appropriate counseling service when it is provided in coordination with other required services, which could include educational, medical, and remedial supports (Tarver-Behring & Spagna, 2004). Leaders must also be mindful that students with disabilities who have become marginalized people due to factors of gender, race, and socioeconomic status may face special counseling concerns. Called double oppression by some researchers and simultaneous oppression by others, minorities with disabilities are often relegated to positions in an invisible and ignored segment of society that is cast well beyond the fringes of the dominant culture (Stuart, 1992).

In serving all populations of individuals with disabilities, professional school counselors must clarify their own feelings and attitudes about counseling students with disabilities, gain knowledge and training to increase competence in this area, and consult and collaborate with other professionals (e.g., supervisors, special educators, physicians, psychiatrists, social workers) and family members in order to provide the best possible counseling service. The following case study illustrates these principles in a school setting.

CASE STUDY 3.3
Disabilities

Ms. Diaz is an elementary school counselor. She is planning to run a third-grade group on resiliency for students referred by classroom teachers and administrators. Through the selection process, Ms. Diaz has decided to include five students. Two of the students, Rochelle and Brian, have been identified as having specific learning disabilities while the other students do not have significant learning problems. In addition, Rochelle is the only African American student in the group.

Anticipating the needs of the students, Ms. Diaz spent weeks observing all of the group members in their classrooms and in less structured school settings (e.g., hallways, cafeteria) and talking with the students' teachers. Ms. Diaz also met with the school's special education teacher in order to gain general information about specific learning disabilities and the needs of Rochelle and Brian in particular. The special educator consented to give Ms. Diaz feedback on the activities and discussion prompts she plans to use for the group to ensure that the activities are appropriate for Rochelle and Brian. Finally, in preparation for the group, Ms. Diaz consulted with one of her former college professors in order to access the most recent literature on resiliency and African American students. Through the pregroup interview with Rochelle, Ms. Diaz begins to suspect that Rochelle's issues of double minority status may intersect in ways that they did not for the other students in the group. Overall, Ms. Diaz has spent many hours preparing for the third-grade resiliency group. Although the time was hard to find, given her busy schedule as an elementary school counselor, Ms. Diaz realizes that the time was not only well spent but also a professional imperative because the new knowledge will come in handy in the future when working with other students with disabilities and multiple oppressions.

SPECIAL ISSUES THAT MIGHT ARISE WHEN LEADING MULTICULTURAL GROUPS

A number of challenging issues might arise when implementing groups with culturally diverse members. These issues are not difficult to overcome but require that the group leader understand and acknowledge the influence of culture on the actions and beliefs of the group members. Following are some common issues that might arise and a discussion of how a group leader might overcome them.

When a Group Leader Is Culturally Different from Group Members

As stated previously, it is important for the group leader to recognize that the group members' cultural backgrounds can have a significant effect on how they participate in the group. The same is true when the group leader is culturally different from the group members. The culturally different group leader should carefully consider how his or her cultural background might affect the students' behaviors in the group. The students may stereotype the leader based on preconceived notions of how the students believe persons from a particular culture behave. For instance, White group members may have faulty beliefs about a group leader of Asian descent. They might base their expectations of the group leader on stereotypical notions of how "Asian people act."

While there is a substantial amount of literature on the composition of multicultural groups (Brown & Mistry, 1994; Davis, Galinsky, & Schopler, 1995), particularly the racial composition of groups, there is very little written on the influence of the group leader's background when compared to those of the group members (Marbley, 2004). When ethnically or culturally different from the members of the group, the leader should consider how members from different backgrounds might view his or her cultural/ethnic background. It can be helpful for leaders to initiate a discussion of difference and to positively frame the discussion so that students can see the benefits of having diversity in a group. By initiating an open, honest discussion about cultural differences, the group leader is modeling a positive behavior for future group sessions.

When a group leader is culturally different from the students, it is also important for him or her to be aware of the personal stereotypes of and reactions to the group members. It is possible that the leader's discomfort or biased perceptions can influence the group's dynamics. Marbley (2004) even suggested that leaders of color may want to seek a co-leader who identifies with the culture of the students. She further suggested that leaders seek a co-leader with a high status of racial identity (i.e., congruence with one's personal racial identity) and an acute awareness of and sensitivity to cultural issues both inside and outside of group work.

When Group Member Hostility Arises

In culturally diverse groups, students may bring their preferred patterns of behaviors, values, and language to the group (Axelson, 1999). Students may also bring experiences with oppression and negative feelings about themselves, their group identity, and the larger society. When student dissatisfaction or hostility among members occurs, the leader should keep in mind that the problems may be caused by the experiences of oppression and marginalization, not by a flaw in the group's process. At the same time, leaders must be aware of the cause for the group member's hostility and label it as such for the students. For instance, consider the example of a heterosexual student who becomes upset when a gay group member complains about being mistreated and discriminated against in social settings. The student talks about his reaction to what he perceives as the gay member's whining and pouting about "everything." The gay member becomes frustrated and explains how the other student's reaction is typical of people in general. The group leader then proceeds to reflect the group members' feelings and engage the remainder of the group in the discussion about gay bias.

When hostility arises, group leaders must not fail to recognize that cultural differences exist and must not diminish their importance. Facing differences is difficult, but it is necessary. Contrary to what many group leaders believe, recognizing and expressing differences does not cause more conflict. Recognizing and accepting differences creates a feeling of safety for members and in turn promotes personal growth among students.

When Advocating for Group Members

Students from historically oppressed backgrounds or groups may need special assistance in negotiating difficult situations outside of the group setting. In working with members from varied cultural backgrounds, the group leader may need to advocate for students. In a support group for Latina sixth-grade girls, for example, the leader became concerned about the girls' lack of knowledge regarding after-school enrichment activities. The leader not only sent the girls' parents information about the activities but also encouraged her colleagues (fellow professional school counselors and teachers) to distribute after-school information to all of their students. Because of the leader's efforts, the students and their parents were more committed to the group experience and trustful of the group leader.

Leaders may wish to consider engaging in other advocacy activities on behalf of students. For example, in a parenting group for adult mothers who are also single parents, the leader experienced a great deal of absenteeism from members who seemed to enjoy the group. It was discovered that transportation and child care were the reasons for these adults' frequent absences. The leader used this information to advocate that transportation and child care be provided by a local social service organization. Eventually, the YMCA provided a van for transportation, and high school students were used for child care, thus enabling the single mothers to attend regularly.

Summary

Given the increasing diversity of the U.S. population, the ability to effectively lead groups consisting of culturally diverse students has become a major challenge for professional school counselors. In this chapter, oppression and marginalization were used as a framework within which to understand the complex issues that students of diverse cultural groups face. In truth, all groups are multicultural because each student brings a different history with different cultural experiences and expectations, whether visible or invisible. With that said, group leaders can no longer ignore the cultural differences among members and treat everyone the same. To do so is to ignore the richness and benefits of different perspectives in the group membership.

Groups are the ideal setting for students of marginalized and oppressed backgrounds because in groups, feelings can be validated and there is a community support atmosphere (Kottler, 2001). Since many oppressed populations focus on the group rather than on the individual as the most significant element of existence, group work is aligned with their cultural practices of cooperation, trust, and relationships. As such, group work provides counseling professionals with an appropriate means of meeting the needs of students from oppressed and marginalized backgrounds.

CHAPTER 4

Distinguishing Group Member Roles

GEORGE R. LEDDICK

PREVIEW

Any discussion of group members should describe what students should both do and not do. This chapter will begin by describing essential tasks for group members (i.e., self-disclosure, feedback) and later identify ways student behavior might prove challenging for leaders. Specific group work techniques include drawing out, giving feedback, I-statements, paradox, reframing, and self-disclosure.

ESSENTIAL TASKS FOR GROUP MEMBERS

Often, discussions of group member characteristics focus on dealing with problem students. A more pro-developmental perspective focuses on what students should be doing in a group. Thus, this chapter will begin with a discussion of two essential member skills, self-disclosure and feedback, and conclude with the more traditional discussion of problematic member roles commonly found within groups.

Self-Disclosure

Among the most important tasks for students is a willingness to take risks to describe themselves (Bednar & Kaul, 1994). Self-disclosure of thoughts, feelings, and behavior is central to participating in the group. In fact, descriptions are valuable substitutes for advice giving. Instead of telling others what to do, members can simply describe how they react to situations. When presented with a variety of reactions, members feel comfortable choosing one that matches their preferences. They have the control of choosing the best match. Understanding how much to disclose and how much to keep private is an early dilemma for most group members. Very young children (preK through grade 3) frequently display less inhibition and readily share private or personal self or family information. As students get older, ordinarily they become more private, although this is certainly always not the case. Self-disclosure is also often situation-dependent. For example, teenagers often self disclose more to close friends than to close adults.

	Known to Others	Unknown to Others
Known to Self	Open, public (e.g., hair color, gender)	Hidden, private (e.g., feelings of inadequacy)
Unknown to Self	Blind (e.g., facial expressions when talking, bad breath)	Unknown, unconscious (e.g., childhood connections to group content)

FIGURE 4.1 The Johari Window.

Describing the Johari Window (Luft, 1984) (Figure 4.1) is one way to help students decide how much they may wish to disclose and how much control they wish to exert to ensure their own privacy. When one first hears of the Johari Window, it may sound mysterious, but it is simply a device invented by Joe Luft and Harry Ingam to help understand the levels of disclosure.

The Johari Window has four "panes." The upper left quadrant symbolizes information you know and others do, too. For example, your name is often public knowledge. The color of the clothes you are wearing is known to anyone who can see you. Such information is not risky to divulge. The lower left quadrant symbolizes information about you known to others but not known to you. Sometimes even your best friend won't mention the bit of lunch still stuck to your teeth or the piece of toilet paper stuck to your shoe. The upper right quadrant of the window represents information known to you but not to others. It is private information. Whether you disclose private information sometimes depends on whether it is pertinent to others. If you have an ingrown toenail, you might not share this fact with other group members. In addition to relevance, another consideration might be whether you trust the group sufficiently to guard confidentiality. A topic that seems too risky in the beginning of group might feel easy to disclose later on.

The remaining quadrant of the Johari Window is information that is unknown to you and to others. It represents the unconscious. Group leaders often introduce students to the idea of the Johari Window to provoke a discussion about responsible risk-taking and personal boundaries. Discussion of the Johari Window provides structure for the consideration of a continuum of degrees of self-disclosure. Leaders often tell members they are allowed to say "pass" if having difficulty articulating a feeling or are unwilling to disclose personal, private information. It is hoped that members who feel in control of their level of self-disclosure exhibit less resistance.

Feedback

When students give each other feedback, they are describing the interpersonal interactions they notice and mentioning their reactions. Bednar and Kaul (1994) identified feedback as a characteristic of effective groups. Students must learn to use skill when giving feedback. Otherwise, it is natural for students who receive feedback to be defensive, feel threatened, or tune out. Good feedback is (1) solicited, not imposed; (2) descriptive, not evaluative; (3) specific, not general; and (4) checked for clarity (by restating or reflecting). If feedback is descriptive, it allows the member to have a choice in behavior. If one labels a student a "loudmouth," that student will get defensive and think of this as a character flaw to blame on his or her ancestors. If instead one tells the student, "You are talking a lot today," he or she will notice there is a continuum. Some days the student talks a lot, and other days the student says little. Thus, the student can take responsibility for the choice of today.

Feedback should also be timed to happen soon after the event so all members can recall the occurrence and share their observations. When feedback is given by a member on behalf of the entire group, the leader should ask if this is the impression of just the spokesperson or if it is an observation shared by the whole group. Leaders do not allow students to assume they are speaking for the whole group without checking for consensus.

It is typical for students to be tentative about giving and receiving feedback. It is often the case that initial feedback is politely positive and sometimes superficial. In groups with topics and/or membership that makes feedback training appropriate, leaders can introduce members to the topic of feedback and allow them to practice developing this skill in a series of dyad activities. For example, in an early session, students might be paired and asked to chat about reasons for joining the group and what they hope will happen (Donigian & Hulse-Killacky, 1999). Each person introduces his or her partner to the group, and the leader remarks on similarities and common themes. In a subsequent group session, when students are paired with different partners, the topic would ordinarily shift to their fears, concerns, hopes, and expectations for this particular group experience. In a subsequent session, new pairs of students might address this question: "When do you feel 'alive,' and why is this important to you?" In each exercise, partners introduce each other to the larger group. Topics should be concise, be appropriate to the initial stage of group dynamics, and become progressively more involved.

If students feel especially inhibited in groups or find communication in early group stages threatening or frightening, Donigian and Hulse-Killacky (1999) recommended using a simple exercise called "Blue Card—Red Card." Each group member gets several cards of each color (blue and red). Blue represents positive feedback, and red represents corrective feedback. At specific points in each session, students are asked to "deal" one card to members soliciting feedback. No verbal explanations are given for the first session, although these might be allowed in later sessions, once members feel less threatened. A blue card (i.e., positive feedback) might be given to point out progress toward goals. A red card might signal to a student that he or she is engaging in a behavior that hinders the group process and/or the task.

If time, ability, or immaturity precludes training in feedback skills, the leader might instead teach students to employ hand signals to indicate approval. When someone makes a statement from the heart or is being genuine or when a group member is able to identify with the speaker's words, the leader and group members could arrange for the use of a hand signal agreed on by the group that group members could use to nonverbally signify agreement. Some groups hold their fingers in the sign language symbol for "I love you." Alternately, others make a "V" and sweep an arm from the heart toward the speaker. If too much verbal feedback is a problem, leaders may wish to invoke a "talking stick," traditionally employed by Native Americans, to ensure that members take turns speaking. Only the member holding the stick may speak.

One simple way to teach members about feedback is to describe how to make I-statements. I-statements substitute for giving advice. The purpose of an I-statement is to use descriptive feedback to empower students and encourage them to explore their choices. Hopefully, this structure reduces defensiveness. I-statements describe the speaker's reaction to a situation by completing three sentence stems:

1. When I see/hear _____.
2. I feel _____.
3. I want to _____.

For example, during a classroom guidance lesson on bullying, a second-grade student, Brianna, might say, "Jason, when I see you picking on my friend Joshua, I feel sad and that makes me not want to play with you anymore." The leader explains the rule that I-statements will replace advice giving and will cut off future attempts at giving advice, substituting a request to translate it into an I-statement.

In addition to building students' confidence in their disclosure and their feedback through the use of progressive dyads and group exercises, the leader can make process comments about the whole group's growth in trust levels and cohesion. In this way, the leader encourages individuals' conscious and responsible risk-taking to confront their issues.

Outstanding leaders manage classrooms and group environments with both discipline and encouragement. In order not to devote too much attention to problem behavior, leaders know they must "catch them being good." Regardless of the maturity level of the group, leaders should make (age-appropriate) comments when members are "caught" helping, guiding, respecting, being friendly, trusting, cooperating, being forthright, displaying confidence, being realistic, obliging, asking for help, supporting, being sensitive, or telling what they need.

CONSIDERING MEMBERS' MULTIPLE CULTURES

Group work in a pluralistic country like the United States cannot avoid the dynamics of multiple cultures, and leaders must attend to member differences. DeLucia-Waack (1996a) identified the group work myth of believing that group member differences do not affect the process and outcome of groups. Group members are affected by the beliefs, interactions, and experiences that constitute their cultural backgrounds. Cultures influence how and when students interact. DeLucia-Waack and Donigian (2003) gave an example of a time DeLucia-Waack tried to lead a stress management workshop for a group of eight male Italian students who had recently immigrated to the United States. She discovered that these men believed it improper for a woman to be a "teacher" for men. Also, their cultural norms did not permit the disclosure of weakness to other males, so there was even less possibility that such disclosure would happen in the presence of a woman.

Hulse-Killacky, Killacky, and Donigian (2001) believed that one of the first tasks of a group leader is learning as much as possible about each student in the group. The challenge is to look past our own stereotypes and also to view each member in the context of his or her own sense of identity development. Doing so contributes to building a group culture in which all members feel more understood.

What if a person identifies with several cultures? It might be possible that a student is the child of a Cuban mother and an African American father and is gay. How do this student's cultures blend together at this point in time? Salazar (2006) described a systematic way to conceptualize plural identities in a student's life. For each group member, a leader can note the strength of belonging to subcultures and also detect the proportionate stage of identity development. Having the group spend time appreciating multifaceted identities and inviting each other to see beyond polite first impressions can establish an atmosphere of acceptance and help members notice both differences and similarities.

CHALLENGES WORKING WITH GROUP MEMBERS

All group leaders get anxious at first. What if there is something you can't handle? Are there resistant, problem members lurking about who wish to make trouble in your next group? Or is the problem actually a nervous and inexperienced leader? Boys' Town's Father Flanagan said that "there is no such thing as a bad boy," and Haley (1987) provocatively reported that client resistance doesn't exist but that counselor misunderstanding does. Students' challenging a group leader is a normal and healthy part of the transition stage of group dynamics.

What follows is an attempt to help leaders learn what to expect so they can feel grounded and prepared to deal with challenging group members. Group leaders' problems with members usually fall into two main areas: (1) problems understanding members and (2) problems with the group process.

Problems Understanding Members

We have all spent time as students and can recognize these student roles: the Class Clown, the Beauty Queen, the Complainer, the Jock, the Critic, the Goody-Goody, the Brooding One, the Volunteer-for-Everything, the Lover, and the Happy One (McCourt, 2005). Experienced educators juggle such characters while creating a cooperative classroom atmosphere and focusing on the day's topic. Group members also adopt roles: the Monopolizer, the Joker, the Silent One, the Distracter, the Intellectualizer, the Attacker, the Rescuer, the Resister, the Lover, the Grouch, the Get-the-Leader, the Crier, and the Insensitive One. In fact, these occur so frequently that they are easily detected by other group members. Schein (1969) indicated that these roles provide a function for group members. Before students can feel comfortable in the group and attend to others, they may orient themselves by resolving personal emotional issues through adopting one of these group member roles. These personal issues may include the following:

1. *Identity:* Who am I to be in this group?
2. *Control–power–influence:* Will I be able to control and influence others?
3. *Individual needs and group goals:* Will the group goals include my own needs?
4. *Acceptance and intimacy:* Will I be liked and accepted by the group?

In the process of resolving these issues, group members experience tension, frustration, and anxiety. Schein said that in order to deal with these feelings, three basic coping patterns emerge:

1. *Tough aggressive responses:* fighting, controlling, and resisting authority.
2. *Tender responses:* helping, supporting, forming alliances, and being dependent.
3. *Withdrawal or denial responses:* being passive, being indifferent, and overusing logic and reason.

Each of these personal issues and basic coping patterns can result in a member adopting a particular group member role. Group member roles are attempts to become self-oriented and feel in tune as a member of the group. If the roles become distracting, leaders can encourage students to verbally explore the roles they have adopted, rather than demanding that they give up their ways of protecting themselves. A leader can describe the behavior of a member and challenge him or her in a caring and respectful manner to try alternative methods to attain the same goals. Corey and Corey (2006) made a number of very helpful suggestions for approaching members in a nondefensive manner:

- Do not dismiss members.
- Express your difficulty with a member without denigrating the character of the person.
- Avoid responding to sarcasm with sarcasm.

- Educate members about how the group works.
- Be honest with members, rather than mystifying the process.
- Encourage members to explore their defensiveness, rather than demanding that they give up their way of protecting themselves.
- Avoid labeling and instead describe the behavior of the member.
- State observations and hunches in a tentative way as opposed to being dogmatic.
- Demonstrate sensitivity to a member's culture, and avoid stereotyping the individual.
- Avoid using the leadership role to intimidate members.
- Monitor your own countertransference reactions.
- Challenge members in a caring and respectful way to do things that may be painful and difficult.
- Do not retreat from conflict.
- Provide a balance between support and challenge.
- Do not take member reactions in an overly personal way.
- Facilitate a more focused exploration of the problem, rather than offering simple solutions.
- Do not meet your own needs at the expense of members' needs.
- Invite members to state how they are personally affected by the problematic behaviors of other members, while blocking judgments, evaluations, and criticisms.

Even though typical group member roles are expected and normal, when textbooks highlight strategies to cope with the most common roles, readers sometimes interpret these roles as deviant behavior. Students may select these roles due to their popularity, not out of some desire to express deviancy. Thus, it is most productive for leaders to perceive these transitional roles as a member's attempt to "fit in," while avoiding the appropriate levels of self-disclosure, feedback, and personal responsibility discussed earlier in this chapter. For example, the monopolizer is a role often spotlighted, perhaps due more to the intimidating effect this member has on a novice leader than to its frequency in groups. Jacobs, Masson, and Harvill (2006) reported that there are three types of monopolizers. The nervous monopolizer chatters to alleviate anxiety. The rambling monopolizer is self-absorbed and unaware of others' signals. The show-off monopolizer is insecure and craves attention. Jacobs et al. recommended directing two types of responses to a monopolizer, depending on whether it is early or late in the group's evolution. At the beginning of the group, leaders should provide structure and redirect members toward cooperative habits. Once the group begins its transition to the working stage, roles may be gently challenged. Early in the group, the leader wishes to curb nonfacilitative behavior but not to be verbally critical. Jacobs et al. suggested three ways to challenge the group's structure when a monopolizer is emerging:

1. The leader uses eye contact and nonverbal body language to convey the movement of "air time" to the next member.
2. The leader opens the floor to new speakers by announcing, "I'm going to ask a question and would like to hear from some of you who haven't talked yet."
3. The leader presents the dilemma of the "group hideout excuse." "In order not to hide behind those brave enough to talk first, I'm going to cut everyone off after 15–20 minutes. That way we can explore member issues serially, in 3–4 segments each week, instead of waiting to move on until the first soul becomes perfect!"

Jacobs et al. (2006) recommended that during feedback training exercises, the leader pair with the talker to provide structure for communication and to ensure privacy for the monopolizer's issues. Later in the group (i.e., during the working and termination stages), the monopolizer's defensiveness and anxiety can be gently confronted. Corey and Corey (2006) offered these examples:

a) Tanya, you talk often. I notice you typically identify with many of the problems raised. I have difficulty following you. I'm confused about what you are trying to tell us. In one sentence, what do you want me to hear?

b) Tanya, you seem to have a lot to say. I wonder, Tanya, if you are willing to go around the circle to each group member and finish this sentence: "What I want you to hear about me is . . ."

> **(Alternatives)** "When people don't listen to me I feel . . ."
> "I want you to listen to me because . . ."
> "If I didn't talk . . ."

Alternatively, Gazda, Ginter, and Horne (2008) suggested three responses to a monopolizer: (1) verbally respond to feelings of insecurity, (2) make specific suggestions about appropriate group behavior, and (3) model these. While more than a dozen group member roles have been identified, several occur more frequently than others. Table 4.1 describes helpful responses to deal with these challenging member types, as suggested by various

TABLE 4.1   Member Roles and Leader Responses

Problem Role	Leader Coping Strategies
Aggressor	Avoid negative confrontation. Encourage the member to be specific about the personal feelings. Place the member in a role-play situation that involves personal self-disclosure, and look for clues to the aggressiveness. Ask for a private conference, share your feelings, and ask for cooperation; point out the harmful effects on others; as a last resort, ask the member to leave the group.
Recognition seeker/ attention getter	Avoid negative confrontation. Respond to the member's feelings of insecurity, if present. Avoid eye contact. Do not respond to off-task comments/behavior. Ask for a private conference, and evaluate the member's reasons for the behavior.
Hostile/acting out	Avoid negative confrontation. Respond to possible negative transference phenomena. Keenly observe nonverbal behavior, and set limits firmly but not angrily. Ask for a private conference, and try to resolve the member's feelings toward the leader or significant others; refer the member to a counselor for individual counseling services if problems cannot be resolved.
Advice giver	Avoid negative confrontation. Respond to feelings of insecurity. Observe the reaction to the advice by the member who receives it. Encourage self-disclosure on the part of the advice giver. Place the advice giver in a role-play situation that limits his or her responses to identifying feelings. Avoid reinforcing the advice giver's inappropriate advice.

scholars including Dye (1968), Gazda et al. (2008), Schein (1969), and Morganett (1990, 1994). The group member roles not listed in Table 4.1 ordinarily can be addressed by facilitating appropriate member self-disclosure and feedback, using the pro-developmental procedures discussed earlier in the chapter. Importantly, the leader should never pathologize the student for adopting one of these challenging group member roles and should always keep in mind that students adopt these roles to fulfill personality needs, to avoid group goals, or to "fit in" with the group.

Problems with the Group Process

There are times that challenging student behavior is shared by either a few or most of the group members, not just a single individual. It can be unsettling for the leader, who worries that the group's process will become nonfacilitative. For example, how should a leader react when the group becomes increasingly silent? It is important to explore the meaning of the silence. Sometimes members are confused about what they are supposed to do next. Other times they are mulling and pondering about what was recently said, gaining insight. Sometimes they are embarrassed and withdrawn. Sometimes they are hoping that someone else will speak, not knowing how to draw that person out. Gazda et al. (2008) declared that leaders should, in general, respect silence. Leaders should verbally recognize members when they do contribute, use the skill of drawing out (Jacobs et al., 2006), and emphasize incremental sharing. Leaders can describe the body language they see in the group. They can also use the skill of linking to encourage members to respond to other members.

When two (or more) people in a group whisper and comment only to each other, it is called pairing. Sometimes members are trying to liven up their experience by making an entertaining running commentary as an aside that they believe only they can hear. However, this commentary is distracting to others in the group. Pairing also affects group dynamics by stimulating cliques or subgroups. When members make asides to each other, ask that these be shared with the whole group. If they persist, separate the whisperers by changing their seating.

New group leaders are sometimes embarrassed when a student in a quiet group announces, "I'm bored!" Instead of becoming flustered or berating yourself for insufficient structure, check to see what the student means by the statement. Leaders need not take personal responsibility for anxiety about transitions between issues. Always poll the group, instead of allowing one person to assume to speak for everyone. The leader might also declare the necessity for a new group rule: When bored, members will contribute something new/different to the group. Should the group agree that the new idea has priority, they will pursue it; if not, the group will explore other avenues.

Leaders familiar with advanced counseling techniques will find they are also useful in a group setting. Gladding (1998) mentioned reframing, paradox, and ordeal as potentially useful techniques when working with problematic group member behavior. Reframing is the art of attributing different meaning to a behavior so it will be seen differently. For example, instead of describing an unruly child in a divorce group as "incorrigible," the child's behavior could be reframed as "sensitive." "Dale is a sensitive group thermostat; each time the tension gets too thick, Dale acts out to direct our attention and protect the group." Alternatively, female African American teens once labeled as "rebellious and defiant" might be reframed as "independent and autonomous." "There's that attitude of independence again—it's important to be able to stand up on your own!" Reframing does not change the situation, but the alteration of meaning invites the possibility of change (Piercy & Sprenkle, 1986).

When using the technique of paradox, the leader gives the group members permission to do something they are already doing in order to lower their resistance to change. With a *restraining paradox,* the leader tells the group members, without sarcasm, that they are incapable of doing anything other than what they are now doing; this outcome was inevitable because there is no way to do something differently. With a *prescribing paradox,* the leader reenacts a role play of dysfunctional behavior before the group.

Haley (1987) described the technique of ordeal as helping the students give up behavior that is more troublesome to maintain than it is worth. The ordeal is a constructive or neutral behavior that the member must perform immediately prior to an undesirable behavior. For example, an ordeal might be for the client to perform aerobic exercise (e.g., 30 minutes on a stationary bike or treadmill) as soon as the client detects the onset of a depression state. An ordeal for a group member who wishes to stop smoking might be to donate one dollar to a despised organization before smoking a cigarette. The ordeal is never harmful, but it is not an activity the member wants to engage in. Will the member give up the behavior in order to avoid performing the constructive ordeal?

Clarity for Member Behavior

It is not uncommon for new group members to be confused about what they should do during group. Leaders who favor theoretical counseling orientations (e.g., person-centered, reality therapy) believe leader modeling is sufficient to establish member roles in groups. However, even when careful explanation is provided during initial group meetings, sometimes members forget, or they need role definitions reinforced. Kottler (2001) provided the following list of member behavior guidelines:

1. Speak only for yourself in the group. Use "I," rather than "we."
2. Blaming, whining, and complaining about people inside or outside the group are discouraged.
3. Racist, sexist, or otherwise disrespectful language will not be tolerated. There will be no name calling.
4. All members should take responsibility for making sure they get their own needs met in the group.
5. Nobody will be coerced or pressured into doing something they do not feel ready to do. Each may "pass."
6. What is said in the group is considered confidential information. Everyone is responsible for maintaining privacy.
7. Time must be equitably distributed among all members.
8. Any member who is late more than three times or misses more than three times will be asked to leave the group.
9. Instead of giving advice, members will tell the story of what they felt and did in a similar situation.
10. Feedback will be descriptive. (pp. 49–50)

Any similar list of guidelines should be brief, parsimonious, and modified so as to be appropriate for the developmental level of the students. The number of items on the list becomes fewer when members are younger. One such list for second graders during class-room guidance sessions consisted of three rules:

1. No one is allowed to hurt another's feelings on purpose.
2. No one can interfere with another's right to learn.
3. If the group sees the need for a new rule, we will establish one.

Finally, the feedback members receive on the kind of group member they are now can be used to draw comparisons to the kind of group member they would like to be. Corey (1981) provided a self-assessment scale that can be used as an in-group activity to provoke independent thoughts and group feedback about self-perceived and other-perceived group member behaviors. Kottler's guidelines above serve a similar function. If other group members tell a student his self-perceptions are not accurate, the group can discuss what changes the student can make in order to get where he wants to be. Self-assessment activities can be powerful mechanisms for changing member behaviors.

Summary

Two essential tasks are required of students in a successful group: self-disclosure and feedback. Self-disclosure involves students' describing their own reactions and experiences and emerges as trust and cohesion build from the group process. Exercises such as the Johari Window can help members understand the nature of self-disclosure and determine how much information about themselves they want to disclose. Feedback helps students understand the effects of their behaviors on others, leading to insights and potential behavior changes. Teaching group members to use I-statements can be particularly helpful when giving feedback.

Challenges related to cultural differences and specific group member roles were also addressed. Members frequently use the group experience to resolve personal emotional issues involving identity, control–power–influence, individual needs and group goals, and acceptance and intimacy. Schein (1969) proposed that members frequently address these personal issues using tough aggressive responses, tender responses, or withdrawal/denial responses. The literature has identified numerous difficult member types, including the aggressor, monopolizer, attention getter, hostile/acting out, and advice giver. Each requires a different leadership approach to effectively deal with the challenging member behaviors. In addition to encouraging student self-disclosure and feedback, commonly used techniques involve drawing out, reframing, paradoxes, and ordeals. Frequently, students alter challenging behavior patterns when they are helped to gain insight into their behavior and its underlying, often subconscious, purposes. This insight is most effectively supplied by other group members engaging in the appropriate use of feedback and self-disclosure.

CHAPTER 5

Leading Groups in the Schools

Amy Milsom

PREVIEW

The thought of leading a group can feel overwhelming for many school counselors-in-training. For counseling students who are just starting to feel comfortable conducting counseling sessions with one student, thinking about how to effectively attend to and facilitate interaction among many students might seem nearly impossible. Basic information on important styles, characteristics, and skills for effective group leadership is provided in this chapter. Specific group work techniques include active listening, blocking, clarifying, confronting, empathizing, evaluating, initiating, instructing, linking, modeling, providing feedback, questioning, and summarizing.

GROUP LEADERS

How do I make sure everyone in the group gets involved? Do I have to lead groups by myself? How can I pay attention to so many people? These questions are common among students in a group work course. As they think about the variety of groups they might eventually lead, these school counselors-in-training often experience anxiety about meeting the needs of all group members, attending to all students, and, in general, being effective in group work. By developing an understanding of different leadership styles, characteristics, and skills, school counselors-in-training will be better equipped to assess their readiness to lead groups.

Group leaders can use a variety of leadership styles, usually described according to how much structure a leader chooses to impose on a group and how much control a leader exercises over the interactions and communications within a group. Choosing which style is best for a particular group involves assessing the needs of the group members, establishing the goals of the group, and identifying the leader's personal preferences and tendencies. Most professional school counselors naturally lean toward one style or another. For example, some leaders have a more difficult time relinquishing control, while others prefer giving a lot of responsibility to students. At this point, it is essential to understand that various leadership styles can affect the outcomes of the group. By varying the amount of structure and control afforded to the group itself, a group leader can positively or negatively affect group outcomes.

Controlling Group Process

Leadership styles can be understood by visualizing a horizontal continuum of low control to high control. Leaders who provide less control fall at the left end of the continuum, while leaders who maintain high levels of control over the group process fall at the right end. The ideal amount of control provided by the group leader will depend a lot on the group's topic, goals, and agenda and on the members' characteristics (e.g., age, abilities).

HIGH-CONTROL LEADERSHIP   Group leaders who provide high levels of control have often been referred to as authoritarian or leader-centered group leaders. High-control leaders might best be described as in control and often take on the role of expert. Their power is evident in that they tend to direct conversation, dictate the group's agenda, and provide clear structure. Students are offered little to no opportunity to influence the direction of the group. Group leaders who fall at the high end of the continuum control interaction. Frequently, group members communicate with and through the leader as opposed to communicating directly with other group members. Thus, communication in groups with this type of leader is often limited to interactions between the group leader and the individual members. For example, in a task group with a time limit and a full agenda, the leader will frequently move the group actions and discussions from agenda item to agenda item, gaining quick consensus and decisions, even when some group members believe greater deliberation of the complexities of the decisions is warranted. High-control task group leaders sometimes do not "hear" these concerns in order to stay on schedule and reach closure as quickly as possible. Efficiency is prized. Classroom guidance leaders frequently move into "teacher mode" and impart information students need to master. Again, given the time constraints in a class schedule, discussion may be minimized so that students will receive all of the information needed in the time allotted.

MODERATE-CONTROL LEADERSHIP   Group leaders who use moderate amounts of control have been described as democratic, group centered, or collaborative. These leaders believe that the group process functions best when all members are actively involved and feel their opinions and efforts are valued. This type of group leader communicates, either explicitly or implicitly, to students that responsibility for the group belongs to everyone: leader and members. Leaders who use moderate control provide structure and support, encourage members to share, and maintain flexibility in order to allow group members to provide some direction. For example, the leader of a psychoeducational group often demonstrates moderate control and structure as he or she imparts information necessary to student learning, but the leader is also quite aware of the need for group members to integrate and process this information via discussion in order to apply it to their everyday lives.

LOW-CONTROL LEADERSHIP   Group leaders who provide little to no structure or control might be classified as laissez-faire or leaders in name only. Although leaders displaying low control might be officially considered the leader, these individuals take on virtually no responsibilities in the group. This type of leader forces members to assume responsibility if they want to make progress. Leaders of self-help groups or groups in which self-awareness is the primary goal may demonstrate low control. For example, in a counseling group for high school senior honor students who are worried about the transition to college and who are low on assertiveness (e.g., shy, inhibited), the leader may take a low-control (nonassertive) approach to "force" students to assume more assertive roles and take responsibility within the group process. While this approach is initially anxiety producing, the students will realize their own abilities to behave assertively and transfer those abilities to social and academic situations when transitioning into the college environment (i.e., demonstrate a success experience).

Member Responsibility

The amount of control provided by the group leader is inversely related to the amount of responsibility placed on students, that is, the more control the group leader provides, the less students need to or are able to take on responsibility for group process and outcomes. Group members must always take responsibility for working on personal goals; they must be willing to spend time and energy during and in between group sessions and be open to self-exploration. However, the group leader controls how much opportunity students have to influence the direction of the group and help each other.

Choosing a Leadership Style

In many ways, group leaders need to be true to themselves and choose a leadership style that fits their personality. Someone who highly values structure and organization might struggle to design and lead a less structured group. Developing skills in and comfort with different leadership styles, however, can help group leaders more easily adapt to students' needs.

For example, psychoeducational groups would logically require more leader-driven structure and control than would some types of counseling or psychotherapy groups. The instructional or educational component of a psychoeducational group would be challenging to implement effectively if group members were required to take on more responsibility than the leader (Brown, 2004). The assumption could be made that a group leader designs and implements a psychoeducational group because the leader possesses more knowledge of the topic (e.g., anger management skills) than do the students. In that sense, the expert role is inherent, and a fairly structured approach is necessary for the leader to ensure that all relevant content is covered. This does not mean that the group could not be run in a fairly democratic manner at certain points in time; the group leader could still engage the students by allowing them to guide the discussion (i.e., process) that follows instruction and skill practice (i.e., content). Nevertheless, flexibility to shift back and forth between more and less structure and control, both during sessions and throughout the group, is important.

Group leaders must also consider the benefits of using different styles during different group stages. Recommendations to provide more structure during the forming/orienting and termination stages of a group suggest that group leaders would benefit from using a style more toward the high end of the control continuum during the first few and the last few group sessions. As students become more comfortable with each other and enter the working stage and as they begin to better understand how the group works, they can benefit from less leader structure. As such, knowing when to allow or encourage group members to take on more responsibility can help the group leader facilitate the movement of the group through to termination.

Group member characteristics should also be considered when choosing a leadership style. The age and developmental level of group members might indicate a need for more structure. For example, children in the early years of elementary school would benefit from higher levels of leader structure and control, since they would not be capable of taking on as much responsibility as adolescents can. Additionally, students who have never engaged in group work might need more structure from the leader as compared to others who have participated in groups in the past. Knowing what to expect and having previous experience might make a group member more willing or able to take on responsibility earlier in the group.

Finally, theoretical approach will dictate leadership style to some degree, or perhaps theoretical approach simply serves as a reflection of group leader preferences. No matter which way you look at it, a direct connection between leadership style and theory appears to exist. Think about which theories lend themselves well to leader structure and control. Theoretical approaches such as cognitive behavioral and solution-focused/brief counseling require group leaders to educate students and lead them through interventions such as skill or thought rehearsal. Naturally, greater amounts of structure from the group leader would be required for success with these types of theoretical approaches as opposed to when group leaders use person-centered or existential theoretical approaches.

Group leaders are encouraged to think about their preferences and comfort level in relation to structure and control: How much responsibility do you want group members to have? Which theoretical approaches are you drawn toward, and how might they influence the amount of structure and control you afford to students? Group leaders are also encouraged to consider the needs of students: Which type of group would best meet the needs of potential members? What special needs might participants possess? All of these questions should be considered when group leaders are in the planning stages so that they can intentionally consider how to incorporate leadership styles that will positively affect the group process.

GROUP LEADER CORE CHARACTERISTICS

Counselor educators often look for evidence of certain personal qualities in potential counseling students during the admissions process, usually focusing on interpersonal skills, insight, or other qualities that would indicate their likelihood for success working with and understanding students' concerns. Qualities that make for a school counselor who is effective with individual students (e.g., genuineness, self-awareness) are also important for leaders. A few counselor characteristics essential to leading groups include adaptability, belief in the group process, enthusiasm, self-confidence, and a willingness to model positive behavior.

Adaptability

Working with more than one student requires that group leaders be adaptable. Leaders cannot always predict student behavior, and they often have limited control over student behavior. Although planning and organization are important, effective group leaders must be able to continuously assess the students' needs. Logically, meeting the needs of multiple students is challenging and requires the ability to identify and prioritize whose needs are the most important to address in the moment.

Group leaders must keep in mind that there might be times when not all students are satisfied and that some member concerns might simply reflect normal anxiety or discomfort with the process. Leaders who are adaptable, however, will be flexible enough to change the direction or focus of the group if necessary, to increase or decrease their control and structure if relevant, and to solicit student feedback throughout the process.

Belief in the Group Process

Group leaders should be able to instill hope and explain to members how and why groups might benefit them, and referencing therapeutic factors is one simple way of doing just that. For example, a group leader might tell a group of third-grade students attending a changing families group that they might benefit from knowing that other students also are struggling to cope with their new family situations (universality). Similarly, a school counselor could inform a group of ninth-grade students attending an anger management group that students who have participated in the group in the past have said it was helpful and it was good to be able to talk about things that frustrated them.

Enthusiasm

Enthusiasm for group work is closely connected with a leader's belief in the group process. Because the nature of group work prevents all members from being actively engaged at all times (i.e., students can't all talk at once), the leader must work hard to maintain student involvement and help students realize the importance of engaging in the work of other members. This might be particularly challenging when working with children and adolescents who are in a more egocentric developmental stage. Demonstrating enthusiasm for the group work students are doing can help leaders maintain member interest and motivation. However, too much enthusiasm might turn some group members off. The enthusiasm must be genuine, but leaders should monitor the reactions of group members. Leaders who tend to be very bubbly might frighten or even annoy some group members, so leaders must be prepared to assess what an appropriate level of enthusiasm might be for each group, depending on the topic and its members.

Maintaining enthusiasm for group work can be difficult at times, even when a leader truly believes in the work being done. We all have bad days or times when we are distracted or tired. Group leaders must find ways to rev themselves up prior to the group session, and planning activities or interventions that students find enjoyable or that engage students will help to keep everyone's energy levels up. Because one negative or withdrawn group member can at times influence the whole group process, proactively planning for ways to generate and maintain group member enthusiasm and motivation is critical. To do this, leaders can start with bringing their own enthusiasm to each session. Additionally, school counselors who lead groups not only can play off of the energy and enthusiasm that so many school-age students exhibit but also can proactively try to guarantee good group energy by choosing at least one student group member who tends to be more extraverted.

Self-Confidence

Group work can be intimidating. Some counselors-in-training who demonstrate confidence and solid basic counseling and attending skills with individual students may experience difficulty when placed in front of a group. Just because someone can work well with an individual client does not mean he or she will necessarily work well with a group. Managing many individuals at once can be challenging and does require practice. Nevertheless, basic individual counseling skills serve as a strong foundation for group work. The idea of attending to more than one student can be overwhelming, and concerns about giving everyone equal attention might cause anxiety. Just as when working with individual students, group workers who enter a session believing they can be effective and knowing that they do not have to be perfect will likely experience success.

Bandura (1997) suggested that self-efficacy, a construct closely tied to self-confidence, can be enhanced through mastery experiences (e.g., successful performance of a task), vicarious learning (e.g., modeling), and verbal persuasion (e.g., encouragement). As a result, in order to increase their self-confidence in relation to leading groups, leaders should consider ways in which they can experience success, observe others, and receive feedback. For example, setting and achieving realistic, progressive goals for each group session can allow leaders to experience success. Those goals might include using any number of the group leadership skills described later in the chapter. Also, by observing groups and/or participating in a group, school counselors-in-training can observe and reflect on effective and ineffective leader behaviors. Finally, by co-leading (discussed at the end of this chapter) with an experienced group leader or providing supervisors with either video- or audiotapes of group sessions, school counselors-in-training can receive feedback regarding their skills. Engaging in all or some of these activities could help group leaders improve their confidence.

Willingness to Model Positive Behavior

The "do as I say and not as I do" attitude will not work well for group leaders. Students often receive that type of message from adults. School counselors who lead groups must maintain an awareness of opportunities where they can demonstrate desirable behaviors to group members with the knowledge that group members will, over time, pick up on and demonstrate acceptable and desirable behaviors. For example, rather than immediately chastising one member for harshly confronting another, an effective group leader will acknowledge the concern and model appropriate ways to confront. Leaders who are unwilling or unable to model the behaviors they expect their group members to exhibit will likely not see those behaviors.

Not only must group leaders be willing to model behaviors that members want to obtain (e.g., social skills), but they also should use opportunities to model behaviors that will help students develop trust and cohesion. Modeling in group work can be different from modeling with individuals. By helping students understand how to interact in respectful ways, group leaders can facilitate growth and movement through group stages. Leaders cannot expect students to give honest, caring feedback if the leader cannot do so to group members. The same holds true for accepting negative feedback and for exhibiting a number of other interpersonal skills.

SKILLS OF EFFECTIVE GROUP LEADERS

A variety of counseling skills learned when working with individual students is very applicable to working with groups. The following listing is presented in the approximate order each might occur in group work and is not comprehensive. However, it includes skills that may take on new importance in groups. In addition, a few skills that are unique to group work are presented. Some of these skills will be highlighted again as appropriate throughout the remainder of this book because of their applicability to the specific stages of the various types of group work. Used intentionally and in combination, these skills can help leaders effectively facilitate groups. While it is difficult to trace the origins of many of these skills to specific sources, the earlier editions of books by Jacobs, Masson, & Harvill (2006) and Corey (2007) are sometimes noted as the creative originators of some of the skills discussed below.

Initiating

Just as students who come to counseling often need some direction or guidance in order to feel comfortable or continue making progress, group members can benefit from leaders' initiating skills. Students, and particularly elementary school students, understandably might need more direction from a group leader or assistance in knowing what is and is not okay to discuss. School counselors who lead groups can provide direction by initiating a topic for discussion in an effort to help members focus their energy in productive ways. Group leaders can also implement activities designed to increase student participation or to move the group to a different level of intensity. Initiating skills will likely be more necessary during the earlier stages of a group, when group members are more anxious and uncertain of what to expect or how to behave. Initiating skills can also be important both in later stages when group members get stuck and in the final stages when students might begin to shut down and resist terminating.

Active Listening

Group leaders use active listening skills (i.e., attending to verbal and nonverbal behavior) to communicate to group members that the leaders are paying attention and to help establish an environment where students feel safe to self-disclose. The effective use of active listening skills might benefit the group in different ways. For example, by giving minimal encouragers (e.g., "uh-huh," head nods), the group leader can encourage Jane to continue sharing a new idea on how to solve a problem. Also, by smiling at Miguel, a group member whose nonverbal behavior indicates he might feel anxious, the group leader can help Miguel feel safe and accepted. Groups are most effective when all students are engaged, and through active listening skills, group leaders can help to establish the group as a safe environment.

Clarifying

Group leaders can use clarifying skills to check their own understanding of a student's concern or to help the student identify a main concern. Leaders can also use clarification for the benefit of other group members. For example, when noticing a look of confusion on Dante's face after Jessica described her problem, a leader might use a clarifying statement to make sure Dante understands her problem: "Jessica, I'm getting the sense that a few group members didn't quite understand your concern—did you mean that you didn't initially feel sad about your mom, but now it seems like you can't concentrate?" Also, some students have short attention spans or engage in storytelling. Although these behaviors often can be developmentally appropriate, group leaders must be ready to address them. For example, Brad tends to give a lot of details and often jumps from one topic to another. In order to identify his main concerns and help him to focus on one thing, the group leader could use a clarifying statement: "So it sounds like the thing you're most concerned about is your problems getting along with your brother and the trouble you get into at home when you two argue." The effective use of clarifying skills in a group requires that the leader pay attention to the reactions of other members, picking up on signs that they do not understand what was stated or that they could benefit from clarification. Nonverbal cues can serve as clear indicators of confusion.

Questioning

Group leaders use questioning in the same way they do with individual students. Questioning can be used to elicit more information from group members. It can also be used when the leader wants to help students focus on an important aspect of their concern or when the leader thinks group members could be more helpful if they knew more about the background or context of the situation. For example, after Melissa shares limited information about her father's recent imprisonment, the group leader says, "You have talked a lot about your little brother's reaction, but please tell us how *you* are feeling about the situation." Questioning can also be used to link group members and help them brainstorm ways to cope: "Dean's situation sounds pretty similar to yours, Kim. Did you find any helpful ways to get through it?"

Providing Feedback

Providing feedback is a skill that allows leaders to help students develop greater self-awareness. Students develop insight through feedback provided by the leader and by other group members, making it critical that leaders model how to give and receive feedback, encourage members to share feedback with each other, and, most importantly, facilitate and maintain an environment where feedback can be shared and received respectfully. Feedback might address nonverbal behaviors: "Colby, are you aware that you smile every time you talk about your grandfather?" It could also be used to express honest reactions to behaviors: "I am upset that you are late again, especially since you promised to be on time"; to convey perceptions of group member progress: "It seems like you're really working hard, and you appear a little more comfortable speaking up"; and to point out patterns: "I noticed that for the past three sessions you have been fairly negative when talking about your mom, and I don't remember hearing that so much from you in the past."

Empathizing

Empathy is important in any relationship. Leaders can communicate understanding and promote trust through the use of empathic statements. For example, it is not uncommon for students to hesitate to share information during the early stages of a group. By making a statement such as "It can be difficult and maybe a bit scary to share things about yourself with people you don't know very well," a leader communicates an understanding of the feelings many students might be experiencing. Through empathic statements, leaders also help students consider how other members might feel, providing them with a greater understanding of others. Trust and cohesion are so critical to the success of a group, and empathy is one group leadership skill that can greatly influence the overall climate and eventual progress of the students.

Blocking

Blocking is a skill that is unique to group work, and it is used mainly to protect group members. Blocking can be done verbally or nonverbally and can be used to protect a group member from someone else or from himself or herself. For example, students in the early stages of a counseling group might not understand how to appropriately confront each other. When the leader hears a 10th-grader, Tyler, confronting his peer, Nate, in a very attacking manner, the group leader can block Tyler's behavior by verbally stating, "I feel the need to cut you off, Tyler, because while you picked up on the inconsistency in Nate's story, I'm concerned that you are attacking and criticizing Nate more than helping him to explore that situation. Nate, were you aware that you told us something different last week?"

Another example might occur in a psychoeducational group focusing on career development. A seventh-grade group member, Sheri, starts to share information about a loss she experienced a year ago. Sensing that the other students are becoming very uncomfortable and determining that the information is not appropriate, given the context of the group, the leader can block Sheri from continuing to share that information by refocusing the group members: "Sheri, it sounds like this stirred up some strong memories for you, but let's shift back to how you might narrow down some potential careers." A follow-up meeting with Sheri after the group session would help the school counselor determine whether or not Sheri could benefit from individual attention to work through the previous loss.

Linking

Linking, another counseling skill that is unique to group work, helps group members connect with one another. A leader who uses linking points out similarities among students' experiences, feelings, or concerns. For example, during the forming and orienting stage of a group, students might share basic information about why they are there. As they talk, the leader can make connections among members, using statements such as "So it sounds like you and Ben are dealing with some pretty similar stuff."

Linking is a very useful skill in facilitating universality as well as in developing group cohesion. As students become more and more aware of the ways in which they are similar, they develop bonds and support each other. When working with adolescents, who often believe that no one else could possibly understand what they are going through, linking becomes a critical skill for leaders. Leaders who are able to model linking skills often find that group members start to link themselves; one member might say to another, "I had almost the same experience with my brother, but he and I still don't talk about it."

Confronting

Confrontation is used to point out discrepancies in an effort to promote self-awareness. A group leader might confront Gene, pointing out that he just shared a very happy story about his sister but that his face appears to express sadness. A group leader might also note discrepancies in information shared from session to session. For example, a fifth-grade student, Telisha, had consistently expressed anger related to how her best friend treated her, but this week she said that everything was fine. Pointing out this discrepancy might allow a group leader to help Telisha honestly explore the situation and her feelings. Has the situation really changed? If so, how did that happen? Are the problems resolved, or is Telisha just tired of working on it and now willing to live with things the way they are?

Confrontation is important in a group setting because leaders not only want to help members honestly explore their own concerns but also want to avoid the need to use their blocking skills. For example, if one student, Meena, frequently shares information that is inconsistent, but the leader never confronts her, chances are that other group members will eventually become frustrated and attack her. A leader who confronts Meena's inconsistencies early on is able not only to prevent unnecessary attacks but also to model appropriate confrontation skills.

Instructing

Not surprisingly, instructing skills are critical for classroom guidance and psychoeducational group leaders (Brown, 2004). These group leaders must be able to present information in an organized manner and tailor the content to match the developmental level of the students. However, instructing skills can benefit the leaders of any type of group. The need for instructing skills is not restricted to psychoeducational group leaders. For example, a counseling group leader can use instructing skills to explain to members how they can best engage in and benefit from a specific counseling intervention. Skills in evaluation, when used in relation to instructing, can help group leaders ensure that students learned or understood the content presented. For many school counselors who have education backgrounds or who possess experience leading classroom guidance, these instructional skills should come easily.

Modeling

As mentioned previously, leaders must be willing to serve as models. Leader modeling may occur naturally, as students want to emulate the individual who holds power in the group. Intentional use of modeling, however, can help a group leader establish behavioral norms. In addition to the examples provided earlier, group leaders can model commitment to the group by arriving on time and being prepared, ways to give feedback, respect for group members by being nonjudgmental, professionalism to a co-leader or trainee, and a variety of other skills and behaviors.

Summarizing

Summarizing is essentially pulling the important elements of an interaction together into a concise statement. Leaders can make summary statements to help ensure that students all take away the same message from another member's work: "So after thinking about it for a long time, you have decided to try speaking up in math class and we can best help you by letting you practice and giving you some feedback." By hearing that type of statement, other group members might have a better idea of how they can be useful. Summarizing is also useful at the end of a session and, in particular, at the end of the group—and in these situations, the summary might reflect the overall group process or content, rather than focusing on one student. This type of summarization can be used to help the students reflect on how hard they worked, how similar their experiences have been, or how they should prepare for the next session: "So it sounds like everyone is excited to practice their I-messages this week and we all should come back next time ready to share how things went."

Evaluating

Evaluating skills are critical to monitoring and affecting group outcomes. In this age of accountability, professional school counselors are often required to demonstrate the effects of

TABLE 5.1   Self-Assessment of Basic Group Leader Skills

At the conclusion of a group work session, rate yourself on the following counseling skills using the following scale: 0 = Did not demonstrate (DND); 1 = Demonstrated, but need improvement (NI); 2 = Demonstrated with skill (SK).

	DND	NI	SK	Comment
Initiating...............	0	1	2	_____
Active Listening......	0	1	2	_____
Clarifying..............	0	1	2	_____
Questioning..........	0	1	2	_____
Providing Feedback.	0	1	2	_____
Empathizing..........	0	1	2	_____
Blocking...............	0	1	2	_____
Linking.................	0	1	2	_____
Confronting..........	0	1	2	_____
Instructing............	0	1	2	_____
Modeling..............	0	1	2	_____
Summarizing.........	0	1	2	_____
Evaluating............	0	1	2	_____

their efforts to supervisors, administrators, or others. Evaluating skills can be used to identify issues that might influence group dynamics and group process as well as the overall outcomes of the group. Group members who struggle to develop cohesion might not be able to achieve positive outcomes. Leaders can evaluate group dynamics and group process throughout the entirety of the group in an effort to identify such potential problems and address them early. Additionally, evaluating the effectiveness of various interventions and techniques can help leaders to determine if or how modifications should be made for future groups. Chapters 10 and 17 contain more information about evaluating groups. Table 5.1 provides a listing of leader skills with a self-assessment that leaders can use at the conclusion of a group session.

LEADER FUNCTIONS

Effective leaders must do more than possess desirable leader characteristics and use group counseling skills. They must assume a number of functions in order to help students get the most out of their experiences. Considering these functions ahead of time will allow group leaders to plan activities and interventions that will enable them to successfully carry out these functions.

Executive Functioning

Leaders have to engage in a number of administrative tasks in order to get their groups up and running as well as to keep them running smoothly. To effectively execute these functions, leaders must possess organizational skills and have access to relevant resources. Professional school counselors will need to set aside time to plan the group and attend to logistical issues, including talking with teachers to determine when the best time will be to allow students to leave their class, determining when a room will be available, ensuring that passes are sent to students, and so on. They will also need to make sure that photocopies of worksheets are made, if relevant, and that group-related materials are available. Groups that are disorganized may not run as smoothly and might result in less-positive outcomes for members. Tasks such as advertising the group, recruiting and screening members, and addressing accommodations fall under this function. Refer to Chapters 6 and 7 for more specifics regarding the other types of executive functions.

Helping Members Gain Insight and Attribute Meaning

Just as leaders must do more than possess basic skills and characteristics, students must do more than simply engage in activities, self-disclose, or share feelings. They must reflect on or make sense of their experiences if they are to gain the most insight. By using processing skills such as questioning, providing feedback, empathizing, and summarizing, leaders can help members to process their experiences on a deeper level—what it was like to finally say something out loud, how it felt to learn that they are not the only ones coping with the loss of their pet, or how they feel about their progress.

While processing skills are associated primarily with counseling and psychotherapy groups, Hulse-Killacky, Kraus, and Schumacher (1999) recommended that task group leaders spend more time processing group dynamics and experiences, rather than focusing mainly on content. Task group members who take the time to focus on processing might gain a better understanding of how they contribute to or impede the work of the group. The group as a whole can more clearly assess its effectiveness as well as determine the types of changes that could be implemented in the future to avoid potential problems and identify the components of the group that are working. Additionally, Furr (2000) suggested that psycho-educational group sessions include some sort of processing component or activity.

Emotional Stimulation

Group leaders must also consider the ways in which they can help facilitate the safe expression of emotion by group members. Creating a supportive environment and helping students feel safe to share are the critical first steps to facilitating emotional stimulation. Group leaders can use skills such as reflecting feelings, empathizing, and questioning to elicit emotion. Importantly, the goal here is to provide a safe environment for members to display emotion if they choose to do so, not to convey the expectation that all students must display intense emotion (e.g., cry) for the group experience to be considered a success.

Johnson and Johnson (2006) identified many benefits associated with group members' experiencing emotions and emphasized that it does not matter whether or not the emotions are actually expressed. Emotions, whether positive or negative, can lead students to desire change. For example, a group member who feels strongly enough about something will be more motivated to take action (e.g., "I'm really tired of getting into trouble, and I do want my parents to be proud of me, so I want to learn how to stay out of fights at school"). Emotional stimulation can also help students bond and can be cathartic (Yalom & Leszcz, 2005). For example, members who express anxiety during the initial stages of a group may find comfort in knowing they are not alone. Finally, emotional stimulation can provide opportunities for group members to work through a number of issues with support from other members and can often lead to insight.

Focus on the Here and Now

One of the main benefits of group work is that it allows members to work through concerns and try out new behaviors in a safe and supportive environment in the hopes of carrying over some of the benefits into regular life. By focusing on the here and now—what is happening in the room at that moment—group leaders facilitate open and honest interactions among members and also help group members to develop increased self-awareness. Leaders can do this by making summary statements that facilitate students' focus on immediate events: "Mary, I've noticed the progress you have made in improving your grades, and it seems like you feel really proud of yourself right now."

Promote Interaction

Groups cannot be effective if members do not interact; all of the benefits of the group will be lost. Many therapeutic factors (e.g., cohesion, interpersonal learning) rely on group members' interacting with and providing feedback to each other. Group leaders can use many of the skills discussed earlier (e.g., initiating, linking, blocking, modeling) to promote healthy interaction among group members. They can also design and implement activities that require group members to get to know one another. School-age students have likely participated in many icebreaker activities and might know a lot about each other, especially if they are in the same classroom. For that reason, when choosing icebreaker and other activities to help students interact with and learn more about each other, school counselors might consider choosing activities that are related to the focus of the group. For example, for a career exploration group, students could be asked to talk about jobs their relatives hold or careers they would and would not like to have. Similarly, in a counseling group whose purpose is to empower students, members could be asked to describe their heroes or people they admire.

GROUP CO-LEADERS

CASE STUDY 5.1

Jan

Jan works as a school counselor in a high-needs elementary school: 87% of the students receive free and reduced lunch, and 62% of the population speaks English as a second language (ESL). Jan is the only school counselor, and her caseload is 520 students. She believes that she can target many students through small groups. A potential school counseling intern, Megan, has approached Jan to inquire if she can help out with some of the groups. Megan indicates that she has completed a graduate course in group dynamics and has volunteered at community agencies serving ESL families and children in the past. Jan currently would like to run more groups, but she cannot because of her other responsibilities. By taking Megan on as a co-leader, she believes she could increase the number of children in the group from 6 to 10 and still meet the needs of the children. Jan needs to consider how she might approach co-leading the group and also weigh the pros and cons of taking on a co-leader, as well as other ethical/legal considerations, such as school board policy, principal permission, and liability.

School counselors might choose to lead groups by themselves, but there are good and not-so-good reasons to consider co-leadership. Just as when determining their leadership style, leaders should consider their personal strengths and weaknesses. When deciding whether or not to work with a co-leader, leaders must also assess their own ability to work with others as well as the characteristics of the other leader. Nelson-Jones (1992) suggested that effective co-leaders respect each other's skills; work collaboratively; are honest with each other; share in the planning, implementation, and evaluation of the group; and clearly understand and agree on each other's role in relation to the group. Co-leaders must also determine the most effective style to use.

Group Co-Leadership Styles

Several types of co-leadership have been identified, including alternated, shared, and apprenticed. Each of these types will be reviewed in the sections that follow.

ALTERNATED   The alternated style of co-leadership occurs when leaders take turns being in charge of specific sessions or parts of sessions. Some leaders alternate from week to week, and others might alternate depending on the topic to be addressed (e.g., the leader with more expertise on the topic might lead) or the intervention to be used (e.g., the leader who has more experience conducting the intervention might lead). Alternated co-leadership can be useful when two group leaders work together but find they possess very different leadership styles. Rather than struggling to match their styles exactly, alternating leadership can allow the group to benefit from both styles without experiencing awkward co-leader interaction.

SHARED   Shared co-leadership occurs when both leaders accept shared responsibility for each group at each session, that is, they do not predetermine who will lead at certain times. Rather, these co-leaders play off each other, interjecting when they can. There might be times when one co-leader assumes more control, but these decisions will be made in the moment and will occur without discussion between the leaders. Understandably, shared co-leadership should be most effective when the two leaders know each other well, respect each other, and have previous experience co-leading together. They must be able to monitor each other in order to avoid interrupting each other.

APPRENTICED   School counselors-in-training might participate in an apprenticed style of co-leadership. This style involves an experienced leader working with a less experienced leader. Co-leaders working in an apprenticed style might choose to alternate or share responsibility for the group, but the main purpose of this style is for the more experienced leader to serve as a model and to support and provide feedback to the less experienced leader.

Potential Advantages and Possible Problems of Group Co-Leadership

There are various benefits and drawbacks of group co-leadership. The following is a summary of potential advantages and some possible problems. Co-leadership affords a group the benefits of two individuals who may share different levels of experience, expertise, and skills. A leader might hesitate to implement a particular intervention because he is not very familiar with it. By bringing on a co-leader who has experience with unfamiliar approaches or techniques, the leader will not only allow the group to benefit from a potentially helpful intervention that they would have missed out on but also benefit himself by directly observing the implementation of that intervention.

Furthermore, efforts can be shared when more than one leader is involved. Co-leaders can share in recruitment and screening activities as well as potential follow-up with group members. Additionally, if one group leader has to miss a session for some reason, the group can still continue in that leader's absence. Having co-leaders also allows for the group size to be increased. Trying to attend to more than 8 group members might be challenging for one leader, but when another leader comes on board, the group might realistically be increased to 12 members.

Groups that are fortunate enough to have co-leaders might benefit from those individuals' modeling interactions or other behaviors. Co-leaders can practice skills in advance and come to the group prepared to demonstrate specific interactions or skills (e.g., communication skills) that they are preparing to teach students.

Additionally, an ongoing evaluation of the group can help to affect positive outcomes. Co-leaders who schedule a regular meeting after each group session can take that time to reflect on what went well and what did not go well during the session. They can compare perspectives and discuss different things each noticed during the group. As one leader is more actively involved, the other can observe and pick up on things possibly not seen by the first leader. Additionally, when the group does not go smoothly or when the leaders decide to try something new, they can serve as the sources of support and feedback for each other.

Finally, using co-leaders makes it more likely that group members will feel a connection to at least one of the leaders. When possible, co-leaders should consider the type of group and the composition of members in order to determine which type of co-leaders might benefit the group. For example, for a heterogeneous group addressing study skills, having male and female co-leaders might help group members feel as if at least one of the leaders could understand their gender-based perspective. Co-leaders could pair up in many ways to reflect group member diversity in relation to race, age, disability, sexual orientation, religion, and a number of other characteristics.

Several potential problems might also arise with co-leadership arrangements. Depending on the size of the group, the use of co-leaders might result in the leaders dominating the members. This can also occur when co-leaders both have strong personalities. Participating in a group might be anxiety provoking for many students, and to enter a group where the leaders clearly dominate might be too overwhelming for some students.

Another possible problem of co-leadership results when the leaders operate from different agendas. As mentioned previously, co-leaders can effectively lead a group even when they possess different leadership styles—using an alternated style allows for this. Co-leaders who cannot agree on a theoretical approach or who disagree on the direction to take the group will likely create confusion among group members.

Similarly, group co-leaders who fail to share in or agree on an equitable division of responsibilities may struggle to work effectively together. Planning between sessions and conducting follow-up after sessions are important if group leaders want to monitor the effectiveness of the group. Co-leaders who do not take time to prepare together may not co-lead sessions as effectively or smoothly.

Finally, group co-leaders who do not get along or who feel competitive toward each other might end up creating an environment where group members feel like they have to side with one over the other. Group cohesion cannot easily develop in an environment filled with tension.

Summary

This chapter included a review of various leadership styles, characteristics, and skills that can help school counselors successfully implement group work. Leaders must be able to assess their own personal and professional characteristics in order to determine the likelihood of their success as group leaders. Understanding which style of leadership they would be most comfortable with will help leaders to determine not only the types of groups they could most likely lead well but also the ways in which they could become more comfortable using various leadership styles. The amount of structure and control offered by the leader will affect the amount of responsibility the group members are able to assume for the group. Theoretical approach, group type, and group member characteristics should also be taken into consideration when determining an appropriate leadership style.

Qualities that make for an effective group leader overlap quite a bit with the qualities that help someone become an effective school counselor in general. Yet leaders must recognize the unique power that groups have to make a difference in the lives of students. Leaders must consider how their personal characteristics—such as adaptability, willingness to model, and

self-confidence, to name a few—can be critical to the overall success of the group. Similarly, general counseling skills can be used by leaders to facilitate group development and student progress toward goals. These skills take on new importance, however, when considering how they can be used to help group members bond. Without student interaction, the power of groups is lost. Therefore, school counselors are encouraged to use general counseling skills, as well as the skills of linking and blocking, to facilitate the development of healthy working relationships among students, while at the same time using those skills to facilitate group members' self-awareness. Finally, leaders can use those skills to help students attribute meaning to their experiences.

No one needs to work in isolation, and for school counselors-in-training, the use of co-leaders can be a beneficial way to gain confidence and skills in group work. The potential advantages and the possible problems associated with co-leadership should be considered in advance of agreeing to co-lead. By observing and working with experienced group leaders, school counselors-in-training can obtain feedback about their progress using a variety of leadership styles and skills.

Systemic Group Work: Planning and Process

CHAPTER 6

Planning for Group Work in the Schools

F. ROBERT WILSON*

PREVIEW

Planning is an essential component of successful school-based group work. This chapter identifies and discusses the key elements of planning, drawn from group work best practices (ASGW, 2007, Best Practice Standard A7.a) and group work training standards (ASGW, 2000), including screening, selecting, and preparing members; selecting methods for deriving meaning and transferring learning; determining needed resources; measuring outcomes; and using closed or open groups.

PLANNING FOR GROUP WORK

An effective group leader carefully plans for the group experience. Contrary to the laissez-faire, "go with the flow" leadership style evidenced by some of group work's pioneers, clinical wisdom and research evidence combine to suggest that the key to success is planned flexibility. Nowhere is this truer than in school-based groups.

Careful planning is required to even launch a program of group-based interventions within the school setting. The academic culture of the school sometimes mitigates against a leader's wish to launch group-based interventions (Bowman, 1987a; Schmidt, 2003). However, a carefully crafted program of collaborative planning and team building can reduce administrator and teacher concerns and embed group interventions into the fabric of school policy and procedure (Ripley & Goodnough, 2001).

Once a group intervention has been launched, a wealth of group process research has revealed that group development follows a relatively orderly developmental progression (Trotzer, 1999). From a starting point of dealing with inclusion and identity issues,

---

* The author is indebted to Susan B. Warm, a group work specialist employed by a suburban high school to design and run ongoing counseling groups and to maintain their extensive group counseling program, for providing rich stories from the field, insights into the realities of group work in the schools, and editorial feedback, all of which helped to ground and vitalize this chapter.

which in this book is referred to as the forming and orienting stage, most groups move through a transition stage of dealing with resistance, into a working stage characterized by cohesion and productivity, and finally to a termination stage in which members can be guided to consolidate their gains and conclude their involvement in the group. Prior to the group, successful group leaders immerse themselves in the realities of the school and its students (e.g., school norms; concerns within the school about its students; competing demands for students', teachers' and administrators' time; current school crises; community norms and concerns). Leaders must plan groups that not only fit with prospective students' needs but also fit comfortably within the culture and climate of the school. In this chapter, the key elements of planning for successful group leadership are identified and discussed.

The cornerstone for developmental guidance programs is found in the American School Counselor Association (ASCA) standards within the domains of academic, career, and personal/social development (Campbell & Dahir, 1997), and *The ASCA National Model* (ASCA, 2005), which refers to the importance of planning for group work in broad terms. In addition, the *ASGW Best Practice Guidelines* (Association for Specialist in Group Work [ASGW], 2007) have established a list of best practices for planning group work activities that are far more detailed and specific. Whether one is consulting with task or work groups in the school, conducting psychoeducational or developmental classroom guidance lessons, or providing group counseling interventions, a solid grounding in these best practices will help the leader achieve greater success in planning group offerings.

A third source of guidance is the *ASGW Professional Standards for the Training of Group Workers* (ASGW, 2000). These training standards outline the knowledge and skills necessary to establish one's scope of practice, assess group members and the social systems in which they live, plan and implement group interventions, become a skillful leader and co-leader of groups, evaluate group outcomes, and observe ethical, diversity-competent best practices while leading groups.

The two ASGW foundational documents identify the key specific elements of successful planning for group work:

- Grounding oneself in the legal and professional regulations governing the practice of group work.
- Clarifying one's own scope of group work competence.
- Establishing the overarching purpose for the group-based intervention.
- Identifying goals and objectives for the intervention.
- Detailing methods to be employed in achieving goals and objectives during the intervention.
- Detailing methods to be used in screening, selecting, and preparing members to be successful in the group.
- Selecting methods to be used in helping students derive meaning from their within-group experiences and transfer within-group learning to real-world circumstances.
- Determining resources needed to launch and sustain the group.
- Determining methods for measuring outcomes during and following the intervention.

The first element was discussed in detail in Chapter 2; the remaining elements will be discussed in turn throughout the remainder of this chapter.

Clarifying One's Scope of Group Work Competence

Not only is it critical that group leaders limit their activities to those that are permitted under their school counseling license or certificate, but also group leaders must limit their activities to those for which they have been adequately trained (ASGW, 2007, Best Practice Standard A2; Conyne, Wilson, & Ward, 1997; Rapin & Conyne, 1999). Said most simply, different leader competencies are required for different types of groups (Remley & Herlihy, 2005). A counselor who is skillful at working with individual students or conducting structured psycho-educational interventions in classrooms may be ill-prepared to lead a more loosely structured self-esteem, bereavement, or anger management counseling group.

Beyond the basic knowledge and skills described in accreditation standards for counseling programs established by the Council for Accreditation of Counseling and Related Educational Programs (CACREP; 2009) and the core group work competencies (ASGW, 2000), group workers are expected to acquire advanced knowledge and skill in the specific types of groups they intend to lead (i.e., task, psychoeducation, counseling, psychotherapy). Specialized knowledge may be acquired through reading and didactic instruction, but the skills and attitudes necessary for specialized practice are best acquired through training and supervision that feature feedback-guided practice while being a member and a leader of groups consistent with the specialization being sought (Wilson, 1997).

The classical counseling theories (e.g., psychodynamic, person-centered, cognitive, behavioral) provide frameworks for organizing the planning for group interventions. These theories have been categorized according to their central goals (gaining insight vs. taking action) and core strategies (rational techniques vs. affective techniques). Many elementary school students may lack the cognitive development that would allow school counselors to rely on insight-oriented approaches, although more-mature adolescents may have the necessary capacity to engage in insight-oriented, meaning-making activities. Instead, counseling with children often focuses more on action-oriented goals and may use role playing or other small-group exercises to generate affective awareness in addition to using cognitive-behavioral, interpersonal, solution-focused, rational-emotive, or reality-oriented approaches to stimulate knowledge and foster skill acquisition and attitude change. What is critical is the goodness of fit among the leader, students, and broader school and community environment in which the intervention is to take place.

Self-knowledge and multicultural sensitivity are continuing processes. Best practices in planning (ASGW, 2007, Section A.3) require that group workers not only "actively assess their knowledge and skills related to the specific group(s) offered" but also "assess their values, beliefs, and theoretical orientation and how these impact upon the group, particularly when working with a diverse and multicultural population." Continuing exposure to feedback is necessary for maintaining an awareness of one's impact on others. Wilson (1997) suggested that continuing education and participation in professional and peer supervision can facilitate the acquisition of new knowledge and skill and increase the awareness of the impact the counselor's personal attitudes and values may have on the students served. Continuing education can be obtained through reading professional literature on group work in schools. By attending conferences in which group interventions with children are demonstrated and discussed, professional school counselors may at least have opportunities to learn group facilitation skills via modeling.

Establishing the Overarching Purpose for the Intervention

Skilled group leaders engage in thorough, ecologically grounded needs assessment (ASGW, 2007, Best Practice Standard A3; Rapin & Conyne, 1999). Ecological assessment refers to gathering information about students in their home and school environments, providing the leader with a comprehensive understanding of (1) students' psychological needs, problems, and dynamics; (2) students' primary relationships with family and schoolmates and their other important relationships; (3) the economic and sociopolitical environment in which the school is embedded and in which students live; and (4) the broader cultural forces that shape students' lives and the culture of the school they attend (Addison, 1992). Drawing from suggestions by Rapin and Conyne (1999), a list of important assessment questions might include the following:

- What needs exist in this school that group counseling might be able to address?
- What resources could be mobilized in order to launch group-based services within this school?
- Which group work model or theory fits best with the needs and culture of this school?
- Which group-based strategies are culturally appropriate for this school?
- How can we get the school community, administrators, teachers, and students to embrace and use the group interventions designed?

To be successful, leaders must involve the school administrators and teachers in the needs assessment and the subsequent design of group-based interventions (Ripley & Goodnough, 2001). Needs assessment will be covered in much more detail in Chapter 16.

Identifying Goals and Objectives for the Intervention

Following a thorough needs assessment, the leader is in a position to develop goals and an intended outcomes framework for the group intervention. Best practices for planning in group work require a leader to set explicit goals that are stated in terms of expected group member benefits (ASGW, 2007, Best Practice Standard A4; Rapin & Conyne, 1999). In addition, the leader may set goals for personal performance or for the climate and process flow the leader intends to establish in the group. For example, the leader of a counseling group may set a goal of using moderate structure and control and may assess that goal by monitoring the amount of verbal interaction contributed by the leader versus the amount of verbal interaction contributed by the rest of the group members.

GLOBAL GROUP MEMBER OUTCOME GOALS   *The ASCA National Model* (ASCA, 2005) poses the critical question: "How are students different because of the school counseling program?" To ensure that group interventions target outcomes viewed as important by both the students and the larger community of administrators, teachers, and parents, the *National Model* suggests the establishment of clear outcome goals. Outcome goals are based on student needs and describe what group members are to acquire as a result of participation in the group. What knowledge, skills, or attitudes will group members learn or develop as a consequence of having participated in the group intervention being planned? The ASCA standards (Campbell & Dahir, 1997) provide clear guidance for goal setting for academic, career, and personal/social development. Under these personal-social standards, for example, professional school counselors are responsible for facilitating student acquisition of self-knowledge, interpersonal skills, decision-making and problem-solving skills, and personal safety skills. Goals may be set to increase or improve group members' knowledge (e.g., "learn the goal-setting process"), skills (e.g., "identify alternative solutions to a problem"), or attitudes (e.g., "develop positive attitudes toward self"). Conversely, goals may be set to decrease or eliminate counterproductive beliefs (e.g., "reduce the stereotypic views of cultural differences"), behaviors (e.g., "reduce or eliminate aggressive talk and combative behavior"), or attitudes (e.g., "reduce the devaluing of others").

By way of illustration, one could write knowledge, skill, and attitude goals for anger management such as these:

- Group members will identify people and situations that trigger angry feelings and lead to aggressive responses (*knowledge goal*).
- Group members will demonstrate assertive responses to role-played trigger situations within the group (*skill goal*).
- Group members will demonstrate increased regard for other people's right to personal safety by choosing to use assertive responses rather than aggressive responses when experiencing conflict with parents, teachers, siblings, and schoolmates (*attitude goal*).

SPECIFIC INDIVIDUAL OUTCOME GOALS   In addition to goals set prior to the launching of the group, a professional school counselor might design a process for students to identify and commit to personally selected goals. As Trotzer (1999) observed, "General group goals are important in organizing a group program, but specific individual goals are necessary to determine outcomes" (p. 376). To comply with the accountability expectations of *The ASCA National Model* (ASCA, 2005), individual goal setting should include an explanation about how to set personal goals, a description of the sorts of goals that fit within the scope of the planned group, and feedback about the feasibility of each group member's proposed goals. A common teaching model for goal setting uses the mnemonic SMART as a guide: Effective goals are *S*pecific, *M*easurable, *A*ttainable, *R*ealistic, and *T*imely (Nikitina, 2004). A leader might plan to facilitate individual goal setting during a pregroup screening interview, assign goal-setting homework to be completed between the screening interview and the first group session, or conduct structured exercises during one of the early group sessions. An example of an individual student goal might be "Students will learn two assertive responses to anger trigger situations."

COUNSELOR PROCESS GOALS   A leader may also set goals for the kind of group process atmosphere necessary for the accomplishment of the student outcome goals set for the group. These leader process goals are typically drawn from the overarching theory of group work to which the leader subscribes, and focus on describing the characteristics of group life necessary to get the group to the working stage. For example, different group member characteristics might require different process goals:

- Group members will commit to attending seven out of eight scheduled group sessions (*a leader process goal for students having problems with chronic shyness*).
- Group members will take turns speaking and refrain from interrupting others during group discussions (*a leader process goal for a group for students with attention and hyperactivity problems*).

Detailing Methods for Achieving Goals and Objectives During the Intervention

With the preparatory self-grounding and goal setting completed, the leader is ready to plan the specific approach to be used to accomplish goals in the group. Best practices in group planning require that leaders choose the techniques and leadership style that fit with the needs and abilities of the students, the type of group being planned, and the personal abilities and skills of the leader or co-leaders (ASGW, 2007, Best Practice Standard A4; Rapin & Conyne, 1999).

Information collected during the comprehensive, ecological, school-based needs assessment helps the group leader to select both a group type and the group techniques that are a good fit for the students and for their school setting. Paraphrasing from suggestions made by Cook, Conyne, Savageau, and Tang (2004), ecologically sound interventions could include any or all of the following:

- Explore the inner feelings and conflicts that cause students to have unproductive, unsatisfying interpersonal relations.
- Use consciousness-raising techniques to heighten student awareness of school environment problems (e.g., bullying, cyberbullying, rumor spreading, cliques and gangs, school expectations, transition problems) and student strengths that could be applied to solving them and to encouraging commitment to take action.
- Use strategies for meaning making to help bereaved group members regain their ability to function at school.
- Use rational-emotive exercises to help group members rid themselves of maladaptive habits of perception and thinking.
- Use role-playing and skill-acquisition techniques to practice core interpersonal skills necessary for finding a friend, making a friend, and keeping a friend.
- Use the philosophy and techniques of reality therapy to foster the recognition of and respect for others' rights and boundaries.

A leader's choice of group type and intervention techniques rests in part on the prospective members' individual and collective readiness for change. Prochaska and DiClemente's (1982) model for the stages of change (i.e., precontemplation, contemplation, determination, and action) and Miller and Rollnick's (2002) motivational interviewing strategies can be helpful guides in selecting the type of group approach that fits best with students' readiness for change.

Students who have not yet realized that they do have problems worth addressing (e.g., those at the precontemplation stage) may not be ready for a group where one is expected to commit to making change and to learn new knowledge, develop new skills, or change certain attitudes. To enhance preparedness for change and eventual success, a leader might instead plan a psychoeducational group that focuses on consciousness raising—that is, increasing members' awareness of the risks or problems associated with their current behavior and lifestyle and helping them evaluate their own mixed feelings about their current approach to school life. As students reach the contemplation, determination, and action stages of change, a less-structured counseling group may be of more benefit. Students may at this point be ready to focus on articulating reasons for changing and the risks of not changing, developing their sense of change self-efficacy, and increasing their commitment to trying by developing action plans and implementing their planned change. Maintaining the current status and coping with relapse may be supported through both psychoeducational and supportive counseling group interventions, the choice of intervention being guided by how acute or chronic the student's problems have been and by what other things are going on in the school and in the student's life that may complicate the counselor's attempts to intervene.

Detailing Methods to Be Used in Screening, Selecting, and Preparing Members to Be Successful in the Group

Another important aspect of planning is preparing to admit participants to the group. In school settings, candidates for group interventions are typically staff referred, counselor identified, or self-referred (Hines & Fields, 2002). Naturally, group leaders seek to include

members who need and can profit from the group's activities, but for a group to be successful, leaders must also exclude those who do not need the services provided and those who,
because of the acuteness of their problems, cannot participate in the group at a level adequate for success.

SCREENING AND SELECTING   Both the ASCA ethical standards (ASCA, 2004) and the ASGW
best practices (ASGW, 2007, Best Practice Standard A7.a; Rapin & Conyne, 1999) encourage
leaders to screen prospective members. Even though dedicating the time required for formal
screening may be challenging to accomplish in school settings, the benefits of screening out-
weigh the difficulties. Even brief screening activities help initiate the counseling relationship,
give prospective group members an opportunity to explore their expectations and concerns
about the group, and give the leader a basis for deciding whether the prospective members
are appropriate to the type of group being offered (Hines & Fields, 2002). During screening,
the leader can answer these questions:

- What are the student's needs? Does the applicant need the sort of intervention or
  experience offered in the planned group?
- What are the student's abilities? Does the applicant have the knowledge, skills, and
  attitudes necessary to succeed in the sort of personal and interpersonal challenges that
  will be posed during the group?
- What are the student's personal and interpersonal limitations? Does the applicant have
  personal or interpersonal qualities that would make success in the group difficult or
  impossible to achieve or that would seriously interfere with others' success?

A counselor may use a variety of data sources for screening, including individual interviews, group interviews, student responses to screening instruments, observations of student
behavior in formal and informal settings, interviews with or written comments from staff,
and historical knowledge gained from personal interaction with the students (Hines &
Fields, 2002). But screening is not only about whether the leader deems the student to be a
good fit with the group. The screening process also helps the student to answer this question: "Is this group right for me?"

PREPARING MEMBERS   In addition to screening, the ASCA (2004) and the ASGW (2007)
hold that it is the responsibility of group workers to facilitate a process by which a student
(and the student's parents/guardians, if appropriate) can give informed consent to participate in the group (ASGW, 2007, Best Practice Standards A7.b & A7.c; see Chapter 2 for a
sample professional informed consent statement). The ASCA ethical standards (2004) indicate that the professional school counselor should notify parents/guardians when students
are involved in group interventions if the counselor deems it appropriate and if such notification is consistent with school board policy or practice. To avoid the frustration of not
being able to secure parental permission for some or even all students chosen to be members of a group, one might seek parental permission for all possible prospective group participants first, with the understanding that not all may be chosen to actually join the planned
group (Hines & Fields, 2002). In addition to the verbal descriptions of the purposes of and
methods to be used in the group, prospective members should receive written descriptions
that they can keep and review at a later date. Bergin (1993) suggested preparing a written contract for prospective group members to sign that lists the purposes of the group
and details the general guidelines for how the group will be conducted. This makes the

group work expectations more concrete for students of all ages and gives students the opportunity to review and recall the group's purpose, goals, and specific operational details (e.g., attendance expectations, confidentiality, responsibility to respect others' opinions and perspectives).

One exceptionally effective, though energy-intensive, way to conduct pregroup screening and member preparation is to offer pregroup role-induction training in which members are provided with information about the group, its purposes, and its goals and with training in the sorts of personal and interpersonal process skills that are deemed useful for successful group participation. The first few sessions of the group could be spent talking about what the group will be about and how to be a constructive group member. Pregroup training has been found useful in a variety of group contexts (DeRoma, Root, & Battle, 2003; Zarle & Willis, 1975).

Selecting Methods for Deriving Meaning and Transferring Learning

The main purpose of group work is to experience interactions in the here and now in order to derive personal meaning from these experiences and then to transfer this learning to life outside the group. The purpose of the following section is to outline this process.

MAKING MEANING FROM THE EXPERIENCE   Group work is much more than a set of techniques. A leader's ability to help students derive meaning from their experience has more impact on promoting growth among group members than does procedural competence (Yalom & Leszcz, 2005). As discussed earlier, a solid theoretical foundation for group interventions provides a consistent frame of reference for helping students ascribe meaning to their experience and for planning, assessing, and evaluating the outcomes of a group intervention.

EXPLORING WITHIN-GROUP EXPERIENCE   Skilled leaders engage in within-group processing to help the students make meaning from their experience. In fact, the ASGW standards emphasize the crucial role of processing in helping members integrate their experiential learning and helping leaders obtain the formative feedback needed to guide the unfolding of their group (ASGW, 2007, Best Practice Standards C1, C2, & C3). Just as ecological needs assessment focuses on the person, the environment, and their interaction, so within-group processing includes the leader, the members, and the ongoing patterns of group interaction. Certainly, valuable lessons can be learned from spontaneous within-group processing; however, effective group leaders plan for processing to ensure that it occurs regularly and is conducted skillfully (Rapin & Conyne, 1999). Group leaders may avail themselves of a variety of sources for gathering group process data:

- The observations of the students, using carefully crafted processing questions to stimulate within-group disclosure and discussion or brief questionnaires or more formal instruments to collect formative feedback data.
- Systematic observations made by a member who has been designated to serve as a within-group process observer.
- External evaluation of the group activities and interactions made by an outside observer based on live observation or a review of recordings of the group. (Trotzer, 1999)

In its most simple form, processing may involve no little no clarifying "Who said what to whom?" and "What did the receiver hear when the speaker spoke?" Skilled leaders use questions designed to elicit what the members observe (e.g., "What do you see happening in our group?" "What stands out about other group members' behavior?") and what they experience inside themselves (e.g., "What are you feeling?" "What do you find yourself thinking about?" "What memories or images come to mind?"). Group processing is just as important for task groups and classroom guidance experiences as it is for counseling and psychotherapy groups.

Modest evaluation tools for helping students examine their experiences in the group include the method described by Trotzer (1999) in which the leader simply distributes small index cards and asks members to write down their honest appraisals of the group. Responses may be stimulated by questions such as these: "How did you feel during today's group?" "What did you learn that might help you in your day-to-day life?" "What could we do next time to be more helpful to you?" As an alternative, these within-group process evaluation cards could be preprinted with a set of evaluative scales like boring–interesting, phony–real, and honest–dishonest. More-sophisticated and standardized group process instruments and evaluation methods will be covered in much greater detail in Chapter 16.

TYING WITHIN-GROUP EXPERIENCE TO LIFE OUTSIDE THE GROUP   Because leaders are responsible for helping students apply their within-group learning to the external world, meaning making may be enhanced by asking members to think through potential real-world applications of within-group experiences. Corey (1995) encouraged members to keep a journal of their experiences during the group and in their daily life outside the group. In his words, "this writing process helps participants focus on relevant trends and on the key things they are discovering about themselves and others through group interaction" (p. 129). Students may also be put in structured role-play situations to practice using the skills learned in group into simulated real-world situations. If the overall group plan includes a follow-up meeting after the group has formally ended, one can plan to ask students to write postgroup reaction papers in which they recall significant occurrences during the group and describe how they have applied their learning to situations that have arisen since the end of the group. They can also be asked to record what they liked and did not like about their group experience to guide the future offerings of the group experience.

Determining Resources Needed to Launch and Sustain the Group

In addition to careful planning for the content and process of their groups, leaders must attend to the practical necessities of securing permissions, cooperation, and resources. School-based group interventions require staffing (e.g., leaders, support personnel), advertising, group meeting space, materials (e.g., audiovisual materials, handouts, evaluation tools), and record-keeping supplies. Many of these resources will be underwritten by the general school or guidance budget. Others may require additional funds.

Even though a school psychoeducational or counseling group is not really a business venture, it is wise to think as though it is. In any business venture, one must consider not only "start-up costs" but also "sustainability." Because of a personal commitment to the value of the group for the students, a professional school counselor might be willing to personally finance part of the start-up costs of a group (e.g., buying special materials, "donating" time that could be spent in other activities); however, few counselors could afford to take the operational costs of a group out of their personal resources for very long. It is a bitter disappointment to design and launch a group that proves to be successful for its participants and then realize that the group cannot be offered again because no sustaining resources are available. In addition to thinking through the purpose of and methods to be used during a group intervention, group leaders would be well served to develop a "business model" for each group they intend to offer in which they detail both start-up and sustaining resources needed to implement the group as planned. Professional school counselors should explicitly discuss with their administrative leaders what the costs will be and how the group will be resourced, whether the group-in-planning is expected to be a one-shot offering or a continuing group.

Getting a specific group offering resourced is one thing; building a culture in which group interventions for students may thrive is quite another. Ripley and Goodnough (2001) suggested a systematic approach to developing a group-friendly culture in a high school that focuses on building collaborative support, institutionalizing group work in the school, and standardizing group rules and procedures to provide a trustworthy product. Ripley and Goodnough launched an ongoing effort to garner and feed faculty support throughout the school year. They institutionalized group work in the school by (1) getting group counseling written into existing policies that regulated excused absences from class, (2) passing a new policy that stipulated the time spent in group counseling would not be counted as an absence from class, (3) passing another new policy barring teachers from denying a student the opportunity to attend group counseling sessions, and (4) getting the start of group sessions incorporated into the policy requiring students to arrive at class on time. Finally, they developed standardized procedures for all groups to ensure that group offerings were consistent, ethically appropriate experiences that had high visibility and credibility among the staff. By creating a group-friendly culture through collaborative engagement with the administration and the teaching staff, Ripley and Goodnough were able to resource and support their group work offerings.

Determining Methods for Measuring Outcomes

The final step in implementing program development and evaluation principles as one plans for a group is to create an evaluation plan to assess the degree to which group member outcome goals and counselor process goals have been met (ASGW, 2007, Best Practice Standard A4). The evaluation of group outcomes must begin during the planning phase.

ASSESSING STUDENT OUTCOMES   According to the ASCA (2005), it is incumbent on the school counselor to document how students are different as a result of the group interventions. For each group, there should be an evaluation plan that identifies how the global group outcome goals and specific individual member outcome goals will be measured. Though group leaders have many evaluation options from which to choose, the evaluation plan should dovetail with the school's results-reporting system and must also be consistent with the school policy and practices regarding collecting evaluative data from students (ASGW, 2007, Best Practice Standard A4).

ASSESSING LEADER GROUP PROCESS GOALS   In addition to evaluating whether students achieved their outcome goals, it is important to evaluate whether the leader's process goals were achieved. To facilitate continual quality improvement, leaders should plan to gather information during and after the group regarding whether the group developed a constructive atmosphere. Many leaders use simple member satisfaction questionnaires at the end of their groups to gather feedback. Typical questions include the following: "What did you most like about this group?" "What didn't you like about this group?" "What did you learn from being in this group?" "What didn't we do that you wished we had?" "Would you recommend a group like this to one of your friends?" "What other kinds of groups should we offer at our school?"

Although member satisfaction surveys can provide information that is useful for planning future group offerings, they do not provide the kind of precise information needed to understand the communication patterns within a group. Counselors who want to analyze how their interventions during a group impacted the development of the group atmosphere might use more formal methods. Because Bales's Interaction Analysis Scale (Bales, 1950) and the Hill Interaction Matrix (Hill, 1966) are observational techniques, these classic procedures work well for studying within-group communication patterns across all developmental levels. With adolescents, Moos's Group Environment Scale (Moos, Finney, & Maude-Griffin, 1993) could be used to get more detailed feedback about group climate. These and the other scales of their kind, though more time consuming, provide a wealth of data on the personal reactions of, and the pattern of interactions among, group members. Group process instruments and evaluations will be covered in much greater detail in Chapter 16.

PLANNING FOR CLOSED GROUPS VERSUS OPEN GROUPS

The standard model for group work in the schools ordinarily is the fixed-membership, time-limited, theme-oriented group. Group work literature is filled with examples of such groups: The multiweek anger management or stress management group, the semester-long children of divorcing parents group, and the brief new student school orientation group are but a few possibilities. Each of these groups might be designed to be a closed group, a group with fixed membership to be conducted within a predetermined time frame.

However, not all groups fit this model. Sometimes the purpose of the group precludes establishing a fixed membership or fixed time boundaries. Open groups, such as groups supporting bereaved students or students from families with chronic illness, may be designed to have no fixed membership. One gains admittance to the group simply by the death or serious illness of a close family member. Open groups tend to have no fixed near-term ending date, staying operational throughout the school year. Students enter and terminate participation in the group according to their own needs.

Group leaders who are accustomed to fixed-membership groups may find that having old members leave and new members join their groups disrupts the cohesion and flow of the group (Capuzzi & Gross, 2002; Corey, 1995). They may also find that the presence of people who are at different developmental levels creates a management problem for them (Corey, 1995; Jacobs, Masson, & Harvill, 2006; Trotzer, 1999). But open groups have a number of advantages as well. With fluctuating membership, new members may infuse the group with new energy, and the group is less likely to get stale. Further, the group can repopulate itself when members leave, avoiding the risk of not having enough members in the group to remain viable. Old members can acculturate new members, helping them learn the knowledge, skills, and attitudes necessary to be successful in the group.

A group with fluctuating membership requires a slightly different planning mentality than does a closed group. As much as the best practice guidelines encourage the use of a flexible structure for organizing closed groups, open groups may require even greater structure and even greater flexibility. To manage the shifting membership of the group, the leader may find that a tightly structured format for each session provides stability for the group. Yet, at a moment's notice, the leader may have to abandon the session's plan in favor of addressing an unanticipated group crisis or need.

PROGRAM DEVELOPMENT AND EVALUATION IN OPEN AND CLOSED GROUPS   Although individual members may have personal goals, it is important for leaders to have a small set of clearly articulated goals for the group as a whole in order to provide focus for the group and to keep the scope of the group within their personal area of practice. Leaders can provide structure for the group by developing self-contained units to be used on a rotating basis. Each of these units should be designed as a self-contained unit that does not rely on the attendance at the previous sessions for a member to be successful. The units should also be designed to accommodate small, medium, and large groups so the leader can adapt to the number of students who happen to be present on a given day. To accommodate new group members, each session's activities should begin with a reiteration of the purpose of the group and group goals and with an acculturation exercise to welcome the new members and help them learn the purpose, rules, and behaviors that promote success in the group. Finally, in order to have data for formative and summative evaluation, the leaders of groups with fluctuating membership should prepare or select brief tools for collecting evaluative data after each session of the group.

Although it is good planning to be prepared for the slow acceptance of new group members, most students in groups are reasonably accepting of a new member in the group. The first group session with the new member in the group may be a bit more "on the surface" (i.e., returning to an earlier stage of the group process), but often the group will quickly get "back to business." A planful group leader is aware of the shifting level of acceptance of new group members and adjusts the expectations of the group accordingly.

GROUP AND MEMBER PREPARATION IN OPEN AND CLOSED GROUPS   With open groups, the prescreening of members is often quite difficult. When conducting an open group, leaders of open groups should plan to conduct screening during a new member's first group session to assess the goodness of fit of the new member with the group's ecology and the goodness of fit between the new member's needs and the group's goals. Critical questions include these:

- Are the new member's needs and goals compatible with the goals and methods of the group?
- Does the new member have the skills necessary to be successful in the group?
- Does the new member have obvious psychological problems that might prove to be an insurmountable impediment to the member's success in the group and that might interfere with the success of other members?

Leaders should be prepared to meet after the group session with the new member to conduct a more thorough screening if initial signs suggest that this is warranted.

Preparation of students for productive involvement in the group may be facilitated by giving each new member a handout at the beginning of the group that outlines the purpose of the group, its goals, its rules, ways the member can gain maximum benefit, and member rights and responsibilities. To increase the stability of membership in an open group, some leaders include a contract for attendance (e.g., for six weeks) with an explicit statement that missing meetings (e.g., two consecutive unexcused absences) will result in dismissal from the group.

PROTECTING ONESELF FROM WHAT ONE DOES NOT KNOW

The wisest group leaders are those who know that they do not know all of what will be required for them to be successful. They know that professional growth is a continuous, developmental process that will extend the length of their careers. Thus, as a part of the planning process, the wisest of group leaders identify the sources of professional consultation or supervision to help them see themselves, their group members, and the process of their group as clearly as possible. Consistent with the *Ethical Standards for School Counselors* (ASCA, 2004), the leader strives to maintain professional competence by arranging for continuing education and professional consultation or supervision to

- Increase group work knowledge and skill competencies (ASGW, 2007, Best Practice Standard A8.a).
- Identify and deal responsibly with ethical concerns that interfere with effective functioning as a group leader (ASGW, 2007, Best Practice Standard A8.b).
- Process personal reactions, problems, or conflicts that threaten to impair his or her professional judgment or group work performance (ASGW, 2007, Best Practice Standard A8.c).
- Ensure appropriate practice when working with a group that stretches the boundaries of the leader's accustomed scope of practice (ASGW, 2007, Best Practice Standard A8.d).

Summary

Planning is critical to success. Where once group leaders avoided advance planning for fear it would impede group spontaneity, contemporary leaders know that a well-planned group provides a safe environment in which group members' goals may be pursued, while encouraging and supporting group members' spontaneity and creativity.

This chapter provided insights into key elements in group planning, examining the importance of grounding oneself in the legal and professional regulations governing the practice of group work and of clarifying one's own scope of group work competence. It addressed the necessity of establishing the overarching purpose for the intervention, identifying goals and objectives for the intervention, detailing methods to be employed in achieving these goals and objectives during the intervention, and detailing methods to be used in screening, selecting, and preparing members to be successful in the group. The chapter next described methods for examining group process during group meetings and at the completion of the group intervention,

and it underscored the necessity of selecting methods for helping members derive meaning from their within-group experiences and transfer within-group learning to real-world circumstances. It also reviewed methods for measuring outcomes during and following the intervention. In addition, this chapter emphasized the importance of determining resources needed to launch and sustain the group.

To illustrate the importance of planning, this chapter examined the special considerations that arise when planning for open groups, which may have a fluctuating membership or no fixed ending date. Finally, this chapter emphasized that the most critical element in planning is recognizing that the wise group leader must constantly engage in ongoing training, collaborative consultation, and personal supervision. Only through systematic participation in activities where we are exposed to new developments in group work theory and practice and where we expose ourselves to examination and feedback can we protect ourselves against what we do not know.

CHAPTER 7

Forming and Orienting Groups

NATHANIEL N. IVERS AND DEBBIE W. NEWSOME

PREVIEW

The purpose of this chapter is to provide an overview of the forming and orienting stage of group work in schools. Provided are descriptions of the primary tasks that are accomplished during the forming and orienting stage, discussion of the responsibilities of the group leader during this stage, and a case example that illustrates what might occur during an initial group session. Specific techniques include using enthusiasm, drawing out, holding the focus, shifting the focus, cutting off, and using journal writing.

GETTING STARTED: FORMING AND ORIENTING

Carlos, an 11-year-old male, has decided to attend a counseling group at his elementary school in order to gain greater insight into how he can cope with some of his personal problems. He goes through the screening process of the group, understands the rules and responsibilities of being a group member, and feels prepared for the group. Notwithstanding his excitement about and interest in beginning the group, Carlos feels some angst about what to expect from the group. He wonders about proper etiquette and holds some skepticism about whether this group experience will truly help him.

Some questions that Carlos might ask himself before, during, or after the group sessions include the following: How safe am I in this group? Can I risk sharing my thoughts and feelings with these people? Do I belong in this group? With whom can I identify, and from whom do I feel disconnected? Will I be rejected or accepted by other members? Can I really be myself in a roomful of strangers?

The forming and orienting stage of a group can be defined as a time of orientation and exploration. Group members attempt to figure out their place in the group, get acquainted with fellow group members, and explore their expectations. In this stage, students must endeavor to understand how they are going to achieve their primary goal or reason for joining the group. In addition, during the forming and orienting stage, students attend to ways in which they will relate to each other. Focusing on social relationships within the group helps foster feelings of security, comfort, and satisfaction, thereby creating an environment that will facilitate the students' capacity to achieve their primary task.

Consider the case of Allison, a 16-year-old single mother who is struggling with social anxiety. Her case provides an illustration of the relationship between a group member's primary task and the task of developing social relationships within the group.

> Allison could feel her anxiety rise as she entered the room for her first group counseling experience. She experienced many feelings, including doubt, anxiety, hope, and fear. As the session began, Allison had a hard time interacting with the group. She was nervous about being rejected and about opening up too much. After a while, through interaction with the group members and the group leaders, Allison began to feel more comfortable and accepted. Hence, she no longer felt threatened, rejected, or judged. As a result, she was able to consciously begin working on her primary task (i.e., social anxiety) within the group. She began to feel comfortable enough to test many of her irrational beliefs with the group— beliefs such as "Everybody's rejecting me and judging me; I'm annoying everybody; I make people feel uncomfortable." By expressing these beliefs and allowing the group to process them, Allison was able to begin to recognize the irrationality of her beliefs—and therefore begin to change them. Furthermore, through changing her perceptions of the people in the group, she began to change some of her perceptions of people outside of the group (a process known as generalization or transference of learning to the external world), which increased her confidence and security in social situations.

Without the security and comfort that came from acquiring acceptance and membership in the group, it would have been very difficult for Allison to work on her social anxiety. In fact, had she not attended to her social relationships in the group, it is likely that she would have succumbed to her anxiety and quit coming to group meetings altogether. Allison's case illustrates the connection between focusing on primary tasks and attending to social relationships during the initial sessions of group, the two key aspects of successful group formation.

Two primary tasks that students attend to during early group formation are identity and inclusion. Finding one's identity in a group involves figuring out who one is in the group in relation to others. It is related to feeling accepted by and connected to other group members. Likewise, inclusion involves a sense of connectedness to the group but also includes determining to what degree one will actively participate in the group and its tasks. In the example of Allison, she took the risk to interact with other group members. She began to identify with the group, increased her comfort in interacting with group members, and thus was able to begin working on her personal goals.

Inherent in the case examples of both Carlos and Allison is the concept of trust. Trust leads to deeper levels of social interaction and self-exploration by giving members confidence to drop superficial interactions. As in the example of Allison, if she had not been able to gain trust in her fellow group members, as well as in the group leaders, she most likely would have hidden her irrational beliefs about group members (e.g., "I make people uncomfortable"; "They are judging me and rejecting me"). This in turn would have hindered

Allison's ability to self-explore and possibly would have thwarted her capacity to overcome her feelings of social anxiety.

It is a mistake to suppose that people in the group will openly trust each other at the onset of the first session of a group. Group members must come to recognize that the group is a safe and accepting environment, a setting that offers more security and approval than the society at large. Group leaders are largely responsible for creating such an environment. One thing a leader can do to foster trust in the group is to acknowledge mistrust, thereby encouraging students to discuss factors that impede their decision to trust the group. In discussing "the elephant in the room"—in this case, a lack of trust—the leader models openness, risk taking, and congruence. This modeling helps develop the therapeutic atmosphere necessary for students to acquire trust in the group. There are many ways in which a skilled leader can cultivate trust within group members, and these and other responsibilities are discussed next.

LEADER RESPONSIBILITIES IN THE FORMING AND ORIENTING STAGE

In the forming and orienting stage, leaders have many functions and responsibilities. Listed below are some of the functions and responsibilities of a group leader in this initial phase of a group; these serve as an outline, and each will be analyzed individually throughout the remainder of the chapter:

1. Reviewing group goals
2. Helping members establish personal goals
3. Specifying group rules
4. Modeling facilitative group behavior
5. Assisting members in expressing their apprehensions
6. Establishing and maintaining trust
7. Promoting positive interchanges among group members
8. Teaching members basic interpersonal skills (e.g., as active listening)
9. Instilling and maintaining hope
10. Resolving possible group problems that manifest in the forming and orienting stage

Reviewing Group Goals

During the planning phase and pregroup interviews, group goals are formulated. Goals are outcomes desired either by individual members or by the entire group. Because it is important for students to keep group goals in mind throughout the group process, the leader should restate the goals and purpose of the group in the opening session. It is also helpful in the initial session to have group members elaborate on their personal goals for the group.

This process of having group members express their goals in the group can be accomplished directly (i.e., by asking each member specifically to state his or her goals) or through the use of a modified icebreaker (i.e., an activity that facilitates cohesion among the students and the leader) or other facilitative activity (see Chapter 15 or Keene & Erford, 2007). An example of an icebreaker that could be incorporated in the initial session is Gifts I Bring (Keene & Erford, 2007). The core of this icebreaker is to have students make a gift card that lists or describes one positive thing they bring to the session. The students then pair up and share their gift ideas with their partners. Finally, group members take turns introducing their partners and the gifts they bring to the group. A group leader could modify this icebreaker into a goal-setting activity by having members express one thing they would like to get out of the group that day (i.e., their goal for the day) or into a closing activity by positioning it at the end of the group session and having members announce the gifts they were given during the group that they will take with them as they leave the session (i.e., the goal or need that was met).

Helping Members Establish Personal Goals

Typically during the forming and orienting stage of a group, students have imprecise ideas about what they want to get out of their group experience. Therefore, one of the main tasks of a leader during this stage is to facilitate the development of positive, measurable, and specific individual goals. For example, a vague goal a third-grade student might have is to get along better with his parents. The leader may help the member develop his vague goal into one that is more specific through open-ended questions. Some examples of open-ended questions that the leader might use include these:

- How will you know when you have achieved a good relationship with your parents?
- What will you do to achieve your goal?
- What keeps you from accomplishing this goal?
- How will you feel when your relationship is better?

By the use of open-ended questions, the leader helps the member narrow down his desires into more succinct, concrete goals.

With respect to making the goal positive, it is important for the group leader to help the members avoid negative goals such as "I will quit fighting with my parents." Instead, the leader should help students state their goals positively (e.g., "I will improve my relationship with my parents"). After stating the goal in a positive manner, it is important to help students make the goal measurable (e.g., "I will talk to my parents at least three times a week about what is going on in my life in order to improve our communication and closeness"). By guiding students in developing positive, specific, and measurable goals, the leader is establishing a group environment that engenders growth and development in individual students and in the group as a whole. Phrasing an objective or goal in measureable terms helps everyone involved know when the goal has been reached. Setting measurable goals is essential for any kind of group work, including classroom guidance and task, psychoeducational, and counseling groups.

Another important aspect of helping students develop individual goals is bringing hidden agendas that they might have out into the open. For instance, students might have goals that run contrary to the group purpose. Members might take up as much attention as possible in the group because of an excessive desire to be in control, or they might attempt to be humorous when topics become deep because of their fear of intimacy. It is important that leaders recognize these covert goals and help members work through them in an overt, explicit manner. Covert personal goals often undermine classroom and small-group effectiveness.

Specifying Group Rules

Group rules are basic guidelines for how a group will operate. During the pregroup planning phase (discussed in Chapter 6), leaders formulate the rules by which the group should abide, and during the initial and subsequent sessions, students may make contributions to the rules of the group. No matter how the rules are developed and introduced in the group, a rationale behind the rules should be in place. When rules are made arbitrarily (e.g., group members should wear only dress shoes during group time), the leader creates an atmosphere that may promote rebellion or game playing (Yalom & Leszcz, 2005).

Confidentiality is one of the key rules that should be explained during the screening process and clearly reiterated in the initial session. Confidentiality is the agreement among all students and leaders that what is said in the group stays in the group. Without a guarantee of confidentiality, group members will rarely develop trust and cohesion, and, thus, they will fail to engage in the productive work that leads to accomplishing goals. Therefore, the agreement to keep things confidential should be addressed not only in the pregroup process but also during the initial session of the group, periodically throughout subsequent sessions as needed, and during the final group session. Just because a group experience has ended does not release members from a promise of confidentiality.

It is imperative that leaders describe confidentiality and insist on it. Because of the powerful influence that confidentiality has in engendering trust, cohesion, and productivity within a group, it may be wise and effective for leaders to take the time to specifically describe problematic situations in which a group member might break confidentiality by accident, and even without knowledge or understanding. A leader may choose to do this anecdotally. For example, the leader may describe a situation in which a group member becomes friends with another group member and they decide that they are going to get together after school. They begin to talk about an issue that they witnessed in the group the week before in which a female group member talked about her personal problems with her boyfriend. In talking about someone else's issues outside of the group context, even with another member of the group, the two students are breaking confidentiality. In fact, even initiating a conversation with a fellow group member outside of the group context about things brought up in the group is construed as breaking confidentiality and is potentially harmful to the group process.

In addition, group members or leaders may breach confidentiality when they speak of group members by name to outsiders, even if it is just a first name, and when leaders initiate a conversation with group members in public. When a leader happens to run into a group member in public, the leader should wait for the group member to initiate any acknowledgment or greeting and avoid talking about the group or any content from the group.

Modeling Facilitative Group Behavior

During the forming and orienting stage, students are oftentimes greatly dependent on the leader. As in the case study of Carlos, members may wonder to what extent they want to participate, how much the group will even benefit them, and what the appropriate etiquette is for a group. This confusion around group norms can generate feelings of anxiety and apprehension within group members.

Leaders, who are more experienced with group culture and group norms, can play a very influential role in soothing students' concerns about how to act. This can be done through modeling appropriate participant behavior. Group leaders can establish and model group norms and set the tone for the group. As the model-setting participants for the group, leaders must openly state their own expectations for the group during the initial session as well as model honesty and spontaneity. It is quite common not only for students to feel some anxiety upon beginning a new group experience but also for leaders to experience some anxiety surrounding the initial group meeting(s). Thus, in honoring honesty, it may be relieving to students if leaders express their own feelings of nervousness about starting a new group. Furthermore, by expressing his or her own feelings of anxiety, the leader may open up some dialogue among members concerning their own anxiety about beginning a group. This disclosure and dialogue may be very therapeutic and conducive to developing group trust and cohesion. Given the importance of honesty and genuineness, students need to understand that leaders truly believe in what they are doing, and honestly care about the group process.

Along with honesty and confidence in the group process, it is very important that leaders model respect and positive regard for each student. By expressing cognitive and affective empathy, sensitively attending and responding to what is said, and understanding and replying to subtle messages that are communicated without words to both individual group members and to the group as a whole, the leader is able to model care and positive regard toward members individually and toward the group as a whole.

Assisting Members in Expressing Their Apprehensions

As illustrated in the case examples of Carlos and Allison, apprehension around membership in a group can inhibit group success. Too much anxiety and too little anxiety can impede group members' performance in the group. On the other hand, a moderate amount of anxiety is appropriate. The following example of two elementary-aged students, Joaquin and Maria, illustrates how too little or too much anxiety can deter member growth:

> Joaquin and Maria both are members of a group. For Joaquin, this is the third group he has attended in the last two years. He is skeptical about whether it will be helpful, since he believes the two previous groups were not. He enters the group with a nonchalant attitude and swagger. He feels very little anxiety and listens halfheartedly as the leader describes confidentiality. When the leader does the rounds, Joaquin describes his thoughts and feelings about the group but really cannot pinpoint anything salient about the session or a goal he would like to work toward because he was not really paying attention. Maria, on the other hand, is very nervous. She struggles to pay attention to the group rules and limits. She wonders if she is going to make a mistake. Therefore, when the floor is open for people to talk, she just sits in a panicked silence, counting down the minutes until the group session ends.

Because high and low levels of apprehension can impede individual and group progress, it is important that leaders appropriately recognize and address apprehension in the session. For example, in working with Maria, the leader may use a technique called drawing out, in which the leader purposefully asks more withdrawn or silent students to speak to a particular member of the group or to the group as a whole. For example, the leader might say to Maria, "I am interested in knowing your thoughts on this particular topic." This technique could be beneficial in helping Maria get over her anxiety surrounding how to act appropriately in the group.

Another technique used in group sessions is dealing with group members' apprehensions at the end of each group session. For example, the leader might interject, "Joaquin, I notice that you seem very withdrawn today. Tell me a little about that." The observation that he is withdrawn and the invitation for him to participate give Joaquin the opportunity to express his skepticism surrounding the group process. Expressing this doubt can be beneficial not only to Joaquin but also to the leader and to the group as a whole. It is possible that others might also be feeling doubtful about the group's potential effectiveness; therefore, having someone express that concern might allow members to process their skepticism in an open and therapeutic manner, thereby helping the group gain trust and cohesion.

Establishing and Maintaining Trust

The importance of establishing a trusting environment during the forming and orienting stage cannot be overemphasized. There are many ways leaders can facilitate the development of trust in a group. One way is through acknowledging that it is normal to experience mistrust in the beginning stages of a group. This process of acknowledging mistrust, as described earlier in the chapter, is very important, as it helps the leader to break down student defenses and express congruence and openness to the group. Other ways in which leaders can establish trust in a group include structuring the group, demonstrating care, and encouraging group members to express their fears.

Groups that are structured are more likely than unstructured groups to engender trust earlier in the group process. The more unstructured the group is, the greater the ambiguity and anxiety students feel about how they should behave. Structure is oftentimes accomplished both during the pregroup preparation and screening of the planning phase and during the initial group session. Leaders who have chosen group members wisely and have a clear purpose for the group are more likely to nurture trust within the group. Furthermore, setting ground rules, explaining group procedures, and expressing the importance of confidentiality are important in creating a group structure where trust can be cultivated among students.

While describing the importance of confidentiality, as well as the rights and responsibilities of group members, it is important that leaders communicate feelings of caring toward each member individually. This can be accomplished by emphasizing the need to respect all members of the group. By seriously dedicating time to the issues of confidentiality, members' rights and responsibilities, and the need to respect others, leaders elicit a serious attitude toward the group.

As members begin to feel invested in the group, they will feel more motivated to "test the waters" of the group through self-disclosure. Generally speaking, during the initial sessions, testing the group waters comes in the form of disclosing "safe" information (e.g., talking about past situations, conversing about other people). As leaders demonstrate care toward each individual, students will find it easier to explore more important issues and self-disclose personal information, thoughts, and feelings.

Another important technique that helps members feel trust in the group is encouraging group members to express their own fears. For example, if Maria is fearful about speaking up and she hears Bill, another member of her group, self-disclose his own fears and anxieties about participating in the group, she may feel more empowered to describe her own fear and anxiety.

After trust has been established, it is important for the leader to help the group maintain it. Trust can be lost when students give unwanted advice, often in an attempt to be helpful, or express negative feelings about other members, the leader, or the group process in general. With respect to giving advice, it is important that the leader stop this behavior before it stifles open communication and trust.

There are many different ways leaders may choose to address advice giving among group members. One such method is both preventive and didactic, and it calls for the leader to present an anecdote that links a particular problem to a quick and apparently easy solution. For example, a group leader might relate this story:

> A parent notices that her child is sitting on the bench during baseball games (the problem). She tells him that he needs to practice at least an hour every day so that he will get better (quick solution). The boy does not heed her advice and continues sitting on the bench.

After relating the anecdote, the leader may ask the group some questions: "What other reasons might there be for why the boy is sitting on the bench?" "How can the mother better improve her communication with her son?" "How might advice giving impede open communication and trust?"

Using this technique, leaders correlate advice giving in groups to an everyday problem. Here, the leader offers a simple solution (i.e., practice an hour each day) and demonstrates how this solution does not bring results. By having members hear the anecdote and answer questions related to advice giving, group leaders facilitate group members' understanding of some of the potential pitfalls of advice giving. By facilitating understanding, group leaders may be able to lessen the amount of advice giving among members.

Promoting Positive Interchanges Among Group Members

Promoting positive interchanges among group members is one of the key responsibilities of a leader during the forming and orienting stage of a group. In fact, if positive interchanges are not appropriately developed, students may discontinue coming to the group altogether. Conversely, as already touched on earlier in the chapter, when group members attend to social relationships and receive positive feedback, they are more able to focus on their reason for joining a group; hence, they become more motivated to continue attending the group. Consequently, it is very important that leaders be active in facilitating the establishment of positive interactions among students. Additionally, although promoting a positive interchange among members is discussed in the context of the forming and orienting stage, techniques and interventions described here may also be used during all stages of the group process to facilitate healthy interchange among students. A few ways in which group leaders can establish a positive tone and interchanges are presented in Table 7.1.

Other ways of producing positive interchange include having group members engage in interactive journal writing and performing icebreaker activities (discussed later in this chapter and in Chapter 15). Interactive journal writing is a process in which students keep journal entries containing their thoughts, impressions, feelings, and behaviors in a group and then exchange these entries with the other members of the group as well as with the leader. Exchanges occur in all directions: member to member, member to leader, and leader to member (Gladding, 2008; Parr, Haberstroh, & Kottler, 2000). Some advantages of effectively engaging the students in interactive journal writing include greater group cohesion, improved trust in individual members and in the group as a whole, increased hope, enhanced self-understanding, and stronger social relationships.

Teaching Members Basic Interpersonal Skills

Several techniques introduced in Chapter 5 are particularly applicable to the forming and orienting stage. The term *interpersonal skills* refers to a broad range of aptitudes that allow

TABLE 7.1   Examples of Positive Interchange Techniques

Positive Interchange Technique	Example
Using enthusiasm	*Leader:* "I feel optimistic and excited about what the group has accomplished today, especially in regard to your willingness to open up and express your feelings and insights."
Drawing out	*Leader:* "Tim, I wonder what your feelings might be concerning this topic."
Holding the focus on interesting topics	*Leader:* "Now, before we move forward, I would like to return to this feeling of mistrust that a few of you have shared concerning the group process."
Shifting the focus	*Leader:* "I, too, was interested in how the basketball game turned out last night, but rather than focusing on why the team lost, I would like to understand a little bit more about how you felt when your sister changed the TV channel in the middle of the game.
Cutting off hostile interactions	*Leader to Marsha (group member):* "Instead of stating what Bill [another group member] is doing wrong, tell us what you are feeling and what you think is making you feel that way."
	Marsha: "I feel frustrated and disrespected when I do not have enough time to adequately express myself."

a person to interact effectively with others. Some specific skills included under the umbrella of interpersonal skills are active listening, empathy, genuineness, and respect. Of course, it is essential that group leaders possess a high level of interpersonal skills in order for the group to function; it is also very important that group members possess, increase, or acquire interpersonal skills. If students are lacking in these skills, even if the group leader possesses exceptional interpersonal skills, the group may have difficulty coming together and ultimately may struggle to grow and progress. Therefore, it is important that the group leader must teach group members basic interpersonal skills. The forming and orienting stage is a good time to do so.

One of the interpersonal skills necessary in group counseling is active listening. As discussed in Chapter 5, active listening is the process of actively attending and listening to people's verbal and nonverbal expressions. Engaging in active listening is not only essential for group leaders but also very important for group members. One key way in which a leader can facilitate active listening in group members is by appropriately listening and attending to each group member. When members recognize that they are being heard and that their thoughts, feelings, and behaviors are being attended to, then they are more likely to sharpen their own active listening skills as they attend to others in the group.

Another important interpersonal skill for students to increase is empathy, which is the ability to "walk in another's shoes" or the capacity to understand and be sensitive to the feelings and situations of others. The development of empathy among group leaders and members is very important to the group process. Empathic understanding motivates leaders and members to open up and share important feelings and thoughts. Thus, it is important for group leaders not only to develop their own ability to empathize but also to help students increase their capacity to demonstrate empathy. As with the teaching of active listening, when group leaders are able to model empathy for group members, the latter are more likely to increase their ability to engage in empathic communication with fellow group members.

Some students, and even group leaders, may feel that they are unable to express empathy because they may not have had the life experiences of other group members. For example, a student who comes from a wealthy family may have a difficult time empathizing with a fellow group member who describes the stress and anxiety she feels around the possibility that her family will be evicted from their apartment for not paying the rent. As group leaders, it is important to model, teach, and convey that it is not always essential that members experience others' situations to truly express empathy.

In the above example, although the group member from a wealthy family has not experienced all of the hardships of poverty, she has no doubt experienced feelings of stress, fear, and anxiety, even if those feelings have come in different contexts. Therefore, she may still be able to demonstrate empathy by being sensitive and attending to the feelings that her fellow group member expresses. For example, the member from a wealthy family might respond: "I felt an uncomfortable knot in my stomach when you described your fear and anxiety about being evicted. It seems really scary." By expressing her feelings, she demonstrates an understanding of and sensitivity to her fellow group member's difficult experience, thereby facilitating further communication. Another response, which might be less therapeutic and could even close down communication, might be "That's awful, but I'm sure your family will come up with the money." In this response, the group member from a wealthy family may be attempting to demonstrate empathy, but she does not meet her fellow group member at the point where she is. The anxious group member most assuredly is not at a point where she can be reassured. Therefore, hearing something that is the opposite of what she is experiencing and feeling may make the member feel unheard and not understood, thereby closing the door to further group cohesion and self-disclosure. Hence, it is important that empathic communication be taught and then developed by both group leaders and members.

Another interpersonal skill that facilitates group cohesion and growth is genuineness—that is, a congruency between what an individual says and does and what he or she truly feels inside (Raskin & Rogers, 1989). For example, it is oftentimes normal for leaders to feel some anxiety before the initial meeting of a group. By self-disclosing their own fears and anxiety around beginning a group, leaders model genuineness, thus making it more likely that group members will learn genuineness and how to appropriately display it within the group and in real-life situations. Conversely, if students feel some anxiety upon beginning a group, yet they state that there is no reason to feel anxious in a group, they may be setting a precedent that it is not necessarily alright to be genuine in the group. Hence, some trust and honesty may be lost in the group. Therefore, in order for group members to develop genuineness within the group context, it is important that group leaders model their own congruency among what they feel, think, and do.

Respect is another important interpersonal skill that helps group members grow and progress. When respect is not developed within a group, students may struggle to participate and may feel a sense of insecurity within the group. Therefore, it is important that leaders help group members develop feelings of respect for each other. Along with modeling respect (e.g., demonstrating positive regard for all group members), it is important that group leaders curtail situations in which disrespect is exhibited between group members. For example, if one group member is interrupting another or is speaking or behaving in a derogatory manner, it may be important for the leader to intervene (Ferencik, 1992; Posthuma, 2002). It might also be important that group leaders intervene to make sure members are included in group discussion. This may be accomplished using the technique of drawing out group members.

Instilling and Maintaining Hope

Instillation and maintenance of hope are essential to the success of a group. In fact, faith in the group's effectiveness is not only therapeutic in keeping members in the group but also therapeutic in itself (Frank & Frank, 1991; Kaul & Bednar, 1994; Yalom & Leszcz, 2005). Yalom and Leszcz (2005) compared the therapeutic power of instilling hope to a placebo effect that patients may experience in scientific experiments. An example of the placebo effect would be members of an experimental control group who are taking sugar pills rather than an antidepressant medication. Because the control group participants believe they are receiving the actual antidepressant medication, they feel hopeful that their depression will get better. As a result, the depression subsides. On the same note, if leaders can instill and maintain hope in group members during pregroup sessions, as well as during the initial sessions of a group, they can facilitate growth and progress within individual students and the group as a whole.

One way hope may be instilled in members during the first few sessions of a group is through recounting success stories. For example, a leader with some prior experience working with groups might describe instances in which she was able to see the progress that a student made while participating in the group. She might describe some of the fear and doubt this particular member had during the forming and orienting stage of the group, the strides that he made in accomplishing his primary task, and how the group facilitated his growth and progress. Furthermore, if the group is open-ended, the leader might be able to rely on veteran group members to describe either their own positive experiences through membership in a group or the success they have seen in fellow group members. For example:

> Richard has decided to enter a group, but he is very nervous about it. He wonders whether he will feel comfortable enough to participate and even whether the group will benefit from him participating. On his first day, he is really nervous because the majority of the people have already been coming to the open group for a while. Danny, a member who has been attending the group for four months, recognizes Richard's anxiety and recounts how he felt during his first few meetings. Danny describes how he was nervous and scared and was not sure he would come back, but once he started participating, Danny began to become more confident. Hence, Danny was able to decrease many of his problems and achieve some of his personal goals. Hearing Danny's experience with the group helps Richard understand that he is not alone in his fear and that if Danny can decrease some of his life struggles and accomplish his goals, then maybe Richard can, too. Consequently, Richard dedicates himself more fully to attending and participating in the group.

In essence, Danny's empathy for Richard and his description of the growth that he had experienced in the group helped instill hope in Richard, which in turn engendered a motivation to actively participate in the group. On a similar note, a leader who is beginning the first session of a closed group may be able to relate his or her own positive growth experience from previous counseling groups.

In addition to relating success stories, it is vitally important that group leaders believe in themselves and in the efficacy of the group in order to instill hope in group members (Frank & Frank, 1991; Yalom & Leszcz, 2005). When group leaders truly believe that they can help every motivated member of their group to progress and are able to succinctly express this belief to each member, they begin to help students experience hope and confidence in themselves and in the group.

CASE ILLUSTRATION OF AN INITIAL GROUP SESSION

This case demonstrates an initial session with a group of high school students, but the principles can apply to elementary and middle school students with some developmental modifications. Michael and Samantha, two experienced professional school counselors, have decided to form a counseling group. They have collaborated on the purpose for the group, advertised the group to receive referrals, interviewed potential group members, selected group members, engaged in pregroup interviews with each member, and set a time for the first group meeting. Now the day and hour are finally at hand, and it is time for the group to begin.

Michael and Samantha greet students as they enter the group room before the first session. In doing so, they feel that they have been able to build rapport more quickly with some members and to decrease some of the anxiety inherent in first sessions. After everybody is seated and even though the students already know who the counselors are, Michael introduces himself and then turns to Samantha to introduce herself. After introductory remarks about themselves and about the group process and purpose, Samantha and Michael reiterate group rules, specifically focusing on confidentiality.

Samantha describes the importance of respecting each group member, including showing up on time and keeping confidentiality. While illustrating confidentiality, Samantha is careful to specify some simple ways in which confidentiality might be breached by group members. She decides to relate an incident that she encountered in a past group that she led.

SAMANTHA (LEADER): Two male group members, Richard and Ted—I changed their names because of confidentiality—decided to go out to eat one afternoon after school and discussed what happened in the group meeting that day. Ted recounted a problem that Melissa—also a made-up name of a fellow group member—presented. "I really think that she needs to get out and do something, and then she won't feel depressed all the time," said Ted. Richard responded, "Yeah, I bet she would enjoy hanging out with us. We should invite her next time." During the next group session, Ted and Richard presented their solution to Melissa. Melissa, rather than thinking that they were being helpful, felt that they had been talking behind her back. Consequently, she lost her trust in the group and wanted to quit the group. You see, it is important that what is talked about in the group stays in the group. Otherwise, confidentiality may be breached, trust may be lost, and potential group and individual growth may be undermined.

After discussing group rules, Michael and Samantha engage the group in an icebreaker. Michael explains that in this icebreaker, members should describe themselves in the third person (as though they were an outside observer); while the members' descriptions should be factual and accurate, they should also focus on how the members would like others in the group to see them. Michael instructs the group members that, in addition to describing themselves, they should state their reasons for joining the group. Following are three examples of information shared by group members in the icebreaker.

CLARENCE (GROUP MEMBER): Clarence is a very caring and sensitive person. Also, he is very good with math and science. Clarence is from a big family. He has four brothers and three sisters. All of them are going to college to become doctors, lawyers, or engineers. Clarence, on the other hand, wants to be a high school science teacher. I believe that his reason for joining the group is to learn new ways of relating to others and his family. You see, during family get-togethers, Clarence feels like he is the odd guy out, being the youngest and not motivated to be some brainiac.

MANDY (GROUP MEMBER): Mandy is a, uh, a nice person. She is fun to talk to. I think that is why we get along. She likes reading and has a really nice boyfriend. Some think that she shouldn't be dating him so seriously, but she seems to be happy. I am not 100% sure why she joined the group, but I do know that she has been struggling in school and she has had a falling out with some of her friends. Maybe she is just curious about the group process and wants to learn ways to better cope with everyday stress.

MARSHALL (GROUP MEMBER): Marshall is 15 years old. He has an older brother and an older sister. He likes to play basketball. He is in this group because he gets a little upset sometimes on the court, and maybe a little bit at other times as well, and he maybe reacts, you know, without thinking. He wants to control himself before he does something he might regret, if you know what I mean.

After giving all the members of the group an opportunity to describe themselves in this manner, Michael begins discussing some of the insecurity and apprehension that he is feeling in this first session. He describes some of the fear and mistrust that he felt before the group session began and how some of that anxiety persists. After opening the discussion by talking about anxiety, Michael makes it possible for other students to express some of their apprehensions and preoccupations surrounding group membership and etiquette.

ELIZABETH (GROUP MEMBER): I am so glad that you said that about feeling nervous. I thought that everybody sounded so together and so comfortable when they described themselves. I thought that I must be the only person in here feeling insecure. I didn't want people to think that I didn't belong in this group, but instead in some group for crazy people. I mean for a second there I thought it was a group prerequisite to have yourself completely together.

FELISHA (GROUP MEMBER): Oh, I feel nervous as well, and I'm sure I don't have all my stuff together. I don't know about you guys, but this is my first time ever being in one of these group things.

	I just don't want to start talking about my problems and have people thinking that I'm hogging all the time or something. I just want to make sure that I'm not wasting y'alls time with my own problems.
MARCUS (GROUP MEMBER):	I can understand that. It would be hard for me to express all my problems knowing that other people might have more important things to get off their chests.
SAMANTHA:	So part of what I am hearing is a fear or anxiety about wasting other people's time with your problems.
CLARENCE:	Yeah, I think that's accurate. I'm not even sure that my issues are even appropriate for this group.
MICHAEL (LEADER):	Well, Clarence, let's analyze that a little. You mentioned that one of your reasons for joining the group was to relate better with others, especially family members. In fact, as you were describing yourself as the "odd guy out" in your family, I noticed you looked away from everybody. Tell me a little about that.
CLARENCE:	Well, as I mentioned, my dad is a rocket scientist working for NASA, two of my older brothers are studying to become physicians, two of my sisters are studying to become lawyers, my oldest sister is an ophthalmologist, and my two other brothers are studying to be chemical engineers. I, on the other hand, just want to be a science teacher at a high school. I feel that I am being looked down on when I tell them my career goal, like they think that their jobs are more important than being a teacher because they make more money. Or they think that they are more intelligent than teachers because they make more money. Of course, being the youngest in the family doesn't help you, you know? I don't know. It feels bad!
MANDY (JUMPING IN):	I understand exactly what you mean by not fitting in. I feel like I cannot relate to most of my best friends, whom I have known since elementary school. Recently, they got into the drinking and partying thing, and I'm not really into that. Now when we're together, they just talk about the parties they've been to and how drunk they get. I just don't feel comfortable with them anymore.
MICHAEL:	OK, so, Mandy, you feel that you can understand to some degree what Clarence is going through because you don't feel like you fit in with your friends who like to party and drink alcohol. Let's explore this a little further.

The group continues to focus on Clarence and Mandy as they process feelings of being left out. When there are about 10 minutes left, Samantha decides that it is time to begin the process of ending the session by checking in with each member of the group. Because it is the first session, she makes sure to focus on group trust and apprehension. The following are some responses from group members as Samantha and Michael are doing the rounds:

ELIZABETH: I am so grateful that we were able to talk about being scared and anxious about being here. At first, as I mentioned, I felt alone in my fear, but hearing from others really helped.

FELISHA: I would like to thank Clarence and Mandy for being so willing to jump out and talk about things. It was really nice to be able to hear their perspectives on things. I think all of us in some context or another feel left out or looked down on. Thank you for sharing. I can't speak for everybody else, but it sure was helpful to me.

CLARENCE: I really appreciate you saying that. I was really beginning to feel nervous about all the focus being on me for such a long time this session. Don't worry, I won't be a time hog.

MARCUS: No way—you don't have to apologize. I would like to thank you for stepping up to the plate and really talking about this. It was really beneficial to me. I feel a lot less anxiety now than I did at the beginning. I noticed that even though some sessions might be focused more on one person, all of us can still gain things from it. I think that may help me when I have stuff to talk about in future sessions.

After going around and letting all the members express themselves, Michael once again reviews the group rule on confidentiality, thanks the members for coming, and explains that trust and apprehension can be discussed further in the subsequent sessions.

CASE ILLUSTRATION OF A SECOND GROUP SESSION DURING THE FORMING AND ORIENTING STAGE

It is now the second session of the group that Michael and Samantha have begun. Some of the anxiety and fear that accompanied the first session have decreased, and trust and cohesion are beginning to appear. Along with trust and cohesion, an openness to take some risks in expressing true feelings has emerged.

Also, Michael and Samantha begin to notice hints of some potential group problems, especially with some members who hardly participate. For example, Marshall, a group member who is a few years younger than the oldest group members, has displayed a tendency to shy away from discussions and participation. In this session, Samantha and Michael make a point to encourage Marshall to participate before he clams up completely or quits coming to the group altogether.

At one point in the session, Elizabeth begins to talk about some anger problems that she is having in regard to her English teacher. After discussing the situation with Elizabeth for a few minutes, Michael involves Marshall.

MICHAEL (LEADER): Marshall, I remember that in the icebreaker of our first session, you mentioned a desire to work on your anger. Tell us a little bit more about that.

MARSHALL (GROUP MEMBER): Well, I guess I just lose my cool sometimes.

SAMANTHA (LEADER):	What is it like when you lose your cool?
MARSHALL:	I don't really know. I just get mad, and it's like nothing else matters after that. I just blow up.
MICHAEL:	What happens when you blow up?
MARSHALL:	I usually either end up in a fight or say something that I regret later.
ELIZABETH (GROUP MEMBER):	That sounds kind of scary. I feel that sometimes, too.
MARSHALL:	Yeah, it's not real fun. Like I said, I want to put these angry explosions in check so that I don't have to regret stuff anymore.
SAMANTHA:	OK, so tell me your goal.
MARSHALL:	To not get angry anymore.
MICHAEL:	How could you change that goal into something positive?
MARSHALL:	Man, I don't know. You're the counselor. How do I make it positive?
SAMANTHA:	Well, how do you feel when you are not angry?
MARSHALL:	Calm.
SAMANTHA:	OK, then maybe your goal can be to stay calm during basketball games.
MARSHALL:	Yeah, but how?
MANDY (GROUP MEMBER):	I know when I begin to get upset, I sing my favorite hymn. I know if you do that, then you will feel better. One time I was so mad at my little two-year-old sister for spilling grape juice on my new purse that I could hardly stand it. In fact, I didn't know what I was going to do until I remembered to sing a song from the hymnal. I felt much better.
MICHAEL (ATTEMPTING TO KEEP THE FOCUS ON MARSHALL):	Marshall, tell me about a time in your life when you were able to control your anger.
MARSHALL:	I guess a few years back when I was in middle school, whenever I began to get upset, Coach Brown took me aside and told me to keep my focus on the fundamentals, like staying active, boxing people out, and running the plays. When I stayed focused, I found myself not getting angry as much, and I enjoyed myself more.
SAMANTHA:	So keeping your focus on what you need to be doing helps you stay calm.
MARSHALL:	Yeah, so I guess I can remind myself of the fundamentals of the game when I recognize that I am getting upset. I'll see how that works.
ELIZABETH:	I sure could use some goals for my anger with my English teacher. She's really a pain.

The session continues with Elizabeth describing her issues as well as other group members participating in the session. The group leaders continue to take an active role in the group through modeling, facilitating the establishment of goals, recognizing potential problems, and establishing trust. In effect, the group members begin to progress through some of the apprehensions and doubt that are pervasive in the forming and orienting stage, and they enter and move through the next step in the development of a group, known as the transition stage.

Summary

The forming and orienting stage of a group is a time of orientation and exploration for its members. During this time, students become more cognizant of their reasons for joining the group. Through interaction with fellow group members, they develop a sense of who they are in the group (identity). They also make decisions about the degree to which they will participate, take risks, and relate to other group members (inclusion). If group members are to interact productively in groups, it is essential that trust be established early on. The group leader plays a key role in helping to cultivate an environment in which trust develops.

In addition to describing these general tasks, which are a part of the forming and orienting stage of a group, this chapter discussed ten responsibilities of leaders: (1) reviewing group goals, (2) helping members establish personal goals, (3) specifying group rules, (4) modeling facilitative group behavior, (5) assisting members in expressing their apprehensions, (6) establishing and maintaining trust, (7) promoting positive interchanges among group members, (8) teaching members basic interpersonal skills (e.g., active listening), (9) instilling and maintaining hope, and (10) resolving possible group problems that manifest in the forming and orienting stage. At the end of the chapter, case illustrations of two group sessions provided examples of group tasks, leadership responsibilities, and membership interactions that are often evidenced during the forming and orienting stage.

CHAPTER 8

The Transition Stage in Group Work

D. PAIGE BENTLEY GREASON

PREVIEW

The theory behind the developmental tasks of the transition stage in groups is explored, including the internal and external determinants of transition dynamics, how these dynamics manifest in the group, and what leaders can do to effectively work with the sometimes overwhelming emotions and behaviors of this transition stage.

TRANSITION IN CONTEXT

Professional school counselors work with a variety of types of groups, including task groups, psychoeduational groups, counseling groups (Akos, Goodnough, & Milsom, 2004; Newsome & Gladding, 2007; Ripley & Goodnough, 2001), and sometimes psychotherapy groups. No matter the type, all groups pass through what is often called the transition stage, although this stage may be quicker and less anxiety producing in some group models (e.g., classroom guidance, small psychoeducational groups, task groups) than others (e.g., counseling groups, psychotherapy groups). For this reason, much of the content and many of the techniques covered in this chapter on the transition stage, while pertinent to all group models, are perhaps most applicable to counseling and psychotherapy group models.

Modern group theorists consider groups to be dynamic and changing systems (Agazarian, 1997; Agazarian & Gantt, 2003; Connors & Caple, 2005; Donigian & Malnati, 1997; McClure, 1998). Like any system, groups are relatively unstable in the early stages of development and progress toward more stability and complexity over time. Early in their development, groups pass through a type of adolescence. Just like a rebellious teenager, the group in transition is testing boundaries and power structures. Depending on the group, this stage manifests as overt or subtle rebellion and conflict and represents a transition from the superficial niceties and enthusiasm that dominate the beginning of the forming and orienting stage to the more complex and challenging, albeit more cooperative, focus that marks the working stage.

If this turbulent transition stage is successfully navigated, the group moves on to a norming period, where cohesiveness grows, and then to the working stage, where the productive, goal-focused work of the group can begin. If the forces that manifest in the transition stage are not adequately dealt with by the leader and the members, they have the potential to keep the group stuck in the transition stage and adversely affect the group process and outcomes. Because of the potentially challenging, even destructive nature of transitional forces, it is important for leaders to be aware of the origins of these forces and how to effectively deal with them.

Much of our understanding of the dynamics of the transition stage in groups is based on research involving adult groups. That research suggests that the dynamics of the transition stage are driven by anxiety and fear, which manifest as defensiveness, resistance, and interpersonal conflict around power and control (Billow, 2003). Very little research, however, has been conducted on the process dynamics of groups in schools or involving children and adolescents (DeLucia-Waack, 2000; Shechtman, 2004).

TRANSITION AS A CRITICAL GROUP TASK

A number of theorists have hypothesized about the reasons for transitional conflict in the group and about the value of this conflict for group development. It is instructive to view transition from two important perspectives: group developmental theories and group systems theory, both of which help to explain why conflict is an important developmental task for groups.

Transition From a Developmental Theory Perspective

Despite the different names given to this transition stage, developmental theories are in agreement that as groups develop, they enter a period characterized by increased tension and testing of the environment. Members may test each other to see whether the environment is safe and to understand what the various relationships within the group will be like. Students may also test the leader to see if the leader will keep them safe, or they may simply use the leader as a safe target for the expression of their inner anger or hostility. Alternatively, they may become overly dependent on the leader. They may hold the irrational expectation that the leader will not only understand their innermost problems without their having to say anything but also make the group itself free of anxiety or tension. Developmental approaches to group work are evident in stage models, such as the one provided in this book, and are readily understandable and applicable to task, psychoeducational, counseling, and psychotherapy groups. However, to truly understand the power and promise of group dynamics in counseling and psychotherapy groups, systemic models should also be considered.

Transition From a Systems Theory Perspective

A review of the scholarly literature on groups reveals that systemic approaches to group counseling and psychotherapy are becoming more prevalent and influential (Connors & Caple, 2005). Group systems theory provides a framework and language for understanding, defining, and working with the dynamics and processes in the group as a whole, particularly those dynamics that present themselves in the transition stage. Leaders operating from a systemic perspective focus on the big picture of the group, while also maintaining awareness of the needs of the individual members. Understanding group dynamics from this perspective enables the leader to be more effective in helping the individual group members and the group itself to attain goals.

Systems theory posits that behaviors and attitudes that manifest during the transition stage are necessary for the optimal growth and health of the group (Agazarian & Gantt, 2003; Connors & Caple, 2005). The group continues to be useful as long as it is changing and evolving. Once the patterns of behavior become so rigid that the group can no longer adapt to a changing environment, the group ceases to serve its purpose, and, ultimately, it ceases to exist. As such, transition is a normal phase of group work, and changes in behavior and responsibility are expected and essential elements.

General systems theory was first postulated in the classic work of Ludwig von Bertalanffy (1968) and was based on the concept of holism—that the whole is greater than the sum of its parts and that the parts are interdependent. Ludwig von Bertalanffy proposed that systems are dynamic and ever-changing and that they evolve from disorder, instability, and simple structure into greater complexity through such processes as self-organization and self-stabilization. All the while, systems attempt to maintain homeostasis in the face of an ever-changing environment. Systems theory maintains that every system includes boundary and power structures that guide its development and growth. In order for the system to survive and grow, its boundaries must be flexible enough to allow input in the form of new information and resources. These boundaries are rarely fixed; rather, they are more open or more closed, depending on the situation.

Likewise, counseling groups can be defined as a system—hence, the term *group systems theory*. Groups are self-defining, self-organizing, and self-regulating (Conners & Caple, 2005). From a systemic perspective, the individual members of a group are in a dynamic, interdependent relationship with each other. Each person within the group plays an essential role in the group's development and growth. A change in one person will have an impact on the rest of the group. According to the group systems theory, behaviors and attitudes that manifest during the transition stage, however conflict laden or anxiety producing, are necessary for the optimal growth and health of the group (Agazarian, 1997; Agazarian & Gantt, 2003; Connors & Caple, 2005; McClure, 1998). Conflict, boundary testing, feedback, and adaptation help create a group environment where member issues can be effectively addressed. Each will be considered in turn below.

CONFLICT   Stability within the group, or in any living system, cannot be maintained forever, no matter how comfortable that stability might feel. Conflict is viewed as necessary for effective growth and functioning. Conflict in a group may arise for a variety of reasons. Consider an example in which students may react to the leader's failure to provide complete safety and freedom from anxiety. Elementary school students in a counseling group for students facing issues of grief and loss may expect that the leader will run the group like teachers run classes. They may have difficulty accepting that this group will require them to open up to other people and share their feelings. Members may become irritated with each other over how they should behave in the group. Students may have differing views of the group and its potential and how to handle issues in the group. Individuals who have less tolerance for anxiety may advocate for a continued focus on safe topics. Individuals with high needs for affection may want to spend time getting to know each other. In contrast, members with high needs for control may want to get on with the business of the group. These events are important to the evolution of the group because they open up interpersonal boundaries between members and create an opportunity for the exploration of defense mechanisms and the establishment of group norms (Rybak & Brown, 1997). Groups that become too rigid in their norms and rules risk stagnation and possible dissolution.

BOUNDARY TESTING   Boundaries in group work are defined as "the amount and kind of contact allowable between members" (Becvar & Becvar, 1996, p. 191). Boundaries are part of the overall structure of the group, which includes leader actions, group norms, goals, individual boundaries, and even group activities (Connors & Caple, 2005). In order for the group to move to higher levels of development and complexity, the boundary structures of the group itself and of the individual members must be permeable and flexible, while preserving enough integrity to maintain safety. For instance, students who are unwilling to share personal information or consider the opinions of others are considered to have impermeable boundaries. If the group as a whole has rigid boundaries and is unwilling to share, the group may become stagnant and uninteresting. Members who are easily influenced by the emotions of others have highly permeable or diffuse boundaries (Nichols & Schwartz, 1998). Leaders need to help members learn how to effectively open and close their boundaries so that group members can interact in meaningful ways and change and growth can occur.

FEEDBACK   Systems theory suggests that the group receives input from the environment that either encourages change or supports the status quo or homeostasis. Connors and Caple (2005) referred to these types of input as change-provoking and change-resisting feedback, respectively. Change-provoking feedback refers to feedback that pushes the system toward growth. In a group, it might be in the form of verbal or nonverbal feedback. For instance, a group member might make an unpleasant facial gesture when a typically self-centered member starts talking about himself again. This gesture sends a message that the usual way of doing things (e.g., listening passively to the group member recount another story) is no longer going to work. The leader could use this opportunity to promote self-disclosure by the first member, perhaps through use of an I-statement about how he feels in response to this self-centered member's storytelling, as well as through feedback that will help both members change the status quo. Change-resisting feedback supports the usual way of doing things. For instance, the same self-centered group member may change the subject when confronted about his patterns of behavior in order to avoid facing the issue and making changes, or other group members may simply allow the facial gesture to pass without any further comment.

From a group systems perspective, change-provoking feedback is the source of conflict because of its challenging and disturbing qualities. Coming face to face with something fearful is difficult, and group members experiencing change-provoking feedback are often very uncomfortable. The sense of chaos that can ensue can be disturbing, though it is seen as, at times, necessary for progress. When faced with these challenges, the group can decide either to retract or expand boundaries or, in rare instances, to collapse and terminate the experience.

ADAPTATION   Interactions in the group are seen as attempts to maintain homeostasis and regulate behavior in order to alleviate the anxiety of the unknown. These interactions result in the establishment of group norms. When something (e.g., a heated exchange between group members) disrupts the norm, the group will seek to reestablish homeostasis. This could mean that the students may avoid emotional subjects for some time after the event or that the group may develop a new norm around the acceptable level of emotional sharing and intimacy. It takes some time to consolidate the event and accommodate the new information, but once a group survives a conflict event, the group may move more quickly toward greater intimacy and growth (Billow, 2003).

Many students can be resistant to change. Early on, individual group members and the group as a whole will attempt to maintain the status quo in order to alleviate the anxiety of the unknown. It is often easier and more comfortable to stay with what is known than to confront difficult areas of growth. In order to avoid the challenging work of growth and change, groups will often lapse into repetitive patterns that maintain the status quo.

Groups are a microcosm of society. Patterns within the group mirror patterns in the individual group members' lives. For example, a male in the group may be loud, dominating, and somewhat egocentric. He tends to talk down to females, in particular. This behavior parallels his behavior with significant women in his life, including his sister, his mother, and even his teachers. As he grows older, this dominating stance may manifest in difficulty establishing strong and stable relationships with women. It may be easier for the male to maintain this behavior than to look at the underlying source of the behavior. Unfortunately, this rigid, patterned approach to life may cut him off from the very intimacy he seeks. Successfully working with these resistances to change will move group members and the group as a whole to a place where change is no longer feared. Instead, change is embraced within the safety of the group (McClure, 1998).

During the transition stage, it is incumbent on leaders to find a balance between some discomfort in the system and complete chaos, which is usually more destructive than constructive (Nitsun, 1996). Consider an example in which a group member verbally attacks another member who has a pattern of dominating the discussion. Such verbal attacks are reflective of the power struggles typical of the transition stage. Imagine that the dominating member cracks under the attack and begins to cry. A sense of tension settles over the group. At this point, the group faces a decision: Should the group rush to the defense of the dominant member, thus maintaining the status quo? Should the group gang up on the dominant member with character attacks? Should the group gang up on the attacking member? How the leader and group members work with these issues will determine whether or not the group survives and grows, maintains the status quo, or devolves into chaos.

ANXIETY AS THE SOURCE OF CONFLICT

Anxiety is considered the driving force in the group (Donigian & Malnati, 1997). But it is important to understand that the reasons for the anxiety experienced and expressed during the transition stage are qualitatively different from those present in the forming and orienting stage. The anxiety related to "Will I fit in?" or "Will I get anything out of this group?" is less pronounced. In the transition stage, students are being asked to confront fears about themselves rather than ignoring them—and to do so in a very public way. This amplifies such core fears as making a fool of oneself, losing control, and being rejected. For example, if Jane becomes angry about the way Jose treated another group member, she may worry that if she expresses the full force of her rage, she will be ostracized by the group or, worse, she won't be able to control her anger. It's no wonder group members feel anxious.

Despite the fact that anxiety is normal in group work, too much anxiety can inhibit the group process. It is important for leaders to understand the sources of great anxiety in order to create a safe environment for reflection on the myriad ways members deal with their anxiety. This is the premier leader challenge of the transition stage. The group setting itself can trigger these defenses against anxiety, as can core interpersonal issues among group members. Fortunately, individual psychology and choice theory provide some insight into the sources of transition forces among children and adolescents, which contribute to the sources of anxiety that are qualitatively different from the anxieties apparent in the forming and orienting stage.

The Group Itself as a Source of Anxiety

Groups are inherently anxiety provoking. Individuals are being asked to be vulnerable, to open up to strangers, to come face to face with change and possibly with parts of themselves they would rather not see. For many years, the source of anxiety in groups was considered to be within the individual members (Donigian & Malnati, 1997). Moreover, literature focused on aggression *in* the group rather than aggression *toward* the group (Nitsun, 1996). This approach does not address the impact of group dynamics or the group setting itself on the elicitation of defensive behaviors. Group work scholars now assume that anxiety and conflict in groups have both an internal and an external origin.

In his work on the aggressive forces in groups, Nitsun (1996) stated that the most commonly voiced anxiety about groups is that they can be destructive. He suggested that both constructive and destructive forces exist on a bipolar continuum in the group and that the tension between these forces is necessary for the continued growth and development of the group and its members. He coined the term the *anti-group* to describe those forces that threaten the integrity of the group and suggested that the anti-group is an important complement to the creative processes within the group. Nitsun outlined a number of characteristics of counseling and therapy groups, presented below, that make them challenging and anxiety provoking for members.

GROUPS ARE COMPOSED OF STRANGERS—OR NOT   One of the first "rules" of member composition in counseling and psychotherapy groups is to fill the group with people who do not know each other so that interpersonal dynamics can start fresh. In a school setting, the reverse of this rule may be true: School groups may be composed of students who interact with each other in many other school settings. Both situations create the possibility for tension in the group. Entering a room full of strangers can be a source of anxiety for a group member, as can entering a room full of school acquaintances who know the member in very different settings. Members often turn to group work because of interpersonal issues, and the group format is forcing them to talk about their most private experiences in front of others. Students may feel frustrated and scared that they are being asked to open up to people they are not even sure they can trust, in the case of strangers, or to people they may have to deal with under different circumstances, in the case of acquaintances.

THE GROUP IS UNSTRUCTURED AND UNPREDICTABLE   Task and psychoeducational groups aside, counseling and psychotherapy groups typically lack a structured agenda or program. This method invites a here-and-now focus on the dynamics within the group (Yalom & Leszcz, 2005). However, this lack of structure can be frustrating for group members who may be looking to the leader to provide direction. The lack of structure can also arouse anxiety around the unpredictable nature of the group. Members are uncertain what to expect from week to week, and the lack of structure makes it more difficult to feel safe.

THE GROUP IS CREATED BY ITS MEMBERS   The paradox of group work is that the very people who are seeking help are the ones who are responsible for the fate of the group itself. Nitsun

(1996) likened this to the blind leading the blind. Students may enter the group with hopes of being "fixed" by the leader. These members believe that responsibility for healing and health is external rather than internal. When it becomes clear that this external cure they dreamed of will not materialize, members may become hostile toward the group or the leader.

THE GROUP IS A PUBLIC ARENA   Because the group is outside the typical bounds of members' private lives, it is often experienced as a public space. Because confidentiality cannot be guaranteed in a group, members' anxieties about exposure and humiliation extend beyond the boundaries of the group. In a school setting, this fear is magnified. Students may become anxious, for example, that they will be treated differently by peers after disclosing something deeply personal or embarrassing about themselves. They may also worry that their self-disclosures will be shared with other students or teachers outside of the group. It is important that counselors in school settings encourage students not to discuss what happens *in* the group *outside* the group, while also reminding members that confidentiality in a group setting cannot be guaranteed (Corey & Corey, 2006; Newsome & Gladding, 2007).

THE GROUP IS A PLURALISTIC ENTITY   A diverse membership creates myriad opportunities for the growth of individual members. However, having to relate to a group of diverse individuals rather than a single counselor can test even the healthiest of individuals. For students, learning to understand and accept the differences of other people is a key developmental task. Furthermore, students can begin to learn different ways of solving problems or interpreting events from individuals who are different from them (Newsome & Gladding, 2007).

THE GROUP IS A COMPLEX AND INCOMPLETE EXPERIENCE   Communication within the group occurs on many different levels (e.g., explicit and implicit, verbal and nonverbal), and individual members construct meaning of the group experience based on their own phenomenological viewpoint. Moreover, due to the inherent limitations on the amount of material that can be covered in the group, individual members may be left with unresolved or unaddressed issues. This can lead to frustration with the group as well as aggression.

Participation in the group forces members to come face to face with change, which is often very difficult, even if it is change for the better. In a school setting, many students are referred to groups by teachers or parents (Newsome & Gladding, 2007). Although the adult wants the child to change, the child may have very little motivation to change. He or she may see the group as an unnecessary waste of time and be resistant to the counseling process.

Core Needs as Sources of Anxiety

In addition to the group setting itself as a source of anxiety, core needs fuel anxiety and concomitant anxiety-driven behaviors. Anxiety is fostered when a discrepancy exists between the needs and the present attainment of those needs, as is often the case in groups. The effective leader is cognizant of the underlying needs and fears that generate anxiety and drive defensive behavior. Being mindful and respectful of those reasons helps when deciding on an appropriate intervention. A number of theories exist regarding basic human needs. Three of these—psychodynamic, individual psychology, and choice theory—are outlined here, as they are particularly relevant to understanding group dynamics with students.

Psychodynamic theories suggest that a student's previous failed attempts to get basic needs met, as well as the resultant fears and core beliefs about one's ability and adequacy, fuel defensive reactions to perceived threats (McLeod & Kettner-Polley, 2004). In a classic analysis, Schutz (1966) identified three primary needs—inclusion, control, and affection— and suggested that these are satisfied through relationships with others. "Inclusion is concerned with the problem of in or out, control is concerned with top or bottom, and affection with close or far" (Schutz, 1966, p. 24). While inclusion behaviors are related to forming a relationship, control and affection behaviors relate to how one deals with relationships that are already established. To be free of anxiety, the student needs to find a balance of these three needs with respect to others. Students differ in the extent to which they are deficient in these areas, reflecting their prior successes or failures in getting these needs met. Schutz suggested that the dynamics within the group reflect these interpersonal needs. For example, a student with strong inclusion needs might try to be "best friends" with everyone in the group, and a student at the opposite end of the spectrum (i.e., with low inclusion needs) might withdraw and avoid contact with others. When the typical defense mechanisms do not fully protect the individual from negative feelings associated with the discrepancy between what is needed and what is attained, anxiety ensues. In the optimal state of equilibrium, defenses are required only minimally.

Individual psychology theory (developed by Alfred Adler) provides an insightful explanation of the needs of children and the related goals of misbehavior (Thompson & Henderson, 2007). According to this theory, children who feel good about themselves attempt to achieve their basic goal of belonging by cooperating and collaborating with others. However, children who are discouraged pursue one of four mistaken goals: attention, power, revenge, or inadequacy or withdrawal. These mistaken-goal behaviors may become more extreme during the transition stage in group work as students try to find their place in the group. For instance, a student who has been mistreated in life may seek to get even by hurting others, or a child who thinks she is inferior or incapable may "act stupid" in order to avoid being challenged by the leader.

Finally, choice theory (primarily developed by William Glasser) suggests that humans have five basic needs—survival, freedom, power, fun, and love—and that psychological problems are the result of an inability to fulfill these needs. Glasser (1999) suggested that students often try to fulfill their basic needs by infringing on the basic rights of others through control tactics, resulting in relationship issues. He proposed therefore that all psychological problems are relationship problems that stem from attempts to control others. The road to mental health, according to the choice theory, is the development of healthy relationships in which each student takes responsibility for personal behavior as opposed to trying to change the behavior of others.

Regardless of theoretical orientation, these basic needs are associated with a plethora of fears and core beliefs about the self. A number of other common fears observed during the transition stage have been identified by group work authors (Corey, 2007; Corey & Corey, 2006; Ormont, 1984, 1988; Schutz, 1966; Yalom & Leszcz, 2005):

- If I show my true self, I will be ignored or, worse, rejected.
- If I speak up or take responsibility, I will make a fool of myself and be seen as incompetent.
- If I look too deep, I'll discover that there is nothing there.
- If I express my anger (fear, sadness, etc.), I will open up Pandora's box and will lose control.
- The group or the leader will expect me to disclose more than I'm comfortable sharing.

- If I get close to people who will not be available to me after the group ends, I will not be able to handle that loss.
- What I say in the group will not stay in the group.
- If I tell people about my past behaviors or my deepest fears or fantasies, they will judge me.
- This group will be a waste of my time. I don't see how this can help.
- The group leader will not be able to help me if things get rough.

The group setting creates a rare venue where the student's unique issues with intimacy and contact with others can not only play out but also be examined (Yalom & Leszcz, 2005). These theoretical perspectives about how groups develop and the underlying internal and external issues that challenge group members provide a backdrop for understanding the member and leader behaviors that arise during the transition stage. Leaders need to know what specific, concrete behaviors to look for and understand that these behaviors may be driven by anxiety.

THE EXPRESSION OF TRANSITION ISSUES

The interpersonal and intrapersonal dynamics mentioned above manifest in the group during the transition stage in predictable ways. While the forming and orienting stage of group development is characterized by acclimation to the group process and some testing of boundaries to identify "ground rules," the transition stage is marked by more overt hostility and conflict (Yalom & Leszcz, 2005).

Some of the most common behaviors observed during transition are identified and described in this section. All of these behaviors should be viewed in light of their role in the development of the group. For instance, rather than being an act of protest, active defiance in the group may actually represent a growing trust in the process and a willingness to express more difficult emotions. Certainly, it could also indicate complete distrust in the process. It is important that the leader explore the origins of various behaviors rather than assuming understanding. Some of these member behaviors can become quite problematic, as was discussed in substantial detail in Chapter 4, and the leader must display skillful, intentional interventions to facilitate member self-disclosure and feedback.

Struggle for Control

During the transition stage, issues around control are present in every group, although they may not always be obvious. To maintain optimal functioning, the group as a whole must find a level of relative equality among members. Conners and Caple (2005) suggested that unequal power dynamics or dominating members must be addressed or else groups will "fall into destructive interpersonal patterns and create negative outcomes" (p. 100).

In this transition stage, students struggle with issues of dependence on the leader's authority and the comfort of the status quo versus the independence and freedom of expression (Billow, 2003). As students seek to find their preferred amount of autonomy and power, they must confront all the other group members, who, likewise, are struggling with the same issues. Furthermore, they must deal with the leader, who has been given tacit power simply by virtue of position. The result is conflict and hostility between members and the leader or just among members.

HOSTILITY TOWARD THE LEADER   Some hostility toward the leader occurs normally as part of a group's development. In the typically high dependency state leading up to the transition stage, the group members tend to look to the group leader for guidance and reassurance, as if they are unable to take care of themselves. Kline (2003) stated that members "deskill" themselves and depend on the leader to understand them without members having to say anything (e.g., "The leader should be able to read my mind"). During this period, group members often engage in magical thinking about the group leader's power in the group. Students may expect the leader to be all-knowing and capable of reading their innermost thoughts and concerns. They may also hold the secret wish that the leader will choose them as the "favorite child" (Yalom & Leszcz, 2005). From this perspective, the behaviors of the leader may be misinterpreted as illustrative of a deeper, individual connection between the leader and the member. For instance, when the group leader made eye contact with Sally while another group member was speaking, Sally interpreted the contact to mean "Ah, he understands exactly what I'm feeling over here. He agrees with me that this person is ridiculous." This illusion of a secret alliance between the leader and the member is quickly shattered as the student comes to realize that the leader may have equal interest in the issues of all group members.

When it becomes clear that the group leader will not fulfill these unrealistic expectations, the group members may become angry and lash out at the leader. Hostility toward the leader may take the form of explicit attacks on the leader's character, competence, or methods. Members may call into question the leader's dedication to students as well as the overall purpose and utility of the group. More passive members may resort to silence in the group or may engage in discussions about the leader with other members outside of the group setting (e.g., in the hallways, during other school events).

Aggression toward the leader may come disguised as a challenge or overtly as an attack. An attack typically reflects a judgment about the group leader's character (e.g., "You are insensitive and uncaring") and leaves no room for discussion. A challenge, on the other hand, opens the door for discussion. It reflects a willingness on the part of the challenger to own his feelings. The member who says, "I am nervous about coming to the group each week because I am afraid that you will allow other group members to attack me," is questioning the leader's behavior rather than attacking the leader's character and opens the door for more dialogue. Young children can also challenge the leader by doing such things as ignoring the leader's requests that the group get quiet, talking back, and acting out. Challenges reflect students' growing sense of autonomy and independence and a testing of boundaries. Attacks may be indicative of more rebellion to come, particularly if they are not handled skillfully by the leader (Billow, 2003). Recommendations for handling these issues will be discussed later in this chapter.

Certainly, not all group members will attack the leader. Some will rally to the leader's defense. Yalom and Leszcz (2005) suggested that who lines up as "attackers" and "defenders" provides good information about the core issues of each member. Challenges or attacks on the leader generally subside as reality sets in and the members begin to recognize the leader's role and limitations.

HOSTILITY TOWARD OTHER GROUP MEMBERS   As students come to the realization that they are not the favorite child and that they do not have a special alliance with the leader, feelings of rivalry toward other members may emerge. The very nature of the group setting, as mentioned above, fosters frustration and aggression. As members try to make room for themselves in an environment with limited time, space, and attention, they are likely to hurt the feelings of others (Ormont, 1984). Some of the behaviors that may elicit negative reactions in other group members and that reflect the struggle for control in the group include the following:

- *Engaging in excessive storytelling or dominating the group by always turning the discussion back on oneself.* This behavior gives the student control in the group and protects the student from being confronted by other group members, who cannot get a word in edgewise.
- *Making comments that are off topic.* This behavior may be an attempt to change the subject, or it may simply be an indication of the difficulty the student has in following the thread of the discussion. Either way, it can be irritating for other group members and may be an impetus for conflict.
- *Abdicating responsibility.* Some members of the group may be more submissive in how they handle life events. This tendency will emerge in the way they talk about themselves or handle group events. Other group members may see this as "weak" or "victimlike"; they may become frustrated by the lack of personal responsibility for change.
- *Giving advice or rescuing.* These behaviors tend to keep the discussion in a "fix it" mode and may inhibit deeper exploration of feelings. Occasional advice giving is a typical reaction to the pain of others. However, when this behavior dominates, it may indicate a need to be in a "power" position or a tendency to avoid deeper work.
- *Always having to have the last word or assuming a position of moral authority.* This behavior tends to generate negative reactions in group members even if they agree with the student's position (Trotzer, 1999).
- *Withdrawing from the group and appearing aloof.* This behavior needs to be distinguished from the supportive silence that gives individuals time to think and the silence that is related to cultural factors. Obvious indicators of withdrawal are physical distance from the group, body language such as rolling one's eyes or crossing one's arms, and criticism of the process.
- *Using humor or sarcasm to deflect attention from difficult topics.* Initially, this behavior is welcomed by group members, as it takes the pressure off of them to do serious work in the group. Over time, however, the jokes may begin to wear on group members who begin to see it for what it is.

Reactions to these behaviors may be flagrant or subtle, and they reflect the interpersonal and intrapersonal issues of the individual group members. Some may lash out verbally at group members or resort to character attacks such as "You think you are the most important person on the planet." Others, perhaps frustrated by the student who monopolizes the conversation, for instance, may not have the courage or the skills necessary to express their feelings or aggressive thoughts. Instead, they may use nonverbal behaviors such as crossing their arms, fidgeting, and looking at a watch to indicate their annoyance.

Just as the group members may "gang up" on the leader, they may unconsciously collude to attack a particular member of the group. This is referred to as scapegoating. The scapegoat may be an innocent victim, but more often, it is someone who provokes attack by specific behaviors in the group (Clark, 2002). Yalom and Leszcz (2005) suggested that this phenomenon often occurs when the group leader cannot be openly criticized for some reason. Attacking a peer is less threatening than attacking the leader. Clark (2002) suggested that the phenomenon of scapegoating reflects the displacement of intolerable feelings for another person or the projection of personal characteristics that are perceived to be intolerable or offensive to others. By turning the focus on one target, the group members exert some control over the content of the session and avoid the work of exploring their own feelings.

Resistance to Intimacy

Closely related to the struggle for control is resistance to both interpersonal and intrapersonal intimacy. As group members seek out their place in the group, they are also establishing personal boundaries around how much they will divulge about themselves and how willing they are to explore their own feelings. Members may be particularly sensitive about those feelings that are ordinarily socially unacceptable (e.g., anger) or indicative of weakness. Therefore, many of the behaviors listed above reflect not only the power drive but also the mechanisms members use to protect themselves against the anxiety inherent in genuinely connecting with others and delving into painful or difficult feelings.

Resistant behaviors can be indicative of an inability or unwillingness to commit to the group process. Ohlsen (1970) suggested that this lack of commitment in any form should be discouraged. Because resistant students have less investment in the group process, they are more likely to break confidentiality, engage in disruptive behavior within the group, and resist moving beyond superficial topics. However, leaders should be careful not to assume that resistant behaviors are always reflective of intrapersonal issues. Resistant behaviors can also be indicators that something is not working in the group. If group events have been handled ineffectively by the group leader, for instance, group members may rightfully be resistant to opening up and making themselves vulnerable. The group does not feel safe.

It is important to note here that expressions of frustration and anger and avoidance of intimacy in the group are not necessarily problem behaviors. They are a natural part of the process of becoming more genuine and authentic. Labeling group members as resistant or the Intellectualizer or Advice Giver only reinforces stereotyping and character attacks, even if these labels are never actually spoken in the group.

HANDLING TRANSITION ISSUES: IMPLICATIONS FOR LEADERS

The overarching objective for a leader during the transition stage is to establish a group environment that supports student goals and involves members in this interpersonal learning process. Working through transitional forces, however, can be challenging. Because of the self-perpetuating nature of the interpersonal and intrapersonal phenomena that occur during the transition stage, if they are not dealt with appropriately, the group risks being harmed by these forces. For example, underlying resistance to the group can lead to a negative perception of the group experience. A negative perception of the group experience can reinforce resistance and aversion to participation. Conversely, if these forces are addressed skillfully, the group moves to a place of greater cohesion, intimacy, and growth and is ready to begin the working stage.

Handling transition dynamics is therefore a key task for group leaders. The overt conflict and resistance can be extremely challenging to a leader's sense of accomplishment and sense of self if not viewed as a natural part of the process. Trotzer (1999) reminded group leaders that a common factor among group members is a "deep and sincere desire for success" (p. 206) and that this simply gets covered by the defensive reactions members have to the now group environment. Conflict in the group is the very material necessary for personal growth and change and for the cultivation of intimacy.

The work of the leader then is to bring these student defenses into play and work to resolve underlying anxieties. The goal is to increase members' tolerance for anxiety so that they can let go of maladaptive defensive behaviors and become more accepting of themselves—fears and all (McClure, 1998). Yalom and Leszcz (2005) encouraged group leaders to "plunge the members into the source of the resistance—in other words, not *around* anxiety, but *through* it" (p. 196). Billow (2003) suggested that after a group has survived the inevitable rebellion and "defenses are sufficiently undone and frustration is contained, the group may move away from authority and dependency preoccupation to phases involved with intimacy and self-affirmation" (p. 334).

Seen in this light, transition issues become an exciting opportunity rather than an intimidating obstacle for group leaders. The next section outlines some common mistakes that leaders make during the transition period and provides an overview of key topics that leaders need to keep in mind to work successfully with transition issues.

Common Leader Traps

Working with transition dynamics is challenging even for experienced leaders. Leaders often do not know what to say or where to respond amidst a variety of potential issues. Edelwich and Brodsky (1992) outlined four common traps that leaders fall into when trying to handle transition issues, particularly issues around resistance: doing individual counseling with one group member, justifying the group, inducing guilt in order to gain compliance, and generalizing the feelings of one member to the whole group.

FOCUSING ON ONE MEMBER ONLY   A common tendency among leaders is to lapse into individual counseling in a group setting. For instance, when a student states that he does not want to participate in the group because he feels uncomfortable, the probing leader might ask the member to explain more about his feelings. Certainly, this is an important step in uncovering emotions and defense mechanisms. However, the goal of group work is to cultivate the capacity of the group to be self-sustaining and autonomous. Complete reliance on the leader to guide the discussion and handle uncomfortable feelings leads to lack of creativity and stagnation (Connors & Caple, 2005).

JUSTIFYING THE GROUP   Hearing negative comments about the group or the process can easily lead to defensive internal reactions in leaders. Reacting defensively, however, by rushing to explain the benefits of the group does little to increase the motivation of the individual to stay in the group or to participate fully. For instance, explaining all the potential benefits of group participation to a member who has just disclosed that the group does not have anything to offer him only sets up a power struggle. Edelwich and Brodsky (1992) argued that it is not the leader's responsibility to keep the group member in the group. A more empowering approach is to put the responsibility for making the group useful in the hands of the group member. The leader might say, "We have discussed previously that you are making a choice to come to this group—even those of you who were recommended to the group by someone else. I do care if you stay or go, but that is your choice. Since you are here, you can also make a choice to use this time to your benefit. I'm wondering how you might use the group time today to get something out of it?"

INDUCING GUILT   Another defensive reaction that leaders sometimes lapse into is responding judgmentally to a group member's rebellion. A leader might, for instance, accuse a group member of not caring about other group members or might suggest that the member's actions reflect a lack of concern for the individual's family. The leader might say, "Don't you care about how your teacher would feel if you dropped out?" Clearly, this type of defensive reaction only perpetuates anxiety, fear, and mistrust of the group process among all group members.

GENERALIZING FEELINGS OF ONE MEMBER TO THE GROUP   In an attempt to bring the group into the discussion of a topic raised by one group member, leaders sometimes fall into the trap of generalizing the feelings of that one member to the group as a whole. Leaders might say such things as "I sense a lot of people are frustrated with my leadership style." Rather than encouraging true dialogue among members about an issue, this approach is likely to elicit feedback designed to "pump up" what appears to be a demoralized leader. At worse, it may become a self-fulfilling prophecy.

CASE STUDY 8.1

David

In the following scenario, explore how you would conceptualize David's core anxieties around group participation and what you would do to work with him in the group.

David, a Caucasian elementary school student, is a member of your group for children experiencing divorce. David, who has typically been an average student with no behavioral problems, has been missing classes, and his grades are slipping. In your preliminary meeting with him, you learn that his mother moved out of the home four months ago to live with her boyfriend in another town. David and his younger brother are living with their father, who works full-time. After school, David is responsible for caring for his younger brother and beginning dinner. David talks very angrily about his mother and states that he hopes he never has to see her again. Other than negative comments about his mother, David doesn't talk much about the rest of his life. He answers questions with a shrug or "I don't know." David has been in trouble in school recently for getting into fights during lunch or recess with other students.

In the group, David has a difficult time sharing about his parents' divorce. He is often silent in the group, and his body language indicates that he is not interested in participating. He has started arriving late to group. You suspect that David's behaviors reflect feelings of discouragement and helplessness. You also recognize that other group members are getting irritated with his behavior and his tardiness.

What core needs is David having difficulty with in fulfilling in his life?

How would you conceptualize David's situation?

How will you handle the growing tension?

Focal Points for Handling Transition

Although some group leaders may fall into the traps listed above from time to time, these traps can also become opportunities for working with conflict in the group. This section outlines specific areas that leaders need to be cognizant of when working with transition issues

PAY ATTENTION TO DEVELOPMENTAL LEVEL   When working in a school setting, it is critical that counselors take into account the developmental level of the student. Young children in the early years of elementary school require very different interventions than do students in middle school. Likewise, middle school students require different approaches than do high school students. In fact, approaches that may be helpful with adolescents may be ineffective or even harmful with young children or preteens (Newsome & Gladding, 2007; Vernon, 2004). Although developmental characteristics must be kept in mind when tailoring an intervention for transition issues, there are some fundamental practices that cut across all developmental levels. These are presented next.

REINFORCE CONFIDENTIALITY   In a school setting, the boundaries of the group are often blurred. Participants will generally see each other in many other school situations (e.g., cafeteria, classrooms, halls). During transition periods in groups, emotions run high, and participants may be tempted to talk to each other or to other students or adults who are not in the group about events that take place within the group. Adolescents, in particular, are often acutely concerned with issues of confidentiality (Newsome & Gladding, 2007). It is important that leaders consistently reinforce the expectations of confidentiality beyond the initial group meeting. How confidentiality is discussed will vary based on the age of the group participants. With young students, the leader can use puppets or role plays to help illustrate issues of confidentiality, or the leader might say something like "In this group, we keep what happens in this group private. That means that if Shawndra says something or does something in the group, we don't talk about it out in the hall or on the playground or in your classroom. If something that happened here hurts your feelings or makes you uncomfortable, you can let me know."

COMMUNICATION IS KEY   Communication is the key to adequately dealing with conflicts as they arise. The expectation of honest and genuine communication needs to repeatedly be made explicit, starting from the earliest planning stages of the group. Edelwich and Brodsky (1992) suggested that group leaders emphasize the importance of honest communication in the group by saying, "There is no issue so sensitive that we cannot talk about it in this group." With younger students, the leader can set the stage for open communication by saying, "In this group, we will try to be honest about how we are feeling. That means that if you are feeling sad, you can say, 'I'm feeling sad today.'" Setting the stage in this way opens the door to allow members to voice their frustrations and irritations. Leaders can also prepare members for the inevitable letdown that can occur as members move from the initial excitement and bonding of early group sessions to the hard work of sharing. By being explicit about what this might look like and emphasizing the importance of discussing this shift when it occurs, leaders lay the groundwork for changes to come (Jacobs, Masson, & Harvill, 2006).

Setting an expectation of communication early sets the stage for productive work in the group rather than stagnation. For instance, in their classic work on focal conflict theory, Whitaker and Lieberman (1964) suggested that conflict in groups is dealt with in one of two ways: restrictive solutions or enabling solutions. Restrictive solutions reflect an avoidance of the conflict. Group members' anxiety is lowered because the issue is ignored. This is illustrated by such behaviors as changing the subject and engaging in storytelling. Enabling solutions are associated with confronting underlying fears and may temporarily increase the anxiety of group members. However, if the solution is successful, tolerance for anxiety will increase, and the group will become more cohesive.

For students of all ages, it is important that expectations about group participation be discussed prior to the start of the group. In screening interviews, the leader can assess what areas might be difficult for the student. For example, a student may have a passive approach to life and could be expected to be quiet in the group. Having a one-on-one discussion prior to the start of the group about the expectation of participation and the issues that may be keeping a student from participating can clarify for the leader what may be happening with the student in the group. It also gives the leader some fodder for encouraging the student to participate in the group without pushing the student to participate (Greenberg, 2003). How these expectations are communicated, of course, depends on the developmental level of the student. Leaders can also use the group itself to develop norms about participation.

Take, for example, Sarah, who is afraid that if she voices her opinion, the group will judge her as stupid or incompetent and reject her. She takes a risk and verbalizes this fear. Rather than being rejected as incompetent, Sarah receives the support of the group. Her willingness to be open about her fears prompts others in the group to share some of their fears as well.

Many times students simply have not learned how to effectively communicate. Research shows that specific instruction in the form of relevant information at critical moments in the group's development is helpful (Morran, Stockton, Cline, & Teed, 1998). It is incumbent on the leader to model effective communication and perhaps even provide more concrete education about what effective communication looks like. Modeling the use of I-statements, for instance, can set the tone for the ownership of feelings and the expression of those feelings. For example, during an uncomfortable silence following some act of rebellion, a leader might say, "We've just sat in silence for a full minute. I know I am feeling uncomfortable and at a loss for words. Does anyone else share my feelings?" Similarly, Edelwich and Brodsky (1992) suggested that the leader can use self-disclosure to address group members' fears. A leader might say, "When I first started working in groups, I was afraid to say anything very close to my heart for fear I would lose control and become emotional in the group. I wasn't sure I could handle that. Who else has had that experience?" Opening the door to discussion about sensitive issues can be followed with this: "When I don't speak up about something that concerns me, it's because I'm afraid I won't be accepted or may sound stupid or because I'm afraid of expressing myself about issues. That's why I've found I don't speak up in groups" (Edelwich & Brodsky, 1992, p. 47).

Members may be helped by concrete psychoeducation about effective communication. Topics might include the differences between a character attack and an expression of personal feelings, between being assertive and being passive (or passive-aggressive), and between feeling and thinking. The author has found it effective to provide group members with lists of feeling words so they have a vocabulary with which to work.

In time, group members begin to realize that voicing their fears actually helps them deal with core interpersonal issues. Through this process of conflict, communication, and resolution, the group begins to become more comfortable with the uncomfortable. Yalom and Leszcz (2005) referred to this as "unfreezing" habitual ways of being and relating to others.

PROCESS THE PROCESS   A common mistake made by group leaders is to become so involved in the content of a group session that the process is neglected. The *Association for Specialists in Group Work (ASGW) Best Practice Guidelines* (ASGW, 2007) suggest that effective group leaders process the workings of the group by attending to the session dynamics. This could not be more important than in the transition stage, when interpersonal and intrapersonal dynamics are running high. Stockton, Morran, and Nitza (2000) defined processing as "capitalizing on significant happenings in the here-and-now interactions of the group to help members reflect on the meaning of their experience; better understand their own thoughts, feelings, and actions; and generalize what is learned to their life outside the group" (p. 345).

Processing therefore includes not only "first tier" descriptions of the ongoing group experience but also "second tier" reflection and extraction of meaning from those experiences (Ward & Litchy, 2004; Yalom & Leszcz, 2005). The leader must help the group members make cognitive sense of what is happening. When used effectively, here-and-now processing serves as a catalyst to deepen interaction among group members and move members toward their personal goals. The object is to shift the discussion from "outside to inside, from the abstract to the specific, from the generic to the personal, from the personal to the interpersonal" (Yalom & Leszcz, 2005, p. 158).

The leader is in a unique position when it comes to here-and-now processing. When group members comment on the process for defensive reasons (e.g., to take themselves out of the client role), they set themselves apart from the other members and may become the target of rage. "Who is he to think he is better than us?" As the observer–participant, the leader has the responsibility of providing objective comments about the cyclical patterns in the group and tying individual goals back into the unfolding of group events. This is not to say that members should never make process comments, particularly as they relate to themselves. In fact, members' learning to observe the process can be an important outcome of group work.

Process statements can be either general or more directive. Ormont (1984) suggested that leaders can encourage group members to think in terms of the group and address the holistic nature of the group by asking such questions as "How is the group operating right now?" and "How is what's happening affecting the feeling of the group?" For elementary-aged students, however, this type of abstract thinking may not be possible. Instead, the leader can ask more direct, concrete questions such as "Emma, you have your arms crossed, and I'm wondering why. Are you angry?"

Yalom and Leszcz (2005) suggested that a more directive approach is often well received by group members. For example, a leader sensing guardedness or withdrawal in the group might say, "We've done a lot of work here today. I sense, however, that something more is going on beneath the surface. I suspect that everyone here has been trying to size up the other group members. Let's take the remainder of the group time to share what we've come up with so far." A less threatening approach—though still directive—is to focus on internal experiences in the group and how those manifest: "Everyone here is coming to this group with very personal goals and hopes for success that require opening up and being vulnerable. I know that I tend to close up when I feel threatened. I wonder if we could spend some time talking about what each of us is likely to do in this group when we feel threatened or unsafe."

Several models exist for helping leaders process group dynamics. These include Conyne, Rapin, and Rand's (1997) "grid for processing experiences in group," Glass and Benshoff's (1999) PARS model, Stockton et al.'s (2000) cognitive map, and Yalom's (Yalom & Leszcz, 2005) two-tiered processing model. Although each model has a slightly different approach to organizing and making sense of the ongoing group experience, all of the models have a common focus on bringing attention to the "what" and "how" of critical incidents in the group, illuminating member reactions, and helping members derive meaning that can be applied outside the group.

CASE STUDY 8.2

Michael

In the following scenario, explore how you would conceptualize Michael's core anxieties around group participation and what you would do to work with him in the group.

On the first day of group, Michael, a middle school student, begins to joke with you before group begins about how counselors only repeat back what is said. He states that he doesn't really believe in counseling and cites a quote from a website about the efficacy of computerized counselors versus "live" counselors to make his case. You let the comment drop for the time being and soon see similar behaviors appearing in the group sessions. Michael continues to remain distant from other group members by joking to deflect attention. Recently, he has begun to enlist other male members of the group in making fun of you and the process as a whole. You realize that there are a number of members in the group who are getting something out of the process, and you fear that if Michael's behavior continues, they will begin to question why they are there.

What core anxiety is Michael displaying?

What aspects of Michael's behavior warrant attention?

How will you enlist the group to work through this resistance?

TIMING COUNTS   Although communication and process orientation are critical for effective work during transition, this must be balanced with proper timing. Asking groups to do work that they are not yet ready to do may backfire, resulting in increased anxiety, frustration, and aggression (Agazarian & Gantt, 2003). It is important to remember that defenses are in place for a reason and to respect these reasons. Penetrating students' defenses too early will not lead to permanent change. Readiness for change involves the ability to discriminate information within the system (Agazarian & Gantt, 2003). If participants are confronted with too much information, the system will be flooded and will falter.

Aspects to keep in mind when deciding whether to focus on a critical incident in the group include the impact the focus will have on the group as a whole, the psychological ability and willingness of the group members to handle the topic, and cultural factors that may influence behavior in the group. For instance, ordinarily it is not worth engaging highly defensive individuals who are attacking other members in an exploration of their underlying causes. It may, however, be worth exploring the impact of the attacking behavior on other group members. It may also be beneficial to wait until a defensive method has played out on several members of the group. Pointing out similarities allows students to see their own defenses in others and reduces embarrassment or shame.

Stockton et al. (2000) suggested some types of events that are worth in-depth examination, although they stress that ultimately the decision is based on the leader's judgment and the empathic understanding of group members. These events include the following:

- Events that evoke heightened emotional or behavioral reactions,
- Events that reflect a recurring pattern,
- Events that directly relate to goals,
- Explicit hostility or conflict in the group,

- Emotional self-disclosures, and
- Body language suggestive of unspoken reactions.

BALANCING CLOSENESS AND DISTANCE   As mentioned above, rebellion against the leader is an important factor in group formation and process. As group members band together in this rebellion process, they not only become more cohesive but also take on more responsibility for the group experience itself. As Vella (1999) said, "Independence cannot be granted by Authority, but must be wrested from it" (p. 17). Therefore, in relating to the group members, the leader must be cognizant of balancing closeness and distance. If the leader is too distant, aggressive feelings dominate the group, and the group may become stuck in rebellion. On the other hand, if the leader is too friendly, no resistance is necessary, and group formation takes longer.

Related to balancing closeness and distance are learning to trust the group process and releasing the reins. This does not mean that the leader is passive. Rather, the leader uses the dynamics of the group to guide from within. For example, this strategy could be used when working with a student who constantly criticizes other group members in the name of "just being honest" but crumbles when the group members retaliate. As the student's school counselor, the leader knows that this is a pattern that is repeated outside the group when the student is in class or in other social settings. The leader recognizes that the member needs to take responsibility for her actions but that, at least initially, she will need support in order to withstand the building anger of the group. Taking on the role of the group member's supporter, the leader can provide comfort anytime another member speaks harshly toward her. This may free other group members to voice their aggression because they know that the leader will support the offending group participant.

CULTIVATE SELF-AWARENESS   Perhaps the most difficult aspect of the transition stage is the impact it can have on the leader's self-esteem if the dynamics are taken personally. It is vitally important that leaders be aware of their own defense mechanisms and underlying anxieties, as these may be triggered when conflict arises (Ward & Litchy, 2004). The leader needs to get comfortable with personal insecurities and "dark sides" in order to help others do the same. Self-awareness also includes the awareness of one's limitations as a group leader. Glass and Benshoff (1999) warned that leaders must have a strong understanding of group dynamics in order to work effectively in here-and-now events within the group.

CASE STUDY 8.3

Kristen

In the following scenario, explore how you would conceptualize Kristen's core anxieties around group participation and what you would do to work with her in the group.

Kristen is a 16-year-old high school sophomore who was referred to counseling for issues of extreme disrespect and impulsive behavior. In the initial interview, you learn that Kristen has a history of self-cutting and had been sexually abused by her mother's boyfriend when she was in elementary school. For the past five years, she has been living with her father and stepmother, and she has very little contact with her mother. At her stepmother's encouragement, Kristen has started working part-time at the local pizza restaurant, where she has met a number of high school males with whom she has engaged in sex.

Kristen has a lot of anger toward her mother as well as her father and stepmother. She believes that her stepmother just wants her to "grow up" and get out of the house and that her father never stands up for her. She states that her stepmother is constantly calling her a "liar," and she admits that she often does lie, particularly about her sexual encounters, to keep the peace. Despite this "goal" of keeping the peace, Kristen often ends up in shouting matches with her stepmother and runs to her bedroom or even out of the house. She states that she never knows what kind of mood her stepmother is going to be in and therefore feels on guard all the time. In the past year, she has become increasingly angry and has developed a reputation at school for being sexually "loose" and emotionally volatile.

You decide that in addition to some individual and family work, Kristen will benefit from a more structured psychoeducational group based on Dialectical Behavior Therapy (DBT). During the past three group sessions, Kristen has regaled the group with a never-ending stream of hardships and obstacles. When group members suggest that she try some DBT skills to help her cope, she shrugs this off as impossible. Her standard line is "I tried that already, and it doesn't work." Finally, Sam, who has previously remained quiet, bursts forth with a stream of criticisms toward Kristen and you. He charges that you should never have allowed her to go on like this. "It is unproductive and boring."

What are the core anxieties being expressed?

What is your highest priority here?

How can you bring the other group members into the conflict?

Summary

Change is challenging. For some, the fear of change can make it nearly impossible to move out of a comfort zone. Students in groups come face to face with the need for change and their concomitant anxieties and fears. Developmental and systemic theorists propose that the dynamics of control, conflict, and resistance that appear in the transition stage are important steps in the process of change and growth. Like rebellious teenagers testing their wings, members in transition-stage groups are testing the group's ability, and their own abilities, to survive the strain of their real selves. It is up to the group leader to help individuals in the group see how they are resistant to change and how their natural defenses against those things that are fearful and anxiety provoking alienate them from others and cheat them out of the fullness of life.

CHAPTER 9

The Working Stage

KEVIN A. FALL, H. GEORGE MCMAHON, AND
DANICA G. HAYS

PREVIEW

For as long as groups have been studied, researchers have noted the time in the life of the group when members actively and freely work on group and personal goals, honestly share aspects of self, courageously give feedback, and feel a sense of "we-ness," all of which enable members to truly believe in the process of group like never before. This chapter provides an overview of the working stage of group work with emphasis on student and leader functions during this important stage of the group process. Additionally, components of this stage related to group foundation and design are discussed to illustrate indicators for optimal working-stage process.

OVERVIEW AND ELEMENTS OF THE WORKING STAGE

"So this is the moment I've been waiting for?" This quote, uttered by a counseling intern as she was leading her first "real" group, captures the sense of awe and relief felt by leaders and members as they begin to experience the benefits of the working stage of group. As a group successfully navigates its way through the conflicts, role confusion, and general tension that characterize the transition stage, it begins to enter into the working stage. The working stage occurs when group members address the purpose of the group and focus their energies on meeting the individual and group goals articulated during the planning phase and the forming and orienting stage. Although group workers have used a variety of terms to describe the stage where the group goals are accomplished—including the performing (Tuckman & Jensen, 1977), action (George & Dustin, 1988), commitment (Berg, Landreth, & Fall, 2006), and middle (Jacobs, Masson, & Harvill, 2006) stage—they all describe this working stage as the time when the most significant accomplishments are realized by group members. Ideally, the working stage will last longer than any other group stage. More important than the amount of time spent in the working stage, however, is what is accomplished during that time. The working stage is where members are expected to derive maximum benefit as they strive to meet group goals and work toward increased personal effectiveness (Berg et al., 2006). In many ways, the previous stages are an investment of time and energy to fully prepare members to do the dif-ficult work of the group. Thus, the forming/orienting and transition stages are certainly crucial to the success of the group because they help to prepare the group for success. That success, however, is realized in the working stage.

The working stage is distinct from the previous stages in several important ways. First, with the struggles for power and positioning within the group resolved, or at least well in hand, the group members fall into a "comfort zone" where each student understands and per-haps even embraces the direction of the group and his or her role in the group. Thus, the time and energy previously spent negotiating internal conflicts are redirected toward fulfilling the purpose of the group, with a more unified and cohesive group ready to "get to work." While usually far from a utopian environment, the working stage is typically characterized by certain dynamics expected to be present in the group, such as group cohesion, trust, open communication, teamwork, and a motivation to succeed. To a large degree, those character-istics are a direct result of the resolution of the conflicts caused by tension during the transi-tion stage. A group that successfully manages the power struggles and role conflicts of the transition stage will develop a certain cohesiveness, where members identify with one another, understand their roles, and share a collective vision of the group and the direction it is heading toward. Part of this cohesion is a deep sense of genuine caring that students develop for each other individually and for the group as a collective entity. A sense of trust in each other and in the group process is also present at the working stage, often a result of members negotiat-ing conflicts during the transition stage with respect and honest communication.

Cohesion is such an important aspect of the working stage that it deserves some spe-cial attention before we move on. Cohesion is not something that "happens" in the working stage but has been developing from the first moment that the group formed. Cohesion is the beneficial outcome of the members' struggling to know one another and find their collective place in the group matrix. It is a fluid element, meaning that it increases when the group participates in those activities associated with cohesion (e.g., sharing, trust building, listen-ing, attendance, constructive feedback) and decreases when the group participates in activi-ties that run counter to its formation (e.g., superficial talk, sarcasm, breaking group norms as set by the group).

Often in the preworking- and beginning working-stage moments, leaders can perceive evidence of cohesion as group attendance becomes steady, as if a group norm has been set that "you miss a lot of good stuff when you don't come to group." Group members also speak directly to each other and rely less on the group leader. As the felt sense of cohesion solidifies, the group members notice a difference, even if they cannot put their fingers on it. For example, it is common to hear group members say, after a strenuous group session, "this is starting to feel like a nice place to be" or "things felt different today."

As the group members become more cohesive, with trust and genuine caring present among students, the group is able to take its attention away from preparation and focus more on action. This orientation toward achievement and accomplishment of goals is a very important component of the working stage. Without it, group members may feel very close to each other and enjoy pleasant group sessions, but they may not be growing or experienc-ing anything therapeutic. Once fully prepared and encouraged—armed with a connection to the group, a sense of purpose, and a feeling of safety that comes from the support of the group—members are motivated to accomplish their goals.

But it is a mistake to characterize the working stage as some perfect environment in which everyone is pulling seamlessly in the same direction and everything is perfectly aligned. Indeed, the working stage still presents leaders and members with plenty of challenges, not to mention that leader and member missteps can lead the group in unanticipated directions or backward into renewed conflict and anxiety. Thus, the leader needs to be vigilant for potential pitfalls, skillful in the implementation of techniques, and mindful of the critical role that group process and dynamics play within successful groups.

The preceding was a brief introduction to the working stage, providing both a definition and a quick sketch of the characteristics that are typical of the working stage. The next section will more fully explore the working stage, specifically presenting the goals of the working stage, the role members are expected to play in the working stage, and the leader's role in the working stage. In addition, the theoretical and conceptual framework often presented in group textbooks will be contrasted with a more realistic, practical view of the development of the working stage from the leader's perspective.

GOALS OF THE WORKING STAGE

There are certain outcomes that leaders expect to accomplish during the working stage. First and foremost, the primary outcome for the working stage is for group members to meet the individual and group goals identified during the planning phase and the forming and orienting stage of the group. For the majority of groups conducted in schools, the ultimate goal of the group will be related to some academic, career, or personal-social success outcome (American School Counselor Association [ASCA], 2005; Carey, Dimmitt, Kosine, & Poynton, 2005). In response to the increased focus on accountability in education, all educators, including school counselors, are expected to demonstrate how their interventions promote student success (ASCA, 2005; House & Hayes, 2002; Paisley & McMahon, 2001). This renewed focus on student success has led to a common misconception among many school counselors that all school groups must have an academic focus. This is not true. The group outcomes may need to be connected to student success, but that does not mean the content of the group needs to be solely academic. Although study skills groups and the like are important parts of a school counselor's repertoire, groups focusing on personal and social issues can also lead to positive student outcomes (e.g., Campbell & Brigman, 2005; Tobias & Myrick, 1999).

To clarify this confusion, Brown and Trusty (2005) conceptualized groups in schools as having both proximal and distal outcomes. Proximal outcomes are the immediate desired outcomes: the stated goals of the group. Developing new skills for studying, increasing one's sense of belonging in the school, improving friendships, and developing coping strategies are all examples of proximal outcomes. Distal outcomes are the eventual outcomes that the proximal outcomes will lead to. For instance, improving study skills should lead to higher grades, developing coping strategies may lead to fewer discipline referrals, and increased school belonging may lead to higher graduation rates. Therefore, while virtually all school groups should have a distal outcome that is related to some measure of student success, it may have a proximal outcome that is more personal, social, or career issues. When talking about the goals of the working stage, one is referring to the proximal goals of the group. When evaluating the ultimate success of school-based groups, however, it will be important to evaluate both the proximal and the distal (student success) outcomes.

The goals of the working stage should be measurable so that students know when they have met their goals. Although this is certainly ideal and worth striving for, developing measurable goals is more difficult in certain groups, and this is also true with some student groups. A school attendance group will have an easily identifiable goal: improving attendance rates.

A group for children of divorce, however, may have a more nebulous goal of "coping better with my parents' divorce." In this case, it may be helpful for group leaders to define specific objectives for the group. Objectives for a divorce group may be (1) understanding that children are not to blame, (2) identifying social supports, and (3) developing strategies for staying out of parental conflict. These objectives will be more easily measurable than the overarching goal of "coping with my parents' divorce."

Alternatively, leaders may ask members to operationalize their own goals so that they can be easily measured, and this certainly can help members to know when their goals have been met and to more easily identify the strides made during the working stage. There are developmental concerns with this strategy when leading groups in schools, however. First, younger students may not be able to identify and select relevant goals. In fact, particularly with younger students, they may have been referred to a group by a parent or a teacher without having a complete understanding of why they were referred and what they need to be working on.

In addition to meeting the individual and group goals, there are several other important aspects of a well-functioning working stage of which group leaders should be aware. For instance, during the working stage, group members should develop an appreciation for being a part of a well-functioning group. The hope is that group members will develop an understanding of both *what* was accomplished and *how* it was achieved. Several writers (e.g., Klein, 2001) have discussed the importance of teamwork to the ultimate success of the group, offering evidence that the act of being committed to and actively participating in a productive team is therapeutic in and of itself (Maples, 1992). This feeling of accomplishment arises not just from meeting goals but also from meeting goals *together*. This can be particularly important for children and adolescents, for whom feeling connected to one's peer group is essential (Berg et al., 2006). Group members can experience satisfaction from knowing they trusted and depended on their peers in their journey and that the personal and interpersonal risks they took were crucial to their success. Moreover, knowing that their peers were able to trust and depend on them can improve students' sense of relational self-efficacy. Whatever the specific goals of the group, the effect of being a part of a unified group that has met and overcome challenges on the way to accomplishing goals can have a great impact on the members, particularly on students who may not have had successful experiences working together with their peers.

Another salient group goal of the working stage is the development of group members' social awareness through their interactions with the group. Research has demonstrated that group counseling and psychotherapy provide certain therapeutic factors that are not prominent in individual counseling, including interpersonal learning, altruism, and family reenactment (Fuhriman & Burlingame, 1990), and that the primary vehicle for such therapeutic change in group settings is the relationships formed within the group (Holmes & Kivlighan, 2000). As group members progress through the working stage, they become more self-reflective, become better able to take an in-depth inventory of themselves, and further develop an understanding of themselves and their ability to function in a social context. In this way, the group members begin to take advantage of the social microcosm provided by the group, using the group as a "social lab" in which to practice new behaviors, role-play new identities, and learn more about themselves through feedback in a safe and respectful environment (Yalom & Leszcz, 2005). This is a particularly important aspect of group work with adolescents, for whom social and interpersonal development plays such a prominent role.

Furthermore, when group members experience genuine feedback about specific behaviors in an environment that is characterized by accurate empathy, trust, and genuine concern, they may be able to distinguish between their behavior and their sense of self, perhaps for the first time (Yalom & Leszcz, 2005). This can enable members to receive feedback on their social interactions without having that feedback shatter or provide a foundation for their entire self-concept. Given their trust in the group and their ability to separate their behavior from their self-concept, members may no longer feel the need to protect themselves from honest feedback. Instead, they can use that feedback to deepen their awareness and, if desired, alter their social behavior.

The group as a reality testing lab has special importance in a school setting. Unlike in groups run by community agencies, where it is rare to know anyone in the group, members of groups in schools may have preexisting relationships. These relationships carry over into the group but should not be seen as static, although some members will want to keep the status quo. Instead, their existence should result in excellent feedback and provide a catalyst for change. For example, in a second-grade friendship group, one boy, Nathan, was particularly shy. Not surprisingly, he was shy in the group. As the group's comfort increased, Nathan began to experiment with more active participation, first through feedback and then through sharing parts of his inner life. Although some group members were hesitant to see Nathan in a new way, as the group progressed to the working stage, the group was actively supporting Nathan's attempts at self-growth. In fact, group members routinely encouraged him to maintain his "in group" personality during the school day. Thus, the group members extended the reality testing lab of the group into real life and then used the group to process both experiences.

MEMBERS' ROLE IN THE WORKING STAGE

In the working stage, the role that the members play in the group can change dramatically. This change is largely a result of the members' developing a sense of identity with other members of the group and buying into the group's purpose and method. In many ways, "*the* group" becomes "*our* group" as the members take on more responsibility for the process of the group within each session and for the overall journey the group is making toward its goals. One of the ways students show the responsibility they have taken for the group is by playing a more active role in group discussions. Group members are likely to communicate directly with each other, rather than through the group leader. In addition, group members are more willing to start conversations, more able to add insights that take the conversations deeper, and more likely to identify important themes in the group's discussion. One group counselor trainee wrote about these dynamics in her leadership journal:

> The group has begun to "take over" the group. It's like they have incorporated my way of leading the group and have started doing it for themselves. For example, today in group, instead of starting the group by saying, "Let's begin today with a check-in. Who would like to start?", one of the group members said, "Well, let's do check-in. I guess I'll go first." The group then just took off. I don't think I said anything for about 15 minutes. I didn't even have to remind them to speak directly to one another. They were talking about trust and they moved deftly between relating trust issues they have had and are having in group (one member was confronted for being consistently late) and trust issues they have with others outside of the group.

Group members are also expected to take more risks in the working stage. Conflict has been experienced and processed in constructive ways in the preceding transition stage, and this sets the groundwork for the risk taking experienced in the working stage. Leaders may notice that members will appear to drop their facades and begin acting in a more authentic, genuine way within the group. This behavior can become contagious, as members who may be more reluctant to take risks can find courage in the successes of other members. Students may also practice new behaviors, first in the group itself and then in the "real world," in an attempt to discover a new way of being that is more effective and healthier. Members of a group in the working stage are also willing to ask for genuine feedback from other group members about their new strategies and are willing to give genuine and appropriate feedback to other members about their behavior.

Finally, group members will engage in appropriate self-disclosure in the working stage. Self-disclosure can be extremely beneficial for a group member as a way to help other members better understand the discloser, as a way to demonstrate empathy for another member, or simply as a cathartic experience. This appropriate self-disclosure is more than just talking about oneself; it is disclosing meaningful and relevant aspects of the individual's self that would previously have remained hidden. For the self-disclosure to be effective, it must be on topic, productive, and appropriate, given the group's stage and level of functioning. During the working stage, self-disclosure is often characterized by immediacy, relating to one's internal reactions to what is currently going on in group. For example:

LESTER: It's weird, but this whole group thing is uncomfortable. I'm not used to talking about feelings and stuff like that. It's weird because I feel like I don't want to talk, but I usually feel good after I do.

ANNA: When I listen to Alexis struggle with her issues, there is a part of me that understands, but another part is telling me to be quiet, to not share, because my problems seem so small compared to hers.

Both of these self-disclosure examples allow for the group to explore the deeper meanings of the feelings, at the group and the individual member levels. Lester's experience of discomfort with emotional vulnerability will be present in many children and adolescents. Instead of scaring group members with the warning that "emotions are uncomfortable," this disclosure at the working stage is an invitation to explore the universal vulnerability. Likewise, Anna's disclosure may produce anxiety in the earlier stages of group as members separate into "those with serious issues versus those who are normal" subgroups, but at the working stage, the flow is not interrupted, and discussion will go deeper into two probable areas: Anna's need to trivialize her issues and Alexis's genuine response to Anna's categorization of her personal struggles. During the working stage, members are expected to make these types of process disclosures without interrupting the flow; in fact, they are seen as enhancing the process.

As students' self-disclosures become more real and immediate, group members also take responsibility for the group by supporting other members' growth and development. Group members can help each other grow from the group experience in a variety of ways. First, by being able to demonstrate accurate empathy and a genuine concern for one another, students can encourage others to take the risks inherent in behavioral change or personal growth. By balancing this genuine concern with a willingness to challenge one another, students can help each other find the courage to take reasonable risks, knowing that, if they falter, the group will be there to make sure they don't fall too far. This will likely look very different from the way group members may have expressed care for one another earlier in the group, when members often attempt to protect or rescue members from difficult situations. Consider this example from a divorce group for seventh graders:

LUCY: It really doesn't matter anyway. It's not like I can do anything about my mom's decision to leave us. I don't even think I care anymore.

CHARLES: I think you do care; otherwise, you wouldn't be so mad.

LUCY: I'm not mad!!

PATTY: You sound mad to me. I think sometimes it's easier to pretend we don't care than admit we are hurt. I know that's how it is for me. I mean, my dad is gone. What's the use of being mad? He'll never know.

CHARLES: That's what is so crazy! Most of us are confused or hurt by our parents' breaking up, and yet we feel that we can't be honest about our feelings or that if we are, it won't matter anyway. That's screwed up.

LUCY: What do you mean "screwed up"?

CHARLES: I mean that we should do better than what most of our parents are doing. We should learn how to express ourselves openly.

COUNSELOR: It sounds like that is what you are all doing right now.

Here, the message that group members send each other changes from "I care about you so I'll protect you from difficult experiences" to "I care about you so I'll support you as you learn from these difficult experiences." In the working stage, members begin to take a much more active role in the process of their group. Capitalizing on the well-developed atmosphere of cohesion, group members more openly share and provide honest feedback to each other in an attempt to solve group and personal goals. As the group becomes more self-sufficient and self-monitoring, the leader is suddenly faced with this question: Now that the group is running like a well-oiled machine, what am I supposed to do? The next section outlines how leaders can make the most out of the working stage.

LEADER'S ROLE IN THE WORKING STAGE

Just as the members' roles begin to change as the working stage progresses, the leader's role must adapt as well. As the members take on greater responsibility for the group's functioning, the leader may become less directive, serving more as a process monitor and group facilitator. The following story from the *Tao of Pooh* (Hoff, 1982) illustrates the possible stance of the group leader during this stage:

At the Gorge of Lu, a great waterfall plunges for thousands of feet, its spray visible for miles. In the churning waters below, no living creature can be seen. One day K'ung Fu-tse [Confucius] was standing at a distance from the pool's edge, when he saw an old man being tossed about in the turbulent water. He called to his disciples, and together they ran to rescue the victim. But by the time they reached the water, the old man had climbed out onto the bank and was walking along, singing to himself. K'ung Fu-tse hurried up to him. "You would have to be a ghost to survive that," he said, "but you seem to be a man instead. What secret power do you have?" "Nothing special," the old man replied. "I began to learn while very young, and grew up practicing it. Now I am certain of success. I go down with the water and come up with the water. I follow it and forget myself. I survive because I don't struggle against the water's superior power. That's all." (pp. 68–69)

In this story, the old man can be a good symbol for the working-stage leader, and the river is the group. The story illustrates that the leader is not absent from the group but is a "part" of the process. By the time the group reaches the working stage, the group should have a way of running itself, and leaders often get into trouble when they try to force their will on the group instead of attending to the underlying process. When we hear group leaders talk about "problems with their group," it is often because they are blocking the forward momentum of the students, the mental image being the group leader as a dam in the river. Group leaders therefore must learn when to trust the group and when to intervene.

Although the leader should support the students' efforts to take more responsibility for the group's functioning, that does not mean that the leader should *give up* responsibility for the group. The members may take more of a hands-on approach regarding group discussion and processing, but it is still the leader's responsibility to lead the group. Ultimately, the leader is still responsible for the group's movement toward its final goals, even if the leader's role is not as obvious. In fact, the functions of the leader during this stage—balancing content and process, modeling behavior, encouraging introspection, and managing difficult situations—are vital to the ultimate success of the group.

Along these lines, the leaders of groups in the working stage must be on the lookout for difficult situations in which they may have to intervene. Even in a high-functioning group, situations can come up that can put the group at a risk of stagnating or regressing. This can be particularly true in school, where common events like students' experiencing disciplinary action, getting poor progress reports, or having fights with friends can carry over into the group setting. Such personal setbacks, particularly if related to the goals of the group, can discourage members, sapping their motivation to continue taking risks. Likewise, topics that are typically very emotional or sensitive for adolescents—such as issues regarding race, sexual orientation, or members' "status" in school—can leave members feeling defensive, attacked, or disillusioned. In times such as these, it is important for leaders to reassert themselves and be willing to manage the situation through open, genuine, and respectful communication.

Managing the situation does not mean that a leader should become authoritarian and "take over" the group, even if the students would prefer that at times. Take, for instance, an anger management group at a high school discussed in Case Study 9.1.

CASE STUDY 9.1
The Anger Management Group

The administration asked me if I would start an anger management group, which I was, of course, happy to do. The members of the group were referred by the administration, and, originally, the group consisted of three members: one white female, one African American male, and one African American female. The group was open-ended, and met once a week for five weeks without any additional members added. I felt we had developed a solid working relationship with each other, and were really starting to get to work. Slowly, additional members were referred to the group by the school's administration, and each time the new members were welcomed.

However, when the group got to six members, five of which were African American, I began worrying about what the members thought about the makeup of the group not looking like the makeup of the school, which was majority White. I was certainly aware of this. I also worried about how they might view me, a White male, in light of this. More than anything, I worried that the racial issues might disrupt a group that was functioning so well. I had a choice. To deal with the issue of unbalanced racial representation would take time away from the group's curriculum and risk damaging the group's working alliance. To ignore the issue might save time for the anger management curriculum, but whatever work would be done would likely be very superficial if it was not the issue that the members were focused on.

I decided not only to discuss the racial issue but also to be the one to bring it up. During the next session, I said, "I can't help but notice that the makeup of this group is not like the makeup of the school, and I'm wondering what it must be like for you to look around and see that the students identified as having anger problems are almost all African American." This led to an important discussion that took up the majority of the group time for the next several sessions. In the end, I know it was productive, and I think many of the members appreciated my asking about it. I think it affected how they saw me and helped our working alliance. It probably took time away from anger management strategies, but it was definitely time well spent.

Although not part of the curriculum as it was designed, the conversation was vital to the group's getting any further work done and established a model for how to deal with difficult and sensitive issues in an honest and forthright manner. In addition, and most importantly, the discussion helped the group function at a higher level than it had previously.

It is no doubt difficult to decide when to let the group go and when to facilitate. The river metaphor encourages leaders to appreciate the power of the group's process but does not give much guidance as to how to interact when a group is regressing to an earlier stage. One metaphor that does provide some guidance is an old childhood game. The game is very simple: Take a large tire (the bigger, the better) and roll it. That's it. That's the game. Like with group work, much of the work comes in the beginning. You have to select a tire, struggle to get it upright, and then push it really hard to get it to roll. Also much like with group work, once you get the tire rolling, your job (here comes the fun part) is to run beside the tire and keep it rolling. When the tire starts to wobble or lose speed, that is when you act. You give it a gentle push, and the tire often corrects itself and continues down the street. Like with the tire game, by the time the group reaches the working stage, it is assumed that the leader has done a nice job of co-creating an atmosphere that builds momentum in the group. During the working stage, the leader's job becomes keeping pace with the group and correcting the "wobbles," as evidenced by behaviors or attitudes that contradict the momentum. Often, these "corrections" come in the form of gentle reminders or process observations that the group can incorporate and then use to self-correct.

One of the most important roles leaders can play during the working stage is negotiating the balance between content and process in the group. In this situation, content is defined as the information related during group discussions, or the *what* of the group interactions, whereas process is defined as the dynamics that occur within the group during group sessions, or the *how* of the group interactions (Geroski & Kraus, 2002). Students with reasonable social and communication skills will likely be able to track the content of the conversation, a more basic communication skill (although when leading groups with very young children, even this can be a challenge). However, it cannot be assumed that children and adolescents will attend to the emotional content underlying the discussion or identify the dynamics present in the here and now of the group session. If allowed to focus on content at the expense of the underlying emotions or group dynamics, the group could miss some important opportunities to build self-awareness. On the other hand, a group of adolescents that has learned to make comments on emotions or to process group dynamics can become a little too enamored with process observations, bogging themselves down as they process and process to the point where little gets accomplished. One can probably imagine this happening with a group of adolescents as they first learn to understand group process and become very proud of their new "depth."

Helping the group maintain the balance between attending to content and attending to process remains the leader's responsibility. This balance can be difficult to maintain but is an important factor in group learning and growth. Consider this example of group members' attending to process from a fifth-grade skills for living group.

BILLY: I just hate school. It's stupid and nothing we learn is really going to help us at all in life. I mean, who needs quadratic equations anyway? [The content issue here is Billy's dislike of school and his inability to find meaning. The process issue is Billy's search for meaning inside group. Could it be that he also sees group as meaningless? That is, the process question is, How does the content comment reflect Billy's perspective of group? At this point, the leader could make that process observation, but in the working stage, group members are becoming skilled at seeing process opportunities.]

STEPHANIE: Billy, maybe you feel group is a waste of time, too. Are you questioning the use of time here? I know I do sometimes, especially when I first started.

BILLY: Well, yeah. It just seems like we don't do much. [Stephanie's process comment brought the discussion into the here and now and avoided the "school is dumb" debate that may have occurred in the earlier stages of the group. The comfort level is such that Billy can explore his current feelings.]

STEPHANIE: Yeah, sometimes we don't do much but talk, but talking is good, too. You have good things to say. Maybe you could participate more by giving feedback? You know, to tell you the truth, I don't know that much about you.

ZACH: Yeah, me either. Maybe if you shared a little bit more, you would think this was more worthwhile. [At this point, the group becomes engaged in helping Billy to find meaning in the group by encouraging him to participate in activities that have made the group meaningful to each of the members—namely, through feedback and sharing. In this way, the members reinforce the norms of the group and attempt to ensure its momentum.]

Another important role that a leader can play in the working stage is that of a role model. Specifically, the leader models the behaviors that he or she would like to see from members during the working stage. This modeling may be different from the modeling that the leader has done in the previous stages, when the goal was to help members develop connections with each other and get accustomed to the novelty of being a part of a group.

The leader may be among the first in the group to challenge members to take risks and to support them in their efforts to stretch, be authentic within the group setting, and self-disclose appropriately. Take the following example in which a group of high school seniors working on building relationship skills talks about what they've accomplished so far.

SARAH: Well, let's see . . . I know I've made it to every group session. I guess that's an accomplishment for me.

LEIGH: Yeah, I've noticed you've been here for each group, and I do think that is a significant accomplishment. And, at the same time, I feel like I still don't really know you well, even though we've been in group together for eight weeks.

SARAH (BEGINNING TO TEAR UP): That's hard to hear. I want to get to know everyone. I guess I'm just still not sure what to do.

KAKKI: I think I know how you feel, Sarah. Even though Leigh didn't say that to me, I was thinking that she probably doesn't know me very well either. Probably none of you do. I guess I thought I could learn a lot from just showing up, but it's harder than I thought.

LEIGH: It is hard to let others get to know the real you, isn't it? But I think that's why we are here. It sounds like you would like to get to know each other on a little bit deeper level—and maybe to let others know you a bit better as well. Any ideas how we start doing that?

The students in this example wanted to do more than "show up," both in group and in life, but the anxiety they felt prevented them from taking that first step. Once Leigh challenged the group in a supportive way, the members realized that they needed to work on a deeper level if they were to get what they wanted out of the group. This realization fundamentally changed the work to be done in the group and challenged the group to strive for more.

It is also important that group leaders continue to deepen and refine their self-reflection, risk-taking, and interpersonal skills throughout the working stage. In reality, the working stage is not a "stage" but a part of a continuum of growth that members will experience throughout the group. Thus, members do not truly "reach" the working stage; rather, they continually develop through the working stage. As group members begin to demonstrate more self-reflective, authentic, and courageous behavior in group, group leaders can acknowledge the benefits of such risks and motivate members to take further steps. As members feel more comfortable sharing their deep thoughts, group leaders can encourage those members to explore their thoughts even more deeply. As members take small risks, group leaders can support their strides and encourage them to take bigger ones. As group members demonstrate trust for one another, group leaders can help them develop an even greater sense of intimacy.

THE WORKING STAGE AND CO-LEADERSHIP CONSIDERATIONS

Although the preceding section provided an overview of leadership roles primarily from the perspective of a single-leader group, the literature asserts that most groups are facilitated by more than one leader (Roller & Nelson, 1991; Rosenbaum, 1983; Yalom & Leszcz, 2005). Co-leadership is a leadership modality in which the relationship between the co-leaders serves as a therapeutic tool. It is interesting to note that co-leader relationships develop in much the same manner as groups do, proceeding through the stages of development (Dick, Lessler, & Whiteside, 1980; Fall & Wejnert, 2005; Gallogly & Levine, 1979; Winter, 1976). Ideally, the two leaders develop in tandem, but they should be mindful of the developmental aspects of the co-leader relationship that can affect the growth of the group.

ACTIVITY 9.1

Brainstorm in dyads the benefits and challenges of having a co-leader, particularly during the working stage. Reflecting on a time when you were a member of a group that was facilitated by multiple group leaders, describe how the experience was more positive, if at all, as a result of having more than one group leader. How, if at all, did it negatively affect your group experience?

Co-leaders who have successfully moved into the working stage specifically use their interpersonal structure as a mechanism to help maintain the momentum of the group and fine tune the co-leader relationship. Similar to the group's management of resistance and conflict, the co-leaders have experienced and managed resistance and processed and resolved their power and expertise issues. In the working stage, co-leaders use two skills, forecasting and open processing, to maintain a smooth flow of communication. Using forecasting, a co-leader may say, "I am picking up on a theme of honesty in what each of you is saying. Why don't we push below the surface and explore this thread?" Instead of abruptly changing the direction of the group, forecasting allows one co-leader to communicate to the other leader and the group as a whole where the line of processing is going. Another key skill is open processing, sometimes called process observation. Open processing is the act of sharing internal dialogue with the entire group. The unique application of open processing for co-leadership includes the discussion or commentary that goes on between co-leaders in addition to the observations made directly to the group. Consider this example: "I noticed a lot of tension in the group as we began to talk about Mark's reaction to last week's discussion" or about specific leadership issues. "Leroy [co-leader], can we stop for a minute and talk about what's going on in the group? I think I might be a little lost."

Although both of these techniques may seem basic to quality group leadership and may occur in different ways throughout the life of the group, it is in the working stage where they are most potent. In earlier stages, group leaders are less likely to forecast and typically change direction as a way to individually gain control of the group. They are also probably less likely to use open processing due to inadequacy fears. The hallmark of the working stage is a high-functioning relationship, and both forecasting and open processing allow the leaders to model the behaviors and skills the group strives to attain. Note how the preceding forecasting example models the importance of communicating with the group as a method for understanding, an important skill for all group members. Open processing models the importance of not censoring one's inner dialogue, of being comfortable with being vulnerable, and of trusting the group as a whole. Two seasoned co-leaders remarked, "Our clients claim the major advantage for them in co-therapy is role modeling . . . part of the process of therapy is teaching people how to be close with each other . . . because we model closeness, we are able to help them achieve it" (Goulding & Goulding, 1991, p. 207).

Much like the experience of the group members, the working stage is a time to reap the benefits of a good working relationship between the co-leaders. Group members move away from their dependence on the leaders and begin to process issues on their own. Co-leaders use the harmony of this stage as a way to deepen the co-leader relationship and its impact on the group. Although in the earlier stages of development, co-leaders are encouraged to receive consultation/supervision to minimize and identify unhealthy trends in the co-leader relationship, in the working stage, co-leaders may become less dependent on supervision, as they find they can address issues with one another in an open and honest manner (Fall & Wejnert, 2005). As with group development, co-leaders who maintain awareness of the relationship can continue the productivity of this stage until the group ends or begins the transition to the termination stage.

THE REAL WORKING STAGE

Although the stages of groups are often presented in a linear model with clear boundaries (as they are presented here), it should be noted that in practice the stages of groups are rarely so clearly defined. In fact, the way group stages are often presented in the literature is primarily an academic concept, as the stages are derived from clinical observation rather than evidence provided by research (Berg et al., 2006). In practice, the boundaries between the stages of group development are more nebulous than the clearly delineated categories presented in textbooks. In addition, the development of groups often presents with an "ebb and flow," rather than a linear progression. This is particularly true when leading groups in schools, where a variety of internal and external factors can disrupt the development of a group at any time. Changes in schedules, student transience, disciplinary action, teachers holding students back, and extracurricular events can all lead to students' missing sessions or dropping out of groups altogether. In addition, events that happen between group members outside of the group can affect the group members inside of group sessions, and a group that is solidly in the working stage one week can regress to an earlier stage the next week. The following example from a group for fifth- and sixth-grade children of divorce (in a K–8 school) demonstrates how quickly the working stage can be threatened:

KARA:	Ms. Jones, we have a problem we need to deal with right now. I had some fifth-grade girls ask me about what I talked about in here last week, and that means that Jessica told them what I said in group. I don't think she should be in the group anymore.
JESSICA:	That's not true, and I already told her I didn't say anything to anyone. And I don't like being accused of lying or talking behind someone's back, so that's fine. I don't want to be in the same group as Kara anyway.
RITA:	Ms. Jones, since they don't want to be together, why don't we just split into two groups? We could have a fifth-grade group and a sixth-grade group. Then Kara and Jessica won't have to be in the same group.
MS. JONES:	Well, maybe we can talk about that as an option, but before we jump to that, let me ask you something. Does this situation remind anyone of anything?
RITA (AFTER A PAUSE):	Oh my gosh! We're getting a divorce!

MS. JONES:	Wow. Can you explain what you mean?
JESSICA:	I get it. We're having a problem, so we just decide to split up, like our parents did.
MS. JONES:	Okay. So, now that we know that, I guess you all need to decide if you want to handle this by splitting up or if you want to try something different.
KARA:	I don't want to split up. I'm willing to try to work this out, even if it is difficult.

As the group members identified that they were, in effect, reenacting a divorce scenario, they reconsidered their plan to split up and rededicated themselves to working through the breach of trust. Although this put the group back to an earlier stage where they were once again managing conflict, it was necessary to do that in order to get back to an effective working stage. Moreover, the process of working out a conflict when it would have been easier to simply split was itself an important therapeutic intervention, especially for this particular population.

Just as a group does not always progress in a linear fashion, the group members may not progress through the stages in unison. Once again, this is particularly true of groups with children and adolescents, where developmental differences within the group can affect how students process the information and the "depth" of understanding the group process. In addition, there are times when some group members are ready to commit to group goals, while others are still holding onto past conflicts or feeling insecure about their place in the group. Consider Case Study 9.2.

CASE STUDY 9.2

The Young Men's Group

The group was a place for seventh- and eighth-grade boys to discuss what it meant to them to "be a man" and to develop strategies to become the type of man they wanted to be. One of the topics that was particularly important to this group was their relationships with their fathers. There was a variety of father–son issues present in the group, with many of the members feeling a strained relationship with their fathers due to frequent conflicts, divorce, or lack of time spent with the fathers. Yet, with the exception of one member, all the adolescent males were highly motivated to work on these issues and make changes in their current relationships with their fathers. The exception was Korey, a young man whose father had left his family and moved away with his "new" family. While other members bonded over their difficult relationships, this student shared very little, choosing instead to focus on his relationship with his stepfather because, as he said, his father "didn't matter to him anyway." Yet as the group became more cohesive and members encouraged each other to share their experiences and try new ways of thinking about or interacting with their fathers, Korey grew more distant from the group. The other members had charged ahead to the working stage, but Korey was still stuck. What was more, seeing the others begin to work on building their relationships with their fathers—what Korey was afraid of most—left him feeling even more left out.

Had Korey been part of a group that was more tentative or slower paced, he might have been more successful in the group. But his vulnerability kept him from taking the risks the others were willing to take, and their excitement to get to work made it difficult for them to know how to encourage him to join them. Although most members of the group were doing the work of the working stage, Korey was not there.

Presenting the group stages in a linear fashion certainly helps novice group workers conceptualize the working stage and its goals and process. However, there is also benefit in realizing that group development is rarely so neat and clean. Knowing that different groups progress at different rates and that students within the same group may progress at different rates can help a novice group leader to be more patient. Like the old man in the river, the leader can allow the group to proceed at its own course and its own pace, rather than struggling against it or giving up. At the same time, understanding that groups ebb and flow can help the leader to identify when a group may be turned around and to look for the opportunities to help the group get reoriented so it can get back to work as soon as possible.

Understanding the differences in group development can also help the group leader identify when a group is not working, even when the leader feels that the group has been running long enough that it "should be" in the working stage by now. This is particularly important in more-structured groups, psychoeducational groups, and classroom guidance, where leaders plan their groups and organize their topics based on a prediction of when a group "should" be in the working stage. But advancing to the working stage is less about time spent in group and more about conflicts resolved. If leaders do not pay attention to where the members are regarding the group stages, they run the risk of forging ahead to the work of the group, while leaving the group members, or many of them, behind. This can lead to frustration on the part of the leaders, who may see the students as "resisting," and to largely ineffective groups.

So how does a group leader know when group members are ready to begin the working stage? The absence of the characteristics mentioned so far (i.e., group cohesion, trust, a willingness to take risks, a commitment to work toward goals) is one indicator that a group is not functioning as it should. However, there are other indicators as well. For instance, if the membership appears to consist of several "cliques" of members rather than a whole group, it is an indication that the group has not come together and developed the sense of "we-ness" that is characteristic of a working group. Rather, there is still some degree of an "us and them" mentality within the group. Until the group members fully form one identity, the members will have difficulty functioning at a high level.

ACTIVITY 9.2

Brainstorm ways in which subgrouping may occur in groups within elementary, middle, and high schools? As a leader, how could you minimize this phenomenon in these settings?

A further complication to recognizing when a group has not yet entered the working stage is that, in many ways, the working stage is a welcome relief from the tension that permeates the transition stage of the group, for group members and leaders alike. The welcome relief from tension, however, can lead group leaders to believe a group has entered the working stage when the group may have simply made an implicit group decision to "move on" without fully resolving conflict. As an example, consider the coping strategies group of advanced placement (AP) students in a high school presented in Case Study 9.3.

CASE STUDY 9.3
The Coping Strategies Group

The members of the group were like most AP students—successful, well liked by teachers, considerate, and compliant. They were also used to getting positive feedback from adults. As the group began, everyone got along well, and they set goals for the group. Like most of their teachers, I was so excited to have a group of students who were so easy to work with. They got along well with each other and were very agreeable. I looked forward to this group for the first few weeks. It seemed almost like a break to me. But as they got to what should have been the working stage, I noticed that the conversation seemed superficial. I began to get bored with the group and wondered exactly where the group was heading. I began to realize that perhaps the group, full of individuals used to being liked and seen as highly sociable, sort of "faked" its way into the working stage. The group members discussed how they would handle conflict in the group but never really allowed a conflict to surface. And I, as the leader, let them get away with it because I was happy to work with students who had no conflicts for a change.

The members of the coping skills group may have said all the right things to indicate they were ready to work and may even have demonstrated some of the characteristics of a true working stage in the group, such as direct and respectful communication and an increased focus on meeting group goals. However, without having truly worked through conflicts, they entered a pseudo–working stage that was pleasant enough but not productive. A group "working around" rather "working through" internal conflict can certainly make things easier during sessions, but without a deep intimacy, the results of the group will be as superficial as the relationships.

In addition, if the goals of the group and the ways in which group members will reach their goals remain unclear to the students, this may be a sign that not all members are on the same page or that the group as a whole is not on the same page as the group leader. Similarly, if the group is displaying some degree of resistance in the work expected of it or if members are missing sessions, being quiet, stalling, or taking the discussion on nonproductive tangents, this may indicate that the members do not trust the group enough to take the risk of being authentic, do not trust the process of group work, or do not feel supported in their efforts to grow.

Finally, the presence of collusion is an indication that the group may not be functioning at a high level. Collusion occurs when group members conspire to work against the growth of the group members and often manifests itself in their protecting or "ganging up on" certain students or the leader. It is probably easier to think of examples where group members gang up on a less powerful member—in fact, such behavior is part of the social norms for many later elementary and middle school students. However, it is also common for students to band together against the leader. For instance, as a group member is being challenged to try a different behavioral strategy, other members may come to that student's "rescue," making excuses for the member and questioning the rationale behind "getting on their case." Or members may rally around a particularly powerful group member and begin challenging the leader's strategy as a way to maintain the status quo, thus protecting themselves from being expected to try new things. These types of behaviors, no matter when they are exhibited in the group, are a sign that the group is not yet in a fully functioning working stage.

Perhaps the most productive way to conceptualize the presence of such collusion is to consider it as evidence of either being stuck or regressing to the transition stage. It is common in the transition stage for group members to practice conflict resolution with the leader being the target of conflict because the leader is often the one member of the group that members can trust to handle conflict appropriately. As mentioned, if the leader avoids the conflict or mishandles it, the group can fail to proceed or can regress. The following example illustrates a leader who correctly identifies the transition stage issue, attends to the process, respectfully handles the cultural issues, and facilitates the group through the confrontation:

RICK (A 14-YEAR-OLD, NEW MEMBER IN AN ONGOING ANGER GROUP AT A MIDDLE SCHOOL): This group is crap. I'm just here 'cause I have to be here. I've been to White counselors and stuff dozens of time, but it never helps. You don't know me; you don't know anything about me; hell, you probably ain't even smart as me. How you gonna teach me anything?

LEADER: You are right, Rick. I don't know you, and because I don't know you, it makes sense that you don't trust me.

RICK: Damn right. I don't trust you or anyone else in this room!

LEADER: That makes sense. I don't blame you for not trusting anyone. I hope that will change, but that's up to you. I don't know who you are as a person, and I don't know if I can teach you anything. For me to assume that I know you, having just met you, would be pretty arrogant on my part. I just hope that you will teach me and the others here what we need to know about you, and maybe when we get to know you, we will begin to understand. But we'll respect you doing that at your own pace.

RICK: Yeah, well, we'll see.

The leader identified that he was being confronted by Rick and was also aware that the group was watching to see how he handled it. He felt attacked and had an urge to attend to and answer the content issue by proving his competence (e.g., by quoting his resume, degrees, etc., or by trying to convince Rick that the leader being White doesn't matter). Instead, he looked for the process issue: What is he really saying? By attending to the process message of "you don't know me," the leader was able to work with the resistance and demonstrate understanding. The group (an ongoing group in the working stage) was able to get a reinforcement of the skills of conflict management, and Rick received an invitation to participate and an orientation to the ways of the group. This three-minute exchange highlights the complex dynamics and interactions of the working stage.

DIFFERENT WORKING STAGES FOR DIFFERENT GROUPS

Group work texts use different names to describe the working stage of a group, but virtually all texts describe the stage in fairly general terms. Many of the designations for the working stages, as they are presented in texts, appear to be drawn from counseling groups that are based on a humanistic perspective, that place a high value on interpersonal learning, and that are designed for adult populations. We know from group work literature and practice, however, that group work varies a great deal and that groups led in schools and with children and adolescents look very different from groups for adults led in agencies or in private practice. With the vast differences in the ways groups are designed and led, it follows that no two working stages would look alike. Depending on the purpose of the group, the group format, and the theoretical perspective of the leaders, group goals may be achieved through behavioral changes (e.g., Gazda, Ginter, & Horne, 2008), cognitive restructuring (e.g., Ellis, 1997), corrective emotional experiences (e.g., Yalom & Leszcz, 2005), encouragement and a sense of belonging (e.g., Sonstegard, 1998), or any combination of the above. The following section describes how working stages may look in schools, depending on important group variables, including the group's foundation, the design of the group, and membership variables.

Group Foundation

The group's foundation provides a basis for many decisions made about the group. The foundation is the starting point for designing a group, but it also plays an important role in the working stage. Specifically, the principles that make up the group foundation dictate what is to be accomplished and how goals will be met within the working stage. Factors that are important components of the group's foundation include the general purpose and the specific goals of the group as well as the underlying theoretical perspective.

One of the most important variables affecting the process of the working stage is the goals of the group. Although the decisions about the goals for the group are usually made during the planning phase or the forming and orienting stage, those decisions will have important effects on the working stage. In a group with a goal that is easily definable, as is the case with many psychoeducational groups and classroom guidance sessions led in schools, the focus of the "work" to be done is often very clear. In a study skills group for middle school students, for instance, the majority of the group process in the working stage will be focused on developing members' organization skills, studying techniques, and perhaps test-taking skills. If the goal of the group is not as clearly defined, as with a group discussing teenage women's issues, the work to be done may be a bit more nebulous. As "teenage women's issues" can mean very different things to different members, the content and process during the working stage may vary from group to group, from session to session, and even from student to student.

The working stage is affected not only by the overall goal of the group but also by how narrow or broad the desired outcomes of the group are. A well-conceived group will be developed around a specific goal and will set objectives that are relevant to the overall goal and are realistic to achieve, given the time allotted for the group and the group format. Unfortunately, goals and objectives are not always well conceived. Furr (2000) noted that a common mistake group leaders make is trying to have a group goal that is too broad, thus trying to cover too many topics in the course of a group. Again, groups led in schools are particularly vulnerable to this urge to cover too much, particularly when expectations from teachers and parents are high, even though the time allotted for group is very small. In these scenarios, the groups can become less like therapeutic experiences and more like survey courses, where a great deal of information is presented but relatively little is absorbed or incorporated into the lives of the students.

Although this is a mistake that is often made in the planning phase, it doesn't come to fruition until the working stage. When group leaders have too much information to cover, it may take so long simply to impart it that not enough time is left for the "work" to be done. This represents a scenario where there is an imbalance of time spent on content at the expense of focusing on process. Even if students learn the information, they may not figure out how to use that information in their lives if they do not have enough time to process it. When leaders in the working stage find themselves in a situation where they feel overwhelmed with pressure to cover a great deal of information, it may be time to reconsider the scope of the group and refine the goals so that members have enough time to integrate what they have learned thus far. It is better to have a group that addresses one issue profoundly than a group that addresses several issues superficially.

The theoretical foundation of a group will influence the working stage, as it can dictate both the type of change that is desired and the process through which that change should take place. Because each theoretical approach has its own values and favors different processes to bring about effective change (e.g., insight, interpersonal learning, behavioral change), we can expect the processes favored in the working stages of groups to be very different as well. Even when groups dealing with the same population are struggling with the same issue, different theoretical perspectives will result in their approaching the issue differently, leading to very different working stages. Consider a social skills group for elementary school students. A group using a cognitive-behavioral perspective will be more content focused and will likely teach new skills for students to practice (Petrocelli, 2002). The working stage in this type of group will likely involve less processing of group dynamics and more practice of new skills that members can use to help manage their anxiety (e.g., calming self-talk) or more use of behavioral techniques (e.g., exposure). A group using a solution-focused approach will be more likely to take advantage of skills members already have by noticing exceptions to the problem and learning from those successes (Murphy, 1997). In this case, the working stage will help students gain insight into behaviors that work for them and generalize their strengths to novel situations. A humanistic group, on the other hand, will be less concerned with directing group members to practice skills, and will spend more time processing the emotional experience of the members in the here and now of the group, disclosing immediate emotions, and empathizing and supporting other group members (Shechtman & Pastor, 2005). In humanistic groups, the "work" of the working stage will be less about incorporating new information and thinking about how to generalize it to the world outside and more about being different in the moment. Finally, an Adlerian group might use aspects of all the above in the working stage, helping members to develop insight into and take responsibility for their social behaviors, encouraging members to practice new behaviors by "acting as if" in group, and using homework to encourage members to actively practice new ways of being outside of the group.

Group Design

In addition to the foundation that underlies the group, the specific group design chosen will affect the process of the working stage. There are many factors to consider as part of group design, including the group type or format, the style of leadership, the duration of the group, and whether the group will be closed or open to new members.

Similar to the effect that the theoretical foundation of the group has on the process of the working stage, the type of group model that is used will influence what the working stage will look like. In a psychoeducational group format, imparting information will certainly be expected to be a central therapeutic factor, while catharsis, existential factors, and altruism may not be emphasized to a great extent. On the other hand, a counseling group will rely more on the interpersonal dynamics within the group for therapeutic growth, utilizing interpersonal learning, catharsis, altruism, and existential factors to a far greater extent. Certainly, a counseling group will still impart information and utilize interpersonal learning, but these factors will not be used as intentionally as with a psychoeducational group.

As an example of how the type of group can affect the working stage, imagine two groups for adolescents from divorced homes. One group is an 8-week psychoeducational group, and the other group is a 12-week counseling group; both are led by a school counselor. The primary goal of the psychoeducational group is for the members to learn about divorce, to learn that divorce is not the child's fault or responsibility, and to learn strategies for understanding and managing their emotions about the divorce. Therefore, a great deal of time is spent imparting the information that is to be learned, while interpersonal factors such as group cohesiveness and interpersonal learning play more of a supportive role in helping members to apply the information to their lives. The counseling group's goals, on the other hand, may include helping members to explore their emotions about the divorce, make meaning of the situation, and find support and encouragement through the group. In this group, the leader in the working stage focuses less on imparting information to members and more on allowing members to share their experiences and explore their beliefs, fears, and other feelings about the divorce. For this interpersonal learning to be effective, group cohesiveness is more crucial than in the psychoeducational group. In addition, interpersonal factors such as catharsis and instillation of hope are more likely to be an important part of a counseling group than a psychoeducational group.

The group leader's style of leadership will also have an effect on the working stage. Whether the leader considers herself to be an educator, a facilitator, or a counselor can have an effect on how she views her role during the working stage. A workshop leader who sees her role as that of an educator will approach the working stage of the group as the time when the most important information is to be disseminated and processed so that it can be effectively generalized outside of the group. A leader who considers himself a facilitator, as in a support group for bereaved children, may view the working stage as the time when the members are best able to get the support and empathy they need from other members. Meanwhile, a leader who considers herself a counselor, working within a male issues group for adolescent boys, may see the working stage as the time when she helps members to develop insight into the masculine stereotypes they hold and to evaluate those stereotypes honestly, something most members would not feel comfortable discussing anywhere else.

Another aspect of group leadership in schools is the leader's use of exercises or activities within group (see Chapter 15). Although not all counseling approaches value the use of exercises in group work, most group leaders seem to agree that exercises can play an important role in group learning when implemented thoughtfully. In addition, for developmental reasons, children and adolescents may derive more learning from participation in exercises than from discussion alone. Therefore, for many leaders in schools, the question is not whether to use exercises in groups but how and when to use them. Leaders who prefer more experiential learning exercises will likely approach the working stage differently than will those who view group process from a purely discussion perspective. For more hands-on leaders who use exercises, the working stage is when exercises are most effective or have the greatest impact on the members. While group leaders may use team-building exercises or other exercises to introduce topics early in the group, the exercises used in the working stage should expose members to more complex or higher-risk topics and should be used to help students apply principles discussed earlier to their own lives in a meaningful way.

Even more important than the exercises themselves is the processing of the exercises, as that is when members are able to develop the interpersonal and intrapersonal learning that is the purpose of the group (DeLucia-Waack, 1997). Processing exercises can help members explore their thoughts and feelings at a greater depth and can stimulate discussion both about the topic and about the group dynamics that were apparent in the exercise. Thus, the processing of exercises in the working stage hopefully will help students to understand the lessons learned from the exercises on a deep level and to develop strategies for applying those insights into the world outside of the group.

Another important factor that needs to be considered during the working stage is the duration of the group—how long the group will run. Preparing for the working stage is an investment, and, generally, the more thoroughly a leader prepares for the working stage, the more effective that work will be. At the same time, given the time limits of groups in schools, there may be a point when any more time invested in laying the groundwork is simply time taken away from the working stage. All groups, whether ongoing counseling groups or full-day workshops, have a working stage (Jacobs et al., 2006). In order to get the most out of a group, the group leader must figure out how to prepare a group to function at a high level, while still ensuring that enough time is saved for the group to actually do the work. If a professional school counselor is presenting a six-hour workshop on cross-cultural understanding, he or she may have to be content with a group cohesion based on the understanding that members share a common goal: to complete the workshop. This may be sufficient for the group to work together for a few hours and meet the goals of the workshop. A high school counselor who is leading a six-session career development group may be able to spend more time helping the group to develop a deeper level of cohesion but is still under considerable time restraints. Certainly, the group needs to have resolved obvious conflicts within the group and established some degree of cohesiveness if the working stage is to be productive, but at some point, the leader may have to sacrifice some of the depth of the group preparation in order to get the group to a working stage. In a longer-term group, the leader may have the luxury of being more patient with the group, allowing time to help the group bond on a deeper level so that the group can get maximum benefit out of the working stage.

The format for membership can also affect the working group, as the stages of a group that is closed to new members will proceed very differently than those of a group with an open membership format. If the group is closed to new members after the start of the group, the group is more likely to follow what would be considered a "typical" process for group development, much like the stages presented in this text. If the group is open-ended, however, the process of group development can be altered. A shake-up in membership can have an effect both on certain individuals within the group and on the group as a whole. When a member leaves, the role that the member played in the group is no longer filled. Often, another member will step into the departed member's role, creating a ripple effect that can change the dynamics of the group as a whole. This sudden shift of roles can make the members feel less safe about group interactions, leading them to pull back and test the waters for a while. In addition, feelings of loss over the departure of a valued member can dampen the members' willingness to take risks in the group, also leading the group to regress for a time.

Likewise, when a new member comes into an open group, there will be a period of trust building, during which the new member learns to trust the group and the group learns to trust the new member. In addition, the new member not only shakes up the group dynamics but also is operating within the group at a much earlier stage than group members who have been there longer. While those members may provide encouragement to the new member, helping the new member become a part of the group faster than he or she ordinarily would, the group as a whole will not be in a true "working stage" while it waits on one or more members to catch up.

Group Membership

Understanding the students participating in the group experience is another vital factor in determining what the working stage will look like. The experiences that make up the working stage, whether discussions or experiential activities, certainly need to be directly related to the group goals, but they also need to be appropriate for and relevant to the members of the group. Some membership variables that should be considered are the age, ability, and cultural factors of the membership, including the diversity present within the group.

Factors that are vital to consider in managing an effective working stage are the ages and the developmental levels of the members. The material discussed and activities used during the working stage must be developmentally appropriate for the members so that they can effectively process the information. Because most of the research on group work has been conducted on adult groups, much of what we know about what makes an effective working stage is based on adult groups (DeLucia-Waack, 2000). School counselors or others leading groups in schools therefore may need to adapt any research-based strategies to make the groups more relevant to and effective with their populations. For instance, we know that children are likely to have shorter attention spans, more-concrete thinking, and a less fully developed sense of self-awareness than adults. In addition, younger students will be more likely to project their feelings onto others and may be more comfortable having a stronger, more directive group leader than older clients would be. Keeping this in mind, the working stage in a group with children is likely to have more experiential learning than discussion, using children's ability to learn through play. These activities should be processed within the group, but on a more concrete level, and this processing should be held to a few minutes.

Groups can be a very effective method for helping adolescents to deal with a range of developmental issues from social skills to values clarification and identity development. However, the working stages of groups serving adolescent populations should also be adapted to ensure that they are appropriate for the developmental stage. As adolescents themselves are in a developmental stage where they can play like children one minute and have a mature discussion about serious issues the next, groups for adolescents may need to be flexible as well. Providing a variety of activities in the working stage can help to ensure that the leader covers a wide range of developmental levels within the group and addresses the many different moods that are likely to appear throughout the group. Many adolescents enjoy hands-on exercises, whether active challenges like team-building exercises or artistic endeavors such as writing stories or creating collages. However, adolescents are able to process these exercises to a much greater extent than are children, and the time spent processing exercises in an adolescent group should be increased accordingly. In fact, having a concrete exercise to process in an abstract way is a good strategy for helping adolescents to further develop their abstract thinking.

The degree of heterogeneity in the group membership may also have an effect on the working stage of a group. Although it is a myth that groups can be truly homogeneous, as the levels of identities within each person are far too vast (DeLucia-Waack, 1996b), members of groups that appear to be more homogeneous may feel safer trusting each other more quickly due to the comfort they feel in sharing similarities, superficial though they may be. In spite of this initial "bonding" that may occur over gender, racial, ethnic, or other similarities, the working stage may not be as rich or fulfilling. The members of a group that is more heterogeneous may have a more difficult time getting to the working stage, as cultural or worldview differences can slow the process of group identification and cohesion and lead to misunderstandings within group process (Jacobs et al., 2006). DeLucia-Waack (1996b) argued that, although conversations about race and culture are difficult to initiate, the act of having those conversations can help groups become more cohesive. In addition to helping the group form a tighter bond, the multiple perspectives that can be shared in a more heterogeneous group can provide members with a wider range of feedback than they would receive a more homogeneous group, making for a potentially richer, deeper experience for the group members.

ACTIVITY 9.3

Cultural issues play an important part in how the working stage plays out in a group. Form dyads to discuss how your personal identities, worldviews, communication pattern preferences, and other sociocultural factors influence your group participation. Consider what potential challenges may occur for you as group leaders. As a large group, discuss how cultural conflicts may be minimized in the working stage.

In addition to the degree of diversity within the group, the leader should be cognizant of the effects the group members' cultural perspectives, as well as the leader's own cultural perspectives, can have on the working stage. Cultural factors can have a strong effect on the way students act and expect others to act within groups. The leader should be aware of any issues regarding communication that may occur in the group, whether they involve language differences or nonverbal behavior. In addition, the leader should ensure that any activities or exercises in the group take cultural differences into account so that differences in how people perceive personal space, comfort level with touching, and other variables do not make members feel uncomfortable or left out. When members do opt out of exercises due to cultural reasons, it is important for the leader to understand it for what it is and not to assume that the member is being "resistant" to the group process. Perhaps most importantly, the leader needs to be aware of any effects that cultural issues may be having on group dynamics and be willing to have conversations about those effects as part of the group process. Although every leader wants to be sensitive to cultural issues, the truth is that, at some point, something will happen that makes members feel uncomfortable. At such a time, the leader must be able to have a discussion about what happened to deepen the understanding among members and get back to an effective working stage as soon as possible. As an illustration of how easily this can come up, consider the example in Case Study 9.4 of a group of high school students in the 6th week of a 10-week psychoeducational group on career development.

CASE STUDY 9.4
The Career Development Group

I felt that this group had gotten to the working stage fairly early, but in recent weeks, they seemed a bit stagnant. I decided to spend some time doing some team-building exercises to boost their cohesion and found some activities that were active and fun but that would require the group members to trust each other, communicate, and break down some physical boundaries. I was unaware, however, that one of the group members was very devout in his religious beliefs, one of which prohibited him from getting physically close with other members of the group. When he opted out of the exercise without explanation, I admit my first thought was that he was showing resistance and that perhaps his excluding himself from the group was related to the stagnation I had noticed in the group. However, I pulled him aside as the activity was starting and asked him for an explanation; he answered by telling me briefly about his beliefs. At that point, we began to discuss what he *could* do to participate in the exercise without putting him in an uncomfortable position from a religious standpoint. After a few minutes, he decided he felt comfortable "coaching" the group and participating in the processing between exercises, which the group enthusiastically agreed to.

The cultural misunderstanding in Case Study 9.4 could have led to assumptions about resistance on the part of the leader and feelings of isolation on the part of the member who opted out of the exercise. Though the initial exercise may have put the member in an uncomfortable position, the ability to discuss and be accepting of cultural differences led to a greater cultural understanding and a stronger connection among the member, his group, and the leader.

ACTIVITY 9.4

Form dyads or triads and discuss and reflect on past group experiences that you have had either as a member or as a group leader. How have you experienced the working stage? What methods (e.g., exercises, discussions) were used? What was positive in your experiences? What do you think could have been done differently to make this stage more effective?

EVALUATION AND THE WORKING STAGE

When it comes to the working stage, leaders have two main questions regarding evaluation: Are we there yet? Are the group members getting what they need? Regarding the first question, the characteristics of the transition stage and those of the working stage must be assessed enough to know whether the group has achieved the momentum common in the working stage. Informal means of evaluation, such as feedback forms asking about members' perceptions of the group, can also be helpful to leaders who are interested in the members' perspective of the process. In addition to informal measures, two more detailed assessments of group interaction, the Johari Window and the Hill Interaction Matrix, are discussed next.

Authors (e.g., Chen & Rybak, 2004) have used the Johari Window (Luft, 1984) to explain relationship development in groups (see Figure 4.1). As described in Chapter 4, the Johari Window can be visualized as a square divided into four quadrants. The top left quadrant, the open quadrant, contains behaviors and thoughts that are in an individual's awareness and are apparent to others. The top right quadrant, the blind quadrant, contains those behaviors that are out of the individual's awareness but are apparent to others. The lower left quadrant, the hidden quadrant, contains behaviors that the individual is aware of but keeps secret from others. The final quadrant, the unknown quadrant, contains behaviors and thoughts that are out of the awareness of both the individual and others. In order to increase self-awareness, a group member must increase the size of his or her open quadrant by moving thoughts and behaviors from the latter three categories to the open category. Material is moved from the blind quadrant to the open quadrant through the feedback of others—in this case, the group members' feedback. As an example, consider a student who says her priority is her academic performance, and, thus, she consistently puts her academic needs first at the expense of her social or emotional needs; she may receive feedback from group members that she appears so stretched and stressed that if she found time to relax and destress, she might find the time she spends studying is more rewarding. Likewise, material is moved out of the hidden quadrant by self-disclosure to the group. A student listening to a group member talk about how her father's view of success skewed her perception of what she needed to accomplish may suddenly realize and share with the group that his pattern of studying so much is an attempt to finally receive his father's approval. Finally, material can be moved out of the unknown quadrant when the individual or the group members gain insight and then moved into the open quadrant through self-disclosure or feedback.

ACTIVITY 9.5

The Johari Window is an excellent model for understanding the working stage. Using a previous group experience as a guide, how is the Johari Window illustrative of your experience at the initial phases of the working stage? At the later phases? How might you incorporate the Johari Window in future groups that you lead?

The Hill Interaction Matrix (Hill, 1956) is another tool used to assess the developmental progress of the group (see Figure 9.1). The cells of the matrix are ordered according to therapeutic benefit as defined by member centeredness, interpersonal risk taking, and interpersonal feedback. The top of the matrix includes the elements of Content Style, which refers to what is being discussed in group. The cell headings within Content Style are as follows:

1. *Topics:* Discussions of "there and then" material—that is, relationships or activities that occur outside of the group.
2. *Group:* Discussions that revolve around the group, primarily concerned with the group's rules, procedures, and goals.

WORK STYLE \ CONTENT STYLE	TOPICS I	GROUP II	PERSONAL III	RELATIONSHIP IV
A -- RESPONSOVE	(1)	(2)	(11)	(12)
B -- CONVENTIONAL	(3)	(4)	(13)	(14)
C -- ASSERTIVE	(5)	(6)	(15)	(16)
D -- SPECULATIVE	(7)	(8)	(17)	(18)
E -- CONFRONTIVE	(9)	(10)	(19)	(20)

POWER QUADRANT

3. *Personal:* Exploration of an individual member within the group, which can include personality issues, behaviors, emotions, thought patterns, and current/historical problems or issues.
4. *Relationship:* The most therapeutic of the elements because of its here-and-now emphasis and focus on interactions between and among group members.

The other axis includes the elements of Work Style, which describes the manner in which members discuss the content elements. The Work Style elements are as follows:

1. *Responsive:* The basic unit of work, characterized by minimal answers to directive questions.
2. *Conventional:* Characterized by social conversation involving general interest topics. The interaction is appropriate, yet superficial.
3. *Assertive:* Interactions that have a conflict-based tone and purpose. This form of interaction usually shuts down conversation instead of facilitating deeper discussions. The speaker is often rigidly opinionated and argumentative.
4. *Speculative:* Open exploration among group members that includes a cooperative spirit in an effort to understand intrapersonal and interpersonal issues.
5. *Confrontive:* Communication that extends below the surface in an attempt to clarify, evaluate and resolve issues, both in the group and within the members. This is the most potent Work Style, as it acts to engage the members in deeper-level processing.

When assessing whether the group is in the working stage, one would most likely look for Content Style/Work Style elements in the lower right quadrant of the matrix, which includes the following combinations:

1. *Speculative-Personal:*

VIRGIL: It seems to me that when you talk about yourself, you feel really scared to open up, like you are afraid to be vulnerable.

2. *Speculative-Relationship:*

RILEY: I feel myself getting angry at you because I think you are ignoring me.

GINNY: I'm not ignoring you. I'm just not agreeing with you all the time. Do I have to agree with you for you to feel heard?

3. *Confrontive-Personal:*

BUFORD: You say you want to come across as more honest and open, and yet you are still the quietest member of the group.

4. *Confrontive-Relationship:*

MIA: I just feel that everyone is blowing me off; like you all don't take my stuff seriously.

JEFF: I find it hard not to be defensive when you accuse me of blowing you off. I want to hear what's behind the insult, but that makes it hard for me. I get the impression that maybe you don't want to connect and you use the insult as a way to distract from the real issue between us.

In addition to evaluating the developmental stage of the group, it is important for leaders of groups in schools to determine if the students are getting what they need to out of the group. Referring back to the focus on accountability, it makes sense that professional school counselors will want to assess students all through the process, rather than waiting until after all the planning and group leading to find out. Toward this end, the ASCA (2005) identified three types of data to be collected for group interventions (see Chapter 16 for detailed discussions): process data (e.g., number of students participating, number of times met), perception data (e.g., students' reactions to group, evidence of new knowledge/skills learned), and results data (e.g., student success or achievement outcomes due to group). The process data are important because they demonstrate the number of students that school counselors work with, and the results data are obviously important because they are what most stakeholders ultimately want to know. The perception data are crucial to examine during the working stage because they can provide information about whether the smaller group objectives are being met.

Timeliness of the perception data is essential so that leaders can make changes to ensure that students learn what they are supposed to learn before the end of the group. For example, think of a group for high school students designed to improve graduation rates (distal outcome); one objective may be increasing career adaptability (proximal outcome). As a result, part of the working stage of the group will be focused on helping students to investigate jobs, take interest inventories, and examine personal values as they relate to work. In such a group, it will be helpful for the leader to know as early as possible if these objectives are being met so he or she can decide whether to move the group along or slow it down to make sure the skills identified as important are learned. The group members may report that the group is cohesive and a safe environment in which to explore personal issues, but if the activities are not giving the members what they need, the desired outcomes of the group may not be met.

Summary

This chapter provided an overview of what one might expect in the working stage of a group in a school setting. The working stage is characterized by a high level of activity, where group members are readily focused on meeting both interpersonal and intrapersonal goals. Students take more responsibility for the process of the group, and interaction is characterized by much more here-and-now communication as compared to other developmental group stages. The members have experienced and worked through group conflict and have developed a sense of cohesion that propels them into the true work of the group. Group members actively participate at this stage, soliciting genuine feedback from other members and electing to take more risks in the group. One common form of risk taking is self-disclosure. Through self-disclosure, group members demonstrate vulnerability in order to gain the great understanding of self and others necessary to meet the individual and group goals set forth at the beginning of the working stage.

During the working stage, leaders often take more of a facilitative role, marked by less direct participation and more maintenance and process observation. The leader serves as a role model for behaviors deemed particularly helpful in this stage, including risk taking, self-disclosure, and the demonstration of vulnerability, all of which "stretch" the group members intrapersonally and interpersonally.

Co-leadership can be advantageous during the working stage. Group leaders may rely on each other to implement skills such as forecasting and open processing, which can help to focus group content and manage group resistance in order to meet individual and group goals. Further, leaders who choose to co-lead groups should be mindful of how the developmental process of the co-leader relationship affects the concurrent growth of the group.

Although common characteristics of the working stage portrayed in linear fashion can be helpful in understanding this stage, readers are reminded of the uniqueness of each group and its process. Components such as group foundation, group design, and group membership were presented to illustrate specific concerns that may arise, depending on the group. To this end, developmental and cultural considerations were presented. Finally, different methods of assessing the working stage were discussed, including the Johari Window and Hill's Interaction Matrix.

CHAPTER 10

Termination in the School Setting

Danica G. Hays, Tammi F. Milliken, and
Catherine Y. Chang

PREVIEW

The purpose of this chapter is to provide an overview of the termination stage, including a general description of termination characteristics, goals, benefits, and challenges. Following these general descriptions, three types of termination for elementary, middle, and high school levels will be discussed: premature termination, termination of group sessions, and termination of the group. Group work techniques reviewed in this chapter include rounds, dyads, sentence completion, scaling, values contracts, summarization, journaling, reunions, scrapbooks, comfort zones, and personal growth charts.

TERMINATION AND GROUP CLOSURE

A high school student drops out of school, prematurely leaving a small group that addresses grief and loss. A large group addressing character education in a middle school setting comes to an end. However, three students in the class will continue to see the professional school counselor in an ongoing small group for students with anxiety. A parent requests to have her elementary school child removed from a small group for children with an incarcerated family member. Toward the end of a large group session on goal setting, a middle school counselor summarizes the session and asks students to reflect on ways to reach their goals both in and out of school. At the end of a small group on test-taking skills for third graders, the counselor brings snacks and gives each student a certificate of achievement. Just prior to graduation, a career development group for college-bound seniors comes to an end.

These examples highlight some of the ways in which termination occurs in group work in the school environment. Termination is a part of all groups; however, it is particularly challenging in the school setting due to the nature of the professional school counselor's overlapping roles. For example, a school counselor may be working with one student individually, in a small group, and in the classroom, while acting as a consultant to the child's parents and teacher, as well as coordinating collaborative interagency services in which the child will participate. These overlapping roles often mean that contact with a child doesn't necessarily cease at the end of a group. Termination is also challenging, given that students may be involved in various types of groups, from a support group lasting for an academic year, to a series of classroom guidance lessons on substance abuse prevention, to a workshop series for career development, to a task group that is planning "career day." Depending on the type and purpose of the group, the termination process can look very different.

Termination may indicate the end of a relationship in its current capacity, the unexpected departure of a group member, the close of a specific group session, or the conclusion of a particular group experience. Therefore, it is necessary to address the multiple ways in which termination can occur and to develop strategies for successfully negotiating these often overlapping roles of the counselor. Although termination is also referred to as closure, for the purposes of this chapter, we will refer to it as termination.

Termination is typically conceptualized as the final stage of the group process. However, it is more than the end of the group. It is an essential part of the entire group process and, if properly executed, serves as a key component in transferring learning to and changing the behavior of students. Thus, successful termination of each group session and the group experience as a whole has the potential to positively affect academic achievement.

Facets of termination are embedded within all stages of group work, as it occurs when a member leaves, at the end of each session, and after the group experience ends. Although termination occurs throughout all group stages and is itself the final stage, it is often minimized in practice. Considering the extent to which professional school counselors engage in group work as a means to address the needs of as many students as possible (American School Counselor Association [ASCA], 2005), leaders need to be skilled in conducting groups effectively during all stages, including termination.

Termination involves reflection and evaluation, activities that vary according to group size, dynamics, and focus (Vernelle, 1994). It addresses past, present, and future experiences of students. With respect to past experiences, termination includes active reflection on individual and group changes. Present experiences are covered by dealing with feelings associated with termination and any unfinished business. Group leaders also assist students with future concerns by co-developing a plan of action, contracting, and assisting members in applying new learning.

Throughout the course of the group, termination as a procedure relates to anecdotal, informal, and formal assessment of individual and group changes. In accord with the *ASCA National Model* (ASCA, 2005), professional school counselors must show how their work with students is having a positive impact on students' academic achievement. Thus, evaluation of groups is necessary to demonstrate accountability. Evaluation involves an assessment of the group's affects on grades, behavioral referrals, and attendance as well as student self-assessments of change, teacher and parent ratings, and counselor observations.

Students cognitively and affectively reflect on personal growth in the context of the group process. As part of this reflection, students consider things they have learned as they have interacted with other group members and prepare to apply new skills to their world outside of the group, both in and out of school, thus translating insight into action. To maximize the impact of the group experience, students need to identify what they learned, how they learned it, and how they can apply it outside of the group.

GOALS AND BENEFITS OF TERMINATION

The general goals of termination at any stage in the group process are consolidation of learning, skills application, and future recommendations for continued growth and development. Consolidation of learning refers to students within the group actively reflecting on knowledge and awareness gained about self and others and integrating this information in order to make changes within their lives. Skills application refers to students applying newly developed skills in the classroom and outside of school. Future recommendations for continued growth and development can range from affirmative statements encouraging students to keep practicing their skills to formal referrals for services, including academic support, special education assessment, additional group counseling, and individual counseling. Termination is a transition or a new beginning for students, rather than an end. As a result, members should view the completion of each session and each group experience as a new beginning that enables them to apply new attitudes and behaviors for success both in and out of school.

Effective termination has several benefits for students that focus on reflection, increased knowledge, and evaluation at various levels. It is an opportunity to apply new learning and make meaning of the group experience. Thus, termination may increase students' awareness of self, others, and their relationships with others. Through this reflection, group members may apply learning, evaluate their growth, and plan for future actions. Leaders should consider how to promote reflection among students in all group formats, from small process groups, to classroom guidance, to large psychoeducational groups.

Self-Awareness

Self-awareness in the termination process refers to recognizing personal attributes and behaviors that facilitate skill development and healthy relationships. Developing self-awareness allows students to improve their decision-making ability as well as their interpersonal relationships within the group, within school, and outside of school. While self-awareness is addressed throughout the group experience, it is assessed and processed in the termination stage. The termination process may increase group members' self-awareness as a result of leader-facilitated interactions among group members. For example, leaders might highlight similarities among members, question students' reactions to one another, and encourage students to give feedback to one another.

Awareness of Others

A key component of the awareness of others involves establishing universality. Yalom and Leszcz (2005) described universality as individuals' sense that their issues are normal and experienced by others. While universality is important at all stages of the group process, termination provides leaders an opportunity to solidify how issues brought up in the group resonated among members. Acknowledging issues that are universal for members may help decrease fears group members have that prevented them from self-disclosing or working on group tasks and goals. This allows members to become aware of how others perceive and respond to their issues. Universality in group process is important to develop because it allows for deeper interpersonal connections.

Planning for the Future

The termination process allows students a chance to plan for the future. This may involve testing knowledge they have gained in group work, bringing up an issue or subject that was discussed in a particular group session, evaluating destructive patterns from a more constructive perspective, and relating to people within their lives in a more positive manner (Grayson, 1993).

As mentioned earlier, one of the goals of termination is skills application. This includes helping members to transfer skills developed in group to the classroom and beyond as well as discussing strategies for and challenges to this task. If the skills application is successful, students not only will be able to apply their skills immediately but also will have developed valuable resources for continuing the process of personal growth and will be able to adapt their learning to new situations.

Having members fantasize about their future can lead to the implementation of new relational, behavioral, or academic skills beyond the group. This can be accomplished through process questions (e.g., "How would you describe your life one, three, and five years from now?" "How would you describe your relationship with [name] one year from now?" "How do you see your academic performance affecting your career goals?"), role plays (e.g., have students role-play different interpersonal scenarios with each other, have students role-play tasks related to possible professions), and creative arts (e.g., have students draw a picture of their life one and five years from the end of the group, have students write letters to each other reflecting their hopes and wishes for each other). To consolidate your understanding of the goals and benefits of termination, read Case Study 10.1 and respond to the reflection questions.

CASE STUDY 10.1

Noah

Consider the following case of Noah, a 17-year-old Caucasian male. At the end of a group addressing career decision-making for high school seniors, Noah discusses things he has learned from the group. The leader initiates closure of the last session of the group. The leader asks students to identify an attribute related to career development that each member possesses that they were not aware of during initial group sessions. Several group members lower their heads and look away from the leader. Noah reports that he has found the group extremely helpful and that he enjoyed getting to know the other group members as well as learning the importance of finding a career that matches one's attributes. He states that group discussions and career value assessments have been helpful in showing him the relationship between values and career decision-making. Noah further states that it was very cool to see his fellow group members connect career values to career decision-making. For example, he turns to Sadie and says that, given her interest in and care for others and her desire for creativity in her work, he can see her being a schoolteacher. When pushed further by the leader to engage more in self-reflection, Noah has a difficult time identifying a specific attribute about himself that he has discovered in the course of the group. The case of Noah displays both the benefits and the challenges of the termination stage. Process the following questions:

1. Identify the benefits that Noah received from the group experience.
2. Identify the challenges that Noah is experiencing as the group terminates.
3. As a group leader, how would you encourage Noah to engage in more self-reflection?

CHALLENGES OF TERMINATION

Particularly in small, process-oriented groups, as students make changes based on skills they have learned, they are becoming increasingly independent from the group. Despite the independence gained, however, many group members experience emotions related to closure, loss, and separation. In dealing with emotions related to termination, there are some developmental considerations for children and adolescents (van Velsor, 2004). Children often formulate their identities within peer and family relationships, and group counseling experiences may facilitate their development. Since group work is a salient medium by which children can define their self-concepts, they may experience sadness and anxiety at termination, making the process particularly difficult for them. This is developmentally normal and appropriate. Since children may quickly form attachments, leaders should prepare for termination early to minimize possible feelings of abandonment. Leaders should model disclosure of feelings, provide individualized positive feedback for the children, and consider appropriate referrals for individual counseling.

Further, peer groups are an important source of both support and stress for adolescents. Adolescents often strive for closeness, yet fear intimacy, making dealing with feelings of termination complex. Thus, adolescents may have difficulty giving and receiving the feedback required in termination, particularly in groups with peers who are similar to them.

During termination of a group, students may display emotions such as withdrawal and aggression that are typically characteristic of earlier phases (Vernelle, 1994). Some students may have conflicting feelings about dissolving relationships formed in the group. Students may express sadness or anxiety, and they may pull back from the group and not introduce new issues. To ease these feelings, they may rely on various defense mechanisms or maladaptive coping mechanisms. For example, students may engage in denial and avoidance as a way to deal with separation and loss, or they may insist that additional group sessions are needed or that the group experience was not helpful.

Sometimes to avoid closure of a group experience, students will reflect solely on positive changes in other group members and not on what they have learned, a dynamic known as the farewell party syndrome. A key indicator that students have successfully completed a group experience is movement toward acknowledging and addressing their problems and specific growth experiences, so deflecting reflection away from personal changes may indicate the farewell party syndrome (see Case Study 10.2).

In addition, members may not be specific about the skills they have learned or about the self-awareness they have achieved. Alternatively, they may not be willing to discuss any negative aspects of the group experience. Leaders should model appropriate responses and challenge students who do not discuss personal and specific examples of growth and skill development.

CASE STUDY 10.2

The Farewell Party Syndrome

Imagine you are a professional school counselor working with a middle school group on cyberbullying during its final session. This group is for students who have been the target of cyberbullying, and its goal is teaching them coping skills. As the group comes to a close, you ask members to describe something they wish they could have addressed during the past group sessions. Several members report that they really enjoyed the group and could not think of anything that could be different. They discuss how much they enjoy each other's company and compliment each other's progress. The group members are easily able to identify the progress other group members have made but are unable to identify progress in themselves.

As the leader in this situation, you realize that the group is engaging in the farewell party syndrome and that this is a way for the students to deal with the termination of the group. It is also important for you not to let the group end without encouraging the group members to acknowledge their own growth and development as well as acknowledging the difficulty some group members may be having at ending this group experience. To address this issue, you conduct an activity that may encourage the individual group members to focus on their own personal learning. You ask each group member to put his or her name at the top of a blank piece of paper and pass the paper to the right. Group members are to write on each paper one thing that they wish this group member would have shared or elaborated on during the course of the group. Members continue to pass the papers to the right and add to the lists until the papers come back to their owners. Then the members write on their own papers what they wish they could have shared. At the end of this activity, you have each group member review his or her list and pick one thing from that list to share with the group. A follow-up to this activity would be to have each group member express one wish for each of the other members as the group ends.

COMMON LEADER FUNCTIONS DURING ALL PHASES OF TERMINATION

Professional school counselors have dual leadership roles related to termination. First, leaders prepare students for the process of termination using various organizational and interpersonal skills. Second, they foster a sense of closure for the students as they move the students through the termination process.

Preparing Students for Group Termination

Leaders prepare students for termination by providing logistical and therapeutic structure. With respect to logistical structure, leaders are cognizant of when to introduce termination. Within a session, they should leave approximately 10 minutes to close the group, although the time allotment will depend on the size and type of the group. They will want to provide the students with at least a 10-minute warning and be the timekeeper for the group. Pertaining to the end of the group experience, leaders should initially make students aware of how many times the group will meet and alert them to the upcoming final session several sessions in advance.

With respect to therapeutic structure, leaders should address termination by reminding students of the importance of maintaining confidentiality between group sessions and at the end of the group as well as adhering to any additional rules developed by the group members. It is also important for leaders to remind the students of the importance of developing a support system outside of the group.

Moving Students Through Termination

Regardless of group format, there are several ways that leaders facilitate movement through termination. These include instilling hope, processing feelings with closure, integrating group member experiences, addressing unfinished business, and assessing the group process. As they move groups through termination, leaders modify how each of these variables is addressed based on the type of group being conducted as well as the developmental needs of its members.

INSTILLING HOPE   Instillation of hope is an important component of the group process because students need to feel supported if they are to take risks in their lives by practicing new behaviors learned in the group (Yalom & Leszcz, 2005) and ultimately to see improvements in school behavior and academic achievement. Hope must be instilled in every stage of group work to prevent premature termination. Leaders should encourage students to apply things they are learning during group work to their daily lives both in and out of school. Further, leaders should reinforce the changes students have made.

In order to prevent premature termination, leaders instill hope through various methods. One way is through the use of outside role models. Outside role models may be former student group members who have successfully completed the group. Highlighting students who have successfully completed the group can encourage group members to continue to develop skills and take new risks.

CASE STUDY 10.3

Ella

Consider Ella, an elementary-aged African American female, who has been attending a grief and loss group due to the death of her mother. This is a general grief and loss group for any students who have experienced a loss in their lives, including death, divorce, and loss due to parental incarceration. Ella is the only group member who is dealing with loss due to death. Ella feels isolated and different from the other group members because the other group members at least have mothers who are living. She shares with the group that she feels like her situation is hopeless and that she should leave the group because she is bringing the others down. The group members tell Ella that she has made progress in the group by just sharing her feelings with them and that, yes, all their losses are different, but they still can support one another. One group member shares that although her loss is different because her parents are going through a divorce, she feels isolated and alone just like Ella described. And she is worried that her father will move away and she won't be able to see him any more. The group members tell Ella that she would be missed if she left the group now and that she is the group member the others can count on for words of encouragement. Ella states that she feels better, and, yes, her situation is different, but so is everyone else's. Ella decides to stay in the group.

What are the primary issues Ella is struggling with?

How did the group members process and respond to Ella's concerns?

As leader, what can you do to help Ella, both inside and outside of the group?

How might you use an outside role model?

PROCESSING FEELINGS WITH CLOSURE   Because negative feelings and defense mechanisms are among the challenges of termination, processing students' feelings with closure may be a difficult, yet necessary, leadership task. Leaders must continue to reiterate the importance of the group experience generally and of termination more specifically to minimize denial and avoidance.

Additionally, leaders should remind students that termination may be difficult because members have developed cohesion with a commitment to the well-being of one another and the group itself. Leaders should process how interpersonal connections were formed within the group so that members can emulate these in other contexts. They may also promote discussion of how students can continue to foster their relationships in other contexts at school.

INTEGRATING GROUP MEMBER EXPERIENCES   Leaders can help members to integrate experiences acquired in and out of group counseling. They can do this by assisting group members in developing specific contracts, completing homework assignments, or reflecting on key turning points within and outside the group. For example, a leader may highlight a student's marked improvement in following the rules of the group from the beginning to the end of the group experience as well as the student's improvement in classroom behavior while participating in the group, as noted by his or her teacher.

Additionally, leaders can help students integrate their experiences by focusing on relationship dynamics among group members. Leaders can encourage students to reflect on reactions to other members in the ending phase versus the beginning phase of the group. If the students note changes, the leader should assess what role members had in changing perceptions or relationships. In the school setting, where "cliques" or closed peer groups are common, counseling groups can act to positively shatter boundaries between students. The termination stage can be used to challenge students to keep these boundaries diffuse and encourage the continuation of friendships beyond the group.

One challenge that leaders may face involves assisting with meaning making for those who do not perceive the group as a forum for learning skills applicable to the outside world. Some students may consider the group an end in itself and not apply learning to their daily lives in and out of school. These members may not perceive that skills developed in a group are useful to other situations in their lives. Additionally, students may not see how skills learned in group can be applied to positively affect their academic achievement. Case Study 10.4 provides an example of the challenges associated with applying learning outside of the group setting.

CASE STUDY 10.4

Kara

The following is a case example of the challenge of getting group members to apply learning posttermination. Imagine you are leading a group on friendship for elementary-aged girls. The purposes of this group are to discuss how to make friends, explore the qualities of being a good friend, understand common friendship problems, learn how to manage conflicts within friendships, and develop a plan to improve friendships. You are beginning to discuss termination with the group with two group sessions remaining. You ask the group members to begin to develop individual written plans for what they will do to improve their friendships outside of the group. Kara, one of the quieter group members, has a difficult time completing this task. She states that she is not sure how what she has learned in the group will help her with her friends outside the group. Of course, she can talk about her problems and express her concern in group, but that is not the same as doing it outside of group. As the leader of the group, how could you ask the other group members to discuss Kara's concerns (content issue) and any issues that may be behind Kara's concern (process issue)?

ADDRESSING UNFINISHED BUSINESS   Another important role of the leader is to facilitate the resolution of unfinished business. Students may have unfinished business related to other group members, the group process, and the goals of the group. Although it is unrealistic to resolve all issues before the termination of a group session or a group, it is the responsibility of the leader to begin the dialogue about remaining issues. In facilitating this dialogue, the leader may motivate students to reexamine their own personal goals for the group and work toward accomplishing those goals before the end of the group.

Group leaders can facilitate this process by asking the following hypothetical questions:

- If group ended today, what would you wish you had said to any of the group members?
- If group ended today, what would you wish you had shared with the group?
- What additional goals do you wish you had accomplished?
- What are your wishes for the other group members?

Leaders may also use this as an opportunity to assess members' needs for additional services. An advantage to school counseling is the opportunity to address students' issues using multiple modalities. Students can be encouraged to voice ideas and concerns generated in small groups during related classroom guidance sessions, they may be encouraged to continue seeing the professional school counselor on an individual basis, and/or they may be referred for other services, such as academic or emotional assessments, tutoring, after-school programming, and outside counseling.

ASSESSING THE GROUP PROCESS   In all groups, leaders assess the progress of the group toward meeting the goals of instilling hope and encouraging the application of learning. To this end, leaders explore with students in various ways how the group is meeting group and individual goals, the degree to which students are satisfied with group content and process, and how successful students are at using their skills in their daily lives. Further, it is ethically imperative that school counselors integrate evidence into their practice. Thus, following up with students at various termination points throughout the group to check on continued progress is essential. Following termination of the group, leaders should assess the group's effect on student behavior (e.g., rate of discipline referrals, teacher reports, parent reports), school attendance, and academic achievement (e.g., grades, standardized test scores, completion of assigned work). This evidence should influence future termination techniques and approaches with student group members (Pollio, 2002). Additionally, these data are essential for substantiating the important link between social/emotional development and academic success as well as for justifying the role of the professional school counselor as an integral component of the academic system (ASCA, 2005).

In summary, termination is a complex process with many challenges and benefits. It takes a skilled leader to move students successfully through the termination process. Thus far, we have discussed termination in general; however, there are three different types of termination: premature termination, termination of individual sessions, and group termination. Each of these three types of termination involves special considerations.

PREMATURE TERMINATION

Premature termination occurs when a leader or a member leaves the group unexpectedly or the group dissolves itself earlier than planned and before the goals of the group have been met. Premature termination is a naturally occurring phenomenon in group work that should be anticipated so that it can be addressed. Leaders realize that premature termination can be minimized or prevented but not altogether eliminated. Ethically speaking, group members are free to leave the group at any time. Also, infrequently, leaders may be unable to continue leading the group.

A group can experience premature termination when the leader leaves due to illness, relocation, reassignment, or some other reason and is not replaced with a new group leader. Premature termination due to the professional school counselor's leaving can cause student group members to feel abandoned and anxious. A leader can minimize the group's fears and anxiety by conducting a final session where he or she processes the reason for leaving and provides group members with referrals for other groups either inside or outside the school. For example, the leader may say, "I'm sorry that we are having to end this group before the agreed-on time, but my doctor believes it is best that I take maternity leave earlier than expected, so I can no longer continue with this group. How are you feeling about having to end this group? I have talked to Ms. XX and Mr. YY, the other professional school counselors here, about the possibility that you can join one of their groups. They will be contacting you to see if you might be interested in meeting with one of them. I will pass out information about their group opportunities as well as information about local groups in the community you might find helpful."

If it is not possible to call together a final group session before the leader leaves, then the leader might consider contacting each group member's parent/guardian via telephone to see if it would be possible to speak with their child. This allows the leader to discuss the rationale for ending the group as well as give the student an opportunity to express fears and concerns related to the premature termination of the group. The leader will want to provide contacts for other counselors in the school as well as outside referrals at this time.

Premature termination of a group member occurs when a student leaves a group prior to the group's ending and without proper closure. Students may exit a group prior to the group's last session because they have met their goals, their parents pull them out of group suddenly, they become frustrated over the lack of progress, the group is no longer suitable for them, or logistics, such as schedule changes, which prevent them from remaining in the group. Premature termination is also referred to as "dropping out" of a group experience. In the school setting, students may opt out of all types of counseling services at any time; however, student-initiated dropping out of a group is much more likely to occur in small groups as opposed to large classroom guidance groups, which are often perceived as another component of the structured educational curriculum, rather than counseling.

Even when a student leaves a group successfully (e.g., goals were attained), it is important that leaders consider that other members may perceive the exit as premature. It is also important for the leader to consider the various overlapping groups that a member may be exiting and respond to each group individually. For example, if a student and her parent decide midyear that the student should no longer participate in counseling services at the school and this results in the student dropping out of a small group addressing grief and loss as well as an ongoing large classroom group on resilience, the leader will want to address the remaining members in both groups to minimize the impact.

There are various views on premature termination (Bostwick, 1987; Lothstein, 1978). Most of the group literature states that premature termination is detrimental to the group process because progress may be disrupted for those who remain in the group. This disruption may cause an increased exodus of other members. Additionally, dropouts may hinder group process for a significant period of time because a group requires stability. In the school setting, the degree of disruption may vary greatly based on the reason for the student's departure from group. A member who leaves a group due to a family move is likely to affect the group process far less than a member who chooses to drop out of a group due to being bored or frustrated with the process. The latter member may model perceptions and behaviors that are then mimicked by other group members. The case of Antwone (Case Study 10.5) demonstrates some of the group issues related to premature termination.

CASE STUDY 10.5

Antwone

Imagine you are a professional school counselor leading a group on "Understanding Yourself and Others." The purpose of this group is to help individuals gain self-awareness related to their characteristics and uniqueness as well as to develop a positive self-image. The group also discusses how to improve peer relationships. This is a voluntary group that meets weekly during the lunch period. After several group sessions, Antwone decides to drop out of the group because he misses having lunch with his friends. After Antwone leaves the group, other group members also state that they miss having lunch with their friends and are thinking about dropping out of the group.

As the leader, how would you help the other group members process Antwone's exit from the group?

What are some reasons that may have caused Antwone to prematurely terminate from the group, and how could these issues have been addressed prior to his exit?

An alternative perspective asserts that premature termination is a natural process in that group members not suitable for a specific group drop out so that other group members' experiences are maximized. However, this may be true only if "inappropriate members" leave the group early in the group process. While the effects of premature termination on the remaining group members are mixed, a group that is cohesive (i.e., the members have a secure attachment to one another) will experience less disruption when a member prematurely leaves a group (Yalom & Leszcz, 2005).

When a student is appropriate for a particular group but is terminated prematurely due to negative experiences, the termination may be detrimental for that student as well as for the remaining members. If a leader does everything to remove the obstacles that have been preventing a particular student from working effectively in a group and nothing changes, other students may experience negative consequences if the student remains in the group. If a member is removed, it is important to emphasize to the student that you as the group leader are looking out for the best interests of that student and those remaining in the group. This will lessen the risk that the student will feel abandoned or rejected. In this case, it may be appropriate to offer other services, such as an alternative group, individual sessions, the opportunity to work with a different professional school counselor (if available), and/or services outside of the school.

A central paradox of premature termination is that those who would benefit most from group work are more likely to drop out of a group. For instance, those who are different from the group in terms of some intrapersonal or interpersonal aspect are more likely to drop out (Yalom & Leszcz, 2005). Thus, students with relational problems with peers at school may be most likely to leave the group prematurely despite the fact that group counseling is especially helpful for addressing these issues.

Why Do Students Terminate Group Prematurely?

Statistics on premature termination (i.e., dropout rates) suggest that 35% of those who join a group (adults and children combined) drop out of group treatment for various reasons (Yalom & Leszcz, 2005). Because the factors that result in premature termination vary, professional school counselors should not automatically assume that students who drop out are resistant to group intervention. Some of the reasons for premature termination include psychological characteristics, group dynamics, logistical issues, and leadership factors.

PSYCHOLOGICAL CHARACTERISTICS   Psychological characteristics such as level of motivation, general comfort level with intimacy and self-disclosure, mental health status, and appropriate personal boundaries play a key role in determining whether students will remain in groups (Gladding, 2008; Yalom & Leszcz, 2005). Students may drop out due to fear of self-disclosure and the subsequent discomfort experienced during group sessions when asked to open up. Alternatively, students may terminate early because they are afraid of experiencing negative effects from hearing about others' problems. This may be an indication of poor boundaries or maladaptive defense mechanisms. However, a higher level of motivation may compensate for students who have moderate levels of discomfort with intimacy and self-disclosure. Students lacking motivation are likely to lose interest in the group process and opt for an alternative to the group experience.

Students may also leave a group prematurely due to their parent's or guardian's fears (see Case Study 10.6). A parent or guardian may become concerned that others in the group are negatively affecting their child. Students from families with rigid boundaries may have a parent or guardian who becomes uncomfortable with the level of disclosure in the group and responds by removing the child. Although a student may be highly motivated to participate in a group, without parental permission he or she may not be able to take part. To possibly prevent this type of premature termination, leaders need to directly address parental concerns.

CASE STUDY 10.6

Nell

Nell is an eight-year-old biracial female who is attending a changing family group. Her father is Caucasian and her mother is Asian. The purpose of the family group is to support children whose parents are going through a divorce or separation. Nell's parents have recently separated. Her mother is the one who gave consent for Nell to attend the group. Although

Nell's father did not want her to participate in the group, he initially agreed that she could attend. After several weeks of the group, Nell's father becomes increasingly uncomfortable with the level of disclosure reported by Nell. He tells Nell that she must quit the group immediately. Nell is very upset and tells you that she does not want to quit. As the leader, you invite both Nell's parents for a consultation.

Is it your role to "convince" Nell to stay in the group? Explain.

Is it your role to "convince" Nell's parents to let her stay in the group? Explain.

What are some issues/concerns you will want to discuss with Nell's parents?

What are some issues/concerns you will want to discuss with the group members if Nell leaves?

GROUP DYNAMICS   Students may terminate prematurely when they perceive unhealthy group dynamics. The term *healthy group dynamics* refers to positive views of a setting, satisfaction with treatment, a willingness to appropriately self-disclose (Bostwick, 1987), a sense of belonging, and a comfort level with group intimacy.

A student's perceived acceptance by both the leader and other group members has a significant impact on the student's psychological characteristics. Sometimes students believe that they do not fit in the group or that other members' issues hinder their own success in the group. Subgrouping, both if members are included and if they are excluded, may affect their sense of acceptance and belonging. Thus, students' satisfaction with a group may be, in part, contingent on the degree to which they have open communication and feel included in the group by others.

Sometimes a student may significantly differ from other group members, a phenomenon termed *group deviancy.* Group deviancy is different from a general sense of not feeling accepted; a deviant member may be different with respect to personality variables, skills, and degree of insight into problems. Group members may be considered deviant if their goals are not congruent with group goals or if they impede the group process due to an unwillingness or an inability to fulfill group tasks. Group deviants are more likely to experience negative consequences from the group, such as being generally less satisfied with the group, viewing the group as not valuable, or experiencing anxiety (Lieberman, Yalom, & Miles, 1973).

Self-disclosure is another key factor affecting premature termination. Students may self-disclose too much too early in the group process, perhaps as a result of poor personal boundaries. This premature self-disclosure may not be reciprocated by others in the group, leaving the disclosing students feeling shame or embarrassment and wanting to drop out of the group (Yalom & Leszcz, 2005).

LOGISTICAL ISSUES   Logistical concerns may also hinder students from continuing group interventions. These may include class schedule changes and family moves. While some of these concerns may arise unexpectedly during the course of the group, leaders should facilitate discussions in initial group sessions about potential logistical barriers to group work.

LEADERSHIP FACTORS   At times, leaders may not adequately prepare group members for a group experience, inadvertently prompting premature termination. Leaders should continually assess students' perceptions about their satisfaction with the group. In addition, leaders should monitor student progress through self-evaluation and consultation. With self-evaluation, leaders may attend to their personal reactions to group dynamics as well as students' feedback when terminating individual sessions. For consultation, leaders can discuss with other professionals their concerns and successes, interventions, reactions to the group content and process, and perceptions of students' progress. These other professionals may include a counselor within the school or from a different school, a guidance director, a school counselor educator, and/or a consultant designated through one's state or national school counseling association. During consultation, professional school counselors should adhere to applicable ethical principles and standards of practice. Case Study 10.7 presents a variety of potential termination scenarios for you to reflect on.

CASE STUDY 10.7

Various Premature Termination Scenarios

The following are examples of how the above factors may cause a student to terminate the group experience prematurely. Reflect on how you could prevent or minimize premature termination in each case.

- Michael, a 17-year-old Caucasian, gay male in a drug and alcohol prevention group, states that he feels that other members of the group are not accepting of him. He states that he feels judged for his sexual identity and wants to leave the group.
- Sydney, a 13-year-old Asian American female in a study skills group, constantly interrupts another group member as he talks about his study skills. She gives advice to the member, stating, "You just need to study harder." The group member, Andy, becomes angry with her interruptions.
- Amber, a 10-year-old Native American female, reports at the end of a group session that she will not be able to attend the group anymore. She states that her mother does not want Amber to share her story with strangers.
- Owen, a 16-year-old Caucasian male in a managing conflicts group, has a difficult time sitting still and staying focused. He is constantly making inappropriate (and sometimes offensive) jokes and getting up and disrupting the rest of the group. Other group members are concerned or upset with his jokes and disruptions and disclose to the group leader after the session that they want Owen to be removed from the group.
- Leigh, an 8-year-old female in a grief and loss group, gets upset as the group members begin sharing the details of their loss. She runs out of the group in the middle of the session.
- Jay, an 11-year-old Asian male in an academic success group, has been a leader of the group and appears to be getting a lot from the group. After one of the group sessions, he tells the leader that he can no longer attend the group. His parents have not seen an improvement in his grades, and they want him to spend his study period actually studying and not in a group talking about studying.

Preventing Premature Termination

Preventing (or minimizing) premature termination begins with screening during the planning phase and continues as a group develops cohesion. Leaders can minimize the risk of students prematurely leaving a group by adequately preparing them for the group experience during the screening process. This includes reviewing risks, addressing group member characteristics, and examining value orientations. Additionally, providing structure and consistency is imperative for retaining members and maximizing their satisfaction with the group experience. In most instances, leaders should attempt to have students commit to the designated number of sessions.

REVIEWING RISKS   Regardless of the group format, it is important that leaders thoroughly describe what the group content and process will be like in general, including the potential psychological and physical risks involved, to minimize premature termination. Potential psychological risks include group pressure to participate, including self-disclosing; scapegoating by other students; confrontation by other students; the inability to guarantee confidentiality; and disruptions in students' lives due to the psychological and logistical resources needed for group participation.

In particular, those participating in small process groups should be alerted to possible reactions from students outside the group. It often happens that students outside the small process group want to join it after they note the positive experiences of members. However, others may respond in a derogatory manner, potentially causing members to feel ashamed of their circumstances and embarrassed to be part of the group. Students who are prepared to handle negative reactions from peers are less likely to terminate the group prematurely.

ADDRESSING GROUP MEMBER CHARACTERISTICS   Because the success of a group significantly depends on the interactions among members and leaders, leaders should attend to idiosyncratic processes in their groups. Early assessment of each member's group experience is necessary because expectations and satisfaction related to group process may influence group continuation. Leaders should inquire about previous group participation both in and outside of school. Throughout the process, leaders should continually encourage members to consider things they are learning and allow them to be heard. This in turn increases a member's sense of belonging and accomplishment.

Leaders should familiarize themselves with group members' vulnerabilities, respect their requests with regard to the degree of participation, develop an invitational style, and use objective statements or nonblaming subjective statements when providing feedback or general interaction. As appropriate, leaders should openly express feelings toward the group process and group members. In addition, leaders should consider the use of concurrent individual and group counseling, if appropriate, for their students.

EXAMINING VALUE ORIENTATIONS   Value conflicts play a central role in premature termination for adults and can result in discomfort and possible termination for children participating in groups at school as well. Leaders should inform and discuss with students their value assumptions related to counseling in general and to group work more specifically. With respect to group work, leaders should articulate typical group work assumptions and values. These include the following: (1) Personal risk taking is essential and beneficial for growth; (2) expression of emotions, thoughts, and personal vulnerabilities is key to building authentic and trusting relationships in group work; and (3) assertiveness and autonomy are necessary for getting what you need from others (Corey, Williams, & Moline, 1995). Acknowledging these expectations inherent in group work and soliciting feedback from group members may prevent premature termination. This information should be disseminated to parents/guardians as well. If parents'/guardians' misconceptions are addressed in the beginning, it is less likely that they will feel that the group process is inappropriate for their children, thus preventing the premature removal of their children from the group.

In addition to discussing group value assumptions, leaders should be clear about their own values in order to minimize the risk of premature termination. These might include values related to their cultural worldview or to group work itself. Leaders should examine how their cultural values interface with the group content and process. For example, leaders who value a collectivistic orientation to skills application (e.g., having students translate newly developed interpersonal skills to family interactions in order to promote harmonious, collaborative relationships) may need to consider how this value would affect those who do not share it. Group members or their parents who may not share similar values may be more inclined to terminate prematurely.

Failure to recognize and attend to cultural values and value conflicts may result in premature termination by members of racial and ethnic minority groups (Leong, 1992). Value conflicts may arise between members' and leaders' cultural values or between members' values and the traditional values of group work. For example, self-disclosure may be deemed an important aspect of healthy group development, yet students may terminate prematurely if their cultural norms frown on self-disclosure.

Leaders should also explore what role group work plays for their students. Professional school counselors following the *ASCA National Model* (ASCA, 2005) use the group format as a means to meet more students' needs. However, some students may not feel comfortable self-disclosing in front of their peers. Because of their large caseloads and the need to show that they are positively affecting all students, it is not feasible for professional school counselors to meet individually with many students. As a result, students uncomfortable with the group process may terminate early. Addressing these concerns and providing a safe, trusting group environment may result in greater levels of comfort, thus preventing some of these students from prematurely dropping out. However, it is important for leaders to have referral sources for those for whom the group format is inappropriate and to coordinate services to meet their needs.

Techniques for Preventing Premature Termination

There are several activities that leaders may use to minimize or prevent premature termination. Three activities are highlighted in this section: values contracts, comfort zones, and personal growth charts. Each of these activities is appropriate at different stages of the group process.

VALUES CONTRACTS   The purpose of a values contract is to ensure discussion of the values that leaders and members bring to sessions. Developing a values contract is one method for articulating leader and member goals and expectations. This contract should be developed in the initial group session so that individuals are clear about the group purpose, group member roles, and implicit and explicit rules. The leader could pose the following questions, which can be modified depending on the grade level of the group members:

- What are your expectations for this group?
- What do you see as your personal role in meeting those expectations?
- What do you see as the leader's role in meeting those expectations?

- What are your personal expectations?
- What are your expectations of the leader?
- What do you view as most important to make this group successful?
- How do you prefer to communicate with others?
- What, if anything, might make you uncomfortable in this group?

After processing these questions and reaching some agreement on group goals and rules from the perspective of the students, the leader should review the group rules, purpose, and goals. The leader should attempt to honor the students' requests as appropriate. This may allow the students to be more invested in and committed to the group process, more willing to openly communicate with others, and less likely to terminate prematurely.

COMFORT ZONES   The purpose of an experiential comfort zone activity is to identify students' vulnerabilities, fears, and other forms of discomfort in the group. This technique may be used in any session when the leader wants to assess group dynamics. The leader should create a large circle in the middle of the floor using a rope at least 18 feet in length. Have the students stand on the edge of the rope, forming a circle outline around the rope. Instruct them to move into the middle of the circle to the degree that they agree with the statements below. Alternatively, if the students do not agree with a statement, they should move outside of the circle, away from the midpoint. Statements explore members' comfort levels with various aspects of daily and group activities, starting with "safer" statements and moving to more "risky" ones. Ask students to move in or out of the circle for each statement.

How comfortable are you . . .

- Talking to a friend?
- Talking to a stranger?
- Engaging in a conversation with several peers?
- Being in a room with strangers?
- Being silent?
- Being the center of attention?
- Taking risks?
- Communicating with others who may have a different opinion than you?
- Communicating with others who may have a different cultural background than you?
- Talking about your strengths?
- Talking about your weaknesses?
- Telling someone when you are dissatisfied with something?
- Giving feedback to others?
- Receiving feedback from a friend?
- Receiving feedback from others?

After the exercise, have the members discuss similarities and differences related to each other's comfort levels with communicating, giving and receiving feedback, and working with different people and worldviews. Brainstorm ways in which the group can handle discomfort in the future to avoid premature termination.

PERSONAL GROWTH CHARTS   The purpose of a personal growth chart exercise is to have members self-monitor their goals and satisfaction with the group. These charts (see Table 10.1) can be shared with the leader to ensure that students are getting their goals addressed,

---

TABLE 10.1   Personal Growth Chart

Please complete the following statements.

Name: _____.

My goal in group today was _____.

I made the following progress today to meet my goal: _____.

On a scale from 1 to 10, I would rate my progress as a _____.

I feel that the group was helpful today because _____.

I feel that the group was not helpful today because _____.

My group participation today was _____.

Things I liked about today's group session are _____.

Things I would like to see change before the next session are _____.

At this time, I am concerned about _____.

I may/may not (circle one) return for future group sessions because _____.

I would/would not (circle one) like to discuss these concerns with group: _____.

---

working well with others, and applying their developing skills outside of the group experience. Have students complete the chart after each session.

TERMINATION OF INDIVIDUAL GROUP SESSIONS

Leaders will want to spend the last few minutes of each group conducting a "mini-termination" of the group session. This includes pretermination, termination, and posttermination. Pretermination is the planning phase of termination; posttermination refers to the follow-up procedures group leaders employ after termination. Throughout these stages, leaders should actively discuss with members what meaning a particular session had for them personally and how the session relates to previous and future learning. Additionally, leaders and members should co-construct meanings related to group development, including assessing each other's growth (Birnbaum & Cicchetti, 2000; Birnbaum, Mason, & Cicchetti, 2002). Now process the termination scenarios presented in Case Study 10.8.

CASE STUDY 10.8

Session Termination Techniques

Discuss the pretermination, termination, and posttermination techniques you would employ to end the following group sessions:

- Psychoeducational group for sixth graders on managing test anxiety
- Psychoeducational group for eighth graders with academic difficulties
- Classroom guidance for elementary students on maintaining good physical health
- Workshop for high school females related to dating violence prevention
- Career counseling session for ninth graders
- Counseling group for recent immigrants in a middle school setting
- Classroom guidance for first graders on sharing

- Support group for middle school students diagnosed with a disability
- Schoolwide psychoeducational group on bullying prevention in a high school setting

Discuss the following in small groups:

In what ways are your techniques similar across these groups?

In what ways do developmental and cultural issues impact these techniques?

The time needed for the termination of group sessions depends on several factors, including the type and purpose of the group, member characteristics, and leader characteristics (Gladding, 2008). Termination of the group session is especially beneficial in short-term groups, open groups, and classroom guidance sessions. Whatever the group type, intensity, and duration, leaders should use an active approach and be intentional about session closures.

Leaders should possess several specific skills for effective session termination: skills in soliciting feedback from students, establishing norms for session endings, informing students of the group process, and dealing with resistance and conflict in the group (Birnbaum et al., 2002). In the early development of a group, leaders need to discuss how sessions will end and what tasks will be involved. They should allocate a specified amount of time (e.g., 5–10 minutes for 30- to 60-minute sessions) to reflect on the content and process of a session.

In terminating a group session, it may be appropriate to integrate feedback from individuals associated with a student in some capacity. Collaborating with parents/guardians, teachers, peers, and administrators may be helpful to gain feedback about the student. Integrating this outside information is important because it could provide insight into how students are progressing toward their goals as well as how satisfied they are with the group process, which helps to assess whether they are making meaning from group sessions and to avoid premature termination, respectively.

Benefits

There are several benefits to having effective session closures. Students may be more satisfied with the group experience and have a greater sense of accomplishment if leaders solicit feedback about the group's effectiveness as well as the members' personal growth. Effective session termination may empower students, encourage reflective thinking, and increase genuine interpersonal interactions within and outside the group (Birnbaum et al., 2002). These positive changes may ultimately translate to the classroom, where teachers benefit from students who are developing in constructive ways that enable them to achieve better academically.

In general, successful session termination may make transitions between sessions progress more smoothly as both leaders and members reflect on limited and focused instances of group content and process. Members have an opportunity to assess their growth within a particular session from several perspectives: their own, other group members', and the leader's. Moreover, session termination may empower students and leaders to demonstrate that they value students' voices in guiding the group's progress. The development of these skills can help students become more confident within the classroom. Members who learn to reflect on and ask for what they need in the group setting will likely be able to ask for what they need from others outside the group as well.

Whatever their ages, students can be asked to engage in active reflection both during and between group sessions. Effective session termination allows members to reflect on the present group experience. What can students take away from today's group session and apply to their daily lives in school and at home? Members should be encouraged to evaluate and reflect on their individual and collective work as they make connections between sessions. As part of this reflection, members may identify issues that they would like to explore in future sessions as well as those that they feel they have not fully worked through by the session's end. Acknowledging individual growth and unfinished business at the end of a session allows students to have a sense of completion even if all issues were not fully addressed in a particular session. Unfinished business could potentially detract from members' ability to focus when returning to the classroom; thus, ensuring that session termination results in a sense of completion is critically important in the school setting.

Further, members can provide suggestions for future groups such as topics for subsequent sessions. This allows for collaboration among the members and between the members and the leader, thus facilitating group cohesion. Members may feel as if they are contributing to future group experiences when they work together in making decisions. Furthermore, students who bond in the group setting are more likely to maintain positive relations outside of group, potentially resulting in fewer instances in which teachers are distracted from teaching by the need to resolve interpersonal conflicts.

In addition to student and teacher benefits, there are several benefits for leaders who terminate group sessions appropriately. By soliciting feedback at the end of each session, leaders can see how effective the group has been and identify what is working and not working. They can gain a greater understanding of members' needs, their acquisitions, and the developmental stage of the group itself. Further, leaders can learn which interventions were most salient for members and had the greatest impact on academic performance.

Challenges

There may be several challenges or barriers to effective session termination. A primary challenge is the members' attitudes toward session termination. For example, members may feel that termination is unnecessary or not useful and perceive that termination should occur only at the end of a group. They may be resistant and may feel that it is repetitious and takes time away from session content and processes. The leader should address these attitudes, discussing the value of termination and the consequences of failing to terminate.

Leaders should also be cognizant that members may be resistant to ending a group session on time. For instance, a member may bring up a new issue in the last few minutes of a group session. The leader should validate the member's disclosure and state that the issue may be discussed in a future group session. Alternatively, the member may be seen individually by the leader, allowed to participate in another group, or referred to outside counseling.

Another challenge is presented when students leave a group permanently, as in the case of open groups. Many schools offer children of alcoholics (COA) groups in an open format. In open groups such as this, group termination as well as session termination can be conceptualized as occurring in each session because at the end of each session, some members may be returning to the group while others may be exiting permanently. Leaders should be cognizant of any resistance they experience when a particular member leaves. Specifically, if a student has been contributing significantly to a group, the leader could be resistant to the member's termination. Self-awareness can prevent this from interfering with the healthy continuation of the group process. Termination must be more individualized in open groups, as students leave at various times. Students should be adequately prepared when a member decides to leave the group, and the impact of an individual leaving a group should be assessed. Communicating to members the nature of open groups at the beginning of the group experience and allowing time during each session to process terminations can prevent disruptions to the group process.

CASE STUDY 10.9
Various Session Termination Scenarios

The following cases are examples of challenges that may occur when leaders terminate group sessions. Reflect on how you would respond to each scenario.

- Shea, a 14-year-old Caucasian female, has been involved in a COA group for four months. Shea has decided that she will no longer be attending meetings. Because it is an open group, there are several students who recently started attending group meetings. As the leader reflects on a session, several members discuss how they have learned so much from having Shea and express their wishes that she continue to come to the group.
- As a leader conducts a round to terminate a session of a study skills group, Chip, a 16-year-old African American male, appears distant and not focused. When it is his turn to participate in the round, Chip discloses to the group that part of the reason that he may be having difficulty in his classes is that he is struggling with how to disclose to others that he is bisexual. This is new information for the group.
- Michele, a 10-year-old Asian American female, expresses irritation when the leader of her stress management group conducts a session termination exercise. The leader asks the members to get partners and talk about what new knowledge they will take with them from today's session. Michele states that she doesn't want to waste time doing the exercise and that she would like to spend the last few minutes learning a new stress management technique instead.
- Shawn, an 8-year-old multiracial male, requests that the leader of his self-esteem group allow the group session to continue for an additional 15 minutes, rather than sending the students back to class. He states that he needs more time to talk to the group about how to prepare for his upcoming talent show performance, which is three days away.

Techniques for Terminating Individual Group Sessions

There are several techniques that leaders may use to terminate group sessions effectively. These techniques may involve leader and member summarization. When used to terminate a group session, leader summarization is characterized as commenting on or reacting to the group process or content in a way that solidifies what was learned within a session, acknowledging specific relationship dynamics among group members, and addressing or calling attention to critical events or learning within the session. When member summarization is used in terminating a group session, one or more group members briefly appraise the group content and process.

TABLE 10.2   Stems

Leaders will find the following stems useful during session termination. Ask members to respond to the following:

- Today I learned _____.
- I feel _____.
- Based on today's group, I will _____ in school this week.
- Based on today's group, I will _____ at home this week.
- Three things I will do differently because of this group session are _____.
- What I like about this group is _____.
- Something discussed in group today that I will continue to reflect on is _____.
- If I could sum up my experience in this group so far using one word, it would be _____.
- I will continue to work on _____.
- I will change _____ before next week.
- My experience with others in this group has been _____ because _____.
- One thing I have learned about how I relate to others is _____.
- One way the group has influenced me is _____.
- I would like to address _____ before the group ends.
- I noticed that the group worked well together today by _____.
- One change I would like to make before next session is _____.
- I noticed that [member's name] benefited from today's session because _____.

Techniques for terminating a session include rounds, dyads, sentence completion, scaling questions, process questions, journaling, and evaluation of a group session (Corey, 2007). Importantly, these techniques can be adapted for use during other facets of group work and modified to match the developmental level of the students.

ROUNDS   Rounds give each group member an equal opportunity to participate in the group by commenting on a statement or question. Usually, each individual is given one to two minutes. Rounds are a positive way to end the group as well as to assure that each member gets an opportunity to participate. See Table 10.2 for stems that leaders can use to begin a round.

DYADS   The leader can have students divide into dyads (i.e., pairs) at the end of the session. As in rounds, the dyads are given stems related to the group session (see Table 10.2) and asked to share their answers. By having students form dyads, the leader is making sure that each student participates in termination, yet less time is taken away from the group work. The leader can assign dyads based on similar issues, or students can form their own dyads.

SENTENCE COMPLETION   Having students complete sentences in written or verbal form can be an important part of preparing group members for the end of a group session. Table 10.2 provides a sentence completion activity.

SCALING ACTIVITY   Scaling is a valuable tool that allows members to conceptualize incremental changes as they move through the sessions. Using this activity, leaders may get a sense of how students operationalize certain changes. One scaling method involves assessing

TABLE 10.3   A Group Session Rating Form

I am interested in improving future sessions so that you have a more enjoyable group experience. Using the following scale, please rate the degree to which you feel the following occurred in today's group session.

1	2	3	4	5
Strongly Disagree	Disagree	Unsure	Agree	Strongly Agree

Please provide a rating to the left of each item and as much feedback as you would like in the comments section.

Group #: _____
Group Topic: _____

_____ The group session was interesting and worthwhile.
_____ My school work will be improved as a result of what I learned in group today.
_____ The group worked toward its goals today.
_____ I worked on my personal goals today in group.
_____ I learned something new about myself today.
_____ I learned something new about others today.
_____ I learned or improved a skill in this group session.
_____ I feel that the group leader was well prepared today.
_____ I feel that the group leader worked toward our goals.
_____ I enjoyed the activities in today's session.
_____ Other group members were supportive and respectful.

Comments:

how satisfied members are with the group in terms of addressing their goals. Table 10.3 provides an example of a scaling activity used to get a sense of members' satisfaction with a counseling group designed to help increase their self-awareness. Case Study 10.10 provides an example of using a scaling procedure in group work.

CASE STUDY 10.10

Using a Scaling Activity to Terminate a Group Session

During the termination of a group session, the leader wants the group to process, consolidate, and evaluate gains made in the group using a scaling activity. The group leader passes out a sheet with the following guided questions and explains:

> I would like you to rate your satisfaction with the group today in terms of learning something new about yourself. To do this, envision a scale ranging from 1 to 10, with 1 being the least satisfied and 10 being the most satisfied with your personal growth in the group today. What would a 1 look like for you on this scale?

What would a 5 look like on this scale? What would a 10 look like on this scale? Where were you on the scale before the group began today? What occurred in the group to change that rating (i.e., what specifically increased or decreased your satisfaction)? Where would you like to be by the end of next session (i.e., how satisfied do you want to be with your increase in self-awareness by the end of the next session)? What can you do to achieve that rating? What can the group do to assist you in achieving that rating? Imagine that this is the last session. What would be your ideal rating? What would your personal growth look like if you reached this ideal rating?

PROCESS QUESTIONS   Process questions should be congruent with the group stage, with more-structured questions used during earlier session endings and less-structured questions used as the group progresses. For example, questions used to summarize initial sessions may focus on group purpose and goals, member relationships, and member roles. In later sessions, members may start closing sessions on their own (Birnbaum et al., 2002). Following are possible process questions to use:

- What stood out to you about today's group session?
- How was today's session different from earlier sessions?
- What would you like to see happen in the next group session?
- How will what you learned in group today help you in school? Outside of school?
- What are your goals for planning for future sessions?
- What did you notice about others' growth in this session?
- In what ways have you begun to meet your goals in this group?
- What has been useful for you in this group experience thus far?
- What are some things that you feel we have not addressed yet?
- What feelings came up for you in group today?
- Which group member did you have the most difficulty relating to and why?
- Which group member did you best relate to and why?
- What things helped the group move toward its goals today?

JOURNALING   Journaling can be an important way for members to reflect on a group session in a private manner. Leaders can encourage members to write reactions to a session during the last few minutes of the group. Alternatively, members may write in a journal daily between sessions as they continue to reflect and apply new learning.

Evaluation of Group Sessions

Evaluation occurs at various junctures throughout the group experience (e.g., end of session, end of experience). Leaders should allow some time to formally or informally assess the group's effectiveness in meeting its purpose. Evaluation related to terminating a group session can occur in many ways, but it is usually done by obtaining verbal or written feedback at the end of the session. Leaders can evaluate the group by asking students directly about their experiences. Alternatively, leaders can distribute questionnaires or rating scales and ask students to complete them periodically or after each group session. Leaders can also assess the effectiveness of a group by asking teachers and parents for feedback about changes noted in students since participating in the group. Much more attention is given to group evaluation strategies in Chapter 16.

TERMINATION OF THE GROUP EXPERIENCE

Groups terminate for several reasons. Termination may occur at a preset time, as with closed groups; when a majority of group members are ready to terminate; or, as discussed earlier, when a leader leaves the group and there are no other leaders available.

In open groups, members have consistent models of the beginning, middle, and ending phases of a group, as membership changes with each group session. In this case, a group may not end until each member has met preset goals. Thus, termination in an open group typically will not occur unless there are changes in the group leadership.

A key indicator that a group is ready for termination is cohesiveness. Group cohesion, a goal of the working stage, involves strong interpersonal bonds among members and yet decreased dependence on one another for support. Students from cohesive groups have more genuine interactions and can provide constructive feedback regarding self, the group, and other members. Since the majority of groups conducted in the school setting are closed groups with a set number of sessions, it is imperative that the leader work to establish group cohesion early on to ensure that the members are able to meet their goals and that the group is ready to terminate when the time arrives.

Evaluation of the Group Experience

Termination of the group experience involves evaluation from both the leader and the members. The leader will want to offer an assessment related to his or her own effectiveness and the effectiveness of the group process as well as to encourage students to evaluate their own participation, the leader's effectiveness, and the group process.

In preparing for group termination, leaders will want to engage in some personal reflections. How do they feel about the group? How do they feel about the group getting ready to terminate? How do they feel about the progress the group has made? How do they feel about their own effectiveness in facilitating the group? Leaders should disclose their own feelings about separation, while continuing genuine interactions with group members and normalizing feelings of termination.

Leaders will also want to encourage members to provide feedback about their group experience. This can be done by incorporating rating scales and process questions such as those described in the previous section but now referencing the entire group experience. Additionally, leaders may consider the following questions:

- What did you like most about the group experience?
- What did you like least about the group experience?
- What aspects of the group were most helpful? Least helpful?
- What characteristics do you feel make a good leader?
- What characteristics do you feel make a good group member?

In evaluating the group, members may provide abstract or vague feedback without concrete examples of what and how they have learned in the group. The leader will want to encourage members to provide more concrete, specific responses. In response to the first question ("What did you like most about the group experience?"), Dee says, "I liked everything—this has been the most positive experience of my life, and I loved every aspect of the group." The leader will want to follow up and encourage Dee to provide more-concrete examples. "I think it's great that you got so much out of this group. Tell us one specific thing that made this group a positive experience for you."

In addition to assessing the group process, following termination, leaders will want to evaluate the impact of the group on students' school performance outside of the group. Academic performance, disciplinary infractions, and attendance are three variables that can be assessed for change following a group experience. To assess change, leaders can use both formal, existing data, such as grades, referrals, and truancy reports, and informal sources, such as surveys of or discussions with parents and teachers. This accountability is essential for showing the viability of the school counseling program in supporting the overall achievement of the students. Group evaluation will be covered in much greater depth in Chapter 16.

Challenges

Students have a variety of feelings related to termination. As termination of a group nears, some students will minimize their improvement because they fear being abandoned by the group. Thus, they may not appear ready to terminate. Other students may overemphasize their growth and may avoid unfinished business or negative feelings. Leaders can minimize these challenges by preparing the group for termination gradually as well as by openly sharing their thoughts and feelings related to termination. Case Study 10.11 provides an example of a group termination challenge.

CASE STUDY 10.11

A Group Termination Challenge

Consider the following case example, which illustrates some of the challenges associated with terminating a group experience. You have been leading a 10-week group for adolescents who self-harm. The group members have made great progress individually and as a group. With two weeks remaining in the group, you begin introducing the topic of termination. The following week three of the seven group members come back stating that they had a horrible week and that they are not ready to end the group. One of the members doesn't show up, and when you call her into your office later that day, she tells you that she isn't cutting herself anymore anyway and that she doesn't need to finish out the group. As the leader, reflect on how you would address these members' concerns.

Techniques for Terminating the Group

The techniques for terminating the group are not all that different from the techniques helpful in terminating group sessions. While all groups, regardless of the model type, should include termination, the procedures may be less formal for task groups, psychoeducational groups, and classroom guidance as opposed to counseling groups and psychotherapy groups. In counseling and psychotherapy groups, students have potentially addressed several personal concerns by the termination stage; therefore, assessment of personal goals and needs is important so that members can see how much they have gained from the group process as well as identify specific areas for their continued growth. For a few sessions before the last group session, professional school counselors should encourage students to consider what they perceive as accomplishments, what they would have done differently, and what they would like to continue to focus on after the group ends. In particular, leaders should encourage the members to reflect on how the things they have learned in the group will continue to positively affect their school performance. In addition, members should consider what interpersonal connections they have made and what feelings they have related to termination.

As with session terminations, rounds, dyads, sentence completion, and journaling can help facilitate termination of the group. Following are sample questions that can be used with these activities:

- What fears did you have coming into this group?
- What fears do you have now as we prepare to end the group experience?
- What is the most important lesson you will take away from this group experience?
- Describe yourself when you first came into the group. Describe yourself now. How are you different? What has made you different?
- How would others close to you describe you before and after the group experience?
- Imagine that you could go back and talk to the person you were before the group began. Based on what you have learned during the group, what advice would you give that person?
- How will your school work be affected by your experience in this group?

PLANNING FOR THE FUTURE   Termination of the group is not only a time for reflection and summarization but also a time for looking toward the future and implementing new skills beyond the group. Members can help each other with plans for the future and implementation of new skills beyond the group through the following activity. Have each member put his or her name on a piece of paper and divide the paper into sections labeled 1, 5, and 10 years. Then have members pass their papers to other group members. Members are instructed to write down where they believe the group member whose name is on the paper will be in 1, 5, and 10 years from today. After each student has had an opportunity to write on every other group member's paper, the papers are returned to their owners. Members are given an opportunity to review what other group members have written. The leader facilitates a discussion related to how the members feel reading what others have written about them. Do they agree with what has been written about them? Any surprises? What additional things would members add to their lists?

Another activity that facilitates planning for the future is to have members draw pictures of their life before the group experience, now as they are ending the group experience, and what they would like their life to be like in the future. Leaders then facilitate discussion related to how members' lives are different and how they brought about that difference for themselves and can continue to make positive changes for themselves for the future.

ROLE PLAYS AND BEHAVIORAL REHEARSALS   During the last several sessions, members can practice what they have learned in the group through role plays and behavioral rehearsals. The leader can have members write down scenarios of issues or concerns that they have and encourage them to play out those scenarios in the group. The leader can either have students participate in their own scenes or watch how others would handle the situation.

GROUP SCRAPBOOK   As a group project, the members can put together a group scrapbook. The scrapbook would include pictures, symbols, and statements relevant to the group. The leader will want to make sure that each person contributes to the group scrapbook. In creating the group scrapbook, members are given the opportunity to reflect back on their experience as well as to see how others experienced the group. The leader can keep the group scrapbook in his or her office to be available to the members and can bring it to follow-up sessions.

A variation of the group scrapbook is to have each member make an individual scrapbook or collage. The leader simply asks members to create scrapbooks that reflect their experiences in the group. As they create their scrapbooks, they are encouraged to reflect on what they have learned about themselves during the group experience as well as what they have learned about others. They also consider what their contribution to the group process was. After members have worked on their own scrapbooks, they are encouraged to walk around and see other members' scrapbooks and contribute thoughts, well wishes, and memories to them. Numerous other closure activities are provided by Keene and Erford (2007) and modified for the school setting.

AFFIRMATIONS   In addition to reflecting on the group experience and planning for the future, the last session of a group in the school setting should include affirmations. This can be accomplished in multiple ways, depending on the nature of the group and the developmental level of the members. For large classroom guidance, the professional school counselor may affirm progress made through a statement to the entire class. For small process groups, affirmations may be expressed through the distribution of certificates and positive statements made to each individual member. Leaders may opt for a party where refreshments are served and progress is celebrated.

FOLLOW-UP

Following up with group members after a group has ended is imperative because it benefits both the leader and the members. Following up with students after termination helps to assess the group experience and individual progress. One goal of follow-up is to measure group change: (1) Are students continuing to work on goals that were contracted in the final session? (2) Have students made and sustained behavioral and attitudinal changes related to the group process? (3) Has school performance improved as a result of the group experience? (4) Did students experience growth in additional areas? Follow-up enables leaders to gain information regarding how effective the group has been for the group members. The length of time suggested for follow-up varies, ranging from six weeks to several months. Some leaders even conduct six-month or one-year follow-ups.

While there are several benefits to following up with members, leaders should determine to what degree they will follow up. This may depend on the length, type, and purpose of the group as well as the developmental needs of its members. This decision may be guided by members' feedback, as leaders should continually assess group dynamics and learning.

Leaders have an ethical responsibility to promote student growth and avoid abandonment. If leaders feel that follow-up sessions would fulfill this responsibility, they should use clinical judgment to determine how many follow-up sessions are needed. Follow-ups can range from formal meetings with students to informal check-ins when encountering students during the school day. Specific methods for following up with students include interviews, group reunions, and survey methods, and leaders may elect to use any or all of these methods for follow-up.

Interviews may be done individually or as a group. In the case of individual interviews, leaders may want to assess individual experiences within the group and the degree to which members have met their goals. Additionally, leaders may want to review referral sources applicable for students who may desire additional group work or individual counseling. Leaders may contact students' parents to provide information about referral sources when applicable. Leaders can conduct a focus group to discuss any changes and new challenges and issues that students have experienced. If new issues have arisen for some members, leaders can provide referrals for additional counseling or other services. During the interviews, leaders may pose the following questions:

- What effects did the group have on you?
- How has the group influenced you in relation to others?
- How has the group influenced you in relation to your school performance?
- What changes have you noticed since leaving the group?
- What recommendations do you have for future groups?

Leaders may consider coordinating a reunion for the group members. This may be helpful for both open and closed groups. Group reunions provide a less-structured social environment where students can reconnect with each other.

Follow-up provides an opportunity to administer any posttests. Leaders may want to use a brief questionnaire to assess members' satisfaction with the group as well as their progress toward meeting goals. Surveys may be used at variable time periods to measure both short-term and long-term progress.

During the last group session, leaders need to explain to group members the purpose of follow-up. They also should review how and when follow-up will occur. As when preparing students for termination, leaders should discuss expectations for follow-up and provide alternatives if members do not wish to follow up in a formal way after termination. One alternative is to provide a referral for another form of treatment, including individual counseling, community services, or another type of group.

Summary

Termination is an essential part of all stages of group counseling, as it occurs when a member leaves prematurely, at the end of each session, and as the group experience ends. If executed properly, termination serves as a critical force in the process of change. Some of the major benefits of termination include self-awareness, awareness of others, and the development of coping skills and interpersonal skills. Despite its benefits, the termination process also involves various challenges, including feelings of separation and loss, difficulty dealing with closure, and conflicted feelings related to ending relationships formed during the group.

There are three types of termination: premature termination, termination of group sessions, and termination of the group experience. Premature termination involves either the leader or a member leaving the group before the goals of the group have been accomplished or before a predetermined time to end the group. Premature termination brings with it opportunities for group growth and challenges. Termination of group sessions refers to conducting a "mini-termination" at the end of each group session that provides an opportunity for both the leader and the members to summarize their learning and to discuss the implementation of skills outside of the group. A group can terminate at a preset time or when the majority of the students are ready to terminate. Rounds, dyads, sentence completion, and journaling are all techniques that can assist with both the termination of group sessions and the termination of the group.

Group Work in Action: Models and Special Issues

CHAPTER 11

Leading Task Groups in Schools

JANICE L. DELUCIA-WAACK AND
AMY NITZA

PREVIEW

If you look hard enough, you can see task groups everywhere in schools. Clubs, classrooms, and meetings all can be defined as task groups. Task groups are groups of people who come together for a common goal. This chapter will provide strategies for using group dynamics, group process, and leadership skills to create successful task groups. Professional school counselors, school psychologists, social workers, administrators, and teachers may all benefit from these suggestions. Guidelines for leading effective task groups are included, focusing on the task groups of students (e.g., classroom guidance lessons, clubs, community service projects, student government) and also on the task groups of staff (e.g., departments or teams, curriculum committees, child study teams). Examples are included to illustrate successful strategies and leadership styles.

LEADING TASK GROUPS IN SCHOOLS

CASE STUDY 11.1

The Book Club

Ms. Dean, a sixth-grade teacher, wants to connect more closely with her students, particularly the young girls. She hears one student saying she wants to be in a book club at the library but can't meet at the scheduled time. Ms. Dean sees this as an opportunity and invites the student to create a book club with her friends to meet after school one day a week. Ms. Dean sees this as a good way to teach about women's history, talk about relationship issues with the girls, and cultivate communication and presentation skills. She chooses the book *Seneca Falls Inheritance* (Monfredo, 1992), the first in a series of historical novels mixed with mystery, as the first book. Her plan is to use the discussion questions on the publisher's website as a place to start. The first meeting goes well, with six girls attending and each talking about what they had read. Some girls had read further than others, so some discussions had to be cut off. Ms. Dean ends the first session by thanking the girls and asking each to read to page 200 by the next meeting (structure). She also e-mails them two days before the next meeting with two discussion questions to start their next meeting (more structure).

The girls are eager to talk at the next session and quickly get into a discussion of the Married Women's Property Act and some of the implications in the book. Ms. Dean then asks how things have changed for women in this century. The girls talk for a while. Ms. Dean then asks about their lives and their plans for the future. One of the girls says, "I didn't know we were going to talk about personal stuff here." Another girl says, "I would rather talk about personal stuff. Let's read something good like *The Sisterhood of the Traveling Pants* (Brashares, 2003) so we can talk about boys." Ms. Dean hasn't read that book, so she wants to check with the librarian to see whether it is appropriate for sixth graders (and maybe check with parents, too) (appropriate structure with minors). She ends the meeting by saying, "Let's finish this book and then we can select another book to read."

The third meeting begins with Ms. Dean asking each member to identify her favorite character (other than the heroine) and explain why. Amanda goes first. She describes her favorite character. Brittany then responds, "How stupid!" Kelsy then says, "Well, I'm not going to answer that question if Brittany is going to be like that." Ms. Dean asks the girls to talk about how they are going to disagree and present different points of view. She reminds them that sometimes it is helpful to ask questions when you don't understand a point of view or when you see it differently from the person speaking. The girls agree to the following rules: (1) One person speaks at a time; (2) no name calling; (3) no saying "that's stupid"; (4) everyone can have a different opinion; (5) no one has to answer a discussion question if she doesn't want to; (6) people can ask you what you are thinking if you are quiet; (7) we are all working on speaking clearly and making our point, so if we don't understand, we will ask for clarification; and (8) we will take turns choosing books and writing discussion questions (with Ms. Dean's OK).

Ms. Dean's intentions with this book club were admirable but not clearly defined. The goals evolved as they began to work together but not without some disagreement and hurt feelings. It probably would have been helpful for Ms. Dean to clearly communicate what she hoped the girls would learn as a result of the book club as well as asking the girls to state what they hoped to get out of the book club. With children and adolescents, it is also helpful to inform parents of the goals, purpose, and content of a group. The book suggested by the girls (*The Sisterhood of the Traveling Pants*) might be viewed as too advanced for sixth graders, and parents might not approve of that book choice. If the girls choose to talk about personal issues, Ms. Dean might want to ask a school counselor to assist or be available to consult or perhaps to use some sort of classroom guidance curriculum on relationship skills appropriate for adolescents.

Group work and team work are an established part of any school. Group learning happens in classrooms, when teams of teachers and staff work together to establish curriculum and identify interventions for students at risk of academic problems, and throughout the school, when students and teachers form clubs, complete community projects, and hold public events. If one considers all of these groups to be task groups, then therapeutic factors and leadership principles can be applied to enhance their efficacy. The Association for Specialists in Group Work (ASGW) published the *ASGW Professional Standards for the*

Training of Group Workers (2000) with two goals: (1) to identify four types of groups (i.e., task/work, psychoeducational/guidance, counseling, and psychotherapy groups) and (2) to specify the focus and goals of each group and the training activities for each type of group. "The focus of task groups . . . is on the application of group dynamics principles and processes to improve the practice and accomplishment of identified work goals" (Conyne, Rapin, & Rand, 1997, p. 117). The section in the *Professional Standards* on Specialization in Task and Work Group Facilitation emphasizes "The application of principles of normal human development and functioning through group based educational, developmental, and systemic strategies applied in the context of here-and-now interaction that promote efficient and effective accomplishment of group tasks among people who are gathered to accomplish group task goals" (ASGW, 2000).

Task groups and work groups come together with a specific group goal. The focus of this type of group is on the accomplishment of the group goal, rather than individual member goals. Task forces, planning groups, community organization, discussion groups, study circles, learning groups, committees, clubs, work groups within organizations, and classrooms may often be considered task and work groups. The activity within a task or work group usually is focused on accomplishing the group goal or on creating an atmosphere or procedure that is effective in accomplishing the group goal. Task groups are commonly used in schools. Their efficacy may vary, however, depending on the applications of group principles and leadership skills. This chapter will provide strategies to use group dynamics, group process, and leadership skills to create successful task groups. Professional school counselors, school psychologists, social workers, administrators, and teachers may all benefit from these suggestions.

Two types of task groups will be discussed in this chapter: those led by a staff person and consisting of staff (e.g., Committee on Special Education, professional development workshops, Student Support Team) and those led by a staff person and consisting of students (e.g., clubs, teams, groups participating in community service projects, student government, groups having classroom guidance lessons). Successful examples of each are included with discussion of the suggested principles.

IMPORTANT PRINCIPLES IN LEADING EFFECTIVE TASK GROUPS IN SCHOOLS

It is important to define a successful task group. Hulse-Killacky, Killacky, and Donigian (2001) stated as follows:

> Successful groups, characterized by accomplishment and personal satisfaction, are those in which people:
>
> - Feel listened to
> - Are accepted for their individuality
> - Have a voice
> - Are part of a climate in which leaders and members acknowledge and appreciate varied perspectives, needs, and concerns
> - Understand and support the purpose of the group
> - Have the opportunity to contribute to the accomplishment of particular tasks. (p. 6)

It is also important to think about why task groups are formed. Why work in a group when an individual can accomplish a task? Why not break down the task(s) or goals of a task group and ask five people to work independently, rather than trying to coordinate group meetings and collaboration? Everyone has been in a work group where it is very difficult to schedule time to get everyone together or where members get totally off topic or where emotional conflict surfaces. So why work in groups? The primary reason is that task groups often create a synergy of ideas, resources, and plans that does not happen when people work individually on a task; also, group interdependence, cooperation, and altruism interact so that group goals are created and accomplished more productively than by individuals.

Conyne et al. (1997) emphasized that certain conditions—particularly leadership by a capable professional practitioner, the application of theoretical understanding of group process, and the recognition of interpersonal interdependence—must be met in order for task groups to be productive. Thus, it is essential, as in other types of groups, to emphasize both the content and the process of groups. Tasks groups must by definition have a collective goal, but group members must also feel connected to and a part of the group in order to contribute and, if it is a voluntary group, to even attend. Task groups that fail often do not pay attention to the importance of group process and how it influences motivation and efforts to accomplish the group goal. The following suggestions are based on the literature regarding effective task groups and teams in schools, business, and industry that use group dynamics principles.

Suggestions for Effective Leadership

The leader of a task group has a significant challenge in creating an atmosphere where the group members embrace the goal(s) of the group and work together cooperatively and effectively. Leadership functions can be best categorized in terms of planning, performing, and processing (ASGW, 2007). The planning phase involves preparation and planning prior to the group beginning. Performing focuses on the group leadership skills necessary to lead the task group effectively. Processing asks each group leader to reflect on the group process, dynamics, and effectiveness to plan for future group sessions and interventions. Group leaders should consider the four guidelines that follow during the planning phase and then adjust and attend to them as they establish and lead their task groups.

1. ESTABLISH CLEARLY THE GOAL OF THE GROUP FOR THE LEADER(S) AND THE MEMBERS

Establishing the goals of a task group requires the leader and members to consider a number of guiding questions: What outcome is to be attained? What problem(s) are to be solved? How will the group know it is successful? Why, how, and by whom has this group been established? How do the goals fit with the needs of the school? Who determines the goals? Have they been predetermined? Does the group set the goals? Are there any parameters or restrictions?

Goals are the defined outcomes of the task group and are sometimes different than the content or the agendas of specific meetings. For instance, the overarching goal of the committee on special education in a school district is to determine whether students need additional services to succeed academically and, if they do, identify what services are needed. The agenda for such a group would vary, depending on the meeting where different students' situations would be placed on the agenda. For a team of fourth-grade teachers, the overall goal might be to coordinate and integrate the curriculum across all subject areas for all fourth-grade students, while the agenda for each meeting might focus on a different subject area. For an ecology club, the goal might be to make the public aware of ways to recycle through public education, with early meetings focusing on the plans for the year and later sessions focusing on the execution of those plans.

If the leader (or an outside force such as the principal or the school district) has defined the goals, then how are the goals communicated to the rest of the task group? How will questions and concerns about the goals be discussed? How will the task group members make the goals their own? How will progress be evaluated and communicated? If the group members are to determine the group goals, will they be informed ahead of time so they can be prepared for the discussion of goals? For example, members of a Wellness Committee might be asked to think about what the focus of this committee should be for this school year so that goals can be established at the first meeting. How will these goals be articulated? How will they be communicated to other members of the school community? How will progress be evaluated?

Conyne, Rapin et al. (1997) emphasized that while most teams or task groups are organized around reaching performance goals, individual goals or the means to achieve them may differ from group to group. Goal clarity is essential. For example, all chapters of Students Against Drunk Driving have the goal of preventing or decreasing the negative effects of drunk driving; each school chapter may select different approaches to this problem, from sponsoring an after-prom party to conducting a communitywide public education campaign. If the task group exists within a classroom guidance activity, then the school counselor needs to clearly articulate what new knowledge, attitudes, or skills the counselor wants the students to learn as a result of the lesson. If the classroom guidance lesson is on preventing bullying, the goals might be to (1) promote the attitude that if you do not intervene when a bullying incident is occurring, you are allowing it to occur; (2) promote the attitude that there are multiple ways to intervene, including telling an adult; and (3) teach assertive statements that could be made to directly intervene.

In addition, Conyne, Wilson et al. (1997) emphasized the mutuality of goals and the importance of group members' collaborating to set goals. It is essential for members of any group to establish and agree on goals as part of the forming and orienting stage; the processes of discussion, the internationalization of group goals and the collective process, collaboration, compromise, and the giving of feedback all begin with this discussion. Whether voluntary or assigned, the group must begin to make the goals its own. One way to do this is to simply ask members to come to the first meeting prepared to talk about their goals for this group and about how these goals can be accomplished. Mullen, Johnson, and Salas (1991), in their meta-analysis, noted that more creativity occurs if group members work individually first. In the case of Ms. Dean's book club, identifying and sharing her own specific goals for the group, as well as asking each member for her own goals and expectations prior to the first meeting or holding a discussion about goals and expectations at the beginning of the first meeting, may have prevented some of the confusion or misunderstanding that occurred during the second meeting.

2. ESTABLISH THE MEMBERSHIP AND GUIDELINES FOR PARTICIPATION How does this task group establish membership? Is it voluntary? If members are appointed, by whom and based on what criteria? Who informs the members of participation in this group? If the principal or administrator appoints group members for a task group of staff members, it is helpful for the principal to inform the members and to share with them a vision and the goals for this group. Members may not be as committed if the appointment is not communicated directly by the administration.

Task groups do not operate in a vacuum. It is essential to understand why the task group was created. Members may also need to know what expertise they are expected to bring to the group. For example, at a local elementary school where the state test scores were lower than neighboring schools, teachers came together to create a task force to more closely tie curriculum to state testing standards. Thus, members were asked to represent a continuum of grade levels and subject matter.

It is also helpful to clarify participation policies. Is attendance mandatory? Will attendance be public information? Reported to administration? If the group is voluntary, it is still helpful to have some kind of guidelines about attendance. How many meetings can members miss before they will be considered a "dropout"? Who should they notify if they will miss a meeting? Who is responsible for informing members of what they missed?

3. ESTABLISH A STRUCTURE FOR GROUP MEETINGS   Meeting structure includes meeting time and duration, group member roles, and guidelines for how members will interact with each other. How often and for how long will the group meet? Will members have assigned roles? Will these roles rotate? How will the roles be determined (assigned, elected, volunteered)? It is helpful to have a convener or leader, a secretary to record meeting minutes, someone to write down ideas during brainstorming sessions, and someone to act as parliamentarian to keep the discussion on task. Who will set the agenda? When? What will be the deadline for putting items on the agenda? For instance, in a student support team that meets every two weeks, it is helpful to decide at the end of a meeting which students or problematic events (e.g., bullying on the bus) will be discussed at the next meeting. The person who puts a particular issue on the agenda then is responsible for providing the team with a description of the critical issues to be discussed a week before the next meeting. Other team members are instructed to bring information to the next meeting related to the issue. Information may be gathered from specific people (e.g., the school psychologist brings information based on assessment and classroom observations, the school nurse provides medical information), while others on the team may bring more general information based on their interactions with and observations of the student or the issue.

Conyne, Wilson et al. (1997) also stressed the multidimensionality of goals, particularly in relation to the structure of task group meetings. "All groups include various combinations of intrapersonal, interpersonal, and task-related goals. A committee, specifically established to accomplish a set of tasks, needs to accommodate intrapersonal and interpersonal goals to be effective" (p. 9). In task groups, those intrapersonal and interpersonal goals relate to how the group will accomplish its task(s). Two related, but different, issues need to be decided. First, group members must reach a general consensus on how they will interact with each other. Hulse-Killacky et al. (2001) emphasized the need for group members to develop an ethic of cooperation, collaboration, and mutual respect as well as building a culture that appreciates differences. Conyne, Wilson et al. (1997) suggested that the composition "must include sufficient members with enough diversity to fuel group interaction" (p. 7). Guidelines for discussion must emphasize cooperation and allow for differences to occur. The task group leader, through the shaping of the group structure, must motivate members and monitor movement toward goals (Conyne, Rapin et al., 1997).

Typically, the discussion guidelines include statements like these: (1) Every person must be treated with respect. (2) Personal attacks are not allowed. (3) It is OK to say, "I do not understand _____. Can you tell me more about that?" (4) Allow others to finish before speaking to avoid interruptions. (5) Listen carefully as a person speaks. If you are planning what you will say or do, you may not fully understand the person speaking. (6) Outside of the group, opinions can be discussed but not people.

Kottler (2001) created a list of guidelines for members of psychoeducational, counseling, and psychotherapy groups, but some of them apply to task groups as well: Speak only for yourself in the group; use "I," rather than "we"; blaming, whining, and complaining about people outside the group are discouraged; racist, sexist, or otherwise disrespectful language will not be tolerated; there will be no name calling.

Now, let's revisit the case of Ms. Dean and analyze her situation from this new perspective. Early on in her first book club meeting, Ms. Dean could have engaged the girls in a dialogue to establish ground rules for all discussions as well as sharing her own expectations for the girls' behavior during the group. Having established ground rules may have prevented the hurt feelings that resulted from the disagreements that took place. If members did behave in a manner that was inappropriate, the ground rules would have provided a structure for correcting the behavior with little disruption to the group. Often, this can occur when the leader, or even another member, simply reminds group members of the ground rules. These guidelines, along with clear goals, would have helped the girls see the multiple levels of conversations that could occur: talking about the content of the book, relating the book to their lives, and using the conversation to practice articulating their opinions and agreeing/disagreeing with others.

If the task of a group is to create and deliver a new intervention or plan, then it is helpful to agree on a problem-solving structure. There are several that are commonly used. With problem-based learning (Duch, Groh, & Allen, 2001), group members complete a series of questions on their own and then share their answers with the group: (1) What is the topic or problem to be addressed? (2) What do we know about it? (3) What do we need to know? (4) How can we get what we need? (5) What can we do with all this information? (6) What does it all mean? (7) What are some of the action steps? Conyne (2006, p. 171) suggested a model for agenda setting for a team that includes the following steps: (1) Engage in team building; (2) discuss and understand the context, problem, and goals; (3) brainstorm; (4) discuss and clarify terms; (5) eyeball the factor analysis into strategy clusters; (6) identify and rank order the top strategy clusters; and (7) use consensus decision-making. Tables 11.1 through 11.4

TABLE 11.1 Guidelines for Leading Classroom Discussions with a Goal of Identifying Critical Issues or Points for Discussion and Application of New Information

1. What are the goals of this discussion? What do you want the discussants to leave knowing? Doing differently? Thinking differently about? Feeling differently about? Describe each goal in terms of knowledge, behavior, or cognition. (For a 20- to 30-minute discussion, two or three goals are reasonable.)

2. From the material to be discussed (either provided beforehand to read or presented in the form of a mini-lecture), what are the key points? Bullet these and then provide an outline of how you will get the members to identify the key points. What questions will you ask? Can you do an activity to help them identify the key points? How can you focus the discussion without giving members the answers?

3. Based on the key points, how can this information be applied and integrated? What questions can be asked? Can scenarios be discussed? An activity implemented?

4. To summarize or wrap up: How will you end? How will you assess what your members have learned?

TABLE 11.2 Feedback Sheet for Topical Discussions

Rate each of the following items using the following rating scale, with 0 indicating "Not at all" and 4 indicating "Very strong".

0	1	2	3	4
Not at all		**OK**		**Very strong**

_____ 1. Use of handouts/outline

_____ 2. Detail of planning outline

_____ 3. Clear opening/introduction to topic

_____ 4. Clear statement of goals of discussion

_____ 5. Help participants to identify key concepts

_____ 6. Redirecting/refocusing when necessary

_____ 7. Shift to application/integration of key concepts

_____ 8. Statements to encourage application/integration

_____ 9. Suggestions of issues/scenarios for application

_____ 10. Clear summary/closure

_____ 11. Facilitation without dominating

_____ 12. Preparation without rote reading

TABLE 11.3 Guidelines for Leading Problem-Solving Discussions to Articulate a Plan of Action

---

1. What are the goals of this discussion? What problem needs to be solved? Describe each goal or problem in terms of knowledge, behavior, or cognition.
2. Outline how you want to structure the discussion in terms of how much time should be spent on each part of the process, such as
   a. A description of the problem (cognitions, affection, behavior)
   b. Relevant background/other interventions already used
      i. Data from multiple sources
   c. Brainstorming for possible solutions
      i. Individually write down all possible solutions within a short period of time (two to five minutes) or come prepared to the meeting
   d. Identification of a plan of action based on group consensus
   e. Identification of key points of the plan
      i. Who, what, when, and where
   f. Timeline for implementation/feedback
      i. Who, what, when, and where
3. Outline what you will say to introduce and move through your model.
4. Identify how you will gently redirect comments and keep members on task.
5. To summarize or wrap up, how will you end? When will you meet to assess progress?

TABLE 11.4 Feedback Sheet for Problem-Solving Discussions

Rate each of the following items using the following rating scale, with 0 indicating "Not at all" and 4 indicating "Very strong".

0	1	2	3	4
Not at all		**OK**		**Very strong**

_____   1. Use of handouts/outline

_____   2. Detailed planning outline

_____   3. Opening/introduction to topic

_____   4. Clear statement of goals of discussion

_____   5. Clear communication of process

_____   6. Redirecting/refocusing when necessary

_____   7. Enough time on each step

_____   8. Statements to encourage application/integration

_____   9. Statements to clearly identify intervention

_____   10. Application/integration for all

_____   11. Statements to clarify plan/timeframe

_____   12. Facilitation without dominating

_____   13. Preparation without rote reading

include variations of these frameworks as well guidelines and evaluation checklists for planning a problem-solving session (e.g., planning group or student services team meeting) and a topical discussion (e.g., professional development workshop, book club, classroom guidance).

If the task of the group is focused on the discussion and application of new information, as in classroom guidance presentations for students and professional development workshops for staff, then an outline that identifies key concepts of the material and then suggests applications of the information is useful. For example, in a classroom guidance lesson on Internet safety, students are shown a short transcript of conversations in a chat room between a 14-year-old girl and a 50-year-old man posing as a 15-year-old boy. Students are first asked to talk about who they have met in a chat room and how much and what kinds of information they have shared online. Students are then asked to identify what clues the 14-year-old girl gave to her identity and how, using Internet resources, the other person was able to figure out where she lived and where she would be at a particular time. Finally, students are asked to collaboratively generate ways to keep themselves and their friends safe and to be able to interact online without putting themselves at risk.

Group guidelines or ground rules are needed to clarify member expectations about what they are to do in group in order to encourage positive member participation (Conyne, Rapin et al., 1997). General guidelines are useful for the life of the task group as is an agenda or organizational structure for each meeting. An estimated timetable for each agenda item is also helpful to keep members on task. It is not useful to plan a meeting for an hour and then spend 50 minutes on the first item. Members are put in the awkward position of leaving if they have another commitment and/or are not devoting sufficient time to important topics. One common mistake in problem-focused meetings (e.g., student support team, child study team) is spending at least half, if not more, of the meeting in identifying the problem. If the problem is identified and clearly stated and distributed to all group members prior to the meeting, five minutes ordinarily is sufficient time to clearly define the problem. Then the majority of the meeting can be spent on identifying and planning interventions for change and a viable course of action.

An agenda is essential to any task group meeting. Often, it is helpful to put out the agenda in advance of the meeting so members are prepared to report on and discuss items and progress. The convener creates the agenda based on input from the members. Following are some questions to consider when establishing guidelines for the task group: Who actually sets the agenda? How does an item get on the agenda? When do agenda items have to be submitted? Is the agenda sent out in advance of the meeting? When? What do members need to do to prepare for the meeting?

When items are brought up in the task group, it is useful to help group members connect their statements to the task group goals. Sometimes group members are not clear about how items relate to group goals and may spend unnecessary time talking about unrelated issues. Hulse-Killacky et al. (2001) suggested the following prompts:

> What I want to accomplish today . . .;
> What I need to do to accomplish my goal . . .;
> The resources in this group that can help me . . .;
> How I will know if I accomplished my goal today. . . . (p. 88)

4. STRIVE FOR A BALANCE OF PROCESS AND CONTENT ISSUES   In a task group, there is both content and process. Content is the task and/or the goals of the group, which need to be clearly outlined and articulated, and much attention in each meeting should be focused on the task(s) at hand. Process is what happens to help a task group (or hinder it) in achieving its goals. While there is always a propensity in task groups to focus on the task at hand and ignore the relationships that create the group, at some point ignoring those relationships will probably become a problem. In any group, members need to feel a sense of connection to other members and to the group. Cohesiveness and connection (or the lack thereof) will ultimately influence the success of the group. Group process must always be attended to, even in task groups. Group leaders must work to effectively shape positive group process and dynamics as well as intervening to redirect those that interfere with achieving group goals. The earlier three guidelines have discussed how to create a structure within which task group members can clearly identify goals and work together cooperatively.

In the initial meetings of task groups, it is important to establish connections and relationships among group members and also connections to the group goal. As mentioned earlier, it is important for group members to articulate in their own words what they see as their goal for the group. For example, the overarching goal of a student support team may be to identify students at risk, but it would helpful for each member to talk about what challenges students in their school typically encounter. Following that, it would be helpful for group members to describe how they have approached such issues on their own to identify multiple perspectives, resources, and strengths within the group (e.g., diversity in experience, perperspectives, and strengths are valued in task groups). Hulse-Killacky et al. (2001) described the initial session as the warm-up phase of a task group. They suggested three questions that need to be answered: "Who am I? (process), Who am I with you? (process), and What do we have to do? (content)" (p. 31). Some sort of introductory activity that identifies group members' names and their connections to the group is necessary.

In groups with members who do not know each other, it is helpful to also use an activity to help to remember each other's names. It is embarrassing for members in the fourth meeting of a group to have to say, "I agree with what that person in the green sweater said." *The Names Activity* (Hulse-Killacky, 2006) helps group members to remember each other's names and begins to establish connections in the group. In a group where members have established relationships (some of which may not be positive), leaders should help them to think about themselves in terms of the goals of the task group. Activities that focus on characteristics or perspectives that group members may bring to the task at hand that will help them to be successful are useful. *What a Character!* (Gillam, 2006) and *Getting to Know Each Other* (Guth, 2006) highlight characteristics and traits that members bring to the task groups.

Activities should never be used just for fun. They should also have a goal related to either the content or the process of the group. If the group members need to connect or learn more about each other, then some kind of appropriate self-disclosure activity might be helpful. *Getting to Know You—Now and Then* (Conroy, 2006) includes 44 different questions that can stimulate discussion. *Map of the World* (Warm, 2006) asks group members to share about themselves and also begin to relate to other group members. DeLucia-Waack, Bridbord, Kleiner, and Nitza (2006) compiled more than 50 activities arranged by group stage, purpose, and type of group. Barlow, Blythe, and Edmonds (1999), Dossick and Shea (1988, 1990, 1995), Foster (1989), and Keene and Erford (2007) all detailed group activities that can be used as icebreakers to promote discussion.

If the goal is to create new interventions with brainstorming and problem solving, then activities that highlight these skills might be useful. *A What?* (Hutchins, 2006) and *Ball in Play* (Halbur, 2006) encourage levity, humor, and laughter within group work as well as asking group members to think about how groups work effectively in a nonthreatening way. *More or Less* (B. Hayes, 2006) is an icebreaker activity that may be used to facilitate self-disclosure, cohesiveness, and a discussion of how groups work without being overly intrusive. *Why are We Meeting Like This?* (R. Hayes, 2006) is a good icebreaker for group members who are somewhat resistant to meeting or who have had trouble in the past working together. In the warm-up stage, it is helpful to accent the positives, the strengths, and the connections of members. At the same time, it is useful to create a structure that allows for open and honest dialogue and brainstorming, feedback, and respect for all members. Creating guidelines for discussion and a template for each session's agenda helps to create a cooperative atmosphere. Activities and discussions in the warm-up phase should result in cooperation, understanding and appreciation of differences, and active participation of members (Hulse-Killacky et al., 2001). "Intentional and thoughtful coalition building actually contributes to successful outcomes" (p. 33).

Group leaders must pay attention to the group process. If the group is working well, then praise should be given: "This was a great meeting." "We did a great job of problem solving." "We worked hard to get some interventions going. Thanks." It is also helpful to briefly ask group members to reflect on how the group worked: "We did a great job of problem solving today. How did we do it so we can make sure it happens again?" "What allowed us to freely generate options and then pick the best one?" "What did each one of you do that contributed to this process?" "Who was helpful to you in being creative (or invested) and how?" Hulse-Killacky et al. (2001) emphasized the importance of allowing members time to reflect on their work, both at the end of the session and when the task group goal is accomplished.

If the process is not working, then this also should be addressed so that group members and the group as a whole can identify and evaluate what the problem is and suggest solutions to solve it. Group members may not appear committed to or interested in a discussion, their feedback may be shallow or superficial, or they may suggest solutions that do not appear realistic or helpful. Questions like these may be necessary: "Something seems different in this meeting. What do you think it is?" "We seem to have trouble focusing (or staying on task or getting into details). What do you think is happening?" "No one seems to be very invested in this discussion (or our solutions or options). What can we do about that?"

Even if the group leader knows what the obstacle may be, it is helpful to start out by commenting only on what has been observed. It is much more helpful if the group members can identify what the obstacle is and then come up with a solution. Sometimes it is helpful to talk about what it is like to disagree or have different perspectives on an issue. It is one thing to intellectually agree that it is alright to suggest different options and another to realize you are the only one in the room voting for a particular option. If the resistance is to the process of problem solving, *Boxed In* (Trotzer, 2006) is an activity that helps group members to identify potential obstacles to problem solving and to generate solutions to overcome these obstacles. *Responsibility Pie* (Smead, 1995) is an activity that is useful in looking at how each group member may contribute to a situation and then at what that member can do to change it. This activity emphasizes that each person has a responsibility in each situation and that even a small change can have a big impact. Another type of activity that may be useful in task and work groups is one that asks members to focus on their relationships with others in the group and how they affect productivity. *What Is My Relationship to the Group?* (Rapin, 2006) is an activity that asks members to describe their relationship to the group. *A Group Image* (Brown, 2006) also asks group members to examine their perceptions of how the group works together and to identify potential areas of difficulty.

It is important to remember that different points of view, feedback, conflict, and disagreement are all inherent in the creative process and are critical elements in group dynamics. Diversity in resources and approaches is critical to problem-solving and task groups. Not all disagreements or differences in opinion are bad. Let's revisit the statement Ms. Dean made in the example that begins this chapter: "Sometimes it is helpful to ask questions when you don't understand a point of view or see it differently from the person speaking." If a task group can put into practice this statement by recognizing that explaining your point of view to someone else often helps clarify it for you and that others may change their views based on a clear articulation of reasons or a point of view, then an open discussion of multiple perspectives can lead to fruitful problem solving, planning, and decision making.

EXAMPLES OF TASK GROUPS IN SCHOOLS

This section provides two examples of the use of task groups in schools. The first example involves a task group of educators, while the second involves a professional school counselor working with a task group of high school students. Table 11.5 provides a list of additional resources with examples of task groups in action.

Student Support Team

A principal of an elementary school attends a conference on student support teams (SSTs) as an early intervention and, without giving too much thought to adapting the process to her school culture, decides that an SST should be implemented in the school. She follows the

---

TABLE 11.5   Suggested Readings with Task Group Examples

Conyne, R. K. (1999). *Failures in group work: How we can learn from our mistakes*. Thousand Oaks, CA: Sage.

Conyne, R. K., Rapin, L. S., & Rand, J. M. (1997). A model for leading task groups. In H. Forester-Miller & J. A. Kottler (Eds.), *Issues and challenges for group practitioners* (pp. 117–132). Denver: Love.

Conyne, R. K., Wilson, F. R., & Ward, D. F. (1997). *Comprehensive group work: What it means and how to teach it*. Alexandria, VA: American Counseling Association.

DeLucia-Waack, J. L., & Donigian, J. (2003). *The practice of multicultural group work: Visions and perspectives from the field*. Belmont, CA: Brooks/Cole.

Duch, B. J., Groh, S. E., & Allen, D. E. (Eds.). (2001). *The power of problem-based learning*. Sterling, VA: Stylus.

Hulse-Killacky, D., Killacky, J., & Donigian, J. (2001). *Making task groups work in your world*. Upper Saddle River, NJ: Merrill/Prentice Hall.

---

model presented at the conference and decides the SST will meet weekly for two hours and ideally will address three to four students. The goal is to identify students early on who are at risk of not succeeding academically or who are struggling emotionally or socially and then to implement interventions. The principal decides that the team should consist of the school nurse, social worker, professional school counselor, psychologist, and principal. Rotating members are all the teachers who currently work with the student being discussed.

When a teacher asks for the SST to discuss a student, the teacher must first fill out a form that provides information about the student's grades and behavior in the classroom and includes a brief statement of the concern; then the teacher must complete several behavioral rating scales. The school counselor completes at least a one-hour classroom observation of the student. The social worker interviews the parents for a psychosocial assessment, and, if not already available, the school psychologist gives an IQ test and a screening for learning disabilities. The school nurse completes a hearing and vision screening and a physical examination. It takes almost a month to convene this group for an initial meeting because once two students are identified, information must be gathered and distributed and it is next to impossible to schedule a time when almost 16 people can meet. Once the meeting finally occurs, it is not very productive. The first 20 minutes are taken up complaining about how difficult it is to get the materials together, so the discussion quickly turns to this question: "Is there a way to speed up this process?" Some of the classroom teachers have no vested interest in this discussion, and one asks if she can go back to her classroom if the SST is not ready to discuss her student.

The principal wisely recognizes that they have moved too quickly and have ended up with an unwieldy process. She agrees that the teachers should go back to their classes. She then poses this question: "Our big goal is to intervene early with students who are having academic or emotional difficulties. How can we best do this? We have a protocol in front of us that has worked for other schools, but it is clear we need to make it our own." Each person has a different view based on the cross-section of the students with whom they work most closely: The school counselor talks about the social-emotional needs, the social worker talks about the family concerns, and so on. The principal asks them to take a step back and think about the students who were helped informally with these issues during the last year.

How did this happen? The social worker talks about a success story where a teacher noticed the student was having difficulty seeing the board and asked the nurse to screen for vision. At the same time, the student confided that some girls were making fun of her clothes. The nurse was able to help out with some clothes from their clothing drive but also talked with the school counselor about the issue. The school counselor first conducted a classroom guidance lesson for the class on friendship skills and then facilitated a conflict resolution session with three girls after an incident on the playground. The school psychologist notes that she did not know of this instance but is working with that student's sibling on some reading strategies and wonders if there is a need for glasses also? The principal comments that this is a good example of some but not all staff working together. She then asks how they can work together in a more systematic fashion.

All agree that the original SST plan proposed by the principal is comprehensive and seems good on paper, but in reality, it is extremely cumbersome because of the amount of information required for every case, much of which doesn't seem necessary. The school psychologist notes that much of the information is what is required for a committee on special education or child study meeting. The professional school counselor then suggests that perhaps the information collected needs to be specific to the student's issue; she recommends that part of each future meeting be spent discussing interventions for students and that the last 20 minutes be spent identifying the students to be discussed at the next meeting and the information needed (e.g., if there are concerns about a student in a particular class, then observations in that class and others can be conducted).

The concern is raised that it is hard to stay on task and it is hard to get teachers to come for a two-hour meeting. The principal suggests that they choose a specific format for discussion with time allotments for each section (e.g., identification of the problem—5 minutes, discussion of related information—5 minutes, interventions that have been tried—5 minutes, etc.) and with 20–30 minutes total for each student so that teachers come only for the part of the meeting they are involved in. The group also agrees to check in with the person assigned to the intervention within two weeks to assess progress.

High School Mentoring Program

A high school counseling department has developed a peer mentoring program that involves upperclassmen leading small groups of freshmen, with the goals of (1) facilitating freshman adjustment to high school and (2) promoting a positive school climate by developing connections among students. The program and its goals have been generated from feedback received regarding the department's previous freshman orientation program. That program included a motivational speaker, panel discussions with upperclassmen, and large-group discussions with counselors. After piloting the orientation, feedback from freshman participants clearly indicated that they found the panel discussions with the upperclass volunteers to be the most useful. It was evident that the freshmen highly valued interaction with the upperclassmen and that they preferred speaking with the upperclassmen more than hearing adults speak on similar topics.

Based on this information, it seemed beneficial to create a program that would foster this interaction on a year-round basis. It was hoped that ongoing small-group discussions would provide the same quality of interaction and connections between freshmen and their mentors that freshmen experienced in the original panel discussions. Additionally, it was determined that the program could support the goals of the new ninth-grade academy program that is scheduled to open in the school the following year. The ninth-grade academy is being developed to provide an environment that will improve the process of freshman transition; thus, a mentoring program that is supportive of incoming freshmen seemed like a natural fit with the academy. In this way, the goals of the mentoring program have been generated by the guidance staff, in response to an identified need and direct feedback from students and in coordination with broader administrative goals. The success of the program may be considered, in part, a result of the goals' being generated from the combined needs of different stakeholders within the school community.

The structure of the mentoring program involves student co-leaders facilitating weekly meetings of small groups of 8–10 freshmen, with a focus on a different topic each week, including such issues as cliques, bullying, teacher expectations, and time management. Topics are assigned by the program directors, but mentors are allowed some freedom to select activities related to the topic that they feel will best fit the needs of their specific group. In addition to these content topics, there is an emphasis within the program on group process, that is, mentors are taught and encouraged not just to focus on the topic at hand but also to use the topic and activities to help the group members to process their experiences in a meaningful way as well as to focus on developing relationships with the freshmen and encouraging them to develop connections among themselves.

Successful implementation of such a program depends heavily on having effective mentors; the program directors have thus developed a comprehensive and thorough program for mentor selection and training. The individuals developing the mentor training program can be considered a task group that is brought together for the purpose of achieving specific educational goals and is an example of a task group in a school that is led by a staff person but is made up of students. An examination of the training process highlights how the program addresses each of the task group principles addressed earlier in the chapter.

The goal of the training program is to provide mentors with adequate preparation to deliver the program as intended. The program directors start with the premise that students are an underutilized resource in schools with the inherent capability to be a significant positive force in a school when empowered. Program directors have identified a specific combination of knowledge, skills, and commitment necessary to enable students to be successful in this new role. Knowledge goals include understanding their role as mentors, the procedural guidelines for confidentiality, the circumstances that require upward referral, problem solving, and ethics. Skills to be developed include communication skills and group facilitation techniques. Finally, the training is intended to foster a commitment on the part of the students to the mentoring program, the school, and each other.

Selection of mentors is done through a careful application and screening process. Criteria have been established based on the characteristics of effective peer helpers, including (1) the personality of the student, (2) the ability to learn new skills and information, (3) the ability of a portion of the student body to relate to the student (i.e., the goal is to select a diverse group of students who represent different types of students in the school), and (4) the student's level of commitment to improving the school climate (Horne, Nitza, Dobias, Jolliff, & Voors, 2008).

Assessment of the potential mentors is based on the established criteria and is done in a multimethod format that incorporates a written essay component, recommendations from faculty and staff, and a group interview process. Each of these components provides a unique contribution to the overall selection of the mentors and helps to ensure that the training has the best possible chance of success.

Once the mentors are selected, guidelines for participation are developed both formally and informally. Very early on in the training, guidelines for being a peer mentor are set out in the form of a Peer Mentor Code of Ethics, which is reviewed and discussed. Specific attitudes and program philosophies are made explicit and emphasized in the discussion, including a commitment to learning and an "always ask questions" philosophy. These guidelines are supported with a clear rationale so that students understand the reasons behind them and are therefore more likely to embrace and take ownership of them (Horne et al., 2008).

The other approach to establishing guidelines for participation is through the informal shaping of group norms on the part of the trainers. Because the students have little idea of what to expect when they begin the training, they look to the leaders as models of appropriate behavior in this setting. Particularly because students are used to interacting with adults in school in a teacher–student manner, the program directors work hard early in the program to establish a different way of interacting. They do this by modeling desired behaviors and attitudes, including energy, enthusiasm, and commitment, and by emphasizing the need to listen to student voices and establish a more collaborative atmosphere. In this case, professional school counselors must remember that the tone they set for training will be the same tone that the mentors develop in their groups, so careful attention to tone is crucial for the overall success of the program.

When training students in this program, careful attention to structure is an absolute key to success. The overall training program is divided into 15 modules: 5 modules from each of the 3 major training goals (i.e., foundational knowledge, peer mentoring skills, and team building). Modules are created using a variety of presentation methods, including lecture, large- and small-group discussion, activities, role plays, games, contests, and skill demonstration and practice. Some of the training actually is psychoeducational in function. A theme running through all the modules and formats is ample opportunity for discussing and processing their learning and experiences. The variety of formats in this particular task group is very intentional. It is designed to deliver the important content in a way that keeps the students interested and engaged and that allows them to have fun while learning, thereby increasing their motivation.

The first session of the training program is planned and organized to accomplish the following goals with the student mentors: (1) develop an understanding and overview of the peer mentoring program (content goal); (2) develop foundational knowledge regarding the characteristics and ethics of effective peer mentors (content goal); (3) develop a commitment to the peer mentoring program (process goal); and (4) develop a group identity, cohesion, and commitment to the peer mentors as a team (process goal). In order to accomplish these goals, a three-hour training workshop is used. The agenda for the training workshop is provided in Table 11.6. Note how portions of the agenda look psychoeducational. As mentioned earlier, the psychoeducational portions are needed to teach the group members what they need to know to accomplish the task.

The same format is used in the subsequent training sessions, including the combination of team-building activities, delivery of content, and team competitions for review. Large-group activities are incorporated as well, once an initial sense of safety and comfort has been established. Additionally, activities that require a greater degree of risk, such as role-playing group leadership skills and crisis situations, are more readily accepted by students after this initial foundation has been established. By the end of the training, the mentors demonstrate a sense of cohesion and connectedness that promotes a commitment to the program as well as the knowledge and skills necessary to begin their roles as group leaders.

TABLE 11.6   Agenda for a Three-Hour Mentor Training Workshop

1. *Introduction and Ground Rules (10 minutes).* These are brief comments by the facilitators that set the tone and create an initial structure by providing an overview of the peer mentor program and the training and by laying out basic expectations and ground rules for conduct during the training session.

2. *Creation of Small Teams (5 minutes).* The large group is then immediately divided into smaller teams; this increases safety by allowing students to break the ice with a smaller number of students initially. The activity *Saying Hello* (Horne et al., 2008) is used to form the teams. This specific activity is used because it necessitates active participation and gets students moving around right away. The teams that are formed using this activity will be used again throughout the training.

3. *Team Building (30 minutes).* In the small teams, two additional icebreaker activities are used that develop safety and encourage communication and cooperation. The activity *Name Game* (Horne et al., 2008) is followed by a cooperative team activity in which students must work together to create a team name and logo.

4. *Break (15 minutes).*

5. *Initial Content Module: Characteristics of a Peer Helper (30 minutes).* Following the team activities, the first content is delivered. The goal of the first module is to help students begin to identify the qualities and characteristics that make a good peer mentor and to define the nature of helping relationships. This is done through the use of the story *Mona's Story*, followed by team discussions to identify the message of the story and the characteristics of peer helpers and to begin to have students reflect on their own strengths and helping qualities. These discussion topics are then reviewed with the large group.

6. *Content Module Two: Helping Skills (40 minutes).* Building on the discussion of the characteristics of peer helpers, this module introduces the basic helping skills necessary to put those characteristics into practice. The skills are introduced, demonstrated, and then practiced in pairs within the teams.

7. *Break (15 minutes).*

8. *Content Module Three: Peer Mentor Code of Ethics (15 minutes).* Building on the previous two modules, the objectives of this module are to establish guidelines and expectations for mentor behavior and to increase the students' understanding of their responsibilities as peer helpers. The Peer Mentor Code of Ethics is reviewed in a large-group lecture and then each member signs the code.

9. *Team Challenge: Pop Quiz (10 minutes).* The closing activity is a team competition to review all the information covered in the workshop. At this point, students have become connected to their teams. The team competition thus becomes motivating to the students and promotes ownership of the content. The students' commitment to their teams also fosters a greater commitment to the overall peer mentor program.

While there is a great deal of content to be learned in the mentor training, there is an equally important emphasis on developing a group identity among the mentors, who are purposefully drawn from different populations within the school and therefore typically do not know each other well. The program directors believe that the program can be successful only if the mentors are highly invested in it and that they must therefore intentionally work to foster cohesion and commitment among the mentors. In addition to the use of team-building activities throughout the training, this goal is accomplished through the use of follow-up training meetings throughout the school year as the mentor program proceeds. While these additional trainings are used to introduce or review content, their primary purpose is to sustain students' enthusiasm and commitment to the program as well as their connections to each other.

The success of the program in general and of the emphasis on process as well as content is evident as peer mentors take on leadership roles with the freshmen and in the school in general. They appear to develop a sense of ownership of their school and a commitment to their group members. Finally, when freshman group members are asked what their group leaders did that was helpful, the clear answer is that while they found discussions of some of the group topics helpful, what they valued most was that the peer mentors listened to them and developed relationships with them. This result would likely not occur without a careful attention to process throughout the mentor training.

Summary

Task groups play an important part in the daily life of any school. The application of group principles and processes can result in groups that are more effective in meeting their goals and thus that contribute to the overall improvement of a school. As potentially the only personnel in a school who are trained in group leadership, professional school counselors have an important role to play in supporting the functioning of task groups. Consideration of the principles of task group leadership suggested here will allow counselors to be successful in facilitating (i.e., leading or consulting with) groups of varying types.

As illustrated by the case examples, these principles can apply to groups made up exclusively of school personnel working together to accomplish particular tasks as well as to those in which counselors or teachers work with students to achieve specific learning objectives. Careful attention to the planning phase, including establishing clear goals for members and leaders as well as guidelines for membership and participation, will increase the probability of success by reducing factors that are likely to result in confusion, frustration, or resistance. Additionally, establishing a structure for group meetings that takes into consideration the intrapersonal and interpersonal goals and needs of members will help to keep the group moving forward in a manner that maximizes opportunities for individual input and collaboration. Finally, the success of any task group will be greatly enhanced by working toward a balance in the attention given to content and process issues in the group. Often, leaders of task groups will focus exclusively on content, while unintentionally ignoring the process factors that contribute to members' levels of commitment, motivation, and effort, all of which are highly important to a group's ultimate success. At the other extreme, groups with too great a focus on process may be experienced as lacking focus or direction, resulting in frustrated members and little progress.

Group work in schools can be a positive experience that results in the accomplishment of tasks and goals that exceed what can be accomplished by individuals alone. Groups can also increase the ability of professional school counselors to successfully identify and meet the needs of a larger range of students. As with any other form of group work, the success of task groups lies in the successful application of group processes and principles by knowledgeable and well-trained leaders.

CHAPTER 12

Psychoeducational Groups in Schools

JULIA BRYAN, SAM STEEN, AND
NORMA L. DAY-VINES

PREVIEW

Psychoeducational groups for students provide unique learning experiences that support the traditional learning that occurs in school settings. This chapter provides information about psychoeducational groups with a focus on both small-group and large-group formats and on strategies for enhancing the delivery of classroom or large-group guidance. A group model, Achieving Success Every Day, and strategies for incorporating bibliotherapy into group work are provided to promote students' academic success. The chapter begins with an operational definition and rationale for psychoeducational groups; enumerates strategies for the planning, implementation, and evaluation of psychoeducational groups; examines issues of diversity in psychoeducational groups; discusses strategies for classroom guidance and management; and describes two models and their application to psychoeducational groups.

CONDUCTING PSYCHOEDUCATIONAL GROUPS

Psychoeducational groups are structured, time limited, leader centered, and usually focused on specific issues and behavioral goals (Aasheim & Niemann, 2006; Association for Specialists in Group Work [ASGW], 2000, 2007; Brown, 2004; DeLucia-Waack, 2006). While counseling groups tend to be less structured and more focused on self-disclosure and extensive processing of feelings, behaviors, and thoughts, psychoeducational groups tend to be more structured, with the group's goals and activities defined primarily by the leader and with processing focused on helping members understand and make meaning of the information presented. As an example, students may have difficulty transitioning from an elementary to a middle school or relocating from one state to another. A psychoeducational group would provide the support and information necessary to help students transition to a new environment, whereas a counseling group might help students explore their feelings of alienation or isolation that come from relocation and then use the group process to help students feel less isolated.

Typically, psychoeducational groups include a teaching component aimed at imparting knowledge and skills to group members with the goals of prevention and remediation. These groups present group members with the opportunity to learn new information and skills, draw connections to previous knowledge, and make personal meaning of the information. However, the functions of psychoeducational groups are diverse, ranging from merely teaching information and skills to promoting self-understanding and self-empowerment (Brown, 2004). Psychoeducational groups often address developmental concerns related to identity, sexuality, parent and peer relationships, college and career decisions, and educational and spiritual issues. The most commonly run psychoeducational groups in the school setting include communication and social skills groups (e.g., friendship groups, anger management groups), academic and career decision-making groups, study skills groups, and self-esteem groups (Gladding, 2008). Psychoeducational groups can help students achieve greater levels of school success and promote student growth and development.

Benefits of Psychoeducational Groups

Psychoeducational groups constitute a critical mode of intervention for professional school counselors, who assume responsibility for meeting the academic, career, and personal-social needs of large numbers of students. It is impossible for school counselors to address the needs of large numbers of students using individual counseling as the primary mode of service delivery. Although individual counseling serves important functions within the school context, classroom guidance and psychoeducational groups allow school counselors to maximize the amount of services delivered to students. Maximizing efficiency in service delivery is especially critical when caseloads for school counselors exceed the recommendations of the American School Counselor Association (ASCA). In fact, the ASCA recommends student-to-counselor ratios of 250:1; however, student-to-counselor ratios usually exceed 478:1 across the United States (Hawkins & Lautz, 2005).

Given the focus on closing the achievement gap and increasing college access for all students, psychoeducational groups offer professional school counselors an appropriate mode of intervention for assisting students with academic challenges and college and career decision-making. Certainly, the focus of psychoeducational groups on learning and skill building easily aligns with the educational mission of schools. Moreover, school counselors can structure and evaluate the effectiveness of psychoeducational initiatives so that outcomes match the educational orientation of specific schools.

Psychoeducational groups are also useful for working with culturally and linguistically diverse students whose collective cultural orientations may cause them to be more comfortable in group work settings. Psychoeducational groups provide both the structure and the direction that some culturally and linguistically diverse groups value. Some cultural groups may find the lesser orientation toward self-disclosure and the greater focus on goal accomplishment more appealing. Nevertheless, counselors who lead psychoeducational groups must be culturally competent and sensitive. It is imperative that they consider the cultural values of culturally diverse members in defining the group's goals. Equally important, professional school counselors must recognize and embrace the strengths of culturally diverse members, rather than viewing them through a deficit lens. Given the increasing number of racially charged incidents in schools, psychoeducational groups offer an appropriate milieu and a format school counselors can capitalize on to teach students tolerance and acceptance of differences. These groups also provide a forum for helping minority and immigrant students cope with issues of cultural identity, acculturation, and relocation.

In school settings, psychoeducational groups provide an effective mode of intervention for working with parents. School counselors sometimes run parent education and support groups to provide parents and guardians with knowledge pertinent to their children's academic and personal success, teach parenting skills, and offer support for parents (Bryan, 2005; Mitchell & Bryan, 2007). Parent education groups increase parents' knowledge of the school system and how to help their children in school; this knowledge in turn increases parents' involvement in their children's education (Chrispeels & González, 2004). It is far more useful for school counselors to conceptualize and design parent groups as psycho-educational groups because, in doing so, counselors apply their group leadership skills more intentionally to relating to parents and to facilitating cohesion and understanding among parents in the group. Increased interactions and networks among parents also increase parents' involvement in their children's education. Parent education and support groups facilitate parents' connection with each other and are especially important for culturally and linguistically diverse parents, who often feel isolated from schools.

In the next section, strategies for the planning, implementation, and evaluation of psychoeducational groups are discussed. Following that, two group models—the Achieving Success Everyday (ASE) group model, developed to improve student academic motivation and engagement, while simultaneously attending to personal-social issues, and a bibliotherapy model that incorporates multiethnic literature to enhance positive identity and literacy among culturally diverse students—are presented.

PLANNING PSYCHOEDUCATIONAL GROUPS

Whether adopting a small-group or a large-group format, planning is critical to the success of a group. Professional school counselors should consider several factors when planning for a psychoeducational group, such as assessing student needs, developing the purpose and goals of the group, recruiting members, deciding on group size and group composition, screening potential members, determining group procedures and techniques, and evaluating the group. While some of these factors are similar to those presented in Chapter 6, planning psychoeducational groups requires specific consideration to these factors because of the more structured and more directive skill development approach. All of these components are best outlined in a group proposal (Corey & Corey, 2006; Smead, 1995). A group proposal provides a road map for conducting a group. The proposal should include a rationale for the group, the overall purpose and goals of the group, the procedures and techniques to be used, and an outline of each group session. The outline for each session should include the purpose, goals, and objectives of that session; the time and materials needed; and a description of teaching and processing activities that will be conducted at the beginning, middle, and end of each session. Smead (1995) suggested dividing each group session into three components, the review, work, and process times, while DeLucia-Waack (2006) recommended breaking each session into four components, the opening, working, processing, and closing times. Accordingly, dividing each group session into an introduction or review time, a teaching time, a processing time, and a closing time allows leaders to intentionally incorporate processing, which is often overlooked in psychoeducational groups.

Professional school counselors who lead psychoeducational groups must recognize the importance of staying current with the school counseling and group work literature. As leaders develop their group proposals, they will find useful techniques and activities in the literature for use in group work with children and adolescents and creative ideas regarding what procedures work best at different stages of the group. Therefore, leaders should include books and resources on groups for children and adolescents (e.g., Morganett, 1990, 1994; Search Institute, 2004; Smead, 2000) and professional journals (e.g., *Professional School Counseling, Journal for Specialists in Group Work*) in their school counseling budget. Other useful resources include professional conferences and workshops offered at the local, state, and national levels (see www.schoolcounselor.org, www.asgw.org, and www.counseling. org for more information; note that membership in these organizations may be required to receive some of these benefits).

The leader should complete the group proposal and select all the group activities prior to implementing any of these activities. This detailed pregroup planning assists the leader in planning for and organizing each session. Table 12.1 provides a suggested format for planning each group session. Lesson plan formats contain logistical information such as group meeting times, length of the group and length of each session, goals, objectives, materials needed to complete the activities, a detailed discussion of the activities, and questions that counselors can use to facilitate dialogue among members. In the event that the leader needs to be away at the time the group meets, another leader can use the group proposal to run the psycho-educational group. In addition, the leader can continue to improve the group proposal by adding new and more effective activities and strategies to the group each time the group is run.

If groups are held during the instructional day, leaders should consider the logistics of getting access to students during class times. Collaboration with teachers, administrators, and parents is critical to the success of groups. Leaders can negotiate with teachers regarding the best strategies for gaining access to students. Some strategies may include staggering the time that the group meets each week so that students do not miss the same class twice, meeting during lunch (although in many cases a single lunch period does not provide sufficient time), and meeting during nonexamination classes such as physical education and health. In order to maintain continuity with students and accountability with school personnel, leaders should

---

TABLE 12.1   Suggested Format for Group Session Planning

Group Session Plan
- Session Name/Topic
- Goals and Objectives
- Materials Needed
- Developmental Activities
  - Review/Introduction
  - Teaching
  - Working/Processing
  - Closing
- Method(s) of Evaluation
- Homework/Between-Sessions Activity

schedule group meetings so the meetings do not conflict with other responsibilities. Although there may be times when cancellations are inevitable, efforts should be made to minimize scheduling conflicts because they disrupt group continuity. Coordinating the distribution of hall/guidance passes in advance helps to inform the student and the teacher of the scheduled meetings. Planning for a psychoeducational group or classroom guidance sessions is essential, as discussed in detail in Chapter 6.

IMPLEMENTING PSYCHOEDUCATIONAL GROUPS

Group development in psychoeducational groups consists of a number of stages. This section describes some important leader tasks of the early (forming and transition), middle (working), and ending (termination) stages with a specific focus on psychoeducational groups.

Early Stage of Psychoeducational Groups: Forming and Transition

Leader tasks in the beginning sessions of psychoeducational groups include clarifying the purpose and goals of the group, discussing confidentiality and its limits, establishing ground rules, normalizing anxiety, teaching and modeling communication skills, encouraging group norms of participation, creating a safe environment, and facilitating cohesion. In the school setting, group members come to the group with preconceived ideas about the upcoming experience. These expectations may stem from the screening process, from other students' discussing their group experiences, or from previous experiences participating in groups, including classroom guidance. In any case, the initial sessions of the group should include an exploration of students' expectations of the group and the group process.

While leaders of psychoeducational groups attend to tasks similar to those of leaders of counseling groups, psychoeducational group leaders should create the norm of teaching and learning by incorporating didactic activities in the early stage. For example, for fifth graders who are struggling to pass the annual state tests, leaders could teach communication skills that are important in both the group and the classroom. Leaders should also focus on creating a balance between teaching new skills and processing students' feelings and reactions to group content early in the group because school settings lend themselves so naturally to teaching that leaders could easily neglect the group process. Additionally, leaders should incorporate interactive group activities during each session.

During the initial stage of the group, students tend to function in a honeymoon state. In other words, students have a greater level of focus and willingness to abide by group rules and work on group goals. During the transition stage, students may be more resistant and reluctant to participate and engage in productive work, especially if they have academic and behavior challenges. Leaders should help students process why they are responding the way they are in group, make connections between their resistance inside and outside of group and the effect of resistance on student success, and support them in finding strategies to avoid undermining their success in group. Leaders will need to be patient and supportive, focus on encouragement and classroom management rather than discipline, and highlight students' strengths. Group leaders who facilitate increased self-disclosure will foster greater exploration and learning among group members. See Chapter 7 for an in-depth discussion of the forming and orienting stage and Chapter 8 for the transition stage of group work.

Middle Stage of Psychoeducational Groups: Working

Although activities (e.g., icebreakers, energizers) continue to be important during the working or middle stage of the psychoeducational group, this is the stage during which the bulk of the teaching of new information and skills takes place. Psychoeducational groups provide information that helps to prevent the onset of difficulties in students' lives or helps students to cope with current challenges. Group leaders should focus on teaching the skills and behaviors that students need in order to accomplish their objectives. It is important to teach skills and behaviors in small, manageable steps and give students opportunities to experience small successes so that they can generalize their learning to their life outside the group. Therefore, group leaders need to be intentional about incorporating time for skill practice inside the group, homework to help students practice their behavior and skills in the classroom and at home, and mechanisms to monitor students' success at trying out these new behaviors and skills (e.g., keeping a journal, recording the number of times they tried a new behavior or skill). Equally important, homework should involve small, manageable steps so that students can experience some success as they practice new behaviors and skills outside the group.

Group leaders should work to make instruction and accompanying activities interesting and engaging as well as developmentally appropriate for students. Effective teachers and, by extension, effective psychoeducational group leaders find ways to make the material being taught relevant to students' lives and elicit and incorporate students' life experiences into teaching. They also help each student feel a sense of belonging to the group. This can be accomplished by using a warm, empathic personal style that communicates the counselor's investment in each group member and his or her belief that each group member matters. See Chapter 9 for an in-depth discussion of the working stage of group work.

Ending Stage of Psychoeducational Groups: Termination

During the ending stage, group leaders focus on termination, which includes summarizing and wrapping up the themes that emerged in the group, discussing and processing unfinished business, and helping members discuss what they learned in group, describe how they have changed, and determine steps they will take to continue working on their new skills and behaviors upon completion of the group. Leaders should help students to process their feelings about leaving the group and separating from each other and to develop a plan to continue working on their goals. In addition, leaders may need to provide support and follow-up for group members who need further intervention.

Another proactive strategy that counselors can use to support psychoeducational group members is connecting them to support networks (e.g., mentors, reading buddies, tutoring programs) outside of the group. These support networks allow students to participate in meaningful relationships that promote personal-social and academic development. Finally, as the group comes to a close, leaders must be sure to administer postassessments for both outcome and process data, as appropriate. See Chapter 10 for an in-depth discussion of the termination stage of group work.

DIVERSITY ISSUES IN PSYCHOEDUCATIONAL GROUPS

Racial and cultural issues are endemic to schools, that is, within schools, culturally diverse children often confront numerous structural inequalities that threaten to undermine their best efforts at school success. Relative to students attending affluent schools, children from poor and minority households are more likely to (1) confront low teacher expectations as well as racial, ethnic, and class-based biases; (2) receive instruction from uncredentialed teachers; (3) have access to fewer accelerated courses and programs; (4) experience over-representation in special education programs and underrepresentation in gifted education programs; (5) attend underfunded schools with inadequate resources; and (6) experience disproportionate levels of suspension and expulsion. Yet the prospect that students would remain disaffected by these differences seems untenable, primarily because schools operate as a microcosm of society and these issues erode students' social and psychological well-being. Professional school counselors must be cognizant of these issues and be prepared to initiate and respond to concerns that arise within the context of psychoeducational groups. The leader's inability to respond authentically to student concerns may create ruptures and schisms within the counseling relationship and circumvent students' academic, career, and personal-social development.

To illustrate, Mrs. Davis, the professional school counselor, convened a group around anger management issues for eight middle school boys, most of whom were African American and Latino. As she reviewed the didactic component of the group, which provided students with new skill sets for improved compliance with teacher requests, several students complained that school personnel were racist and provoked many of the conflict situations that resulted in their placement in the in-school suspension program. Mrs. Davis responded by defending her colleagues and insisting that teachers do not see color. Her response effectively silenced the group participants, who felt revictimized by the leader's denial that race may have contributed to some of their discipline referrals and contributed to the boys' perception that she was not trustworthy, did not understand their sociopolitical realities, and, most damaging, was complicit in racial bias.

Day-Vines et al. (2007) developed a model of broaching behavior that professional school counselors will find useful in running psychoeducational groups in schools. The model enumerates behaviors that the counselors exhibit as they both initiate and respond to the concerns about racial, ethnic, and cultural issues that may be embedded in students' presenting problems. Leaders along the lower end of the continuum ignore and minimize the impact of race, ethnicity, and culture, while counselors along the higher end of the continuum exhibit a level of social consciousness and comfort in examining racial, ethnic, and cultural factors with students. The leader's ability to explore taboo subjects such as race will help members to explore problem situations, normalize issues related to race and representation, exchange ideas about how group members have negotiated similar concerns, and develop improved decision-making and problem-solving strategies for managing issues such as racial bias. Day-Vines et al. provided a detailed discussion of how leaders consider racial and ethnic issues within psychoeducational groups.

When working with culturally and linguistically diverse students in psychoeducational groups, leaders must be aware of their own attitudes, biases, and assumptions that may affect students and the group process and that may interfere with the delivery of culturally responsive group work. At the same time, professional school counselors cannot be inhibited by feelings of guilt and fear, which have the potential to immobilize helpful group leadership practices. Day-Vines et al. (2007) encouraged leaders to normalize student concerns when issues related to race, ethnicity, and culture arise during the group process. Leaders should monitor their own reactions so that countertransference issues do not interfere with their relationship with students. Leaders should also recognize the sociopolitical issues that govern students' experience. An inability to broach racial and cultural factors may limit the progress leaders can make with students. For instance, in the scenario presented earlier, a leader who rationalizes her colleagues' behavior may miss an opportunity to help students gain personal insight and devise strategies for responding appropriately to perceived racism. On the other hand, leaders who openly discuss these issues can help alleviate student anxiety and work to improve student decision-making.

Using the case illustration cited earlier, the leader could have facilitated a dialogue among the boys that would have helped to increase her understanding of their perceptions of racial bias in the school. For instance, the leader might have elicited an example of biased behavior, processed what effect the experience has on students' ability to function in school, explored some of the coping strategies that students have relied on, and acknowledged that students of color experience disproportionate rates of suspension and expulsion nationwide. Such counseling responses would help the students to feel that their concerns were heard, understood, and validated. Additionally, the leader could use the boys' concerns as a spring-board for helping them identify behavioral strategies that would reduce discipline problems. For instance, the leader might assign the students the task of observing how other students respond to teacher reprimands and determining what student reactions elicit positive or negative reactions from teachers. This activity would help the group members observe a wide repertoire of student behaviors that could help them modify their own responses to teachers. The leader could also have the students role-play strategies in which they negotiate conflict situations with teachers.

Professional school counselors must also recognize that some issues are external to students. The leader can support the students as they learn more effective ways to conduct themselves in class, but this intervention may be far from sufficient (although it is necessary) for working with students who are encountering teacher bias and other structural barriers to their school success. The leader may need to push for some structural modifications in order to support the students, that is, the leader may advocate for staff development training among teachers on topics such as cultural sensitivity and inclusive practices.

IMPLEMENTING CLASSROOM GUIDANCE

This section highlights considerations for planning, implementing, and evaluating large-group guidance, also known as classroom guidance. Typically, professional school counselors deliver classroom guidance curricula consisting of units with four to six lessons. These units can be organized in a number of ways; often, they tend to revolve around current initiatives (e.g., bullying prevention, suicide awareness) mandated by a school system's central-office or building-level administrators, critical needs that arise in the school or are unique to the local student body, or a combination.

Planning

In planning a classroom or group guidance curriculum and lessons, leaders must attend to pregroup tasks similar to those involved in planning smaller psychoeducational groups: assessing student needs, developing the purpose and goals of the group, determining group procedures and techniques, and evaluating the group. The needs assessment strategies that are applicable to the small-group format—including surveying students, parents, building-level administrators, and teachers to identify the most pressing student needs, which may serve as potential topics for classroom guidance—are also appropriate when planning for classroom guidance. In addition, leaders may use student-related data (e.g., discipline referrals for bullying, reports of bias and prejudice, performance by grade level on state performance tests, numbers of seniors admitted to college in previous years) as a springboard for the development of classroom guidance units. For example, data related to discipline referrals for bullying may indicate the need for a comprehensive bully prevention program to be delivered to all grade levels. Data concerning racially charged incidents may suggest that the professional school counselor needs to deliver a schoolwide antiracism or antiprejudice curriculum. Data regarding juniors' knowledge of the college admissions process may uncover the need for a guidance unit for all juniors addressing the college search and college choice processes.

Following the identification of classroom guidance activities, professional school counselors can create specific lessons that incorporate American School Counselor Association (ASCA) standards, state standards, or school improvement goals. The *ASCA National Model* (2005) and *National Standards for School Counseling Programs* (——) provide useful information for developing creative, data-driven lessons. In addition, counselors should create lessons that are engaging, stimulating, developmentally appropriate, culturally sensitive, and aligned with schoolwide initiatives and instructional objectives. Furthermore, counselors should seek out resources to generate ideas for activities and materials for lessons. These resources can be found in school counseling and group counseling texts, on professional counseling websites (e.g., the ASCA website, www.schoolcounselor.org), and at professional development venues (e.g., state and national counseling conferences and local workshops). DeLucia-Waack (2006) incorporated numerous resources in her text on leading psychoeducational groups for children and adolescents, including a resource guide on books, videos, and games.

Other practical considerations include planning ahead of time and proactively developing lessons and alternatives just in case things do not go as planned. Integrating technology into classroom guidance heightens the need to have a backup plan because malfunctions can and often do happen when teaching with technology. The lesson here is this: Never simply "wing it." Inadequate preparation creates a potential for disaster, which may include but is not limited to the inability of students to profit from the guidance unit, increased disciplinary problems, loss of counselor credibility, and decreased levels of confidence in the counselor. Group leaders should work diligently to portray organization and high levels of energy, passion, and engagement because these characteristics communicate to students that the information being presented is worthwhile; in addition, the leader is more likely to capture students' attention. Leaders must also explore strategies for effective classroom management in order to decrease issues of discipline in the classroom. In the section that follows, we describe practical classroom management strategies, with attention to the importance of treating all students with respect.

Classroom Management

Classroom management involves managing classroom dynamics in an effort to prevent potential disciplinary problems and minimize any behavioral problems that arise. Effective classroom management is critical to the successful delivery of classroom guidance. Professional school counselors tend to find it easier to manage students in the small-group setting, and working with an entire classroom can present some unique and interesting challenges. For instance, student–teacher relationships commence the first day of school and evolve thereafter. Professional school counselors are not usually in the classroom on the first day. Consequently, when they conduct classroom guidance, it is important that they adopt the classroom management strategies that the teacher has already implemented unless those strategies are poorly conceived and ineffective. If adopting the classroom management system in place is difficult, they should consider building on the work of the teacher. If this is also not feasible, the following strategies can be implemented to decrease classroom disruptions.

First and foremost, leaders need to become familiar with each of the students' names as quickly as possible. They can obtain seating charts from teachers in order to learn names quickly. Addressing students by name enhances familiarity and interpersonal connections between leaders and students. In middle or high schools, leaders can encourage positive counselor–student relationships by getting to the classroom as early as possible and, when appropriate, greeting students at the door with a handshake, a pat on the shoulder, or a small talk that validates and affirms students. Furthermore, professional school counselors can provide students with an assignment such as creating name tags, drawing family portraits, or completing some other developmentally appropriate task as they wait for the lesson to begin.

Establishing classroom rules facilitates the classroom management process. As mentioned previously, the best way to incorporate classroom rules is to adopt or build on those already established by the teachers. Sometimes this is not possible. In this case, leaders should collaborate with the students to generate classroom rules relevant to the context of classroom guidance. For example, do students need to raise their hand before speaking? Are they allowed to be out of their seats? Is music, food, or drinks allowed in the classroom? The resulting rules may be appropriate within the context of classroom guidance activities but not within their typical classroom. Nonetheless, working with the students to create appropriate rules and expectations will increase their buy-in to the classroom process and willingness to adhere to the classroom management system. Additionally, the classroom rules can hold students responsible for each other's behavior and encourage them to be accountable to one another when the rules are not followed. However, counselors must be sure to include a policy consistent with the school's policy for serious disciplinary infractions. Displaying visuals with the classroom guidance rules reduces ambiguity about student conduct, establishes a clear set of behavioral guidelines, and reinforces counselor expectations about student conduct.

Positive reinforcement and redirection should be used to remind students of the leaders' expectations for appropriate behavior. Leaders can acknowledge and affirm appropriate behavior among students to increase the likelihood that students will continue the behavior. Positive reinforcement builds students' esteem while getting the attention of those who need redirection, focuses the entire class on the correct behaviors, and benefits even students who remain on task. A key aspect of positive reinforcement is acknowledging the behaviors of those students who are doing the correct thing. For instance, perhaps Cornelius is not interacting appropriately with his peers, but Antwonn is. The leader acknowledges the correct behavior by saying, "I really like the way that Antwonn is treating his classmates." This gets the attention of Cornelius, Antwonn, and others, who immediately react to the prompt in an attempt to win the leader's approval. Of course, this strategy may not work with every child in the classroom, but focusing on the positive reminds students of the expectations for classroom behavior.

Students also need to be treated with respect. Treating students as valued and respected members of the group helps to decrease the occurrence of discipline issues during classroom guidance. Leaders should use praise to communicate respect to students. This praise should extend to all students, not just the well-behaved students. For instance, Robert has a tendency to blurt out responses, rather than waiting to be called on. Instead of becoming annoyed, the leader asks students to review the classroom rules. Additionally, the leader uses a strategy developed by Bireda (2002) known as the stroke–sting–stroke method. Instead of reprimanding Robert in an exasperated tone, the leader addresses Robert's behavior by prefacing her request with a positive comment (e.g., stroke), making a behavioral request (sting), and following up the sting with another positive comment. As an example, the leader says, "Robert, I am excited about your interest in the lesson, active participation, and willingness to share your perspectives with the group [stroke]; however, when you talk without raising your hand, you interrupt someone who is following the classroom rules [sting]. You are such a confident, competent, and articulate young man. I hope you will use your listening and leadership skills to model the classroom rules for the rest of the class [stroke]." Such a response preserves Robert's dignity, highlights his attributes, communicates the counselor's need for his cooperation, and maintains a healthy classroom climate. The leader must use a vocal tone and quality that express these sentiments toward Robert with an air of genuineness, sincerity, respect, and firmness. If stated sarcastically, the leader's tone may undermine the message. If stated earnestly, the leader can command respect not only from Robert but from other students as well.

A positive climate is critical when delivering classroom guidance. Valuing diverse opinions and viewpoints helps to create a positive climate for all students. When professional school counselors value all students' comments and embrace different opinions, they provide the opportunity for students to be exposed to a variety of perspectives. In turn, hearing a range of viewpoints teaches students about diversity and acknowledges the impact of culture in ways that validate and affirm all students, including those who have experiences and worldviews that are different from the White middle-class culture of most schools. Furthermore, valuing students' responses fosters a sense of belonging and acceptance among students and improves the likelihood of delivering classroom guidance lessons without major disruptions.

Another illustration of the benefit of creating a safe environment where all students and divergent perspectives are valued in the classroom involves an elementary student named Ghulam, whose family was from Afghanistan. This student had difficulty on two fronts. First, he appeared to be less willing to engage in any activities that he was not interested in. Second, he would not actively participate in collaborative activities in which females were involved. We could have attributed his behavior to his gender and the fact that his country of origin is a patriarchal society or to his developmental stage as a third grader. Nonetheless, we were willing to work through these differences in light of the reality that this student's worldview was different than ours. We worked to engage Ghulam in group activities, while allowing him space to be comfortable. Rather than acknowledging his behavior openly, we addressed this situation by modeling genuine acceptance and consistent messages that all members of the classroom were valued.

Other helpful strategies for valuing students utilize the dialogue between classroom guidance leaders and students. As counselors interact with students, they should do so in a manner that involves all students or, at the very least, does not exclude students on the basis of their class, culture, or religious orientation. Leaders should strive to achieve balance in their discussions and interactions with students and scan the class regularly to detect the body language of the class members. This will help to gauge how students are responding to the prompts verbally as well as subconsciously.

TWO EXEMPLAR MODELS FOR PSYCHOEDUCATIONAL GROUP WORK

In this section, we describe two exemplar models that may be used in psychoeducational groups in school settings to enhance student academic success: (a) the Achieving Success Everyday group model and (b) bibliotherapy.

Achieving Success Everyday Group Model

Given the focus on academic development in schools (ASCA, 2005), professional school counselors can best assist students by implementing group counseling and psychoeducational models that simultaneously address personal-social and academic development (Brigman & Campbell, 2003; Steen & Kaffenberger, 2007). A unique contribution of the Achieving Success Everyday (ASE) group model (Steen, 2007) is the intentional integration of academic and personal-social development, using psychoeducational and counseling components. The primary purpose of ASE groups is to enhance students' personal-social development, while helping students to improve academic-related behaviors that contribute to success in the classroom (e.g., attending to tasks, completing assignments, asking questions). Using the ASE group model, leaders teach students strategies to address their personal-social concerns and academic difficulties. Leaders also help students identify and build on their internal assets (e.g., achievement motivation, school performance), while drawing on external assets (e.g., caring and supportive adults, high expectations) available within the school and the surrounding community.

Goals may be selected from the ASCA *National Standards for School Counseling Programs* (Campbell & Dahir, 1997). Examples of academic goals for students include increasing learning behaviors, achieving school success, improving academic self-concept, acquiring skills for improving learning, relating school to life experience, and taking responsibility for actions. Examples of personal-social goals for students include learning to communicate feelings, learning strategies to advocate on behalf of self, learning to identify internal and external assets, learning to deal with events that provoke negative emotional responses, learning strategies to handle stressful situations, and learning to apply social skills outside of group.

GROUP DEVELOPMENT IN ASE GROUPS   The ASE group model is designed to assist students who can benefit from academic as well as personal-social support. ASE groups experience six phases: assessment, review, acquaintance, challenge, empowerment, and support. These phases develop across the group's lifespan. Each session of the group comprises an introduction, a personal-social component, an academic component, and a closing.

The assessment phase occurs prior to the start of the group and involves the selection of the group members. During the assessment phase, the leader gathers information from teachers, parents, and the potential student member for use in assessing the student's academic and personal-social strengths and difficulties. This information may be collected through surveys or at faculty meetings, parent information meetings, or parent–teacher conferences. The leader may choose to design his or her own surveys or to use instruments that are available in the literature.

The leader should then use the data to decide who is most in need of services and to help construct the actual group goals, objectives, and lessons. In addition, the leader may use the information gathered in the assessment phase to periodically update teachers and parents about the students' progress. Students should know about these updates and even help decide what information they would like shared with their teachers and parents.

Sharing student successes that occur inside and outside the group with teachers and parents can improve teacher–student and parent–student relationships. Overall, collaborating with teachers and parents can help the leader, teachers, and parents keep abreast of student progress, support student efforts at goal accomplishment, empower students, and identify new areas for student improvement.

The review phase primarily takes place during the first or second session of the group. The leader reviews the group's purpose, goals, and ground rules, including confidentiality, and helps students identify individual goals. During this phase, the leader may also review data collected from the assessment phase and share the results with the group members. These data can be used to drive discussions about the purpose of the group's meetings and the benefits that may accrue from student participation. Additionally, the data from the assessment phase can be used to highlight the fact that students may be experiencing similar difficulties. This in turn helps students normalize their concerns (i.e., see their universality).

In the acquaintance phase, the leader facilitates connection among the students to provide a cohesive environment conducive to change. The leader encourages all students to begin actively participating in the group process and helps them to discuss positive self-attributes in meaningful ways. One strategy that the leader can use to increase students' comfort in sharing in the group is exploring uncertainties regarding confidentiality. Facilitating cohesion will help members feel more comfortable in a small-group setting. As the group enters into and continues through the acquaintance phase, the leader should spend a few minutes at the beginning of each session helping students to reconnect with each other. However, it will become less necessary to do this over time, as members become more familiar with and willing to engage one another.

During the acquaintance phase, the leader should model appropriate interpersonal skills and help students learn how to communicate effectively. The leader can use engaging activities to encourage students to connect and communicate with each other. Some feasible activities include sentence completion exercises, pair-and-share (i.e., pairing up with another member and then sharing the information with the entire group), and a team drawing activity during which students work collectively in groups of two or three on an art project that represents aspects of themselves. These activities promote safety and self-disclosure among students by highlighting their similarities with one another and examining their differences.

During the challenge phase, the leader teaches group members productive ways to clarify or confront their own unwanted behaviors and those behaviors they recognize in other members. To facilitate constructive confrontation, the leader needs to teach students how to give productive feedback (e.g., stroke–sting–stroke). The leader should also help students explore their feelings about feedback they receive about their own behaviors. Equally important, the leader should use group leadership skills to confront or challenge inconsistencies, negative behaviors and thoughts, and students' misconceptions or misunderstandings regarding issues raised during previous sessions.

During the empowerment phase, the leader should focus on providing students with knowledge, strategies, and skills to overcome academic and personal-social obstacles. This typically is where the teaching component in psychoeducational groups occurs. Empowerment is defined as a process of increasing individuals' personal, interpersonal, or political power so that they can take appropriate action to improve their lives (Gutierrez, 1990). Empowerment is used to help students identify and cultivate personal strengths and take initiative to overcome personal challenges. The leader helps students to recognize their potential to make changes in their lives that they may not have noticed before. The leader also helps students recognize their strengths by facilitating discussion and exploration of the internal and external assets available to them. The Search Institute's list of 40 Developmental Assets may be useful for generating discussion ideas. Assets lists for early, middle, and adolescent years in French, Spanish, and English may be found at http://www.search-institute.org/system/files/40AssetsList.pdf. Other asset-building resources that may be useful with psychoeducational groups include the following books: *Building Assets Is Elementary: Group Activities for Helping Kids Ages 8–12 Succeed* (Search Institute, 2004), *More Building Assets Together: 130 Group Activities for Helping Youth Succeed* (Grothe, 2002), and *Great Group Games: 175 Boredom-Busting, Zero-Prep Team Builders for All Ages* (Ragsdale & Taylor, 2007). In addition to using asset-building activities, the leader should help students brainstorm unique and creative ideas to overcome their personal or academic challenges.

In order to facilitate student empowerment, the leader must recognize the role that environmental and societal pressures (e.g., poverty, institutional racism, stereotypes, negative and unhealthy school climates) play in children's lives. Furthermore, empowering students necessitates that the leader see students from a strength-based rather than a deficit perspective, that is, the leader must identify the strengths in all students regardless of gender, class, race, or religion. Hence, the leader who effectively empowers students has a positive view of children and works diligently to confront his or her own biases and stereotypes.

The support phase is used to bring closure to a group. During the support phase, the primary focus is on helping students support each other as the group draws to an end. The leader should facilitate a discussion about students' initial goals, established early in the group; how their goals may have changed; and whether they accomplished their goals. The leader should also encourage students to give each other feedback about areas of growth they have observed in one another. Students can encourage each other to improve and to accept each other's unique differences and limitations. The leader can also help students to identify supports and resources within and external to the group that will help them to accomplish their goals. The leader should help students to discover resources available within the group (e.g., acceptance, enhanced self-esteem), within the school (e.g., a supportive adult in the school), and within their family and community (e.g., positive role models, youth or community groups). The leader can brainstorm with students how they may draw on these resources for support as they work toward their goals and as the group terminates. A discussion of external resources during group sessions and at the conclusion of the group can help increase long-term positive results for students (Steen & Bemak, 2007). Finally, as the group comes to a close, the leader should help students explore and celebrate their accomplishments.

Bibliotherapy

Bibliotherapy refers to the leaders' use of literature to help students cope with dilemmas that affect their academic, career, and personal-social development. DeLucia-Waack (2006) recommended the use of bibliotherapy in psychoeducational groups to help students process their feelings. Bibliotherapy also supports the educational mission of schools by promoting and reinforcing literacy skills. In some school counseling contexts, the term *bibliocounseling* may be preferred so as to not imply that leaders are conducting therapy sessions with students. For the purpose of this chapter, we will rely on the customary term, *bibliotherapy*. In any case, leaders select literature that corresponds with a particular need or challenge that students confront. Selections are usually based on developmental appropriateness, similarities between the protagonist and the students (e.g., age), and relevance of the book's content to the students' problem situation.

Leaders have several options for presenting the material to students in psychoeducational groups. For instance, they can read the material to students directly; have students read the material orally or silently; and, in some cases, assign reading outside the counseling session. Following exposure to the literature, leaders facilitate discussions with students about the book's content. Discussions permit students to (1) recognize that others experience similar dilemmas, (2) identify similarities between their own experience and the protagonist's experience, and (3) develop a larger repertoire of more effective problem-solving behaviors and coping strategies.

A fairly extensive body of literature documents the use of bibliotherapy across a range of counseling settings and as a conduit for resolving numerous problem situations. Far less attention, however, has been devoted to the inclusion of multiethnic bibliotherapeutic selections, despite the increasing levels of diversity within schools. Day-Vines, Moore-Thomas, and Hines (2005) developed a model of culturally relevant bibliotherapy (CRB), which refers to the purposeful use of multiethnic books in individual counseling and group work contexts to address the culture-specific concerns of children of color. This model identifies criteria that professional school counselors can use as they select culturally relevant literature. According to the model, protagonists in the books used in CRB are from culturally and linguistically diverse groups that reflect the growing diversity in society.

Day-Vines et al. (2007) recommended that leaders using CRB rely on works written within the last 10 years because authors more recently have made greater efforts to avoid bias in children's literature. They also noted that more-exemplary CRB selections are written by people from underrepresented groups because they generally tend to write from a personal, lived experience. Within books used in CRB, the plot generally contains at least two themes, a universal theme that applies to all individuals irrespective of racial or ethnic group membership and a culture-specific theme that addresses the unique experiences and developmental concerns of students of color. As an advantage, CRB serves multiple purpose, that is, CRB allows students from the dominant culture to have exposure to literary and cultural perspectives that lie outside a White middle-class imperative. Similarly, CRB permits students of color to have their heritages and cultural perspectives validated and affirmed. Literature used in CRB depicts the integrity of the ethnic minority experience and provides counternarratives that contest and resist the stereotypes and overgeneralizations that have historically been heaped on people from marginalized groups. Most importantly, CRB can serve as a source of empowerment for culturally and linguistically diverse students. Leaders can integrate CRB seamlessly into their psychoeducational group and classroom guidance activities with students.

Demographers predict that by 2050 students of color will make up more than half of the school-age population (Sue & Sue, 2003). Leaders can respond to these shifts by incorporating literature into their bibliotherapy efforts that better reflects the student population. This increasing diversity implies that a larger segment of the student population will speak English as a second language, accented English, or nonstandard forms of English. In any case, students whose discourse styles do not approximate a Standard English imperative may encounter varying forms of linguistic bias. When confronted with linguistic bias, students may have few resources with which to respond and may internalize their linguistic differences in ways that detract from their sense of well-being, pride, and school success.

Books can assist leaders as they work with students during classroom guidance and psychoeducational groups to address issues pertaining to cultural diversity. For instance, books can be used during small-group guidance to help homogeneous groups of students explore what it means to be culturally different in school settings where differences may not necessarily be appreciated. These books may be included in self-esteem, study skills, or friendship groups to help students gain greater levels of self-acceptance and self-understanding. Far too many students of color are viewed from deficit perspectives when certain cultural markers (e.g., their names, discourse communities) are seen as possessing less status. Leaders can help to restore social and ethnic pride in students by normalizing their experiences and allowing them opportunities to talk about the effects of culture on their educational experience. Leaders can use their training and expertise to promote multicultural dispositions among students. In fact, leaders can develop classroom guidance activities to help students accept and appreciate cultural differences among peers. Whether leaders incorporate CRB within the context of small psychoeducational groups or classroom guidance, Day-Vines et al. (2005) identified strategies that leaders can use to facilitate discussions.

Following the reading of the CRB selection, the leader can elicit students' general reactions and impressions of the literary content. After ascertaining students' reactions to the book, the leader can inquire whether themes presented in the book parallel issues and concerns of students in the school and community. Discussions of the broader meanings and implications of the literature will facilitate more personalized discussions of the material. Next, the leader can have students discuss similarities between their own experience and that of the protagonist as well as implications for their own lives. For instance, the leader may sequence questions to inquire about students' perceptions of the book or to have students consider how the bibliotherapy selection can inform their thoughts, attitudes, and behaviors. Delucia-Waack (2006) suggested that students can write or make their own books to help other students cope with problems similar to their own.

In addition to the discussions cited above, the leader can facilitate additional creative activities in which students prepare drawings, create collages using magazines, write stories or conclusions for their own problems, role-play, and enact new conclusions to the stories read using dramatic play activities. The creative activities, along with the bibliotherapy, permit students to explore their problems and feelings within the safety of the group context. Moreover, the students can use these activities to transfer newly acquired skills and understandings to their personal lives outside the group.

Summary

Psychoeducational groups constitute a vital component of comprehensive, developmental school counseling programs. Essentially, psychoeducational groups permit professional school counselors to maximize their efficiency by working with students in groups versus individually in an effort to stimulate and promote improved decision making, coping skills, personal and interpersonal competence, and academic achievement. Ordinarily, psychoeducational groups tend to be more structured than other group formats in order to provide students with useful knowledge, information, and skills.

Personal characteristics of the leader—such as enthusiasm, warmth, and friendliness—contribute to the well-being of the group, as does the leader's ability to create a safe, nurturing group environment. Requisite skills of the leader include the ability to both teach content and attend to group process, so that all students have a meaningful and substantive group experience.

Given the rapid and explosive demographic shifts in this society, resulting in an increasing number of students from ethnic minority backgrounds now matriculating in U.S. school systems, professional school counselors must address universal and culture-specific issues that affect the lived experiences of students. Group leaders must be aware of their own attitudes, biases, and assumptions to avoid countertransference. Additionally, an important correlate of multicultural counseling competence involves leaders' willingness to broach the subjects of race, ethnicity, and culture, which may arise during the counseling process, in a manner that helps students to gain a heightened sense of critical consciousness and to develop appropriate coping and decision-making strategies so they can maximize their ability to function in a pluralistic society.

In addition to conducting psychoeducational groups, professional school counselors should develop proficiency in delivering classroom guidance interventions. The preparatory activities for classroom guidance—assessing student needs, developing the purpose and goals of the group, determining group procedures and techniques, and evaluating the group—share many parallels with the planning for smaller psychoeducational groups.

Steen's (2007) model, Achieving Success Everyday, holds considerable promise for the delivery of psychoeducational interventions because it integrates academic and personal-social competencies that are relevant for the healthy developmental functioning of children and adolescents. Each of the six phases of the model—assessment, review, acquaintance, challenge, empowerment, and support—is designed to help members achieve school success.

Day-Vines et al. (2005) specified criteria for identifying multiethnic children's literature in an effort to incorporate culturally relevant bibliotherapy into the psychoeducational group process. Culturally relevant bibliotherapy serves as a source of empowerment for students from marginalized groups because it validates and affirms their cultural heritage and addresses universal issues that students from all cultures experience, while at the same time addressing the specific and unique developmental concerns of students from ethnic minority backgrounds. Concomitantly, it helps students from the dominant culture recognize the perspectives of ethnic minority group members.

CHAPTER 13

Theoretically Based Group Models Used in Counseling and Psychotherapy Groups

ANN VERNON AND DARCIE DAVIS-GAGE

PREVIEW

Counseling groups are common in school counseling programs, while psychotherapy groups are far less common. This chapter presents information about the theoretically based treatment approaches commonly used in counseling and psychotherapy groups in schools—the Adlerian, behavioral, Gestalt, rational emotive behavior therapy, and choice theory/reality therapy models.

COUNSELING AND PSYCHOTHERAPY GROUP MODELS

Numerous theoretical models have been developed during the last century to help members meet goals within the structure of counseling and psychotherapy groups. This chapter reviews the models that are more commonly used in schools today—the Adlerian, behavioral, Gestalt, rational emotive behavior therapy, and choice theory/reality therapy models.

ADLERIAN GROUPS

Adlerian theory is a socially oriented theory developed by Alfred Adler and used by him and his colleagues in child guidance clinics in Vienna as early as 1922. Other theorists contributed to adapting the concepts for group work—most notably, Rudolph Dreikurs, who introduced group therapy in the United States in the late 1930s. The basic tenets of Adlerian theory include the purposefulness of behavior, the subjective nature of perception, the holistic nature of people, the importance of a healthy lifestyle, individual self-determination, and the ability to choose from a variety of behaviors after considering the consequences. The notion that people are motivated by social interest and have feelings of concern for others is central to the theory.

Adlerian theory emphasizes accepting responsibility, searching for meaning, and striving for superiority. Understanding an individual is accomplished by learning how the individual operates within a social context; this makes Adlerian theory ideally suited for group counseling, since relationships are addressed in a group setting (Sonstegard & Bitter, 2004).

Another major aspect of this theory is the emphasis on the family constellation and process, which affect personality development during childhood. When children observe family interactions, their values, gender-role expectations, and interpersonal relationships are affected. Analyzing the family constellation also forms the basis for interpretations about the client's strengths and weaknesses and the current influence of the family.

Yet another core concept of Adlerian theory is lifestyle, which is influenced by the family constellation and significant experiences within the family, primarily during the first six years of life. Because people are influenced by their perception of the past, particularly childhood experiences, it is important to help group members become aware of self-defeating or erroneous ideas so that a more adaptive lifestyle can be created.

Types of Adlerian Groups

Adlerian groups often use components of psychoeducational and counseling approaches as well as psychotherapy approaches. Based on the social orientation of this theory, a major premise in all types of groups is that people learn from each other. Because so many problems are interpersonal in nature, a group approach is particularly helpful in promoting change, especially with regard to challenging feelings of inferiority and erroneous concepts that form the basis of many social and emotional problems.

Adlerian group approaches are very applicable in school settings with students, teachers, and parents. For example, the STEP (Systematic Training for Effective Parenting) program, developed by Don Dinkmeyer and consisting of seven components (collaboration, consultation, clarification, confrontation, concern, confidentiality, and commitment), uses an Adlerian approach. Other Adlerian parent education groups stress developmental and preventive parenting approaches, with an emphasis on understanding children's behavior, using logical and natural consequences, and implementing the family council meeting. Adlerian theory can be integrated into groups with children, focusing on the family constellation, encouragement, social interest (e.g., empathy, concern for others, cooperation, listening skills, belonging, relatedness), and mistaken goals of misbehavior.

Role and Function of the Leader in Adlerian Groups

Mosak (2000) emphasized that Adlerian group leaders must be collaborative and open about sharing their feelings and opinions. Their personality is as critical to the functioning of the group as the techniques are. Leaders need to be accepting of others, be open, have a sense of humor and a positive attitude, and be sincere and adaptable. In working with children in particular, leaders must use encouragement to help them see that behavior change is possible.

Stages of Adlerian Groups

Corey (2007) described four stages in an Adlerian group approach. In the first stage, it is important to develop a democratic atmosphere where cooperation and mutual respect are emphasized. In the Adlerian group, an egalitarian relationship is stressed. The second stage involves an analysis and assessment of group members' lifestyles and how these lifestyles affect functioning in the present. Recalling early recollections facilitates an understanding of life goals, motivations, beliefs, and values. This lifestyle analysis is interpreted to group members so they can develop a plan for change. Stage three focuses on awareness and insight, which are the basis for change. Interpretation is used liberally in this stage and helps students develop a better understanding of themselves and their problems as well as what they can do to improve their circumstances. In the final stage, reorientation, group members and leaders strive to change mistaken attitudes and beliefs and to examine other ways of thinking and behaving. Reeducation is an important part of this stage, along with problem solving and decision making.

Techniques Commonly Used in Adlerian Groups

Leaders of Adlerian groups commonly facilitate growth and development within the group setting using several techniques, including modeling social skills, using visual imagery, observing and interpreting members' nonverbal behaviors, using constructive confrontation, and employing paradoxical intention by asking members to increase negative thoughts and behaviors. With young children in particular, leaders must use caution when utilizing paradoxical techniques, since they may be misunderstood. Likewise, confrontation must be used selectively and with care.

Other Adlerian interventions that are especially appropriate for children in group settings include play therapy techniques, art, humor, and acting as if they are the person they would like to be. Corey (2007) identified additional interventions: using the push-button technique, using stories and fables, and catching oneself.

Some Final Comments on Adlerian Groups

Adlerian group approaches can be used with many different populations and are particularly applicable with children, adolescents, and parents in a school setting. The variety of techniques used by Adlerian group leaders enables the members to learn concepts relatively quickly, and the fact that these groups are grounded in a democratic approach and emphasize belonging enhances participation. The emphasis on responsibility makes this approach particularly helpful to school-age children who are developing this disposition. One criticism is that groups based on Adlerian theory may be quite narrow in scope. In addition, some problems, such as Attention-Deficit/Hyperactivity Disorder, anxiety, and depression, may not be socially based and therefore, Adlerian approaches may have little effect on member clinical outcomes.

BEHAVIORAL GROUPS

Behavioral group approaches help students learn life skills and address specific present, as well as future, problems through an emphasis on self-management skills. Behavioral groups can have an interpersonal and interactive focus that helps members pursue specific goals for self-improvement. This type of behavioral group is didactic and psychoeducational.

Several principles underscore behavioral applications in a group setting. First is the notion that problematic behaviors are learned and can therefore be modified. Second is the idea that change can occur without insight. Finally, a variety of techniques, such as positive reinforcement, desensitization, shaping, modeling, contingency contracting, behavioral rehearsal, coaching, and extinction, can be systematically employed to help individuals change maladaptive behaviors. Simplistically stated, behaviorists believe that behaviors that are followed by rewards or positive consequences will occur more frequently than those that are not.

Over the past several decades, traditional behavior therapy groups have been replaced with an approach that is actually more cognitive-behavioral. Behavioral groups tend to be short term, psychoeducational, and action oriented, so they are very applicable to school settings. The fact that participants learn how to apply skills to their everyday life is especially important for school-age children who can, at a young age, develop life-enhancing skills to facilitate their development.

Types of Behavioral Groups

Behavioral groups can be organized around various topics, including learning new social skills, behaving assertively rather than aggressively, and managing weight, stress, pain, or addictions. Learning new ways of thinking and behaving is a focus of the cognitive-behavioral groups. The self-management approach of behavioral groups deemphasizes dependence on professional experts. Instead, group members are empowered to become more self-directed. While self-direction is the ultimate goal, this might be somewhat difficult with younger students, so leaders must be more involved at this level.

Role and Function of the Leader in Behavioral Groups

Behavioral groups are problem oriented and employ short-term interventions. Thus, leaders need to be knowledgeable about a variety of strategies that can be developed from diverse therapeutic approaches. Behavioral group leaders are active and directive, often teaching members to learn and rehearse skills to facilitate problem resolution. At the same time, they are supportive and flexible in their leadership style. As leaders, they also model appropriate behaviors, reinforce members as they learn new behaviors, and collaborate with members on developing homework assignments to practice new skills. Throughout the sessions, leaders assess members' problems, employ strategies to help them achieve their goals, and encourage them to practice new skills in the group setting that they can apply to real-life situations.

Stages of Behavioral Groups

As with most types of groups, the initial stage involves exploring members' expectations and dealing with organizational details. In behavioral counseling groups, leaders also give relevant information about the group process and how sessions will be structured. Often, a contract that identifies leaders' and members' mutual expectations is developed. Building group cohesiveness in order to establish openness and sharing, as well as identifying target behaviors to work on, also occurs during the initial stage. Leaders can build a sense of community in a school setting by implementing a variety of rapport-building activities, such as having students introduce themselves by sharing three things about themselves that others can't tell by looking at them, tear a piece of paper into a shape that identifies something they like to do, or write their initials on a sheet of paper and drawing something beginning with each letter that represents them.

During the working stage, leaders introduce students to the behavioral framework. This is most effectively accomplished by teaching members the Antecedent–Behavior (response)–Consequence (A–B–C) model of behaviorism. In essence, this model proposes that all behavior is purposeful but not necessarily productive. The goal is for group members to learn this model and assess and monitor their own actions in light of specific behaviors. As the group progresses, members are asked to identify behaviors they would like to change and use a variety of behavioral techniques to accomplish this.

Techniques Commonly Used in Behavioral Groups

Numerous behavioral techniques can be helpful as group members engage in the process of change. Leaders often model and demonstrate many of these during group. Positive reinforcement entails praising or giving positive feedback when members make contributions in the group or when they report on other constructive changes. The ultimate goal is for group members to practice positive reinforcement behaviors within and outside of the group setting. Group members are always encouraged to develop action plans, since insight and verbalizing do not produce behavior change. Action plans are extremely helpful for school-age participants because they learn to be accountable and see that change is possible. Group members are also encouraged to contract with others in the group, calling them throughout the week to report on their progress.

Behavioral rehearsal is another popular technique, where group members are encouraged to practice a behavior they would like to change within the safety of the group setting and receive feedback and suggestions from other group members; their goal is to perform this behavior outside of the group setting. This technique is very effective with children and adolescents because they often are better able to assimilate concepts and transfer skills to the "real world" if they have opportunities to practice skills.

Shaping is another procedure that helps students learn new behaviors in a gradual process as they practice parts of the targeted behavior in a step-by-step process until they can do it successfully. Other behavioral techniques include coaching, where leaders (coaches) help group members rehearse a desired behavior by sitting behind them, intervening, and providing direction as needed.

Some Final Comments on Behavioral Groups

The self-help educative approach is a definite strength of the behavioral group approach, as is the fact that a variety of specific, concrete techniques can be employed to facilitate skill development for a variety of problems. This is especially helpful for children and adolescents, who typically need concrete strategies to help them learn concepts. The behavioral approach emphasizes accountability and evaluation of interventions, which increase its efficacy. On the other hand, group members can become too dependent on their leaders, and there is some risk that the methods might be employed too mechanically or stringently. Also, the fact that issues from the past and the exploration of feelings are not emphasized in behavioral groups may make this group approach less appropriate for some types of student problems (e.g., family-of-origin issues, relationship issues).

GESTALT GROUPS

Gestalt therapy, developed by Fritz Perls in the 1940s, uses a humanistic approach to integrate the elements of certain psychoanalytic concepts with existential ideas (Donigian & Hulse-Killacky, 1999). The emphasis in Gestalt groups is on awareness, which is taught in a variety of ways.

Gestalt group counseling, which emphasizes working in the here and now, operates from four central assumptions. First, full integration, or holism, is achieved through group members' examining the internal and conflicting messages about their past and getting rid of their unfinished business through various exercises. Through this process, group members become more complete. Second is the development of awareness, which leads to personal insight and assists group members in taking responsibility for their own behaviors. Third is a focus on figure–ground, which includes an individual's ability to identify the needs and tasks that are central to existence and those that are secondary. Healthy individuals are able to differentiate between the two and meet their primary needs first. Congruence, the final concept, is achieved when members are able to identify parts of themselves of which they were unaware. This can be accomplished using experiments or techniques such as the empty chair (Donigian & Hulse-Killacky, 1999).

Types of Gestalt Groups

Most often, Gestalt groups tend to be classified as counseling or therapy groups, but one could also use the principles in psychoeducational groups. Two general types of Gestalt groups are prominent. In the first type of group, leaders work with individual members one on one, while the other members mostly observe. Particular attention is given to the concepts of self-awareness, centering, and responsibility. The second type of Gestalt group is more interactive, using the here and now and encouraging more direct communication. When working with groups of children and adolescents, co-leadership may be helpful because students may need more individual attention than adults.

Research has found that Gestalt group counseling can be helpful for children and adolescents presenting a variety of problems. Oaklander (1999) advocated using Gestalt play therapy with groups of children to help them learn to express their emotions both verbally and nonverbally. Also, children may become more self-aware by discovering likes and dislikes, which might enable them to make positive choices regarding behavior.

Role and Function of the Leader of Gestalt Groups

Leaders coordinate Gestalt groups by deciding the timing, content, and length of work allotted for each member. When leaders use the Gestalt approach with children and adolescents, they need to provide more structure than when working with adults. Donigian and Hulse-Killacky (1999) noted that one of the main functions of group leaders in Gestalt groups is to make group members responsible for their own behavior, which is very helpful for school-age students. Group leaders are the experts in helping and communicating as well as being the ones who will challenge and teach group members. Leaders must emphasize the here-and-now interactions of the group members, facilitate a safe climate where members will be willing to take risks, and lay the groundwork for members to experiment or try out new behaviors. Facilitating a safe climate is of utmost importance when working with children and adolescents.

Stages of Gestalt Groups

The stages of development in a Gestalt group are very similar to the four general stages of groups described in this book. During the forming and orienting stage, members become acquainted and are most concerned with finding a place within the group. During the second stage, members often compete for attention and at times will question the leader's ability to facilitate the group. In the next stage, members focus on building relationships and completing goals. The final stage, termination, includes reflections on the group's progress, which some members will resist discussing.

Techniques Commonly Used in Gestalt Groups

Many techniques exist for counselors using a Gestalt approach in a group setting. Spitz and Spitz (1999) described the use of various role plays and exercises to illicit strong emotional reactions. Once these strong emotions are displayed, members can be assisted in working on congruence and integration. The technique most commonly used to promote awareness and integration is the empty chair, but this may not be an appropriate technique to implement in some school systems or with young children. With the empty chair technique, a member identifies a person with whom he or she has unfinished business. The leader then encourages the member to dialogue with the empty chair to help gain insight and awareness and to resolve the past issues. For example, an adolescent who is having difficulty communicating with either or both parents/guardians might benefit by practicing a conversation using the empty chair technique. This dialogue might help the student gain awareness of the emotions connected to conversing with his or her parents, while also practicing effective communication. Other techniques used to promote self-awareness are focusing on students' nonverbal communications and helping students to bring the past into the present by discussing how the past is influencing their relationships with people in the group.

Group leaders using a Gestalt approach can teach members how to change their questions into statements and help them to reveal and discuss their internal dialogue. Since the Gestalt approach integrates activities and experimentation into groups, it can be very appealing to and effective for children and adolescents. For example, dream work can be integrated into Gestalt groups. Young children may draw pictures of and share feelings associated with their dreams, and adolescent groups might benefit from the members' sharing their dreams and discussing the themes that arise.

Some Final Comments on Gestalt Groups

When using a Gestalt approach to group work, leaders must be aware of some limitations. Although the here-and-now focus can be very beneficial, leaders must be aware that this can produce very strong emotional reactions and that they must be skilled in handling the emotions brought to the surface and be prepared to process these feelings in group. As a result, leaders must use care while assigning experiments for students and consider the amount of adult support they have outside of group.

Strengths of the Gestalt group approach include members' feelings of connectedness with others as well as the sheer number and variety of effective techniques at the leader's disposal. While sparse, the extant literature does appear to support the effectiveness and benefits of the Gestalt group approach (O'Leary, Sheedy, O'Sullivan, & Thoresen, 2001; Paivio & Greenberg, 1995).

RATIONAL EMOTIVE BEHAVIOR THERAPY GROUPS

Group applications have been an integral part of rational emotive behavior therapy (REBT) since 1959, when Albert Ellis discovered that people by and large improved more from group therapy than from individual therapy (Ellis, 1997). Ellis noted that group therapy has several advantages. First, several group members help to dispute another member's irrational beliefs, which usually makes the disputations better and stronger. In addition, group members can collectively suggest better homework assignments that they are more likely to carry out because they are accountable to several people, not just the leader. Ellis (1997, 2001b) also suggested that since many people seek counseling for help with significant interpersonal and relationship problems and since the group itself is a social situation, these problems may be more easily assessed and addressed in a group setting. The fact that group participants can see that others in the group have changed is another advantage of this approach and motivates other group members to help themselves.

According to Ellis (2001a, 2001b), a fundamental premise of REBT is that students create their own emotional and behavioral disturbance by thinking absolutistically and dogmatically and it is not the event itself, but rather how students perceive the event, that creates problems. Helping students identify and change self-defeating thoughts, feelings, and behaviors by disputing irrational beliefs is a primary goal. Another key concept is that students must learn to accept themselves and others unconditionally and to cope with life's circumstances more effectively.

Types of REBT Groups

Vernon (2004, 2007) identified several types of REBT groups that are very appropriate in a school setting: (1) the open-ended problem-solving group, where group members learn the basic REBT concepts and then help each other apply them to current problems that group members take turns presenting; (2) the topic-specific group, where group members all share the same problem, such as divorce, anger, or substance abuse, and learn to apply REBT principles to problem resolution; and (3) the preventive group, which is psychoeducational in nature as opposed to problem focused. The preventive group is typically more structured and organized around a specific activity or lesson that introduces REBT concepts and encourages group inter-action and application of the ideas. Regardless of the type of group, the main goal is for group members to learn to think more rationally, reduce or eliminate unhealthy emotions, engage in fewer self-defeating behaviors, and apply REBT concepts to typical problems (Ellis, 2001a, 2001b).

Role and Function of the Leader in REBT Groups

In REBT groups, leaders ordinarily display a high activity level and a directive approach (Ellis, 1997). Ellis described himself as a teacher who shows group members how they upset them-selves and what they can do to change. He believes that because group members often choose not to modify their behavior, leaders must actively encourage them to change. "As a leader, I try to maximize honest revealing of feelings, cutting through defensiveness, getting to members' core dysfunctional philosophies" (Ellis, 1997, p. 152). He also helps members dispute, accept their discomfort, and engage in in-group and out-of-group experiential and behavioral exercises.

REBT group leaders do not relate closely to members for fear of creating dependency, but they are collaborative and supportive. Group leaders may also engage in self-disclosure when appropriate and serve as models to show group members how leaders practice REBT in their own lives. Leaders also monitor the group process so that one member does not dominate or obstruct the group in any way.

Stages of REBT Groups

In the initial stages of the group, leaders devote some attention to building group cohesion, which facilitates group participation. With younger children, a game called *Who Are You?* (Vernon, 2002) is effective. The leader asks the child next to him or her, "Who are you?"

The child responds with a characteristic, such as "I'm someone who likes to read." This child then asks the person seated next to him or her the same question, and the members continue in that manner so they become better acquainted. Adolescents respond better to a *Find Someone Who* activity where developmentally appropriate items are listed down the left-hand side of a paper (i.e., loves to skateboard, has a job, is addicted to video games). Opposite each item is a line for an autograph, which students get from other group members who identify with the various items listed.

Following rapport building, leaders introduce participants to the ABCDE (i.e., *A*ctivating event, *B*elief, *C*onsequence, *D*ispute, *E*valuate) theory. In the working stage of the group, members learn to apply REBT concepts to the problems they introduce in the group setting. For example, in a topic-specific group on surviving parental divorce, students can learn how to dispute irrational beliefs such as "Nothing could be worse than this" and "I can't stand it," replacing them with rational thoughts. The final stage emphasizes skill acquisition and completion of homework assignments.

Techniques Commonly Used in REBT Groups

There are numerous cognitive, emotive, and behavioral techniques that have been used effectively in groups with students. Assertiveness training, role playing, behavioral rehearsal, rational emotive imagery, relaxation training, cognitive restructuring, and information giving are among the most commonly used methods. A few additional techniques will also be described.

COGNITIVE TECHNIQUES   A popular cognitive technique, rational coping self-statements, involves asking group members to identify rational beliefs and coping statements to substitute for their irrational beliefs. Members write these on cards and use them repeatedly until they believe them. Following is a rational coping self-statement for a group participant struggling to stay in college: "I know I have to study hard, but I've done it successfully before, so I can do it again."

Another popular cognitive technique is to use psychoeducational methods such as REBT books, pamphlets, audio- or videotapes, and other self-help material (Corey, 2004; Ellis, 1997, 2001b). For example, a young child with anxiety might benefit from reading *What If It Never Stops Raining?* (Carlson, 1992) to learn different ways of reframing thoughts to reduce anxiety. Group members who use these methods learn to apply REBT more effectively.

EMOTIVE TECHNIQUES   Shame attack exercises are consistently used to help group members learn that they can stand the anxiety that comes from guilt, embarrassment, and shame and that they can accept themselves even if others think they are behaving foolishly. Shame attack exercises involve some degree of risk taking and therefore must be used cautiously with elementary and middle school students; they can be used successfully with high school students as long as they are properly structured. Shame attack exercises could include things such as calling out the stops on the elevator and asking for directions to a well-known place when they are standing near it to prove that they can tolerate embarrassment.

Another emotive technique is to use humor to show group members that they take themselves too seriously and to illustrate the ridiculousness of their irrational beliefs. One of Ellis's favorite ways of introducing humor is through humorous songs he has written on a variety of topics (see Ellis, 2001a, for examples). Vernon (2002) adapted this concept for children by introducing "silly songs" and suggested having young clients write their own humorous songs to help them reframe their issues and not take the issues too seriously.

BEHAVIORAL TECHNIQUES   REBT group leaders encourage members to reinforce themselves when they do something to change a negative behavior and to penalize themselves when they don't (Ellis, 1997). Penalties may include giving their allowance to parents or siblings and doing an onerous task such as scrubbing toilets. Group members can also monitor or suggest rewards and penalties for other members. Homework, typically thought of as a cognitive technique, is also a behavioral strategy when group leaders encourage members to do things they are fearful of in order to conquer their fears. Other activity-based assignments can also be used, such as conducting surveys to see if a perfect person truly exists (Vernon, 2002).

Some Final Comments on REBT Groups

A distinct advantage of the REBT approach is that leaders have the flexibility to introduce a variety of developmentally appropriate activities to convey the basic REBT points, rather then relying on discussion alone. This is especially important with children and adolescents, who often learn best by "doing."

Another advantage of the REBT group approach is that the basic theoretical assumptions can readily be taught to students who can then help each other as well as themselves to employ the process to solve typical problems. The fact that both intervention and prevention are incorporated into the group approach is another strength. Another benefit is that homework assignments help members transfer learning from the group to real life.

In conducting groups, REBT leaders must be cautious about being too active-directive, which interferes with a collaborative member–leader relationship. If leaders are too didactic and active, members may become passive. Although Ellis prefers a more active and confrontational style, group leaders can be flexible and adopt their own style, while still adhering to the basic principles of the approach. REBT practitioners who work with students stress the importance of developing a good relationship.

CHOICE THEORY/REALITY THERAPY GROUPS

William Glasser developed choice theory, which is based on the assumption that all behavior is purposeful and a choice. Glasser contended that most people do not have a clear understanding of why they behave as they do; they choose behaviors they think will help them to cope with frustrations caused by dissatisfactory relationships, which constitute many of the problems people have. This concept is particularly true for children and adolescents.

Also central to choice theory is the belief that as humans, we make choices that are based on the physiological need of survival and four psychological needs: love and belonging, power, freedom, and fun. Survival relates to how to maintain good health and a satisfying life. Love and belonging signify the importance of involvement with people and the need to love and be loved. Power refers to the need to be in charge of one's life and to have a sense of accomplishment and achievement. Freedom is the need to make choices, whereas fun is the need to laugh, experience humor, and enjoy life. Individuals attempt to control their world in order to satisfy these five basic needs, which differ in degree.

Reality therapy stresses the present, thereby helping people solve current problems. Instead of emphasizing feelings, the focus is on thinking and acting in order to initiate change (Glasser, 1999). Reality therapy, whether employed in an individual or a group setting, is active, didactic, and directive; it teaches members to look at whether their actions are getting them what they want, to examine their needs and perceptions, and to make a plan for change.

Choice theory and reality therapy principles can be readily integrated into group work, and this approach has been successfully employed in schools in particular, as well as in mental health agencies and correctional institutions. Glasser's (1969) book, *Schools Without Failure,* examined the application of reality therapy principles to classroom groups. In 1986, Glasser published *Control Theory in the Classroom,* which addressed how teachers could motivate students by helping them be responsible for their own learning. Today, more than 200 schools in North America belong to the Quality School Consortium and use choice theory and reality therapy to empower students and improve the school environment. Importantly, choice theory provides the theoretical underpinnings of Glasser's approach, while reality therapy is the counseling application of choice theory.

Types of Reality Therapy Groups

Depending on the setting, various types of reality therapy groups can be employed. For instance, in a school setting, reality therapy groups may involve all students in a classroom meeting. Trotzer (1999) described three types of classroom meetings: the social problem-solving meeting, the open-ended meeting, and the educational diagnostic meeting. Classroom meetings increase student responsibility and enhance classroom relationships. For example, during the problem-solving meeting, a problem common to the group is introduced, followed by a brief discussion. Group counseling participants are asked to evaluate whether or not the behaviors associated with this problem help them achieve their goals, and a plan is developed to address the issue, with periodic follow-up and reevaluation of the plan (Glasser, 1999).

Role and Function of the Leader in Reality Therapy Groups

One of the basic premises of reality therapy is that connection and interpersonal relationships are very important, which leads to the wide applicability of reality therapy to groups. With this in mind, a primary role of group leaders is to establish a good relationship with the group members by engaging in warm and caring interactions but also to use direct and confrontational interactions as appropriate.

According to Glasser (1999), group leaders must be responsible individuals who can fulfill their own needs in order to help others do the same. Furthermore, they must be mentally and emotionally mature, supportive, involved, accepting, and respectful of all group members. Leaders can serve as role models of responsible behavior and help students to assume responsibility for their own actions. Group leaders help members to find effective ways to meet their needs and, in conjunction with other group members, to develop specific action plans that will help members make the changes needed to attain their goals. Group leaders are active, teaching and encouraging members to take control of their lives by thinking and acting differently. Of course, leaders need to develop their own style of leadership so that they can employ it with sincerity. It is critical that group leaders demonstrate an openness to their own growth and a willingness to explore their own values with the groups they facilitate.

Stages of Reality Therapy Groups

In the initial stage of a reality therapy group, the leader strives to create a comfortable, supportive atmosphere and establish good rapport with group members. According to Wubbolding (2000), leaders must be empathic, which is demonstrated through skillful questioning, and use techniques such as incorporating humor and/or self-disclosure appropriately, listening for themes and metaphors, and suspending judgment to help establish a conducive climate.

The basic goal in a reality therapy group is to help members engage in new, productive behaviors that enable them to achieve present goals. To accomplish this, leaders help members to evaluate their current behavior and teach them how to take responsibility for these behaviors. Wubbolding (2000) described how the acronym WDEP (*W*ants, *D*irection and doing, self-*E*valuation, and *P*lanning) is integrated into groups to promote change. The leader first asks group members what they want and, through skillful questioning, helps them to define their needs, what they have, and what they are not getting. Next, members analyze their current behavior to see if what they are doing is consistent with what they want. The leader does not allow discussion of past events unless these events relate to present experiences and facilitate group members' future planning.

After helping members to realize what they are doing and teaching them how to control their behavior in order to make choices to change their lives, the leader's next task is to engage members in a self-evaluation process, viewed as the core of reality therapy. In confronting group participants with the consequences of their behaviors in a nonjudgmental manner, the leader encourages them to evaluate their own actions, which results in greater ownership. With younger children in particular, the leader may need to be more active in helping group members evaluate their actions.

Once group members have evaluated their own behavior, the leader helps them identify a plan for specific behavioral change. Wubbolding (2000) noted that an effective plan is one that is initiated by the student (but can involve input from the leader), relates to his or her needs, and is realistic, attainable, do-able, and easy to understand. In addition, the plan should include positive actions that can be practiced regularly and carried out independent of others and should also be flexible, repetitive, precise, and measurable. Wubbolding suggested that group members give feedback to each other, which is a skill that will probably need to be taught to school-age group members if they are not used to giving feedback. The leader needs to be persistent in helping students work on the plan and revise it as needed in order to be successful.

Techniques Commonly Used in Reality Therapy Groups

Wubbolding (1991) identified three techniques to employ in a group setting: humor, paradox, and skillful questioning. According to Wubbolding, humor helps students to develop an awareness of a situation and should be used only after considering the timing, focus, and degree of trust in the group, as well as the age of group members, since younger children might not understand the subtleties of humor. Paradox, where members are asked to perform the problematic behavior, thought, or symptom they are trying to change, can be effective for some group members but should be used cautiously in school settings. Skillful questioning involves the use of open-ended questions to help students explore issues. It is also important to focus on positive behaviors that group members would like to target.

Some Final Comments on Reality Therapy Groups

Advantages of reality therapy are that it stresses accountability and includes a structure that helps individuals to develop action plans for change. In addition, choice theory is straightforward, flexible, and a relatively brief approach to counseling and therapy. The group applications are very useful in schools. In classroom meetings, students learn to accept responsibility for their behavior, realize that they can control themselves but not others, and develop their problem-solving abilities. In small-group settings, students learn how to engage in self-evaluation and deal with present concerns in a supportive environment. Limitations of this approach include the deemphasis on feelings and the lack of exploration of the past. Furthermore, group leaders are cautioned against being too simplistic or acting as moral experts.

Summary

This chapter highlighted several different theoretical approaches to group counseling and psychotherapy. Various types of groups exist to provide different ways to meet the needs of group members. Regardless of the type of group or the theoretical approach used, many similar principles operate within the groups: For example, group members need to learn to relate to others on an interpersonal level and to learn that other individuals struggle with situations in their lives. With regard to leadership, leaders of some groups may take on a more facilitative, less active role. With other types of groups, leaders may be more directive and active in the group process.

All types of group approaches progress through identified stages of development. These stages help guide leaders as they choose specific techniques and interventions. When working in counseling and therapy groups, leaders usually work within a theoretical framework. The theories described in this chapter provide a conceptual map of human nature and the principles related to how groups develop and how areas of focus for the leaders are identified. Regardless of the group type or the theoretical approach of the leader, research has shown that groups are an effective approach with various populations.

CHAPTER 14

Special Issues in Group Work in Schools

SUSAN H. EAVES AND CARL J. SHEPERIS

PREVIEW

Special issues in group work with children and adolescents are addressed, including the basic principles of group work with children of alcoholics, children of divorce, sexual abuse victims, adolescents struggling with addictions, and children in need of social skills training.

SPECIAL ISSUES IN GROUP WORK WITH CHILDREN AND ADOLESCENTS IN THE SCHOOLS

Having reached this point in the book, you can now see that group work is an effective tool that has been proven useful with a wide range of populations and issues. However, like other forms of counseling, it must be implemented intentionally and should be varied according to the specific population with which it is used. Put another way, in order for group work to be effective, leaders must not only understand a range of basic group skills but also know when and how to apply the various skills acquired. Positive outcomes are more probable when group leaders understand the unique needs of the population with which they are working, match group members' capacities with the treatment approach, and modify that approach to accommodate the specific characteristics of the members. If leaders are equipped with appropriate skills and knowledge, adaptations can easily be made so that group members receive the most benefit from their experience within the group.

Because group leaders need to know when and how to apply their acquired skills and knowledge in various contexts, no group counseling text would be complete without examining group work with special populations and specific issues, including age (i.e., children, adolescents), aspects of the members' personal development, and preferred characteristics of the group leader.

GROUP WORK WITH CHILDREN

Group work can be a means of serving the needs of young children in an effective and efficient way. When children progress through developmental tasks and issues in conjunction with peers, they often develop a greater sense of self-efficacy and resources, leading to fewer problems in the future. Group work can be especially beneficial in this way, as children are provided with healthy modeling from both group peers and leaders. Children are referred for group work with a host of issues; however, the most common typically revolve around low self-esteem, grief, abuse, aggressiveness, inability to get along with others, rule violations, depression and anxiety, or crisis.

Group settings are natural environments for children and come with the enormous capability to harm or heal children. Because of this, extreme care must be taken by leaders when working with this population in order to do the least harm and the greatest good. Oftentimes, group members have more influence on one another than group leaders have on any one member. Because peer influence is so valued at this developmental stage, group leaders must be vigilant in facilitating a group that can be reflective of and validating to a child's development (van Velsor, 2004). There are a number of considerations when counseling small children. The first step is to prescreen members prior to inclusion into the group. When meeting with children as potential group members, it is essential to assess the degree to which they can establish relationships and their capacity to want group acceptance enough to give up any inappropriate behaviors they may display. Additional considerations in working with young students, addressed in the next sections, include confidentiality, interventions, and group size.

Confidentiality With Children

With children as clients, the concept of confidentiality can be difficult to convey. However, children can be taught how to discuss the group experience in general, without breaking confidentiality, in language that is developmentally appropriate for their age level. Leaders are encouraged to develop specific examples that can be reviewed in group as well as guidelines for how to respond when someone asks the children questions about the group. Depending on the ages and developmental levels of participants, written confidentiality agreements can be signed.

Confidentiality can be difficult for leaders to manage in some settings. For example, in schools, counselors often remove students from class to participate in group. Teachers or peers may ask questions about the process. Thus, it is important to develop responses to such inquiries ahead of time. In addition, the location of the group in a school may compromise confidentiality to some degree. As a result, leaders should take care in planning the location of the group.

Prior to beginning, leaders should obtain the written consent or assent of each child's parent or legal guardian. In an ideal situation, both parents and leaders have a common goal to promote the well-being of the child. While parental consent/assent is important and enhances cooperation, parent involvement can also affect the comfort level of the child with regard to confidentiality. While most parents are well meaning, they may ask leaders to break the confidences of the group and give them information about their child's experiences. It is important to strike a balance in this area and explain to parents the purposes of the group in such a way as to satisfy any curiosity or suspicion they may have, thereby minimizing future inquiries and resistance. At this time, leaders can encourage parents to refrain from asking their child questions about the group. Leaders should also discuss their obligation to confidentiality and how this obligation affects the parent's right to know. Leaders can satisfy this right by sharing general group information, such as weekly session topics, and keeping parents updated in general without divulging a child's personal information. Just as a parent has a right to know, a child has a right to confidentiality (van Velsor, 2004).

Interventions

As with any group, it is important for leaders to use appropriate exercises and techniques. An often-debated topic pertinent to group work with young children is the use of verbal versus nonverbal techniques. According to Thompson and Rudolph (1996), children respond better to nonverbal techniques because of their limited vocabularies. In fact, for children under the age of 12 years, leaders may rely less on verbal intervention and more on play- and action-oriented techniques. In contrast, Ohlsen, Horne, and Lawe (1988) stated that verbal techniques are appropriate to use with even very young children and that those who have difficulty expressing themselves with words can be taught to do so.

In a debate such as this, knowledge regarding child development can be of great use. In general, preschool-age children have limited verbal skills, while children above the age of six years may have the ability to learn verbal expression, though they continue to express themselves primarily in nonverbal ways. It is important for leaders to know the capabilities of the children they serve in the group setting and combine verbal and nonverbal activities and techniques in a way that is most beneficial to the age group with which they are working (van Velsor, 2004). In addition, the purpose of any technique or exercise should be explained, and children should not be pressured to participate. For example, consider the following scenario where group counseling can be used to work on social skills with preschool children. One of the ways to achieve group goals is by selecting an appropriate story that exemplifies the theme for the group session. Begin the group with a list of rules (e.g., keep your hands and feet to yourself, use an inside voice), read the story to the children, ask the children to identify the various social skills (e.g., "How did Tommy the Turtle make a friend?") in the book, and then let the children act out the story. In this process, verbal skills and play are combined to achieve group goals.

Group Size

The size and structure of a children's group are important elements to consider. In general, leaders should be prepared enough that each session is structured and yet flexible enough that the group can take its own direction. Opinions vary regarding the size of the group and the length of the sessions. A useful guideline to consider is this: the younger the group members, the shorter the session and the smaller the group. For children, groups larger than nine are considered too large for members to participate, for leaders to prevent subgroups from forming, and for leaders to adequately manage behavior. Leaders need to be counselors, not disciplinarians. Likewise, the younger the children are, the shorter the session should be. The attention span of a 6-year-old is typically very different from that of an 11-year-old. Attention spans and general behavior patterns should be taken into consideration when determining the length of sessions. As an example, ordinarily preschool groups should last no longer than 30 minutes and contain no more than seven or eight children.

GROUP WORK WITH ADOLESCENTS

As any group leader who works with adolescents will testify, working with adolescents requires patience and a clear understanding of the developmental processes at work. Adolescence is a time of change and uncertainty. During these formative years, adolescents attempt to create a unique and separate identity, solidify a value system, and establish connectedness, yet independence, in relationships with others. This is a time of increased freedom but also of increased responsibilities, expectations, pressures, and demands. Teenagers often fluctuate between a need for individuality and independence and a need for connectedness and security. In general, adolescence is a time of polarities, often leading to isolation and loneliness. At the same time, the influence and importance of a peer group increase. For these reasons, group experiences can be of great use to this population and are oftentimes even the preferred choice for treatment.

A group counseling format allows adolescents to vocalize emotions, test boundaries safely and appropriately, and feel heard, all while assisting other members in common difficulties. Further, groups can be used to help adolescents transition from childhood to adulthood, providing support and models along the way. Some themes for adolescent groups include self-esteem, stress management, family addiction, social skills, assertiveness, and grief. Several special issues with adolescents deserve further mention: participation and resistance, leader characteristics, addressing problem behavior, and ethical practice.

Participation and Resistance

Motivation to participate in counseling can sometimes be a problematic issue when working with adolescents. Even with voluntary group members, active and appropriate involvement in the group can sometimes be a challenge. Adolescents typically do better when the group is structured, expectations are given early, and limits and boundaries are made clear. Still, keeping sessions moving in a meaningful direction can prove difficult and may require leaders to actively deal with resistant members, involve as many members as possible, and cut off inappropriate storytelling. Additional problem behaviors seen in this population include purposeful disruptiveness, withdrawal, subgrouping, and inappropriate disclosure. These behaviors can be ignored, discussed openly as a group, or managed individually. Remember that leaders are responsible for facilitating new ways of behaving. Skilled group leaders learn to use resistance and other forms of problematic behavior as learning opportunities within the group. When working with adolescents, leaders must set limits early and be consistent. They must also hold members accountable for their behavior and maintain control over the process.

Leader Characteristics

Perhaps more than with any other population, the personality and behavior of group leaders are of great importance. Adolescents respond best not only to leaders who are caring, enthusiastic, open, and direct but also to leaders who are obviously congruent, are genuine, and have come to terms with their own adolescent milestones and issues. An appropriate amount of self-disclosure is not only preferred but also oftentimes expected from these group members. Leaders' respect for these individuals and their questions about the leaders' experiences will typically result in reciprocity of both respect and openness. Above all, leaders who are effective with adolescents are good role models, promoting the very behaviors they hope to see from the adolescents.

Addressing Problem Behavior

While many leader behaviors and characteristics are conducive to productive group counseling with adolescents, there are a number of behaviors, characteristics, and responses that are not. Group leaders are strongly encouraged to take an active rather than a passive role in the process. Leaders should be fair and firm and address behavior that is not appropriate according to the limits set early in the group. For instance, if confidentiality is breached, it must be addressed in the group setting. If behavior toward the leader crosses the boundaries of what is appropriate, the leader must be assertive enough to say so. Remember that you are the leader—not a peer. While it is important to not be judgmental of a member's slang language, you also do not have to incorporate it into your own style of speaking in an effort to be accepted by the group. Finally, avoid advice giving and siding with adolescents in their complaints against parents, teachers, or administrators.

Group work with adolescents can be especially helpful, as groups are designed to provide a supportive and healthy environment of peers. Because peer relations are so crucial during adolescence, a group format can be even more beneficial than other modes of therapy. Adolescents can vent feelings openly, try out new behaviors, learn through modeling, and receive feedback. Finally, adolescents can gain a sense of connectedness with others and a sense of well-being through helping other members. Despite the many positive aspects of group work with adolescents, there can be a number of disadvantages as well, most of which involve inappropriate member behavior. Because peer-group pressure is so strong during this time in adolescents' lives, group leaders must be vigilant in screening out members with inappropriate or destructive behaviors and in keeping behavior productive and supportive after group begins.

Ethical Practice

One final caution when working with adolescents involves ethical obligations. When working with this population, leaders must be thoroughly familiar with the pertinent ethical guidelines and consult with a colleague or supervisor, as appropriate, if problems arise. Depending on the age of the adolescent and the issue the group addresses, it may be necessary to obtain parental consent or assent. Parents may be determined to know the personal details of their teen's involvement in group, while the adolescent may be especially sensitive to any communication between the leader and the parent. Remember that the adolescent in this case is the one with whom you have entered into a counseling relationship. Be very clear with all group members regarding your communication with their parents or legal guardians. If the group member is being made to participate, you may have to communicate information to a judge or a probation officer. Thus, it is important to be clear with all parties, especially the adolescent, about the amount and nature of the information to be shared. In addition to obtaining consent/assent from the parent, it is appropriate to gain consent/assent from the group members, ensuring they understand the process of this type of treatment and the potential risks involved and also emphasizing their choice and freedom in the matter. Finally, thoroughly explain your duty regarding threats of danger to self or others. Adolescents oftentimes are more prone to statements involving harm, and they must understand your obligation to protect and report.

GROUP WORK WITH MINOR CHILDREN OF ALCOHOLICS

There are an estimated 10 million alcoholics in the United States. For every alcoholic, it is estimated that four or five family members and friends, 35 to 45 million persons, are directly and negatively affected by the drinking (Wilson & Blocher, 1990). Alcoholism has the greatest negative affect on the spouse and children. Approximately 8 million minor children and 18 million adult children of alcoholics (COAs) currently reside in the United States (Riddle & Bergin, 1997).

Children growing up in homes with alcoholism contend with inconsistency and tension on a daily basis, making it the most common reason for severe stress in children. COAs report household arguing and uncertainty about the family staying intact as primary concerns in childhood. COAs are also more likely to experience physical abuse, sexual abuse, and neglect. Their emotional needs are neglected and their feelings are ignored. These children often behave more like miniature adults and become the caretakers of both siblings and parents. Unpredictability in the home, especially concerning rules, norms, and discipline, also contributes to the tension and stress this population feels. Finally, distortion, denial, and isolation are used within these families in order to maintain the family secret. In light of such chaos and turmoil, it is little wonder that these students develop problematic behaviors. As group counseling emulates the family dynamics, it is important for group leaders to keep these family norms in mind in order to better understand within-group behaviors (Wilson & Blocher, 1990).

Presenting Problems

Before discussing symptomology associated with COAs, it is first important to understand that they are not sick. Instead, it would be more accurate and fair to say that they are simply reacting in a normal and self-preserving manner to abnormal and threatening events (Wilson & Blocher, 1990). In general, COAs have higher frequencies of temper outbursts, truancy, fighting with peers, eating disorders, low grades, low frustration tolerance, substance use, depression, low self-esteem, suicide attempts and completions, and psychosomatic complaints. Regarding substance use, sons of fathers with alcoholism are five times more likely to become alcoholic themselves, while daughters of mothers with alcoholism are three times more likely. Alcohol is used to compensate for the poor social skills common to this population as well as to reduce anxiety (Chandy, Harris, Blum, & Resnick, 1994; Harman & Armsworth, 1995; Thompson, 1990; Tomori, 1994; Wilson & Blocher, 1990).

Children raised in such families continue to use the same coping responses that have proved to be necessary and useful in their home environment. As these children continue to develop and mature, their social skills and coping responses may become maladaptive and detrimental to their well-being, preventing optimal functioning. These children will continue to struggle with trust, dependency, control, depression, identification, and emotional expression, as previously learned behavior becomes dysfunctional when applied to relationships outside the home (Glover, 1994). Finally, characteristic personality traits of COAs include having difficulty with project follow-through, taking themselves too seriously, overreacting to change, constantly seeking approval, feeling odd or different, denying needs, having high needs for control, exhibiting an inappropriate sense of personal responsibility, and being impulsive (Seefeldt & Lyon, 1992). These qualities often result in impoverished interpersonal relationships, chemical dependency, co-dependency, and stress-related illness (Downing &

Walker, 1987). Knowledge regarding the problematic results of growing up in an alcoholic home is of great importance in the development and implementation of group work approaches aimed at helping COAs.

Goals and Objectives

Goals listed in the literature for group work with COAs include appropriate and healthy emotional expression, social skills, identification and expression of needs, education about the illness, self-esteem building, assertiveness training, relaxation to reduce psychosomatic complaints, decision making, resource identification, and increased support systems (Riddle & Bergin, 1997; Wilson & Blocher, 1990). According to Downing and Walker (1987) in their classic study of COA group approaches, there should be four specific group goals. First, because secrecy is a typical alcoholic family characteristic, the group should provide a safe place to talk honestly about events in the home. Second, the group should confront denial and guilt, traits often seen in COAs. Third, the group should have an educational aspect, focusing on the disease of alcoholism. Finally, the group should assist members in identifying and recovering feelings that have been distorted or lost. The following format is suggested for the accomplishment of these goals: week 1—building commonality and confronting denial; weeks 2 and 3—confronting denial and educating about alcoholism and co-dependency; weeks 4 through 8—recognizing and recovering emotions. Structure decreases throughout the life of the group, and members' needs increasingly become the focus.

Assessment

While many aspects of the logistics of group work (e.g., number of members, duration, frequency) depend heavily on the age group being served, screening of group members warrants specific attention for each specialty group. An individual interview with each potential group member should be conducted prior to including the member in the group. With COAs, it is important to assess (1) current functioning, (2) the need for intervention, (3) the impact of parental alcoholism, (4) current substance use, (5) expectations for treatment, and (6) the match between potential member expectations and what the group can provide (Downing & Walker, 1987). When assessing current functioning, the need for intervention, and the impact of parental alcoholism, keep in mind that while many COAs display the problematic behaviors discussed earlier, some fit into a role termed the superhero.

Within the home of an alcoholic parent, each child develops a survival mode, leading to the adoption of behavior perceived to cause the least amount of upheaval and the greatest amount of chaos reduction in the home. The five typical adaptive roles are as follows: (1) the enabler, whom the alcoholic depends on the most; (2) the scapegoat, who draws attention away from the chemically dependent person with troublemaking behavior; (3) the lost child, who hides and disappears into the chaos; (4) the mascot, who charms and humors the family to deflect negative circumstances; and (5) the superhero, who strives for perfection, bringing pride to a family that will now be perceived as healthy and happy. The potential hazard for superheroes is that they often appear highly successful with model behavior and as a result are excluded from groups. They seem normal, even extraordinary by society's standards; however, they not only have been neglected by their alcoholic family but also risk being overlooked by group leaders. In fact, they are in need of intervention as much as other COAs (Downing & Walker, 1987; Glover, 1994).

A final note regarding the screening of group members is necessary, as there are some potential members that would prove inappropriate to the group process. Persons currently experiencing an intense crisis may not be ready for group work. Also, persons who abuse substances should first be referred and successfully treated for alcohol or drug abuse before being included in this type of group therapy. Finally, those believed by the group leaders to have the potential for disrupting the group's functioning (e.g., those with certain personality disorders) should be excluded from this type of group as well (Downing & Walker, 1987).

Benefits of Participation

Group counseling and psychotherapy have been shown to be an especially beneficial treatment modality for COAs. According to Riddle and Bergin (1997), the primary purpose of group counseling for this population is to increase effective coping with the parental alcoholism, thereby minimizing the harmful consequences. Whether or not the parents stop drinking, it is important for COAs to learn to attend to their own needs and cope in spite of their parents' behavior. If the children continue to live in the home environment, this purpose can be framed in terms of parent-proofing the children so they can survive, and perhaps even thrive, despite their home environment.

A second major purpose of group counseling with COAs is to enable group members to differentiate between themselves and their parents. Group members are educated about the disease of alcoholism and the resulting family dynamics. They are taught they cannot cause, cannot control, and cannot cure parental alcoholism. Through a kind of demystification process, the disease loses its mystery and therefore much of its power. Family secrets are explored and perspectives become increasingly objective. Through this, children learn to detach from the behavior of the alcoholic, as they come to realize that detachment is neither abandonment nor rejection (Glover, 1994; Riddle & Bergin, 1997).

In comparison to individual counseling, group counseling provides a different type of atmosphere for growth and change. The importance of the group environment's mimicking the family dynamics cannot be stressed enough. Group members begin to take on characteristics of family members, as perceived by each member. COAs also bring to the group their different family roles. Members not only see themselves mirrored in other group members but see their siblings and other family mirrored by other members as well. In this way, they gain valuable insight into their own behavior, feelings, and reactions, thereby increasing their chances for understanding and changing (Glover, 1994).

Format

Riddle and Bergin (1997) offered suggestions for the format of COA groups. Opening activities are suggested for the purpose of providing fun and relaxation. Secret handshakes can be used to close each session and help increase cohesion and camaraderie. Riddle and Bergin also suggested repetition of the group motto: "I can't cause alcoholism. I can't cure alcoholism. I can't control alcoholism. But I can learn to cope with it" (p. 199). In addition, children's books that involve characters who learn to express their feelings are frequently used. Students may also draw family pictures, make collages of feeling words, and act out family roles from the pictures and storybooks. Unspoken rules from home of "don't talk, don't trust, don't feel" (p. 200) are discussed. (Additional activities can be found in Riddle and

Bergin, 1997.) The point is that, while the specific activities of groups may differ according to the developmental age of the participants, the group goals are much the same.

The tasks of group leaders are also universal with COAs. Group leaders play a fundamental role in building cohesion within the group by drawing out and linking members' stories. Further, leaders assist each member in creating an accurate picture of his or her family, free of guilt, distortion, and denial. Group leaders help members to identify the effects that the alcoholic family has had on them personally as well as their emotional reactions to these effects. Leaders should validate and normalize members' reactions, while teaching members that they can control and choose how to respond (Arman, 2000).

GROUP WORK WITH CHILDREN OF DIVORCE

The divorce rate in the United States has become a source of concern. However, because divorce has become so common, the toll it takes on the children involved is often overlooked. Not only does divorce have short-term effects, but also the data indicate that children of divorce often continue to experience adjustment problems for as long as 10 years after the divorce occurs. During the process of a divorce, not only can there be family conflict, upheaval, uncertainty, and loss, but also during all of this change, parents are under such personal stress that they are often unable to be attentive to and provide support for their children. It is no wonder that children experience negative repercussions during divorce. In fact, it is well established that parental conflict and divorce are precursors to adverse emotional and behavioral consequences in children (Yauman, 1991).

Presenting Problems

Children of divorce often experience loneliness, chaos, feelings of responsibility for the divorce, divided loyalties, and loss of stability. Because of these experiences, they often show increased impulsivity, distractibility, aggressiveness, acting-out behaviors, depression, anger, insecurity, fear, and withdrawal and lowered academic achievement. Often, even after the divorce, children have to contend with inconsistent visitation, continued interparental hostility, and parental remarriage (Schreier & Kalter, 1990).

"Group counseling is perceived as the most practical, efficient, and effective treatment mode for children of divorce" (Yauman, 1991, p. 131). Group work is beneficial in a number of ways, as it provides an avenue for reducing feelings of isolation and shame. Simply talking aloud about feelings and experiences takes away some of the negative power of divorce. According to Schreier and Kalter (1990), the group setting provides safety in numbers and facilitates verbal and emotional expression earlier than in individual or family counseling. While providing peer support, validation, and modeling, group counseling for children of divorce can also assist members in gaining new ways of thinking, feeling, and behaving. These changes first occur within the group context and then later are applied within the members' personal lives (Sonnenshein-Schneider & Baird, 1980; Yauman, 1991).

Because divorce leaves parents emotionally and physically drained, they are often unable to provide their child objective support. When parents learn of the possibility of their child's being in a group, they typically respond favorably, as they are often relieved to have the extra source of support and stability for their child (Sonnenshein-Schneider & Baird, 1980; Yauman, 1991). Once consent is given for the child to participate in the group, and the child is willing as well, an interview with the parents is suggested. Basic information-gathering questions should be asked in an effort to assess all the changes that have occurred in the child's life. This is beneficial because it allows the group leader to better understand the dynamics operating within the group and it builds rapport with the parents. Most importantly, however, it assists the leader in separating out what is fantasy and what is reality as the child reports it. Children often speak in terms of what they wish would happen, rather than what is actually happening. If leaders are aware of the facts, they can recognize this as a defense and help group members explore their needs and fears.

It is also suggested that, under optimal circumstances, parents receive treatment separately but in conjunction with the child. Because parents are instrumental in their child's ability to adapt to the changing circumstances, they should, at a minimum, be educated regarding the effects that divorce can have on their child as well as ways in which they can better meet their child's needs during this time. Parent education and support groups can be of great value to both parent and child (Yauman, 1991).

Goals and Objectives

Since children of divorce have and continue to experience excess amounts of upheaval and uncertainty, a structured environment with clear and fair rules is suggested (Yauman, 1991). Within this structured environment, group leaders should make it a priority to offer support, teach coping skills, validate feelings, reinforce appropriate expression, offer resources, and facilitate communication among members. Further, leaders should make sure they reinforce the message that it is not the child's divorce and that no one is divorcing the child. The child did not cause the situation between his or her parents, and neither can the child fix it.

Schreier and Kalter (1990) offered five specific goals for children of divorce groups: (1) normalize the divorce experience, (2) clarify divorce-related concerns, (3) help each child reexperience painful emotions, (4) improve coping, and (5) communicate each child's reactions and questions to the parents to facilitate increased parental support. These goals are met through a structured group that meets for eight sessions. These sessions initially focus on the need for fairy-tale endings and the reality and sadness of the lost family unit. The group then shifts its focus to feelings about parental hostility, loss, fear, divided loyalties, and confusion regarding custody. In later sessions, the group discusses feelings about the noncustodial parent, parental dating, and remarriage. A number of techniques and activities are used throughout the life of the group to address these themes.

Techniques Used in Groups for Children of Divorce

When used appropriately, selectively, and in a flexible manner, specific techniques can assist in stimulating group interaction and clarifying feelings, especially when working with children and adolescents. The group techniques used most often for this population include bibliotherapy, movies, board games, drawings, brainstorming, role-playing, and puppets. One of the most commonly used methods, bibliotherapy, is recommended because it is often helpful to approach the issues surrounding divorce in an indirect manner early in the group. This technique is most productive when used with other techniques and in only one or two sessions. Similar to the use of storybooks, short movies can be used to stimulate group members' discussion and expression of feelings through their reactions to what they've read or viewed. Movies are especially useful for reassuring children that their feelings and reactions are normal. Children also benefit because they can typically identify with the characters they see depicted.

Games can be used to generate enthusiasm and maximize group interaction. Many games have been created for specific subpopulations and foster cognitive restructuring, behavioral rehearsal, feedback, and positive social behaviors (Yauman, 1991).

According to Sonnenshein-Schneider and Baird (1980), one of the most successful combinations of techniques is brainstorming, role playing, and rehearsal. When a group member expresses a divorce-related concern, the group first brainstorms possible courses of action. The members then role-play and rehearse the solution that they agree is most likely and beneficial. Efforts to teach children how to clarify and act on their feelings are greatly enhanced by this process, as it desensitizes the group to the problems, clarifies the issues, generates active problem-solving, and fosters communication.

Remember that techniques should be well thought out, reviewed prior to the group session, and used appropriately, selectively, and intentionally. Keep in mind that the purpose of using specific techniques is to facilitate the discussion and processing of information in such a way that it becomes personally relevant for each child (Yauman, 1991).

Strengths and Resources

One additional suggestion for working with children of divorce involves the importance of attending to the positive aspects of the child's situation. Students must be encouraged not only to mourn their loss but also to consider the positive aspects of their new family structure. Reframing the divorce and considering the positive events and conditions that have resulted from it are invaluable in changing the child's perception (Yauman, 1991).

Finally, group leaders must set realistic expectations for themselves, the group, and the members. A group counseling experience for children of divorce serves many purposes, including offering support and normalizing feelings. It can result in many positive changes, including improved concentration, mood, social skills; resolution of feelings, behavior; and overall well-being and adjustment. However, the group will not radically change anyone's situation, nor will it save any particular child. The loss involved in a divorce is similar in some ways to the loss of a loved one to death. However, with divorce, there is sometimes no closure, and the child often continues to wish for a reunion between the parents. It is important for leaders to recognize this as normal and not as therapeutic failure (Sonnenshein-Schneider & Baird, 1980).

GROUP WORK WITH SURVIVORS OF SEXUAL ABUSE

Depending on how abuse is defined, it can be estimated that between one-third and one-half of all females in the United States experience some form of sexual abuse during their lifetime. Several factors contribute to the level of trauma experienced by the victim of sexual abuse. First, the family atmosphere within which the abuse occurred seems to play the most significant role in terms of outcome. Individuals whose families are viewed as nonsupportive, blaming the victim, or neglectful or are dealing with substance abuse seemed to have the most difficulty coping with the sexual abuse. Second, the younger the age at which the abuse occurred, the more devastating the effects on the survivor. Third, the more violent the abuse, the more traumatic the effects. Finally, of all the forms of sexual abuse, father–daughter incest is considered the most difficult to recover from, primarily due to the beliefs society holds regarding fathers as protectors. The child who is abused by her father has to accept not only that her father did not protect her but also that he caused her direct and purposeful harm (Newbauer & Hess, 1994; Turner, 1993).

A host of psychological effects can occur as a result of sexual abuse, although they will differ from person to person, with no two survivors reacting in the same way. A survivor's history of crisis, support network, emotional stability, coping skills, and unique experience of abuse—including the type of abuse, the perpetrator, and the reaction of others—will all affect the range, duration, and severity of symptoms he or she experiences. In general, survivors of sexual abuse typically report depression, shame, guilt, anxiety, worthlessness, lowered self-esteem, stigmatization, isolation, anger, difficulty trusting others, problems with sexuality, obsessive- compulsive tendencies, self-destructive behaviors, and perhaps dissociation (Darongkamas, Madden, Swarbrick, & Evans, 1995; Turner, 1993).

Benefits of Group Membership

Despite the high number of sexual abuse survivors, and knowledge of the resulting trauma, society continues to send the message that sexual abuse is not to be talked about. Because victims are so often silenced, feelings of isolation and alienation are increased. Belonging to a group designed specifically for survivors of sexual abuse not only allows the communication and open discussion prohibited by society but also provides a safe environment in order to encourage such openness. It is believed that each time survivors speak about their experiences, they distance themselves from the pain. The more they talk, the less power the abuse has, and, therefore, the less victimized they feel. Such a group is believed to foster a sense of empowerment and connection to others and to facilitate the ability to trust, a trait that is nearly always shattered when abuse occurs (Turner, 1993).

Group counseling and psychotherapy are thought to be the most effective and timely treatment modality for survivors, as they allow for the ventilation of feelings necessary for the construction of a new cognitive framework or simply a new perception of the abuse (Darongkamas et al., 1995; Herder & Redner, 1991). These goals can also be accomplished in individual counseling. The difference between group and individual counseling lies in the all-in-the-same-boat idea, described by Shulman (1992). Essentially, a group setting enables survivors to share among others who feel similarly, lessening isolation and providing a sense of relief. Within a group format, the members are as healing to one another as the leader is to each member (Darongkamas et al., 1995; Turner, 1993).

Not only is the group setting conducive to treating the symptomology associated with abuse, but also the therapeutic social interactions can greatly reduce feelings of isolation, aloneness, and shame. Another benefit that a group experience provides is that it replicates family dynamics. Because of this group trait, each member has the opportunity to explore behaviors learned in the family of origin that might be influencing behavior (Marotta & Asner, 1999). Ideally, the group has a skilled leader and restorative and nurturing members and functions as a healthy surrogate family. In this way, members are further supported, learn that boundaries are respected, begin to trust again, and practice new and healthier behaviors (deYoung & Corbin, 1994).

A final note regarding group counseling and psychotherapy as the preferred treatment options for sexually abused individuals concerns one of the dangers of individual treatment with this population. Individual treatment can have characteristics that may in some ways feel similar to the abusive relationship: Both an abusive relationship and individual treatment are emotionally intense, dyadic relationships based on trust, but with an unbalanced power relationship. Group counseling, on the other hand, emphasizes equal and open relationships and reduces secrecy (deYoung & Corbin, 1994).

Group Assessment of Survivors of Sexual Abuse

As with any group experience, decisions have to be made regarding screening and selection of group members. While screening criteria are well documented for group inclusion in general, some specific guidelines are needed when screening members for a sexual abuse group. deYoung and Corbin (1994) stressed the importance of this phase in group preparedness and emphasized that each member selected must be ready for the group experience. Readiness is assumed if the member is no longer being abused, is not in contact with the perpetrator, has a support system, is willing to share with others in the group, and is ready to realize the impact the abuse has had on current functioning and decision making.

In order for the group experience to be therapeutic rather than damaging, it is important for each member selected to have ego strength and be able to cope with what occurs within the group. Potential members should have a positive opinion about their possible inclusion in the group (Darongkamas et al., 1995). Herman and Schatzow (1984) even weighted this factor as more important than other factors in predicting successful group outcomes. Prior therapy and disclosure of the abuse are preferred as well. For instance, if a potential member had just become aware of past abuse or had just recently disclosed it to a helping professional, group participation would need to be postponed until individual work had been done. Those who are new to treatment for this issue tend to be in a crisis mode and require much more individual attention than a group format can provide (Darongkamas et al., 1995).

Potential members' personal lives should be relatively stable from day to day. While stability is a relative term for each individual, it might prove beneficial to exclude those who have had recent hospitalizations or suicide attempts. Further, although it is expected that some mental health symptomology will be present, those with active psychotic symptoms should be excluded. Not only would these individuals be too fragile for the group setting, but also they might overwhelm other group members and become a counterproductive force in the group experience. Finally, potential members should perceive and accept the sexual abuse as a primary problem or the main impetus for the problematic issues currently being experienced.

Conjoint Group and Individual Counseling With Survivors of Sexual Abuse

One final issue debated in the professional literature involves concomitant group and individual counseling with survivors of sexual abuse. Herman and Schatzow (1984) considered an ongoing relationship with an individual counselor a necessary criterion for inclusion in a sexual abuse group. Likewise, deYoung and Corbin (1994) stated the importance of ongoing individual treatment during the course of group work in order for each member to continue gaining insights initiated in the group as well as to work on issues unrelated to the sexual abuse. However, it was the reasonable opinion of Darongkamas et al. (1995) that concurrent individual work may take away from the group experience and that any difficulties that arise from participation in the group should be discussed as part of the group process. In this way, insights generated from the group process are fed back into the group process, rather than becoming topics for isolated discussions with individual counselors.

Format

Less than 4 members and more than 10 members make establishing a healthy group dynamic difficult, especially with this population. For sexual abuse groups specifically, five to six members seems to be the most frequently cited number (Marotta & Asner, 1999). The group's length, duration, and frequency of meetings and whether the group is open or closed will often be determined by treatment goals, setting, and the age range of the members (i.e., preschool children, elementary children, preadolescents, adolescents). However, it is generally agreed that, if possible, groups should be closed and time limited. The closed-group format promotes trust, cohesion, safety, and some degree of predictability, all of which are paramount to survivors of sexual abuse. Further, when groups are time limited, members not only are encouraged to focus on and work toward their goals more efficiently but also are provided a sense of closure and completion (Darongkamas et al., 1995; deYoung & Corbin, 1994; Marotta & Asner, 1999).

Group rules, including those related to attendance, timeliness, and respect for other members, are essential for the development of trust and the protection of members. However, rules without reasons can lead to rebellion for some group members, while others may become overly compliant. When setting rules, keep in mind their purpose, limitations, and exceptions, as these group members have experienced the abuse of power and authority. In addition to rules, structure is important. Each group meeting should have a structured format and yet retain enough flexibility to be responsive to the needs of the group at that moment. The goal is to provide enough structure to promote safety and predictability and yet allow enough flexibility that the members feel they have autonomy and choices, as these are especially important issues for sexual abuse survivors (Darongkamas et al., 1995; deYoung & Corbin, 1994).

In addition to reducing feelings of isolation, shame, oddity, and alienation, sexual abuse groups serve the function of resocialization within a surrogate family. Such groups assist in transforming secretiveness into openness, confusion into certainty, and numbness into expression. Further, members work toward creating meaning from the chaos following the abuse. Hearing others' stories serves as a mirroring process. Giving and receiving feedback is empowering. Seeing rules set, explained, and followed builds a sense of safety and trust in the group, which then transfers to the members' larger environment outside of the group. Insight can be gained into the effects the abuse has on current functioning. Finally, as group leaders normalize the thoughts and feelings of each member, survivors are able to reorganize their perceptions and reinterpret events in such a way that they no longer assume responsibility for those events. Overall, traumatic memories are perceived in a new way so that they may be more easily incorporated, thereby giving them less power (deYoung & Corbin, 1994).

Group counseling and psychotherapy have been so widely advocated for victims of sexual abuse that many formats have been created solely for that purpose. One such model is the trauma-focused sexual abuse treatment group, which focuses on adolescents. Probably the main element of this group is the member's disclosure about the experience of sexual abuse. The leader goes to great lengths to facilitate storytelling and even uses a guided exercise. If a member has already had the experience of family members, law enforcement officers, or child welfare professionals disbelieving the details of her story, she may be very reluctant about having that same experience with the leader. The guided exercise acts as a prompt for sharing details. It begins with an affirmation that reinforces each member's control over the disclosure and relieves each child of responsibility for the sexual abuse. The guided exercise then suggests the details of the sexual abuse that are important to the story, such as who the perpetrator was, how many times the abuse occurred, the pressures for secrecy, the impact it had, and the nonoffending parent's response to it. The exercise then ends with an affirmation of each member's right to respect and safety (deYoung & Corbin, 1994).

Although telling the story has great value, telling alone is not enough. The task of the leader therefore, is to normalize these thoughts and feelings, reorganize perceptions, and provide a new interpretation that relieves the member of responsibility. As a result, traumatic memories are transformed so that they may be more easily incorporated into the member's life (deYoung & Corbin, 1994).

Male Victims of Sexual Abuse

Male victims of sexual abuse are often overlooked because male sexual abuse is underreported and male victims are much less likely to seek help than female victims. Studies show that as many as 16% of male children and adolescents are sexually abused. Some symptoms more common in male than female victims include normalization of the abuse, homophobic concerns, sexual identity confusion, sexual compulsiveness, difficulties dealing with anger, aggression, and wariness of men (Thomas & Nelson, 1994).

A process group for males who were abused as children and adolescents has been formatted to address the specific problems associated with being a male victim. It is recommended that this process group be an ongoing experience with no set time to end because healing from sexual abuse is a process and each member has to resolve a different combination of issues. A structured group with set expectations and time limits may cause more harm than good. It is emphasized that recovery is a process that involves several stages and steps and that no one follows the same pattern. Long-term group counseling is necessary to treat the total problem, rather than simply treating the symptoms (Thomas & Nelson, 1994).

GROUP WORK AND ADDICTIONS

Addictive behaviors encompass a variety of issues, ranging from food to gambling, sexual endeavors, and substances. Many characteristics pertinent to groups dealing with addictions span addictive issues; however, some are specific to a particular addiction and do not necessarily apply to others. For the purposes of this chapter, group work with addictions in general will be discussed; where information pertains only to a particular addiction, such an acknowledgment will be made.

Benefits of Group Membership

Group counseling and psychotherapy not only are the most common treatment modalities for persons with addictions but also are commonly considered an essential and core aspect of treatment (Line & Cooper, 2002; Weiss, Jaffee, de Menil, & Cogley, 2004). In addition to the obvious cost-effectiveness of the group format, the dominant use of group work with members with addictions is related to the strong influence of peer groups. The idea that others who have experienced similar problems are influential is especially relevant in reducing the denial, rationalization, and minimization that are so common among individuals with addictions. The feeling of sameness reduces these common defenses, as does the fact that group members are able to support and confront one another. As group members challenge one another's distorted interpretations of behavior, defenses lessen more quickly than might be expected in individual treatment. Group members who share the commonality of addiction tend to trust other members more readily than the leader, who may be viewed as authority (Line & Cooper, 2002).

In particular, adolescents with addictions can especially benefit from group membership. Because the addictive behaviors of adolescents are so often perpetuated by others in similar peer-group settings, using this same social-based influence for counseling purposes is helpful, and perhaps even necessary (Waldron & Kaminer, 2004). This peer-group condition has been demonstrated in research (Graham, Annis, & Brett, 1996) as most effective in increasing skills necessary to reduce relapse among adolescent substance abusers because it mirrors daily experience.

Goals and Objectives

Not only is group work essential in confronting the typical defenses of members with addictions, but also it is an integral part of healing the shame that is commonly present and that typically contributes to further addictive behaviors. Individuals with addictions often engage in secretive behavior and internalize negative societal perceptions. As members get to know one another, empathy and understanding for other members develop. This in turn leads to self-empathy and self-understanding as members realize that others also have misguided rationales for their addictive behavior and are not inherently "bad." In addition, leaders should provide a safe and nonjudgmental atmosphere to facilitate shame reduction (Line & Cooper, 2002).

Although various treatment approaches have proved to be effective with addictive behaviors, group work is especially promising, as it uses various strategies to increase social support, social skills, coping responses, and role changes. The group itself becomes a microcosm of each member's personal society, so that members may reflect on their lives and the dynamics of their addictions in order to recognize and overcome issues that interfere with their recovery. In addition, group work should ideally contribute to members' recognition of the void created by addiction, reflection of ignored emotions, understanding of their motivations for addictive behavior, and deciding how to behave without their addiction (Washington & Moxley, 2003). A final goal of group work with addictions is to assist members in developing more appropriate coping responses for negative emotions, situations, and issues. Members should learn healthier strategies (e.g., using others for support, honest communication, self-care) to replace old habits (e.g., sexual acting-out, eating, substance use) (Line & Cooper, 2002).

Presenting Problems

Certain characteristics that appear with chemically addicted populations bear mentioning here, as they will no doubt affect group processes. Persons who are chemically dependent oftentimes exhibit behaviors that can interfere with their ability to develop effective communication and interpersonal relationships, both of which are necessary for successful group outcomes. During times of substance use, social, personal, and work activities are negatively affected, as time is diverted away from these life areas and instead used for the addictive behavior. Because of this neglect and preoccupation, dysfunctional and maladaptive behaviors emerge. Among such responses are compulsiveness, impulsiveness, overspending, overeating, hypersexuality, depression, low self-worth, societal estrangement, social isolation, impaired judgment, aggressiveness, rebelliousness, and anger (Campbell & Page, 1993).

Not all persons with addictions are equally well suited for group work. Those who have particular personality features may be unable to emotionally attach, which is a necessary component of successful group work. Many members are openly defiant, rebellious, or conning, all of which can undermine the potential work of other group members. It is preferable to have like-minded individuals in a group, thereby increasing chances of effectiveness. However, as this is not always possible, it is important for leaders to keep in mind that most persons with addictions have a commonality regardless of their addiction or their personality traits. Typically, most members with addictions are looking outside of themselves for an escape that keeps them from facing their inward emptiness (Flores, 1997).

Other factors that call for special consideration with this population are lack of motivation to change, lack of engagement, retention issues, and co-occurring disorders. When working specifically with chemical addiction, symptoms of physiological withdrawal may interfere with group work. Also, research shows that for those who began substance abuse in adolescence and are now chemically addicted, completion of crucial developmental tasks has likely been delayed. For instance, the processes of developing prosocial behavior and interpersonal skills and assuming family and work responsibilities are often prolonged, as the necessary opportunities and coping skills are not realized when engaging in heavy substance use (Waldron & Kaminer, 2004). All of these factors can impede group work and, at a minimum, should be a consideration of group leaders.

Models of Group Work With Addictions

In a review of the existing literature on group work for addiction, Weiss et al. (2004) identified five common models of group work for persons with addictions: (1) the education model, where the leader acts as a teacher, educating members about addiction; (2) the recovery skills training model, where the leader teaches specific skills to decrease relapse; (3) the group process model, where outcomes are a result of group process and interaction; (4) the check-in model, which entails brief individual assessments within the group; and (5) the specific-issue group model, where the focus is on an issue related to the addiction. While these same authors found few differences between group therapy models or focus in terms of treatment effectiveness, Washington and Moxley (2003) urged group leaders to be intentional and diligent in selecting group interventions in such a way that the group experience is tailored to the individual needs of the members. While group work in general has been shown to be effective with individuals with addictions, it is uncertain which group characteristics and interventions truly contribute to recovery. The different phases of recovery, the various needs of group members, and diverse social issues should be taken into account when developing an addiction group.

Flores (1997) and Line and Cooper (2002), among others, point out that group work with persons with addictions should look different in the beginning stages of the group as compared to the latter, as well as for those new to the recovery system compared to those who have done work in the past. Specifically, Flores (1997) stated that group leaders should provide high levels of support and structure in the beginning of group. As members spend more time in the group, confrontation is necessary to encourage them to look honestly at themselves and their lives and to deal with the very feelings they have been avoiding. Forcing this view of members too early, however, can lead to anxiety or depression and possibly trigger relapse. Similarly, Line and Cooper (2002) suggested a high level of structure, psychoeducation, and a cognitive-behavioral approach in the beginning of group as this oftentimes feels *safer* to new members.

Dayton (2005) noted that leaders developing treatment approaches should be concerned with whether issues of grief will undermine a group member's sobriety. Many persons with addictions are self-medicated (e.g., with drugs, alcohol, food, sex, gambling) as a way to manage their emotional pain. This pain may reemerge during the recovery process, as these self-medicating tools are no longer an available option. Members may need to grieve for the lost time, often years that were spent in addiction, and for the pain they have caused others. In general, in early recovery, members with addictions may not benefit from revisiting painful matters from the past, as this can trigger relapse. However, the very opposite can be true in later recovery. Avoiding such painful material after the group member has developed ego strength and support can undermine recovery (Dayton, 2005).

GROUP WORK FOR SOCIAL SKILLS DEFICITS

Group work for children and adolescents capitalizes on the aspect of social interaction, which is pertinent to the developmental process of this age group. According to Bandura (1989), most social learning takes place through observation of the actions and consequences of others. By its very nature then, group counseling provides ample opportunity for this to occur and allows for observation, comparison, interaction, and practice.

Presenting Problems

Positive interactions with others serve as an important protective factor for children and adolescents. Positive peer relationships serve as a safeguard against anxiety, depression, and loneliness and assist in the development of healthy self-worth and social problem-solving. However, when social interactions are negative and entail rejection or aggressiveness, children's self-esteem, academic performance, and feelings of belonging can all be affected (Sim, Whiteside, Dittner, & Mellon, 2006). According to Kupersmidt and Coie (1990), peer rejection is associated with school truancy, suspension, delinquency, and dropping out.

A social skills deficit implies that a child does not have the necessary repertoire of social abilities useful in not only navigating various social situations and avoiding problematic situations but also building connections and relationships. Though not always the case, most children with social skills deficits typically have a number of other risk factors as well. When the lack of appropriate social skills leads to rejection, isolation, and conflict, the original problems are compounded. In addition, social skills are considered a necessary component for success in life well beyond childhood and adolescence. Among other things, parents and teachers can ask themselves if a child has (1) trouble approaching new groups, (2) difficulty waiting his or her turn in a conversation, (3) trouble discerning appropriate distances from other children, or (4) difficulty managing emotional reactivity (Sim et al., 2006).

The use of social skills training is a popular idea in most school settings. Such training has been supported by extensive reviews of the research, which shows three skills to be most important to student success: cognitive skills (e.g., memory, goal setting), social skills (e.g., problem solving, listening), and self-management skills (e.g., motivation, controlling anger). Research findings have been used to support the connection among social, emotional, and academic functioning, with improvements in one area affecting improvements in other areas (Brigman, Webb, & Campbell, 2007).

Specific Leader Qualities

In general, it is both helpful and necessary that leaders be able to personally demonstrate the social skills in which the group members are to be trained. In other words, potential group leaders need to be socially competent. For instance, if a professional school counselor is passive and unable to assert himself, it is going to be difficult for him to then teach and model assertive behavior to a group member. Similary, counselors should be able to distinguish among aggressive, assertive, and passive behavior. At a minimum, they should be able to establish eye contact, share their emotions assertively, use I-statements, and make direct requests (Rotheram-Borus, Bickford, & Milburn, 2001).

Goals and Objectives

While social skills are extremely important, many students do not have ample opportunity to develop them, are lacking the appropriate models or guidance needed to develop them accurately, or are impaired due to emotional or behavioral disorders. The goals of group work for the purpose of social skills training encompass several interrelated objectives. In general, it is important to focus on training children in nonverbal and verbal skills that will assist them in using more prosocial and appropriate behaviors and also in recognizing the impact of their behavior on others. More specifically, children and adolescents should have both the opportunity and the guidance needed to develop skills such as managing emotions, cooperating, compromising, feeling empathy, and listening. Specific goals of social skills training often involve tasks that most adults find commonplace. Meeting friends, making good first impressions, joining groups, praising others, being a good host, coping with teasing, using conversation skills, reading social cues, and solving problems in order to reduce conflict are all examples of such goals. In order to address these goals, groups typically use education, group activities, exercises, behavior rehearsal techniques, peer feedback, and homework. Leaders rely heavily on practice assignments to encourage students to generalize skills to other settings and environments outside of group (Sim et al., 2006).

Techniques or Format

The format of a social skills group can vary, but most are either structured discussion groups involving a specific agenda or activity groups that go beyond discussion and incorporate guided and purposeful tasks for skill acquisition. As an example, a typical activity group might involve a three-phase process for skill acquisition. The first few sessions of group might provide information about social skills deficits and the benefit of counseling. Sessions falling in the middle portion of the program might incorporate skill-building exercises focused on social cues, social problem-solving, assertiveness, and cognitive restructuring. The latter sessions then could provide opportunities to incorporate these skills into actual demonstrations through within-session exposure and homework assignments. It is during this skill generalization process that parental involvement has been advocated (Schindler, 1999).

Researchers suggest that parental involvement can improve treatment outcomes regarding skill acquisition and use outside of group environments (Kolko, Loar, & Sturnick, 1990). Specifically, research findings have shown that parental involvement results in improved social skills ratings and decreased aggression (Frankel, Myatt, Cantwell, & Feinberg, 1997).

A host of social skills training programs have been designed specifically for the professional school counselor and have been shown through research to be effective (Rotheram-Borus et al., 2001). Typically, these programs are theory driven, are enjoyable, and require repeated practice of new skills. Most social skills training programs have a manual that specifies exactly what is needed to conduct the group. Activities, exercises, and oftentimes an exact example for carrying out intended objectives are provided. In addition, it is typical to find role-play scenes, self-assessments, and homework exercises included.

One such skills program, the Assertive Communication Training (ACT) Game, was designed specifically for children in grades three through six, some of whom are lacking in social skills and some who are socially skilled. The idea is to have those skilled members serve as learning models for those who are not skilled. Also, social skills training is considered to improve the adjustment of all children, regardless of skill deficit or attainment, and can be implemented at the classroom level through the use of the ACT Game. Typically, a problematic social situation is presented by the professional school counselor, and students are chosen to role-play the situation, with the roles of facilitative coaches, dilemma-presenting challenger, and problem-solving actor being filled by the children. The school counselor usually plays the role of director and guides the role play in an appropriate and meaningful direction (Rotheram-Borus et al., 2001).

Student Success Skills (SSS), another social skills training program, is designed to teach academic, social, and self-management skills (Brigman et al., 2007). This program focuses directly on improving student behavior and academic achievement and aligns itself with *The ASCA National Model* (American School Counselor Association, 2005). The SSS group meets for eight weekly and four monthly sessions, each lasting approximately 45 minutes. Each session focuses on improving social, self-management, and academic skills. Specific strategies of this group include music, movement, storytelling, role playing, and peer coaching.

The SSS group follows a specific format for each group meeting, meaning that each session is conducted in three parts. At the beginning of each session, the group focuses on setting goals and monitoring progress. During the middle portion of the session, students work toward solving a social problem using dramatization and feedback. Finally, at the end of each group session, members report progress in each area specific to the group through a formal instrument; they are also encouraged to report any useful tools they learned (Brigman et al., 2007).

Children suitable for social skills training groups typically have poor listening, low frustration tolerance, inability to perceive social cues, inappropriate social boundaries, difficulty expressing themselves, passivity, or aggressiveness. These very characteristics that are in need of remediation also contribute to difficult group processes. Because group work is a social environment and because many of the members of a social skills group are likely to have poor social skills, smaller groups—typically around six children—are suggested for optimal results. Including more than this in the group can become counterproductive, as students will learn from one another as intended, but they may be learning inappropriate behaviors instead of newer and more socially appropriate ones (Schindler, 1999).

Summary

Group work is effective with both children and adolescents for a variety of reasons. There are important considerations to keep in mind when conducting group work for individuals in various developmental stages and with specific issues. When group leaders are prepared, are intentional, and understand the needs of the group, positive outcomes are most likely.

Recall that group settings are natural social environments for children and therefore are highly influential. Group leaders need to facilitate a positive group environment because peer influences and feedback actively shape the students. Confidentiality is a concern with this particular population, and group leaders must take extra care to make certain that children understand the limits of confidentiality. Parents of these children can press group leaders for information, and a balance has to be achieved between a parent's right to know and a child's right to confidentiality. The size and structure of the group are especially important considerations. Typically, the younger the members, the shorter the sessions and the smaller the group should be. In general, knowledge of child development can be of great use when planning and implementing group counseling for children.

Group counseling is often the preferred treatment approach for adolescents; however, it is not without special concerns. Disruptiveness, withdrawal, cliques, inappropriate disclosure, and poor boundaries are all special issues related to group work with adolescents. A lack of motivation can be especially problematic. Thus, it is important for group leaders to help members reframe their thoughts about participating in group. Leaders should also remind themselves to use resistance in a therapeutic manner, to remain nondefensive, to resist personalizing adolescent behavior, to model appropriate behavior, and to remain both firm and fair. Finally, because peers are so influential at this stage, it is even more important for group leaders to be vigilant in screening members and keeping behavior productive during group. If group interactions are not appropriate according to the rules and limits set early within the group, leaders must attend to this immediately, keeping in mind that they are the group leader—not a peer.

This chapter offered overviews of five specific groups commonly used with children and adolescents. First, groups used for children of alcoholics can become distorted as group members come to emulate the family of origin within the group setting, with similar dynamics and norms. Group leaders must keep this in mind to better understand within-group processes and use them to facilitate healing and changed behaviors. This environment can be especially helpful because members are able to try out new coping responses in a setting that feels similar to their home environment. Objectives for this type of group include providing a safe place to talk honestly in an effort to combat secrecy, confronting common characteristics of denial and guilt, educating members about the disease of alcoholism, and identifying and recovering feelings that have been distorted or lost.

Second, group work is the most effective treatment modality for children of divorce. Not only does the group setting provide safety in numbers, but also it can be validating, supportive, and encouraging of emotional expression. A group that is structured and has clear and fair rules is especially important for these members, as they oftentimes continue to experience uncertainty and a changing environment. The group techniques most often used for this population include bibliotherapy, movies, board games, drawings, brainstorming, role playing, and puppets. Techniques should always be well thought out, reviewed prior to the group session, and used appropriately, selectively, and intentionally. When working with this population, the positive aspects of the child's situation must be stressed; in other words, children must be encouraged not only to mourn their loss but also to consider positive aspects of their new family structure.

Third, groups designed to treat victims of sexual abuse are most helpful and appropriate for those who have already recalled, acknowledged, and worked on issues stemming from the abuse within an individual therapy setting. Survivors of abuse who have only recently opened up about the abuse are considered to be in crisis and are therefore not appropriate for group work because they need more individual attention than the group setting can provide. Group leaders should bear in mind that not all group members are affected in the same way by sexual abuse. Several factors that may determine the level of trauma experienced by the survivor include family atmosphere, age at the time of the abuse, the violence of the abuse, and the relationship of the perpetrator to the abuser. Similar to groups for children of alcoholics, groups for sexual abuse survivors can begin to take on the characteristics of the family of origin.

The fourth specialty group is the group that works with addictions. Not only is group work the most common approach with this population, but also it is considered essential to recovery. Specific goals pertinent to an addictions group include recognizing the repercussions of addiction, owning previously ignored emotions, gaining insight into motivations for the addiction, and learning new ways of behaving without the addiction. Persons with addictions typically exhibit difficulty communicating and forming relationships. Both of these elements are essential for successful groups, so members' difficulty in these areas can pose an additional challenge within the group setting. Group leaders must remain intentional at all times in an effort to tailor the group to the individual needs of the members.

Finally, social skills groups for children and adolescents were reviewed. The very nature of group work is such that social learning takes place. Such groups are widely used within the school setting, as the relationships between social functioning and behavior, as well as social functioning and academics, have been established through research. Social competence is viewed as a buffer against trauma, crisis, anxiety, and depression.

Likewise, the lack of social skills, which ultimately leads to conflict with and rejection by peers, compounds the effects of risk factors already existing within the child. The school-related concerns most often cited as affected by social skills deficits include school truancy, delinquency, dropping out, and lower grades. Many social skills programs exist that provide for learning that is structured so as to improve the likelihood that social learning will be positive and skill acquisition possible. Due to the nature of the socially deficient child, smaller groups of around six children are recommended. Within these groups, which must be led by socially competent counselors, skills such as nonverbal behaviors, compromise, listening, and emotion regulation are taught through a variety of techniques, including role playing, education, peer feedback, and homework.

Regardless of the developmental stage of the group or the specific issue to be addressed, effective and competent group leaders will be intentional and purposeful in every stage of the development and implementation of the group: conducting the initial planning for the group; screening the members; deciding on the specifics of location, number, frequency, and duration; setting rules and guidelines; choosing activities and interventions, and facilitating the group process itself. Knowledge specific to each group and awareness of member characteristics and needs will assist in this process.

CHAPTER 15

Using Activities and Expressive Arts in Group Work

Bradley T. Erford, Debbie W. Newsome, and Mary Keene

PREVIEW

Group activities and expressive arts are powerful additions to the professional school counselor's toolbox. While these techniques and strategies work well under normal circumstances, expressive arts also allow group leaders to reach resistant, creative, and sensitive members. Expressive arts and activities challenge members to use their creativity and talents to overcome adversity. Likewise, counseling and therapeutic games have been used for years with small groups of children to help them achieve developmental and therapeutic goals when dealing with such issues as social skills, study skills, anger management, and changing families. In addition, the use of creative arts (e.g., drawing, journaling, music therapy) is on the rise in group work, particularly with school-age youth. This chapter surveys the use of each of these procedures within the context of group work to help motivate group members and facilitate the group work. This chapter also explores ways that leaders can expand introductory activities, games, and the creative arts in order to increase the comfort level of students and to add a new dimension to groups.

THE USE OF ACTIVITIES AND EXPRESSIVE ARTS IN GROUP WORK

Effective counseling often requires a departure from traditional talk therapy (Sommers-Flanagan & Sommers-Flanagan, 1997). It is important for group leaders to be familiar with a wide range of interventions. Leaders select which intervention to use based on their theoretical orientation, the members' developmental levels, and the particular issues being addressed. The use of activities and expressive arts with members provides leaders with a repertoire of interventions that are compatible with many theoretical approaches and can be adapted to different developmental levels.

There are several advantages associated with using the arts in counseling. Activities and expressive arts are enriching, stimulating, pragmatic, and therapeutic. Creative interventions get people doing rather than thinking and thus can be more activating than verbal counseling. By their very nature, expressive arts foster different ways of experiencing the world. They can benefit members who are "stuck" by helping them view things from different perspectives, with a variety of possible responses. Counseling is enhanced as the emotional, perceptual, and creative world of the member is engaged through the use of expressive approaches.

The use of creative interventions in group work provides a way to symbolize feelings in a unique, tangible, and powerful way (Nichols & Schwartz, 1998). Artistic expression acts as a metaphor for conflicts, emotions, and troubling situations (Ulik & Cummings, 1997). Providing members with creative outlets allows them to communicate emotions and concerns that cannot be assessed through rational, linear language.

Another benefit associated with the use of activities and expressive arts is that they help members picture themselves or their situations in a concrete, objectified manner. Art can serve as a bridge between the members and the leader, especially when the subject matter is too embarrassing or difficult to talk about, such as family violence or abuse (Brooke, 1995; Trowbridge, 1995).

Many different creative interventions can be used in group work, including visual art, music, imagery, dance and movement, drama and puppetry, therapeutic writing, storytelling, bibliotherapy, therapeutic games, and energizing, creative activities. Counseling techniques using these expressive forms have been described elsewhere by many authors (e.g., Gladding, 2008; Hobday & Ollier, 1999; Kaduson & Schaefer, 1997; Muro & Kottman, 1995; Vernon, 1999). This chapter focuses on examples of activities associated with six creative categories: energizing, creative activities; visual arts; music; creative writing and storytelling; visual imagery; and therapeutic games. The examples selected to represent each category describe only a few of the numerous ways creative interventions can be used by group leaders to enhance the counseling process. Some of the activities are familiar and have been documented in other resources. Other activities have evolved through ongoing work with students. Most of the interventions can be adapted according to members' developmental levels. Note that some of the activities may be used more often in individual counseling, while others are used more often for group experiences, but all can be used in both situations, depending on the issue being addressed.

USING ENERGIZING, CREATIVE ACTIVITIES IN GROUP WORK

Since people are social beings whose growth and development takes place in groups, it seems logical that they would grow through meeting and discussing issues with their peers, especially when they feel comfortable with and enthusiastic about the goals of the group. Various types of energizing icebreaker activities help in setting the comfort level for many different types of groups.

Selecting and Evaluating Group Work Activities

Group work activities should be selected specifically to meet group goals or objectives and to facilitate the processing of important group issues. Activities can be used effectively in nearly any stage of group work but must be carefully selected and appropriately implemented to promote group goals. In group work, leaders must be cautioned against the use of such activities to simply structure or organize group time. These activities are best used to generate members' discussions and provoke thoughts that are helpful in processing group content, not as substitutes for group process. In fact, experienced leaders will frequently interrupt or forego group activities if group members are already engaging in valuable discussions and addressing important group goals. In other words, leaders should use activities to facilitate the ultimate goal of effective group process, never to interrupt or supplant it. Over the next few pages you will be introduced to a selection of exercises meant to acquaint you with some of the possibilities for structured group work and the fun that can be infused into group work. Creative counselors frequently develop or devise their own energizing activities to support the goals of the group and engage in "timely teaching" when group members are developmentally or clinically poised to effectively address issues confronting the group.

You are also advised to peruse the book *Group Activities: Firing Up for Performance* (Keene & Erford, 2007). This book provides detailed instructions for more than 150 activities to facilitate group work, categorized according to these themes: starters, energizers, communication, team building, and closure. Figures 15.1 and 15.2 provide two examples of activities from the book. In addition, Trotzer (1999) and Jacobs, Masson, and Harvill (2006) provide numerous group activities.

The Importance of Processing and Evaluating Group Work Activities

While activities can be fun and entertaining, effective leaders realize the importance of processing and evaluating these activities with group members to enhance learning, insight, and understanding. Evaluation will be covered in detail in Chapter 16, which focuses on accountability. Regarding processing, be sure to take the time before, during, and/or after the implementation of an activity to facilitate the members' group experience and evaluate the effectiveness of the activity. Posthuma (2002, p. 226) recommended guiding discussion about group activities by exploring the following:

1. *Processing the Activity:* What happened? What did you see?
2. *Reactions to the Activity:* What was easy? What was difficult?
3. *The Activity's Effect on Group Process:* What did you learn about others? How did members interact and react?
4. *Reflection of Feelings, Thoughts, Insights:* How did you feel during the activity? What did you learn about yourself?
5. *How the Activity Relates to Life Outside the Group:* How can you use what you learned here? What would you like to change?

Jacobs et al. (2006) made the following suggestions to guide the use of activities:

1. Inform members of the purpose of and procedures for the activities.
2. Avoid confusing or lengthy directions.
3. Allow members to not share or to "take a pass."
4. Inform members of the time remaining to complete activities.
5. Exercise good judgment when deciding to participate as the leader.
6. Give careful consideration to the most effective ways to process group exercises and allow enough time.

B5	We Are Siamese

Goal: Energizer	**Ages**: 8-Adult	**Time**: 10 minutes

Directions:

1. Set up an obstacle course that "Siamese Twins" teams can maneuver through. A sample course is provided in the illustration.
2. Relay teams should be formed with at least six participants per team. An even number of participants should comprise each team. Team members will pair up and tie their legs together with a cloth strip (one participant's left leg tied to their partner's right leg, like in a traditional three-legged race).
3. The goal of the relay is for the teams (one pair at a time and using only their feet) to maneuver the ball around the 3 obstacle cones (chairs) and back to the start/finish line. The first complete team to maneuver the course is the winner.

Variations:

Have the participants discuss ways of improving performance to overcome barriers and obstacles, then repeat the race.

This activity can also be used as a "Starter."

Materials: 3 obstacle cones (or chairs) per team, a marked start/finish line, 1 plastic or playground ball per team, one 3' long cloth strip per pair	**Setup**: See illustration B5	**Group Size**: 12 or more, divided into teams of at least 6, then into pairs

Illustration B5: Obstacle course for the "We Are Siamese" activity

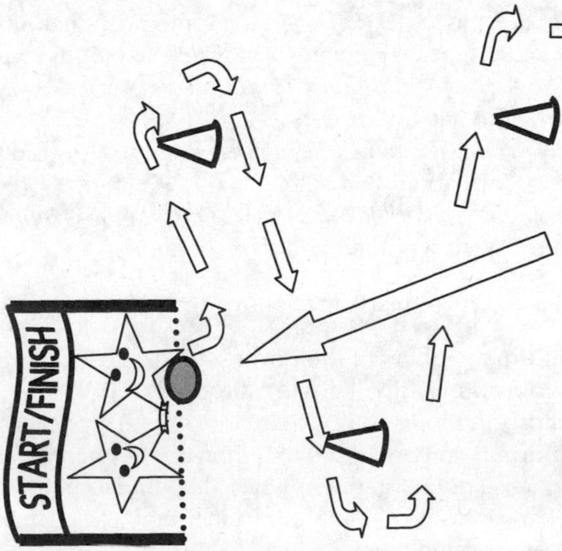

FIGURE 15.1 We are Siamese.

D33   Swat the Balloon Relay

Goal: Team Building   **Ages**: 5-Adult   **Time**: 10-15 minutes

Directions:

1. Have participants in each group (of no more than 10) line up in two rows and face the person in the other row (see Illustration D33).
2. The object is to keep the balloon in the air going up and down the rows.
3. Give the two fly swatters to the first participants in each row (participants 1 & 2).
4. After participant #1 swats the balloon to participant #2, he hands the flyswatter to participant #3, participant #2 swats the balloon to participant #3 then hands the fly swatter to participant #4, and so on until the balloon makes it all the way up the line and back again. In the Illustration (D33), the balloon travels in the order 1-2-3-4-5-6-7-8-9-10-9-8-7-6-5-4-3-2-1. The first fly swatter travels in the order 1-3-5-7-9-7-5-3-1, and the 2nd fly swatter travels in the order 2-4-6-8-10-8-6-4-2).
5. If a person lets the balloon drop, the group must begin over. The first team that goes back and forth five times wins.

Materials: Two fly swatters per group, several inflated balloons

Setup: Open area

Group Size: Any size, divided into groups of about 10

Illustration D33: Swat the Balloon Relay

FIGURE 15.2   Swat the balloon relay.

However you decide to process group activities, be sure to leave plenty of time for in-depth discussion and ask open-ended questions to elicit member perspectives. Finally, be sure to summarize the process comments so that members can learn and internalize the perspectives and ideas of others for future use in their own lives. Many of the activities that appear in *Group Activities* (Keene & Erford, 2007) and that follow in the remainder of this chapter may be used with both adults and children. Others may be appropriate for students of specific ages but can be modified for use with people of various ages by creative counselors.

BOX 15.1

We Are All Alike and Yet All Different

It is often important to group members to feel connected in some way. The use of the Venn diagram in this activity does just that.

OBJECTIVES: (1) Group members will identify at least two ways they are alike and two ways they are different in order to better understand themselves and others. (2) Group members will express at least one misunderstanding that could occur if they do not understand or appreciate group member similarities or differences.

MATERIALS: Venn diagram resource sheet (see Figure 15.3), pen or pencil

GROUP STAGE USED: Forming, Transition

DIRECTIONS:

1. Divide the group members into pairs.
2. Have the members of each pair discuss their alikes and differences and put them down in a two-column list (see Table 15.1).

TABLE 15.1 Alike and Different

Alike	Different

3. Tell members to fill in the Venn diagram as illustrated in Figure 15.3. The overlapping area shows how the members are alike, and the outside areas show how they are different.

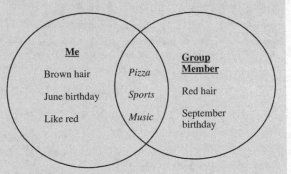

FIGURE 15.3 Example of we are all alike and yet all different.

PROCESSING QUESTIONS: What did you learn about yourself and your partner during this activity? How openly did you share or protect personal information? If you could change any one thing about your differences, what would it be?

EVALUATION: Group members will show, using Venn diagrams, at least two ways they are alike and different. Group members will discuss at least one misunderstanding that could occur if they did not understand or appreciate how they are alike or different.

BOX 15.2

Stress Balls

The center of a table or of the group is a great place to put stress relievers. Stress balls and play dough are inexpensive and easy to make and use.

OBJECTIVES: (1) Group members will create a stress ball to help relieve stress. (2) Group members will identify two situations in which the stress ball might help reduce stress.

MATERIALS: Balloons (10- to 12-inch balloons are best), play sand, funnels or paper cups

GROUP STAGE USED: Any stage

DIRECTIONS:

1. Blow up each of the balloons several times to stretch them.
2. Use a paper cup (you can shape it into a spout) or a plastic funnel to pour the sand into the lip of a balloon.
3. Fill up the balloon until it reaches 2–4 inches in diameter and then tie a knot in the end. Instantly, you have a stress ball that you can use to squeeze away your stresses, worries, and anxieties.
4. Caution: Do *NOT* use flour unless you want drug-sniffing K-9s around your school!

PROCESSING QUESTIONS: How did the stress ball feel as you held it during this session? How did it help you feel more relaxed during the session? What are some other ways that you could make a stress reliever using other materials?

EVALUATION: Groups members will list two situations where the stress ball could help them to relieve stress in their daily lives.

BOX 15.3

Trashing Problems

OBJECTIVE: Group members will identify three current life stressors.

MATERIALS: Trash bag, white paper, pens and pencils

GROUP STAGE USED: Termination

DIRECTIONS: Bring a large trash bag to the last session of the group. Distribute a plain sheet of paper to each member and have members list at least three problematic stress situations they now know how to resolve. Each group member will read his or her statements and solutions, crumple the paper into a ball, and throw it into the trash. This is a helpful way to show that problems have been resolved in the group and that if similar situations come up, group members will have techniques to resolve them.

PROCESSING QUESTIONS: How does it feel to be empowered to rid yourself of these former problems? What are some situations you wish you could trash but have not yet resolved? What was easy about this activity? What was difficult about this activity?

EVALUATION: Group members will provide a list of three current stressors.

BOX 15.4

Caring Circles

OBJECTIVE: Group members will reflect on the importance sharing positive comments and feedback can have for a group experience.

GROUP STAGE USED: Any

DIRECTIONS: Caring circles can be used during each session or at the end of a group. Many groups are conducted in circles, so this is a wonderful way to end the group. Several techniques may be used during the caring circles, but in most cases, the leader should start the circle. For an example, the leader could place a hand on the shoulder of the person on his or her left and say how the leader has appreciated that person during the group. The next person then touches the shoulder of the person on the left and compliments the person.

Instead of touching the shoulder of a person, balls, stuffed animals, or other objects can be passed or gently tossed to the next person. Group issues can also be used in the caring circle for discussion purposes. It is a place where group members can open up and express things that are on their mind. They can also show appreciation for group members in a safe environment.

PROCESSING QUESTIONS: How does it feel to be listened to as you express your views? What have you observed that has been different about other group members during this activity?

EVALUATION: Members will list one way other group members helped them by sharing positive comments and feedback during this activity.

INTERVENTIONS USING VISUAL ARTS

Drawing, sketching, painting, sculpting, and photography are all examples of visual art interventions. Using visual art in group work helps members gain a better understanding of themselves and how they function in groups, relationships, families, and society. As members draw, paint, and sculpt, they communicate thoughts and feelings in ways that the leader can see and understand (Orton, 1997).

A wide variety of art supplies helps provide members with choices of the manner in which they choose to express themselves. Children up to about 11 or 12 years of age typically enjoy using colored paper, colored pencils, and thin or thick colored markers, whereas adolescents and adults may prefer using pens, pencils, and white paper (Hobday & Ollier, 1999). Members of all ages tend to enjoy drawing on dry-erase boards. Other supplies that facilitate artistic expression include watercolor paints, tempera paints, finger paints, glue, scissors, and modeling clay or Play-Doh (Muro & Kottman, 1995).

Introductory Activities for Building Rapport Using Visual Arts

ABOUT ME The purpose of this activity is to help build a therapeutic relationship and give members an opportunity to describe themselves using artistic media. It can be used effectively with members of all ages and is particularly useful in initial counseling sessions, either with individuals or with groups. To begin the activity, each group member is invited to decoratively write his or her name in the center of a piece of poster board or construction paper. The leader then asks the members to draw or select magazine pictures that describe different aspects of themselves, including strengths, interests, relationships, and other characteristics they want to reveal at that point. For members who seem stuck or unsure about what to draw, it may be helpful to provide prompting questions. Examples include the following:

- What do you like to do in your free time?
- What are you good at?
- Where do you like to go on weekends or holidays?
- Who is your best friend?
- What pets do you have?
- What is your favorite food, subject, color, and so on?

After the collages are completed, the leader encourages members to talk about their picture selections. Descriptions serve as a springboard for further discussion, helping the leader develop an understanding of each member's world.

Adolescents may enjoy using photography to complete a variation of this activity. Members take photographs that represent who they are and then arrange the pictures to form a collage. When the leader processes the experience with members afterward, it is helpful to look for patterns, themes, and omissions.

DECORATING MY BAG   This activity can be used with members of all ages and, like the previously described activity, is particularly helpful in the beginning stage of group work. The exercise of decorating and displaying bags requires group members to cut out pictures representing themselves from magazines or newspapers. They then paste or tape these pictures, along with other representative symbols, on the outside of their bags. Also, as part of the exercise, they put loose pictures and symbols that they are not yet ready to share inside the bags.

After completing the activity, members introduce themselves to one another by describing themselves in relation to the pictures and symbols on the outside of the bags. During subsequent sessions, as trust is developed, members are given opportunities to share materials on the inside of the bags, providing a way to help group members make covert parts of their lives more overt as time and desire allow (Gladding, 1997).

As a variation, the exercise can be introduced during the termination phase of group counseling. On the outside of their bags, members paste pictures representing positive changes they have made as a result of group work. On the inside of the bags, they place pictures describing areas in which they are continuing to grow and develop. Rather than selecting pictures from magazines, the members may choose to draw symbols representing issues and changes. As with any group activity, the leader is responsible for sensitively processing the experience with the group members. Through processing, members are provided opportunities to articulate personal changes they have made and affirm changes made by others.

Dealing with Feelings

LINES OF FEELING   This exercise is based on the premise that everyone has emotional lines in their lives (Gladding, 1997). At times, members cannot find words to express their emotions, although they may have a strong sense of what those feelings are. To help with awareness and expression, the leader asks members to draw lines representing their emotions using various art media (e.g., markers, colored pencils, paints, crayons). The leader explains that both the shape and the color of the lines should match the emotions being depicted. For example, jagged, rough lines in red or orange might signify anger or discontent, whereas smooth, flowing, pastel-colored lines might represent peacefulness (Gladding, 1997, 2008).

Depending on the stage of group work and the particular issues presented, the approach the leader takes with this activity can vary. One approach is to ask members to draw lines representing their feelings at the present moment. They then are asked to explain the lines and to draw what they hope the lines will become in the future. As an alternative, the leader asks members to reflect on specific past, present, and future events that relate to the issues with which they are struggling (e.g., divorce, failing grades, violent incident, substance use). Using lines, members draw feelings associated with the events, thereby providing an avenue for exploring thoughts, feelings, and behaviors.

FEEL WHEEL   Professional school counselors frequently use games, books, and drawing activities to help children recognize, express, and talk about their feelings. A simple visual art activity that facilitates the discussion of feelings involves asking members to draw faces reflecting different emotions (e.g., glad, sad, worried, mad) and then to talk about times they experienced those feelings. Instead of drawing the faces, the members may prefer to mold them out of clay. Another option is to use a dry-erase board and play a guessing game about what the faces reflect with the members, leading to further discussion of feelings, thoughts, and behaviors.

An expanded version of drawing feelings, called the Feel Wheel, is described by Hobday and Ollier (1999). Members draw a circle on a paper plate or a piece of paper and divide it into eight pie sections [to resemble a wheel with spokes]. Each section is labeled with a different emotion, with pictures drawn to accompany each one. The leader then describes different situations involving either the member or a fictional character and asks the member to determine how the character would feel. Alternatively, the leader can ask members to describe or draw times they or other people have experienced those particular emotions.

THE VOLCANO   Many members who participate in counseling struggle with anger issues. The Volcano (White, 1998), which is especially applicable at the elementary and middle school levels, is an activity designed to help members with anger management. To begin the activity, the leader asks members to share what they know about why volcanoes erupt (e.g., eruptions are the sudden escape of high-pressure volcanic gas from magma inside the volcano). Members are invited to draw a volcano, and the leader explains how explosive volcanic eruptions are similar to the way people sometimes erupt when they are angry. Members draw steam and lava coming out of their volcanoes and write in words describing harmful ways people sometimes "blow their tops" in anger (e.g., hurting oneself or others, cursing, yelling). Next, they are asked to think about stressful or troublesome things in their lives that might contribute to a buildup of pressure inside their volcanoes. To avoid "explosions," members are instructed to draw several vents leading from the pressure source to the outside of their volcanoes. The drawing of the vents generates a discussion of healthy ways people can vent or get rid of angry feelings. Examples might include breathing deeply, engaging in self-talk, counting to 10, talking to a friend, doing physical exercise, and listening to music. To conclude the activity, the leader asks members to choose one or two vents they will use during the upcoming week to help them avoid angry explosions (see Figure 15.4).

Past, Present, and Future

ROAD MAP   The road map and its numerous variations, such as life maps and life lines, can be used to help members review significant periods in their lives and anticipate the future. One goal of the activity is to help members explore patterns, expand self-expression, and

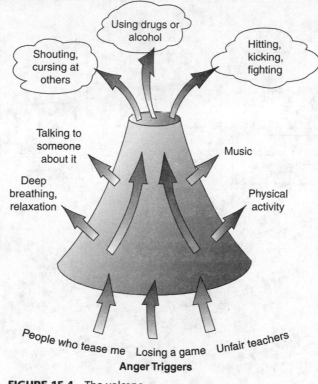

FIGURE 15.4 The volcano.

plan their lives more effectively (Gladding, 2008; Kahn, 1999). The road map provides an opportunity for leaders to help members plan for the future as they reflect on where they have been and think about where they are going. The manner in which the activity is presented depends on members' ages, counseling goals, and interests. One way to introduce the activity is to say, "I want you to represent your life as a road map. Some roads are straight and wide; others are narrow and winding. Some are bumpy, and others are smooth. There may be some road blocks or detours. It is possible that the road of your life has had many of these characteristics." These directions give members free rein to evaluate the life events that have been most influential and to visualize the past, present, and future simultaneously. After the drawing is finished, the leader encourages each member to talk about the map and the events depicted on it. Which events were expected? Which were unexpected? What people were associated with these events? What feelings are remembered? These and other questions encourage self-exploration, while at the same time providing the leader with a picture of the member's contextual development.

For members facing decisions about the future, the following variation of the road map can be helpful. The leader asks members to draw the current road they are on. Next, they are asked to draw three paths branching off the main road: the high road, the expected road, and the low road. Along each path, they draw or paint symbols to represent an ideal future, an anticipated future, and the worst possible scenario. After the paths have been drawn, members are encouraged to explore possible action steps that need to be accomplished to stay on the preferred path (see Figure 15.5).

FIGURE 15.5 Variation of the road map.

Problem Solving and Goal Setting

THE BRIDGE   For members dealing with problem situations, visual representations of the situation and possible solutions can be empowering (Gladding, 1997). The Bridge is an activity that promotes such representations and can be adapted for members of varying ages. To begin the activity, members divide a piece of paper into three panels or sections. On the first panel, members are invited to draw a picture of a specific problem or concern. Next, they are asked to think about what it would look like if the problem was solved and to draw that on the third panel. Between these two scenes, members draw symbols of obstacles blocking their movement toward the "solution." Afterward the members are asked to draw a bridge over the obstacles, providing a connection between the problem and the problem solved. The leader encourages the inclusion of symbols or word phrases on the bridge that represent varied solutions for circumventing the obstacles and living life more effectively.

A variation of The Bridge can be especially helpful for members experiencing particular crises, such as divorce, illness, or death of a loved one. Members are invited to draw a picture of themselves in the present and a picture of how they would like things to look in the future. The sequential drawings can serve as a springboard for discussing coping skills, new patterns of behavior, and emotional responses to the changes being experienced.

THREE WISHES   The Three Wishes activity, described by Denny (1977) and Orton (1997), is especially appropriate for children in elementary school and can be used for assessment or goal setting. It can be employed effectively in both individual and group counseling. To begin the activity, the leader asks members to draw or paint pictures of three wishes. Depending on the situation, the leader may choose to ask the members to think of wishes related to a particular setting, such as school or home. After the drawings are complete, the leader talks with the members about the strength of the wishes, whether they are attainable, and what needs to be accomplished to make what is desired a reality.

The techniques just described represent just a few of the multiple ways group leaders can employ visual art interventions in group work. It is important to consider each intervention within the context of the leader's skill and the members' needs.

MUSIC INTERVENTIONS

Throughout history, music has played an important role in nurturing and healing. Noted for its therapeutic capabilities, music can be used to capture attention, elicit memories, soothe, communicate feelings, and create or intensify moods. For some members, the act of listening to music can enhance self-awareness, reduce anxiety, and provide a springboard for discussing feelings and experiences. For others, performing or creating music can energize, provide emotional release, and promote self-awareness and well-being (Gladding, 2008; McClellan, 1994). DeLucia-Waack (2001) even developed an entire session-by-session group counseling program using music to address divorce issues with children.

As a counseling approach, the use of music can be especially effective with children and adolescents (Newcomb, 1994). Younger children seem to love music and spontaneously sing, listen, or play quasi-musical instruments. Their natural affinity for music can be used to promote fun, learning, good feelings, and bonding among members from diverse backgrounds. Adolescents also have an affinity for music, although their interests may be expressed in ways that differ from those used by younger children. For many, listening to CDs, playing in a band, and composing songs are activities that promote self-expression as well as enjoyment (Gladding, 2008).

Listening to Music

LYRICS   Whereas sometimes the rhythm and melody attract members to particular songs, other times it is the lyrics—or a combination of lyrics, rhythm, and melody. The leader can use the lyrics in music to promote group work in several different ways. For example, the leader might ask members to bring in CDs or tapes containing lyrics that reflect some of the issues with which they are dealing. Due to the explicit nature of some lyrics, it might be necessary to set limits in advance about the types of music that may be brought to the counseling session. After listening to the portion of the song selected by the member, the leader facilitates discussion about how the music was meaningful. What thoughts, feelings, or memories did it evoke? The leader can help members process responses to the music, providing an impetus for self-exploration and growth.

An alternative to asking members to select one representative song is to have them create a music collage by recording short music segments that reflect their lives in some way. The segments may be chosen because the member likes the music or because the lyrics are meaningful. The final result is a collage of musical pieces with an identity and feeling of its own. Listening to the members' tapes can reveal unique perspectives and promote further exploration (Bowman, 1987b).

During the termination stage of group work, music can be particularly effective. When a group is nearing closure, goals include helping members reflect on past experiences in the group, evaluate what was learned, acknowledge feelings, and articulate decisions for new ways of behaving. Ideally, as a result of the group experience, members know themselves and each other on a deeper level. Song lyrics can help them express either what they have experienced in the group or the specific ways they have changed. Members play the portions of the songs they have selected and talk about their reasons for selecting them. Afterward, the leader helps process the activity by pointing out common themes and encouraging members to share their responses to songs brought in by other students.

At times, it is helpful for the leader to select music for the session. The selection should be based on counseling goals, taking into account the members' preferences and needs. For example, the song "Change Your Mind," by Sister Hazel (2000), describes the importance of changing one's thought processes when "you're tired of doing battle with yourself." Playing the song and talking about the lyrics is one way to enhance a cognitive-based approach to counseling, which focuses on changing maladaptive thinking patterns to improve emotional well-being.

STRESS REDUCTION   Members of all ages can benefit from learning ways to relax when they feel anxious or uptight. One way to teach relaxation is to ask members to select soothing music to bring to the group session. Using guided imagery or progressive relaxation in conjunction with the music can enhance the process of helping members reduce stressful feelings (Bowman, 1987b; Russell, 1992).

Another approach to teaching relaxation is for the leader, rather than the member, to make the music selection. There are advantages and disadvantages to using counselor-selected music. Although certain compositions and types of music (e.g., instrumental music with violin, flute, or piano) have been associated with anxiety reduction, there is evidence that the most important factor related to relaxation is the person's liking for the music. Having members collaborate in the choice of music helps to personalize the process, making positive results more likely.

Performing and Composing

Performing or creating music can energize, evoke emotional release, and promote self-awareness and well-being. To provide opportunities for creating music, leaders might include a variety of portable musical instruments in group rooms, such as drums, rain sticks, recorders, and keyboards. Members can be invited to "play out" their feelings, after which they talk about those feelings and the events that precipitated them.

As a homework assignment, leaders can encourage musically inclined members to compose music through which they can represent themselves. At the next session, the members either play the composition or bring in a recording of it. Afterward, the members and the leader talk about the actual experience of composing as well as the personal significance of the music (Gladding, 2008).

Composing does not have to involve recognizable instruments. Instead, members can be asked to tap, snap, click, bang, or hum to represent different emotions (Gladding, 2008). Also, leaders can encourage younger children to improvise and compose during group work and guidance sessions. For example, members can be divided into small groups of three or four. Each group is secretly given a feeling word. Children then use sound makers of various types to create songs representing the assigned feelings. Each group performs its composition, while the rest of the members try to guess what emotion is being expressed.

As with visual art interventions, there are many ways music can be used therapeutically by group leaders, depending on the needs of the students. The various ways music can be used to enhance the counseling process are limited only by the creativity and skill of the leader.

THERAPEUTIC WRITING AND STORYTELLING

Therapeutic writing (creative writing) and therapeutic storytelling help group members express their identities, re-create events and experiences, and communicate powerful emotions. Both forms of imaginative expression can facilitate group work processes.

Scriptotherapy

Scriptotherapy is a term coined by Riordan (1996) to denote the many different forms of writing that are used in counseling. Writing for preventive and therapeutic purposes has a notable history. Since the 1940s, workers in the helping professions have incorporated activities such as journaling, autobiographical expression, and the writing of stories and poems into their work with members (L'Abate, 1999). Although much of the research on the effectiveness of expressive writing interventions is anecdotal rather than empirical, evidence of the therapeutic benefits of expressive writing is substantial (Riordan, 1996; Wenz & McWhirter, 1990).

Scriptotherapy can facilitate counseling processes that emphasize catharsis, the acceptance of emotions, and the objectification of thoughts, feelings, and behaviors. Writing is an expressive act that offers a medium through which emotions can be analyzed and integrated in a personal way. Free forms of writing, such as poetry, elicit the writer's unique subjective perceptions and encourage emotional self-searching. Conceivably, writing brings about healing sooner and with equal or greater intensity than does counseling without writing (Riordan, 1996). Written expression also provides concrete evidence of a member's involvement in the counseling process. Leaders can incorporate therapeutic writing interventions directly into their counseling sessions or give members assignments to be completed between sessions. As with other expressive arts, the types of activities implemented are limited only by the leader's imagination and skill and the members' preferences.

Writing interventions can be structured or unstructured. Journaling is an example of an unstructured therapeutic writing activity that is frequently prescribed as homework (Gladding, 2008). Examples of more-structured creative writing activities include life-review exercises, letter writing, therapeutic fairy tales, and specific group exercises.

JOURNALING   For some group members, the process of writing on a regular basis about life experiences and processes can be therapeutic. Journal writing can take several forms, including poetic reflections, daily logs, stream-of-consciousness responses, and semistructured writing sprints (Bradley & Gould, 1999). People often express a desire to keep a journal but frequently end up not doing so. To help members who are interested in journal writing, Adams (1994) offered several suggestions. One suggestion is for members to prepare themselves in advance for the writing process. Preparation may include selecting an aesthetically appealing space or creating an atmosphere for reflection by playing music or engaging in progressive muscle relaxation.

Another way leaders can encourage members to engage in journal writing is by prescribing the "five-minute writing sprint" (Adams, 1994; Gladding, 2008). To participate in the five-minute writing sprint, the member sets a timer for five minutes and then begins writing about anything of interest. During the five minutes, the writing instrument must be continually in motion, even if that means doodling. When the time is up, the member stops writing and then reads and reflects on what was written. At times, it may be helpful to provide members with a list of possible writing starters, such as "I wish," "When I was angry," "A big decision," or "The best/worst thing about today." On other occasions, a less structured approach may be preferred. Gladding suggested that members write one day and then reflect on what was written the next day to increase their motivation and mindfulness.

LIFE-REVIEW EXERCISES   Whereas journal writing is often used to help members reflect on what is going on in their lives in the present, life-review exercises help them reflect on past experiences and future possibilities. Many forms of life-review can be used therapeutically by leaders. For example, Hobday and Ollier (1999) described an activity called My Life So Far. The activity may take several sessions and can include illustrations as well as written descriptions of significant events in members' lives. Members are asked to think about noteworthy events they have experienced and remember the feelings associated with them. The review, which is a type of autobiography, should include as much information from as many different times in the member's life as possible, including early memories as well as those from the more recent past. Events are described on separate pages and need not be recorded chronologically. Hobday and Ollier stated, "It is less of an emotional load . . . if you move from difficult times to good times" (p. 149). At the end of the activity, leaders help members assemble the pages chronologically into a book or folder. When they review the book together, leaders encourage members to look for themes, patterns, and strengths.

Past, Present, Future is another activity leaders can use to help members review ways they have changed and will continue to change (Hobday & Ollier, 1999). In this exercise, the member is asked to divide a large piece of paper into four columns. The first column is used to record relevant aspects of the member's life, including friends, habits, getting angry, having fun, living arrangements, and other pertinent categories. The next three columns are given the respective headings of "Past," "Present," and "Future." In the second column, the member writes a brief description summarizing the way a particular aspect was manifested in the past. Next, the member writes about the way the aspect is evidenced now. The final column is used to describe the member's realistic hopes and wishes. During the process, the leader helps the member notice ways he or she has changed.

One aim of Past, Present, Future is to help members notice how their lives are improving, so it is important to select several areas in which they have been successful. If members are not experiencing success in particular areas, help them envision positive possibilities for the future. Hobday and Ollier (1999) cautioned that some aspects of members' lives, such as parental relationships, might deteriorate during certain developmental stages. For example, parental relationships may become somewhat strained during adolescence. Leaders can help normalize what adolescents are experiencing, pointing toward the possibility of working toward closer relationships with parents as adulthood approaches.

Instead of focusing on a broad time span, leaders may choose to focus on specific difficult situations members have faced. For example, leaders can encourage members to create illustrated texts about traumatic or painful experiences. The Pain Getting Better Book is an example of an intervention of this nature (Mills & Crowley, 1986). Members objectify painful experiences by drawing or sketching representations of what happened. Next, they write about what they experienced and how they currently view the situation. To help members recognize their personal strengths and resources, leaders encourage them to write or talk about what helped them overcome or cope with what was experienced.

LETTER WRITING   An activity that has been referenced many times in the literature and that has a wide range of applications is letter writing (Riordan, 1996). Letter writing can take a variety of forms, including leader–member correspondence, letters written to specific individuals, and letters written to an abstract concept such as anger, grief, or fear.

Leaders working with members who have experienced the loss of a loved one can use letter writing to help members accept the loss, remember the one who died, and articulate feelings surrounding the loss. Members are invited to write a letter to the person who died, describing what they miss most about the person and what life is like without the person. To illustrate this process, Bradley and Gould (1999) provided a case study about a young girl, Sarah, whose grandfather had died. She felt sad because she missed him and had not been able to tell him good-bye. To help with the grief process, the professional counselor suggested that Sarah write her grandfather a letter, expressing all the things she hadn't gotten to say. After Sarah wrote the letter, she read it to the professional counselor and said, "It's not as good as telling him in person, but I think he could hear me" (p. 93). Over the course of the next few weeks, Sarah wrote several more letters to her grandfather and, through that process and other interventions, began to come to terms with her grandfather's death.

Letter writing can be especially helpful for members who are angry about particular issues. For example, an adolescent might be encouraged to write a letter to a parent with whom he is having trouble communicating; a child might write a letter to an absent parent, expressing her wish to see the parent more frequently; or an adult might write a letter to a partner, expressing his wish to reestablish meaningful intimate communications. In cases of abuse, a member can write a letter to the offender, sharing feelings about the abuse. In most cases, letters are not mailed to the recipients but instead are used to provide a way for the members to recognize and express feelings and explore ways to cope more effectively.

THERAPEUTIC FAIRY TALES   Writing a therapeutic fairy tale allows members to project themselves into another time dimension, where they are able to positively resolve particular issues or conflicts (Gladding, 1997). The activity is especially effective with groups but can also be used in individual counseling. Participants are asked to complete the written exercise in 6–10 minutes, during which time they

- set the scene in a place and time far away from the here and now;
- within this setting, describe a problem or predicament; and
- solve the difficulty in a positive and gratifying manner, even if the solution seems unrealistic or bizarre. (Hoskins, 1985)

After members write their stories, they are asked to read them aloud to the group. To process what occurred during the experience, the leader asks facilitative questions such as the following:

- In what ways are you like the main character in the story? In what ways are you different?
- In what way does the predicament affect the characters? Is the predicament, or the resulting emotion, familiar in any way?
- How is the solution pleasing? How is it implemented? How does it compare with the way you typically solve problems? (Gladding, 2008)

As members read their fairy tales, the leader should pay attention to the use of symbolic or metaphoric language. Metaphors provide insight into how members view the world and understand experiences. Leaders can continue using these metaphors with the members to express empathic understanding (Bowman, 1995).

GROUP EXERCISES   Written exercises can be particularly valuable in group counseling. Carefully selected exercises can help group members become more involved and prevent them from feeling put on the spot. Written activities provide material for discussion and give members opportunities for rehearsal and insight (Wenz & McWhirter, 1990).

Sentence completion exercises can facilitate movement through the different stages of the group process. For example, during the forming and orienting stage, members might be asked to complete the following sentences:

In a new group, I feel _____.

When people first meet me, they _____.

In this group, I am most afraid that _____.

During the transition stage, members can respond to sentence stems such as these:

I feel annoyed when the leader _____.

When people remain silent, I feel _____.

An effective way to help members put closure on group processes is to create a collaborative poem by reflecting on changes they have experienced in the group. The sentence stem may be as simple as "I _____." Gladding (1997, p. 93) shared the following example to illustrate collaborative group poetry writing:

THE GROWTH GROUP

As part of the group that was:

I gained insight into myself and others

I realized anew the power of people together

I was aware of new thoughts and differences

I grew in unexpected ways

I gained feelings of confidence and care

I realized I was a person of worth and substance

Now I am moving on!

A writing exercise that can be used to stimulate group development and heighten intimacy and cohesion is the Personal Logo (Wenz & McWhirter, 1990). In this exercise, members draw a personal logo, describe it in a story, and then share the picture and story with the group. Members are asked to play with doodles they have always enjoyed drawing until they develop a symbol that feels right for them. After creating a logo, each member is encouraged to write a story about it. The story may take the form of a fairy tale, a poem, or some other literary creation of the member's choosing. Members then share their logos and stories with the group. The leader helps members notice common themes, while facilitating the discussion of thoughts, feelings, and insights generated by the exercise.

Another written activity for groups is the Epigram. Epigrams are short, witty sayings or quotations that can be used to highlight important issues for individual group members (Wenz & McWhirter, 1990). Group leaders invite students to select an epigram and then write about the personal meaning it has for them. Wenz and McWhirter suggested, "Do not search too hard for the perfect one—let it find you. Copy it on a fresh piece of paper, then begin to explore and write and wonder about it . . . ." (p. 40). In the group, members share their epigrams and selections of their personal writings that they choose to read aloud. Leaders help them process what was shared so that members can transfer their insights and learning to their lives outside of the group.

Using written exercises in groups can facilitate trust building and affiliation, generate energy and excitement, and clarify issues and concerns. Sentence completion activities, Personal Logo, and Epigram are just a few of the many written exercises that can be implemented to enhance the group process.

Storytelling

For group members who have an aversion to writing, counseling interventions such as those just described may not be appropriate. Instead, a more effective creative intervention for these members is storytelling. Storytelling can take many forms, including the presentation of therapeutic metaphors by the leader (Kottman, 1995), narrative construction (White & Epston, 1990), and mutual storytelling (Gardner, 1971, 1975; Kottman, 1995). In this section, attention will be directed toward the art of mutual storytelling.

Mutual storytelling is a metaphoric counseling technique developed by Dr. Richard A. Gardner (1971, 1975). Mutual storytelling is most often conducted with individual members, particularly children and adolescents, but can easily be modified for group work. In this technique, the leader asks a member to tell a story that has a beginning, a middle, and an end as well as a moral or lesson. Some members may choose to talk into a tape recorder, pretending to produce a make-believe television program. As the story is told, the leader notes its content and possible meaning. The leader comments positively on the member's story and then tells another story, ordinarily using the same characters, setting, and dilemma that were presented in the original story. In retelling the story, the leader includes a better resolution of the conflict and identifies more alternatives to problem solving. This process helps members become aware of the multiplicity of options and recognize that behavior patterns can change. Adapting the technique to group work may be as simple as having other group members contribute resolutions and alternatives or as complex as having members take turns contributing content to the retelling of the story.

Kottman (1995) recommended incorporating the use of puppets or stuffed animals, rather than simply asking young children to tell a story. She invited children to choose a set of puppets or plastic animals and pretend that the puppets or animals could talk. Next, she asked each child to tell a story using the characters. To encourage the use of imagination, Kottman told the children that the story could be something they had seen on television or witnessed in real life. Some members may have difficulty constructing a plot. If so, the leader can ask specific questions about what happens next or what the characters said in a particular situation.

As members tell their stories, it is important to consider how the tales metaphorically represent what is happening in their lives. Kottman (1995) suggested using the following questions to guide the leader's internal thought process:

- Which character represents the member?
- Which characters represent significant people in the member's life?
- What is the overall affective tone of the story?
- How does the member view self, others, and the world?
- What patterns and themes are presented?
- What strategies are used for resolving conflict?
- What might be a more constructive, courageous way to handle the conflict?
- What might be more helpful patterns of interacting or solving problems?

After reflecting on these questions, the leader retells the story, without moralizing, interpreting, or indicating the superiority of any specific problem-solving method. Instead, through the retelling of the story, the leader helps members gain insight into their lifestyles and develop awareness of new perspectives and possibilities.

A CD–ROM version for the personal computer called *The Mutual Storytelling Game* (Erford, 2000) helps members construct backgrounds and offers diverse character sets to facilitate storytelling. Telling stories using puppets, stuffed animals, dolls, and other toys can also enhance the counseling process. Sometimes the stories are invented or fantasy based; other times they focus on real-life situations. Through the process of telling stories about actual concerns or experiences, members can discover new problem-solving methods. For example, a professional school counselor was working with a third-grade student, Matt, who had been disciplined by the school principal for hitting another student. The professional school counselor used several different stuffed animals to represent Matt, Matt's teacher, the principal, and the other student. Matt first used the animals to tell the story as it actually happened. Then he told the story again, but this time he gave the story a more positive outcome. By reenacting the event, Matt was able to explore the feelings he'd experienced when the other student angered him and then come up with alternative, more positive solutions.

Storytelling, whether based on imagination, fantasy, metaphor, or real life, provides a way for leaders to help members see themselves more clearly. It also provides a nonthreatening medium through which members can examine their thoughts, feelings, actions, and choices.

Considerations for Therapeutic Writing and Storytelling

Although therapeutic writing and storytelling interventions have a wide range of applications, there are some precautions to be aware of, particularly in regard to writing activities. Riordan (1996) pointed out the importance of keeping the process interactive so that writing is not used to avoid other appropriate actions. He also recommended that leaders refrain from assigning writing until they are sure that no issues will arise that members are not prepared to handle. Furthermore, leaders should take into account the members' educational levels, abilities, and preferences and whether the writing or storytelling is increasing obsessive thinking about the problem in ways that are not helpful. Guidelines such as these can help direct leaders to use writing and storytelling as tools in group work.

USING GUIDED VISUAL IMAGERY IN GROUP WORK

Visual imagery is used in numerous approaches to counseling with both individual members and groups (Arbuthnott, Arbuthnott, & Rossiter, 2001; Seligman, 2001). More specifically, visual imagery has been shown to reduce anxiety, facilitate relaxation, promote a sense of control, improve problem solving and decision making, alleviate pain (Seligman, 2001), produce positive behavioral change and self-concept (Vernon, 1993), and effectively treat stress, Posttraumatic Stress Disorder, panic attacks, Bulimia Nervosa, phobias, depression (Arbuthnott et al., 2001), chronic pain (Chaves, 1994; Cupal & Brewer, 2001; Gonsalkorale, 1996; Ross & Berger, 1996), asthma (Peck, Bray, & Kehle, 2003), enuresis, and psychosomatic disorders (Myrick & Myrick, 1993). While useful with most members, visual imagery may have limited effectiveness with young children (Schoettle, 1980). Also, the use of guided imagery with school students has been criticized by some religious and community groups. Indeed, the use of guided imagery in public schools in Alabama is prohibited. Good judgment must be exercised when selecting any counseling technique to ensure that it is developmentally and organizationally appropriate.

When implementing a guided visual imagery technique, Erford, Eaves, Bryant, and Young (2010) suggested that leaders

> make sure that the room is quiet and the member is comfortable. Music may be used to create a soothing mode, but be aware that for some people music is a distraction. . . . Help the member relax by suggesting he close his eyes and take slow, deep breaths. . . . Once the member is relaxed, start the guided imagery experience. Speak in a soft, soothing voice. It is preferable to have a story scripted ahead of time to ensure that the words create the desired mood and direction. . . . Guided imagery scripts do not need to be long, and it may take only a minute or two to lead a member through the experience. Keep the exercises simple at first. . . .

Many resources or recordings of visual imagery exercises exist. Table 15.2 provides a transcript of one of the several excellent tracks available on volume 1 of *Stressbuster Relaxation Exercises* (Erford, 2001), available from the American Counseling Association Foundation (see www.counseling.org/Publications). In order to process the visual imagery activity, the group leader should ask several follow up-questions before finishing the activity or moving on to another topic or activity: for example, "What did you like about this activity?" "What did you not like about the activity?"

USING THERAPEUTIC AND DEVELOPMENTAL GAMES IN GROUP WORK

Therapeutic games and developmental games are commonly used in psychoeducational and counseling group work with children in schools because games provide quasi-structured learning content that can, at any time, allow the leader to become more process oriented. Many games are available for use in group work that address a wide range of topics. One series of games developed by Erford and colleagues (Erford & McKechnie, 2002a, 2002b, 2002c; Erford, Schlerf, & Carr, 2000a, 2000b, 2000c, 2000d, 2001a, 2001b, 2001c) is distributed by the American Counseling Association Foundation (www.counseling.org/Publications)

TABLE 15.2   A Guided Visual Imagery Exercise

Stressbuster Relaxation Exercises: Volume 1: The Meadow

Welcome to a world full of sunshine and wildflowers. Before you can see this beautiful place, you need to prepare. Sit in a comfortable chair, place both feet flat on the floor and rest your arms at your sides. Close your eyes. Let's try to relax our bodies with some deep breathing exercises. As you inhale, slowly count to five, hold your breath for five seconds and then exhale for eight seconds. Let's begin.

Inhale, one, two, three, four, five, hold. One, two, three, four, five, and exhale. One, two, three, four, five, six, seven, eight. Good. Now, try it again.

Inhale. (pause)

Hold. (pause)

And exhale. (pause)

Excellent.

Now, envision yourself standing on the edge of a flower-filled meadow. The meadow goes on for as far as you can see. You stand for a moment and admire the beauty of the landscape. You have never seen flowers so bright and vivid. There are flowers of every color of the rainbow. The meadow smells sweet, like your favorite perfume or cologne. You hear the birds chirping in the trees surrounding the meadow and you see the butterflies gently gliding from flower to flower. You decide to walk to the middle of the meadow. As you walk along, the flowers gently caress your legs. (pause)

You spread out a blanket and sit down on the ground. You feel the sun warm your face, arms, and legs. You begin to relax your body by slowly rolling your neck and head in a circular motion. First to the left. (pause)

And then to the right. (pause)

Go ahead, do this again. As you do this, you are releasing the tension in your head, neck, and shoulders. (pause)

Good. Now try this neck-stretching activity a couple more times and say to yourself, "All the tension is leaving my body. The tension is leaving my body." (pause)

Excellent. Next take both hands and reach above your head. Lean to the right. (pause) Then to the left. (pause) Be sure to get a good stretch of both sides of your body. Now, try it once more on your own and say to yourself, "I feel relaxed. I feel relaxed." (pause)

Good. Now move to your legs. Keep your legs straight and point your toes away from your body. Then bring your toes inward and point your heels outward. This should give you a good stretch of the back of your legs. Excellent. Now try it one more time on your own as you say to yourself, "I feel calm and relaxed. I feel calm and relaxed." (pause)

Lie back on the blanket and enjoy the warm sun and feel of relaxation. Take a few moments and enjoy the peacefulness. You feel totally relaxed. (pause)

When you are ready, gather up your blanket, take a deep breath in, and smell the fragrant flowers. Admire for a moment longer the beauty that surrounds you. (pause)

When you are ready, open your eyes. You feel calm and relaxed and ready to meet the challenges of the day.

---

and is particularly useful with school-age youth. The game series addresses 10 commonly encountered childhood issues: good grief, anger management, conflict resolution, changing families, studying skillfully, social skills, solving problems, self-concept, perfectionism, and Attention-Deficit/Hyperactivity Disorder. The games are very cost efficient because each different topic can be used with a single, colorful dinosaur-themed game board and 6-inch dinosaur game pieces.

A variation of play therapy, the structure of the games, coupled with the focus of the statements and questions on the cards, allows intense attention to issues frequently encountered by youth. This focus is accomplished by a preplanned, sequential grouping of the game cards according to specific content. For example, each set of cards in Understanding Anger is composed of 30 cards and is lettered according to the topic and then numbered in sequence. In Understanding Anger, these topics are labeled as follows: a. Learning About Anger; b. Coping with Anger; c. Anger and Friends; d. Anger and the Family; e. Anger at School; and f. Anger and Sports.

Each deck is then subdivided to intensely examine the thoughts, feelings, and behaviors associated with effective coping responses. Through this process, children and youth not only understand the prominent issues related to anger but also develop the resiliency and coping mechanisms to effectively adjust to situations commonly involving anger. Within each deck, the cards are sequenced in a manner that facilitates the exploration of important topical issues. Within each issue, exploration of thoughts, feelings, and behaviors is prompted, leading the children or youth through a series of developmental and therapeutic exercises. Each game comes with standard directions for rules of play. The following section presents creative modifications to get the most out of students and the group process and can be used with nearly any therapeutic or developmental game.

Creative Modifications

The following creative modifications add fun and efficiency to the standard rules of play:

- Often, the best sessions are those in which members deal with pressing issues. Leaders should not feel pressured to rush through a deck of cards. The best sessions don't get past the fourth or fifth card because important issues are discussed in great depth. Remember that group work's purpose is to facilitate communication. When communication is flowing, don't allow the structure of a game to interrupt it.
- Feel free to make up your own prompts. Timely teaching is a characteristic of effective counseling. When a member can benefit from a prompt different from the one on the card, the leader should feel free to modify or supplant the card content.
- Allow all members the opportunity to respond to the card with different responses. Once the member's turn is completed, allow other members the opportunity to give a different response to the card prompt. It is important that others give a different response so members will benefit from differing perspectives, not just mimic others to obtain additional chips. This modification gives all members the chance to process the issue, keeps them in the game when it is not their turn, and allows more frequent reinforcement (e.g., chips, attention, achievement).
- Consider using the chips as a primary reinforcer that can be exchanged for immediate or long-term rewards. Examples include a celebration party at the end of the group, knickknacks or small toys, and more time allowed on favored activities.
- Change "Chip" spaces into "Card" spaces. If competition for chips becomes too intense or when time grows short, consider making "Chip" spaces into "Card" spaces. This virtually guarantees a card will be processed on each turn and substantially lowers the competitiveness of players focused on accumulating chips.
- Change "Chip" spaces into "Earn a Chip" spaces. Have the members who land on a "Chip" space "earn" a chip by performing some task. One favorite is a simple affirmation statement directed at another member of the leader's choosing. The affirmation statement should involve a character trait, rather than something superficial, such as

clothing, hair, or smile (e.g., "Turn to Susan and tell her one thing that makes her such a good friend").

- Give multiple chips for being the first player to finish. Another modification is to count the number of players and award each player a decreasing number of chips as they pass the "Finish" space. For example, if five people are playing, the first player to cross the "Finish" space would get five chips, the second four chips, the third three chips, the fourth two chips, and the last player would receive one chip as the finish line is crossed.
- To speed up the game, consider rolling two dice.
- After landing on a "Card" space, consider having the player roll the die to see how many chips a correct answer may earn. For example, if a member lands on a "Card" space, rolls a four on the die, and responds correctly to the card prompt, she could earn four chips for that turn. Alternatively, the die would already show a number when the player landed on the space and that die could be used to indicate the number of chips the member could earn.
- Consider allowing members who have crossed the finish line to continue playing and earning chips. This will serve to keep them in the game and minimize the distraction of other players progressing toward the finish line.

Flexibility and Efficiency

The flexibility afforded to group leaders who use developmental and therapeutic games will become apparent as you read the information offered above and try the games out in clinical practice. This series of psychoeducational games offers flexibility and tremendous cost-effectiveness. For example, the game boards are printed on two sides, so the leader receives two game boards for the price of one. Also, the game boards are not labeled in any specific way, so the leader can use them for any game in this series, or nearly any other psychotherapeutic game that uses cards to convey information, understanding, and action. However, numerous therapeutic games exist. Table 15.3 provides a list of some of the more commonly used products.

TABLE 15.3 Developmental or Psychotherapeutic Games	
Title/(Topics)	**Available from**
Dr. Erford's Dinosaur Game Series (Understanding Anger, Good Grief, Social Skills, Studying Skillfully, Conflict Resolution, AD/HD, Perfectionism, Self-Concept, Changing Families, Solving Problems)	American Counseling Association
Dr. PlayWell's Amazing Card Games (Coping with Stress, Positive Thinking, Caring About Others, Communicating Feelings, Controlling Your Anger)	Childswork/Childsplay
The Talking, Feeling and Doing Game Series (Original, Anger Card Game, Good Behavior Card Game, Teasing Card Game, Shyness Card Game, Divorce Card Game)	Childswork/Childsplay
Helping, Sharing and Caring Game	
Stop, Relax & Think	Childswork/Childsplay
Berthold Berg Series (Changing Family Game, Anger Control Game, Classroom Survival Game, Frustration Game, Social Conflict Game, Achievement Game, Self-Control Game, Conduct Management Game, Drugs and Alcohol Game, Relapse Prevention Game, Feelings Game, Family Living Game, Self Concept Game, Social Skills Game, Anxiety Coping Game, Stress Management Game)	Western Psychological Services

Summary

This chapter has suggested ways that any group program can successfully attract members and try to maintain maximum participation. The need to develop new ways to reach members calls for the reframing of traditional ways of conducting groups. In an ever-changing world, some counseling techniques must also change.

Counseling interventions using expressive arts and activities provide engaging and effective ways for group leaders to facilitate change in children and adolescents. The visual arts, music, and therapeutic writing and storytelling represent three of the many categories of expressive arts that can be used to help students prevent and resolve problems. Other creative art forms that reach students in ways that go beyond simply talking include imagery, dance, drama, puppetry, games, and play.

These creative interventions enable students to communicate emotions and concerns in unique ways. They foster different ways of viewing the world and consequently facilitate the development of new perspectives and alternatives for behaving. By selecting interventions carefully, based on members' developmental levels, counseling goals, and personal preferences, leaders can expand their repertoire of procedures that can be employed effectively to promote choice and change.

CHAPTER 16

Accountability in Group Work and School Counseling

BRADLEY T. ERFORD

PREVIEW

The following facets of accountability are addressed: needs assessment, program evaluation, process evaluation, and outcome studies. Each facet contributes to a cycle of quality improvement for group work practice.

ACCOUNTABILITY IN GROUP WORK

Research has established that group work is an effective treatment delivery system (see Chapter 17). However, this knowledge alone does not satisfy the public's justified need for continued accountability in school counseling services, particularly on a case-by-case (or group-by-group) basis. In order for group counseling to remain valued by the public, group leaders must provide evidence demonstrating that their work is worthwhile and produces results. Lack of accountability can cause the elimination of school counseling positions, specific counseling practices, and delivery systems. For instance, a new era of educational reform and a lack of accountability in the school counseling profession have caused positions to be eliminated from school districts across the United States. Erford, House, and Martin (2007) stated, "School districts, including superintendents and school boards, are primarily focused on increasing student achievement. Professional school counselors must demonstrate that they are central to the success of these efforts" (p. 11).

Accountability in group work answers the question, How are group members different as a result of the services provided by group leaders? By using assessment techniques to measure outcomes, leaders can provide a means for accountability to members, administrators, and other stakeholders and demonstrate how the school counseling program is affecting member outcomes, development, and even achievement.

According to various scholars (Erford, 2007a; Issacs, 2003; Loesch & Ritchie, 2004; Myrick, 2003), accountability ordinarily involves

- Identifying and collaborating with stakeholder groups (e.g., advisory committees, administrators, parents, teachers, students);

- Collecting data and assessing the needs of students, staff, and community;
- Setting goals and establishing objectives based on data and determined needs;
- Implementing effective interventions to address the goals and objectives;
- Measuring the outcomes or results of these interventions;
- Using these results for program improvement; and
- Sharing results with major stakeholder groups (e.g., administration, teachers and staff, parents and guardians, students, school boards, community and business leaders, school counselors and supervisors).

There are advantages and disadvantages to conducting accountability studies. These are outlined in Table 16.1. It is important to note that many of the disadvantages can be remedied if practitioners work with researchers to evaluate group work effectiveness.

It is the professional and ethical responsibility of leaders to ensure that the services offered to stakeholder groups are truly effective. The focus of this chapter is on the wide-ranging accountability functions of the professional school counselor, including needs assessment, program and process evaluation, and outcome research. The content of this chapter is among the most important in terms of (1) understanding the needs of a student population and community (needs assessment); (2) determining the extent to which a program exists (program evaluation); (3) evaluating leader, member, and group processes (process evaluation); and (4) assessing group work effectiveness (outcome or results studies). This information

---

TABLE 16.1   Advantages and Disadvantages of Accountability Studies

Advantages

1. Data are almost always as good as or better than perception when it comes to guiding decision making about programs, practices, and interventions.
2. Accountability studies help demonstrate necessity, efficiency, and effectiveness of counseling services.
3. Accountability studies can help identify professional development and staff development needs.
4. Leaders can network to share program results, thereby spreading the word about effective practices.
5. Conducting accountability studies is a professional responsibility and demonstrates one's commitment to personal and professional improvement.
6. Accountability results can serve a public relations function by informing stakeholders and the public of a school counseling program's accomplishments.

Challenges

1. Outcome measures and surveys require some training and skill to develop.
2. It requires time and resources to do quality outcomes research and evaluation—time and resources that could be dedicated to additional service delivery.
3. Many do not understand the nature and purpose of accountability because of misperceptions or previous "bad" experiences.
4. Data are sometimes "overinterpreted" or given undue meaning (e.g., the facts may not support the conclusion). All studies have limitations that must be considered when arriving at conclusions.
5. Comprehensive evaluations are seldom conducted. More often, bits and pieces of evaluative information are collected, and the "big picture" is often incomplete.

will also allow leaders to speak the language of decision makers, thus allowing social and academic advocacy for students who have diverse needs or who are encountering systemic barriers to academic, career, or personal-social success. Finally, every professional school counselor should be constantly asking and gathering information to answer the question, Is what I'm doing working with this member?

CONDUCTING A NEEDS ASSESSMENT

At least two primary purposes underlie the use of a needs assessment in school counseling programs. First, a needs assessment helps leaders understand the needs of various subpopulations of a community. These subpopulations may include students, teachers, parents, administrators, community organizations, congregations, neighborhoods, local businesses, and the general citizenry. Each of these groups holds a stake in the success of the total program; thus, they are called stakeholder groups. Second, needs assessment helps establish the priorities that guide the construction of a counseling program or group work intervention as well as the continuous quality improvement of the program. A needs assessment emphasizes what currently exists in comparison with identified goals and objectives (Erford, 2008a). Assessing the needs of a community or community population provides a trajectory for addressing what the community values and desires to pursue. Needs assessments can be classified as data-driven needs assessments and perceptions-based needs assessments.

Data-Driven Needs Assessment

Data-driven decision making deals with real needs and impact, not perceived needs. Data-driven needs assessment is most frequently used in school systems when standardized assessment is systematically conducted, primarily as a result of state and federal initiatives such as the No Child Left Behind Act of 2001.

Data-driven needs assessment begins with an analysis of school-based or community-based performance data. Given the prominence of high-stakes testing and large-scale testing programs required under No Child Left Behind, schools are frequently provided with aggregated and disaggregated performance results. Aggregated means that all student results are lumped together to show total grade level or schoolwide (average) results. Aggregated data are helpful in understanding how the average students perform in a given class, grade, or school—but tell very little about the diversity of learner performance or needs and nothing about how various subgroups or subpopulations performed. In Table 16.2, the aggregated results are represented by the "Total Grade" line at the top for a school with 100 fifth graders.

To fully understand how to use performance data, professional school counselors must become proficient in understanding norm-referenced and criterion-referenced score interpretation. While a comprehensive explanation of score interpretation is beyond the scope of this chapter and is typically encountered in an assessment or testing course, what follows can be considered a very basic primer on the interpretation of norm-referenced scores. (For a more advanced understanding of interpreting standardized test score data, see Erford, 2007b, 2008a.)

Note that in the example in Table 16.2, the mean national percentile rank is 50. A percentile rank is most easily understood if one visualizes a lineup of 100 individuals, all with certain characteristics in common—in this case, they are all fifth-grade math students. Importantly, when interpreting percentile ranks, the 1st student in the line is the lowest-performing student,

TABLE 16.2   Aggregated and Disaggregated Results from a Typical Large-Scale Math Achievement Test for a School's Fifth-Grade Level

	n	NPR	% in Quartile			
			Q_1	Q_2	Q_3	Q_4
Total Grade	100	50	19	31	26	24
Male	48	45	22	34	26	18
Female	52	56	10	31	31	28
Asian	8	72	0	25	38	38
Black	31	37	29	52	13	6
Hispanic	8	43	25	50	25	0
White	52	58	9	30	33	28
Other	1	44	0	100	0	0
Low SES	48	31	36	38	23	3
Non Low SES	52	71	5	24	36	35
English (Second Language)	3	43	0	67	33	0
English (Primary Language)	97	51	19	30	27	24
Special Education	10	25	60	20	20	0
Non Special Education	90	58	11	31	32	26

Note: n = number of students in the sample;
NPR = national percentile rank;
% in Quartile = the percentage of the sample that actually performed in a given quartile.

while the 100th student is the highest-performing student. A student's place indicates his or her relative standing compared to other fifth-grade math students across the country (thus, the term *national percentile rank*). For example, a student scoring at the 79th percentile performed better than 79% of the fifth graders in the national norm group or was the 79th student standing in the line. Likewise, a student performing at the fifth percentile would be standing in the fifth place in line and has outperformed only 5% of the fifth graders in the nationwide norm group. A quartile is a commonly used interpretive statistic that divides the percentile rank distribution into four segments. The first quartile includes percentile ranks ranging from 1 to 25; it is the lowest quarter of a distribution and is designated Q_1. The second quartile (Q_2) includes percentile ranks ranging from 26 to 50. The third quartile (Q_3) includes percentile ranks ranging from 51 to 75. The fourth quartile (Q_4) includes percentile ranks ranging from 76 to 100, the highest quarter of the distribution.

Some test publishers also use an interpretive statistic known as a stanine, which is short for standard nine. A normal distribution is divided into nine segments or stanines, albeit in a manner quite different from quartiles. A stanine actually represents one-half of a standard deviation, so while each quartile represents 25% of the population, stanines may represent varying percentages of the population. The first stanine represents the lowest level of performance, while the ninth stanine represents the highest level of performance.

Importantly, parents, teachers, and students will understand performance most easily and accurately when percentile ranks are used. Other standardized scores can require some

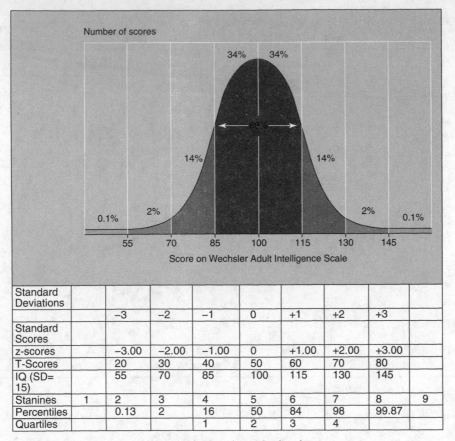

Standard Deviations									
		−3	−2	−1	0	+1	+2	+3	
Standard Scores									
z-scores		−3.00	−2.00	−1.00	0	+1.00	+2.00	+3.00	
T-Scores		20	30	40	50	60	70	80	
IQ (SD= 15)		55	70	85	100	115	130	145	
Stanines	1	2	3	4	5	6	7	8	9
Percentiles		0.13	2	16	50	84	98	99.87	
Quartiles				1	2	3	4		

FIGURE 16.1 The normal curve and related standardized scores.

sophistication and may lead to errors in interpretation. Figure 16.1 provides a graphic of the normal curve and the commonly used standardized scores that leaders may encounter. Note that each of these standardized scores can be converted into a percentile rank for easy explanation to parents, teachers and students.

Disaggregated means the data have been broken down by subpopulations so that performance differences between and among groups can be analyzed. Usually, this analysis involves intergroup differences (e.g., male versus female, by race and ethnicity, special education versus regular education status). Most test publishers can provide this level of information upon request, broken down by school, by grade level, and even by individual classes. Differences can be determined using statistical methods or by informal comparison. Disaggregated data provide evidence of gaps in performance between groups of students; they also provide direction for the types of strategies and interventions needed to close these gaps.

Returning to the data provided in Table 16.2, one can see several noticeable gaps in achievement. First, students from the Low SES (socioeconomic status) grouping performed at the 31st percentile rank, on average, while students from the Non Low SES group (middle class and upper middle class in this example) performed at the 71st percentile rank, on average.

Second, there is a noticeable difference between the average math performance for Black and Hispanic students (37th and 43rd percentile ranks, respectively) and that for Asian and White students (72nd and 58th percentile ranks, respectively). Third, females outperformed males, on average (56th versus 45th percentile rank, respectively). From these comparisons of disaggregated data, discussions can ensue and strategies can be developed to decrease the math performance gap. But importantly, it all starts with the data—thus, the name data-driven. In this way, data provide the impetus and drive behind school improvement plans and responsive school counseling programs.

Perceptions-Based Needs Assessments

In contrast to a data-driven needs assessment, a traditional needs assessment process is more content and perception driven. Group leaders are often interested in what members, community leaders, citizens, teachers, parents, and students perceive as primary needs to be addressed. Prior to undertaking a perceptions-based needs assessment, group leaders are wise to consider issues of how often to conduct a needs assessment, which stakeholder group(s) to assess, and how to design an efficient needs assessment.

FREQUENCY OF CONDUCTING A NEEDS ASSESSMENT   While it may seem tempting to design and conduct a global needs assessment on an annual basis, such an endeavor would be a massive and costly undertaking. It is probably best to follow a continuous cycle of programmatic needs assessment. This will allow ample time for program development and improvements over the course of the cycle. For example, the ASCA National Standards (Campbell & Dahir, 1997) and National Model (ASCA, 2005) designate the areas of academic, career, and personal-social development as cornerstones of a comprehensive, developmental guidance program; therefore, it makes sense to assess schools' needs according to these components on a rotating basis. For a new program or one undergoing tremendous renovations, years one and two of a six-year cycle can be spent in conducting needs assessments and implementing programmatic changes to address horizontal and vertical articulation issues surrounding student academic development. Years three and four can be spent on student career development needs; years five and six can focus on student personal-social issues. On the other hand, the six-year cycle could alternate among the three domains, addressing each of the domain issues every three years (i.e., year 1: academic, year 2: career, year 3: personal-social, year 4: academic, year 5: career, year 6: personal-social). An established school counseling program in good condition and requiring only fine-tuning may be put on a three-year continuous improvement cycle.

The main point here is that assessing needs is part of a much bigger endeavor: that of implementing programmatic changes to continuously improve the school counseling program. Importantly, implementing changes can be quite time intensive and simply a waste of time if not guided by accurate needs assessments and program outcome research. An effective program uses this information to fine-tune its efforts in data-driven decision making.

POPULATIONS TO BE ASSESSED   In the broadest sense, any stakeholder group can provide helpful information about the needs of a population or community. However, it is most practical and efficient to seek out those who are informed and likely to respond. Community leaders, teachers, administrators, students, and parents are the most likely to be informed about community and school issues and needs and under most circumstances will be the primary stakeholder groups surveyed during a needs assessment. Valuable information can be garnered from community organizations, local businesses, and the general citizenry as well. It is just more difficult to obtain a large sample of responses from these groups. Information from these stakeholders is probably best obtained through personal contacts and interviews.

Return rate is an important factor in the needs assessment process. Return rate is the percentage of surveys returned out of those sent. As in any research sampling procedure, the higher the return rate, the lower the sampling error; this leads to greater confidence in the accuracy of the results. Return rate is generally maximized when the participants are a "captured audience." For example, if a social skills needs assessment of fourth-grade students is conducted in the classroom, the response rate should be nearly 100%. On the other hand, if a needs assessment for parents is sent home, the professional school counselor may be lucky to receive 25–50% of the surveys back. Whenever possible, surveys should be distributed and collected immediately during community gatherings, faculty meetings, class meetings, and parent gatherings.

Triangulation of needs across populations should be attempted when possible, that is, the highest-priority needs should be those agreed to by all or most populations assessed. This ensures that the community's needs, not an individual's agenda, drive programs and services. For instance, if an administrator has decided to place a high priority on social skills, but community leaders, parents, and group members indicate this is a low priority—and far below other issues such as depression, career development, and substance abuse—the triangulated responses of the teachers, parents, and students can provide compelling evidence to guide the program's focus.

DESIGN ISSUES IN AN EFFICIENT NEEDS ASSESSMENT   Designing an efficient needs assessment is essential in order to obtain meaningful results. While some advocate for a comprehensive needs assessment that simultaneously assesses all goals and topics associated with a comprehensive counseling program, others have found it more helpful to focus the assessment on specifically defined topics or issues that are being updated or altered (Erford, 2007b, 2008a). This chapter will focus on the latter method.

Stone and Bradley (1994) recommended seven methods for determining needs: questionnaires and inventories, records analysis, personal interviews, counseling statistics, classroom visits, use of outside consultants, and a systematic evaluation of the guidance program. Perhaps what is most important is that the needs assessments use objective methods for data gathering and analysis. It is essential to understand that some questions are addressed by different methodologies. Although all of these methods are important and useful, questionnaires (formal or informal surveys) are most commonly used and will be focused on here. Importantly, while open-ended questionnaires are generally easier to design and yield rich and diverse information, such questionnaires are usually more difficult to interpret and translate into goals and objectives.

From a return-rate perspective, it is good practice to design a needs assessment that is only one to two pages in length and can be completed in about three to five minutes. The content of the needs assessment should be topical (e.g., social skills, changing families, substance abuse, college application procedures) rather than service related (e.g., individual counseling, group counseling, consultation). Group leaders should keep in mind that services are simply methods for meeting needs, not needs in themselves. Of course, the topics should be related to the program goals or organizational mission so that priority status can be placed on addressing the most pressing needs in comparison to mission/goals. A good needs assessment directly translates into program development.

In general, the following steps form the basis of an efficient needs assessment:

1. Decide what you need to know.
2. Decide on the best approach to gather the information you need to know.
3. Develop the needs assessment instrument or method.
4. Enlist the support of colleagues and a few individuals from the target groups to review and try out items for understanding.
5. Implement the final version with the target groups.
6. Tabulate, analyze, and interpret the results.
7. Translate the results into programmatic goals and objectives.

The design of the scale itself deserves some mention. The survey should ask for the name of the individual completing the form unless the form is to be completed anonymously. Teacher surveys may ask for the grade level, the number of students in class, or other pertinent information. Parent surveys should ask for the names of the parents' children in case their response to the survey requires contact by the professional school counselor. Student surveys should ask for the student's grade and homeroom teacher's name.

Questions or response stems should be short, to the point, and easily understood. The reading level of the items should also be appropriate for the target audience. Figure 16.2 provides an example of a topic-focused needs assessment for students.

Substantial consideration should also be given to the response format. If the purpose of the survey is to determine the importance or frequency of a potential problem, it is generally

Name: _____

Place a check mark (✓) In the appropriate space below to indicate how well you handle each issue.

	Almost Never	Sometimes	Often	Almost Always	I need help with this	
					Yes	No
1. I am able to focus my thoughts when I need to.						
2. I have a good workout schedule.						
3. I have good time management skills.						
4. I can control my breathing when upset.						
5. I can control my level of stress.						
6. I have good organizational skills.						
7. My muscles are relaxed.						
8. I have good nutritional habits.						
9. I think positive thoughts about myself.						
10. I can readily identify stressors in my life.						

FIGURE 16.2   A focused stress management needs assessment.

best to use a multipoint scale with four to seven choices. For example, Figure 16.2 asks about the frequency of display of stressors, so the response choices "Almost Never," "Sometimes," "Often," and "Almost Always" are appropriate. Note that the response choices "Never" and "Always" do not appear. It is rare that behaviors never or always occur; to include these descriptors may force responses to the center of the distribution and truncate the range of possible results. Also notice how each category has a descriptor. Thankfully gone are the days in survey construction when a survey would list the response categories of 0 ("Almost Never") and 3 ("Almost Always") and then provide the center points of 1 and 2 with no accompanying descriptors. The reliability problems of such a scale are obvious: Will all respondents agree on what the unlabeled 1 and 2 represent? All choice categories must be accompanied by descriptors.

Another important response component of a needs assessment is a frequency count. Suppose a group leader wants not only to assess the importance of an issue but also to determine how many potential group members are likely in need of services to address the problems stemming from the issue. When possible, the needs assessment should be designed to include an indication of whether the student should be targeted for intervention. In Figure 16.2, notice how the right-hand column asks for a Yes or No response to the statement "I need help with this." An affirmative response targets the potential member for intervention to address a self-perceived weakness.

Tallying or computing the information from a needs assessment is relatively simple. Tallying involves counting the number of potential group members who may benefit from intervention. Computing the results of a needs assessment is probably best accomplished by assigning a number value to each response category and averaging all responses for a given item. In Figure 16.2, assume that the response categories are assigned the following values: Almost Never = 0, Sometimes = 1, Often = 2, and Almost Always = 3. For item 1, "I am able to focus my thoughts when I need to," simply add all the student response values and divide by the number of responses. Using the data in Table 16.3, for item 1, if 50 members completed the needs assessment and 10 members marked "Almost Never" ($10 \times 0 = 0$), 12 members marked "Sometimes" ($12 \times 1 = 12$), 21 members marked "Often" ($21 \times 2 = 42$), and 7 members marked "Almost Always" ($7 \times 3 = 21$), simply sum the points ($0 + 12 + 42 + 21 = 75$) and divide by the number of member responses to compute the average frequency rating (sum of 75 divided by 50 students = 1.50). Although this assumes an interval or ratio scale and is somewhat nebulous from a statistical interpretation perspective (that is, what does a 1.50 really mean?), it does offer a reasonable estimate of the average frequency of a behavior or the importance of one issue in comparison to the other issues under study. For example, when viewing the mean computations of the 10 items in Table 16.3, the leader gets a good idea how important item 1 is in comparison to the other nine items in the needs assessment.

HELPFUL TIPS FOR DEVELOPING A NEEDS ASSESSMENT   A helpful set of commonsense guidelines for questionnaire or survey development was provided by Worthen, Sanders, and Fitzpatrick (1997):

1. Sequencing questions
   a. Are later responses biased by early questions?
   b. Does the questionnaire begin with easy, unthreatening, but pertinent questions?
   c. Are leading questions (ones that "lead" to a certain response) avoided?

TABLE 16.3 Data from the Stress Management Needs Assessment (n = 50)

	AN(0)	S(1)	O(2)	AA(3)	Yes	No	Ave(rank)
1. I am able to focus my thoughts when I need to.	10(0)	12(12)	21(42)	7(21)	21	29	1.50(9)
2. I have a good workout schedule.	22(0)	17(17)	7(14)	4(12)	33	17	0.86(3)
3. I have good time management skills.	15(0)	12(12)	14(28)	9(27)	22	28	1.34(6)
4. I can control my breathing when upset.	29(0)	12(12)	7(14)	2(6)	42	8	0.64(1)
5. I can control my level of stress.	24(0)	9(9)	10(20)	7(21)	33	17	1.00(4)
6. I have good organizational skills.	14(0)	9(9)	17(34)	10(30)	19	31	1.46(8)
7. My muscles are relaxed.	28(0)	8(8)	8(16)	6(18)	35	15	0.84(2)
8. I have good nutritional habits.	19(0)	15(15)	7(14)	9(27)	35	15	1.12(5)
9. I think positive thoughts about myself.	17(0)	12(12)	7(14)	14(42)	23	27	1.36(7)
10. I can readily identify stressors in my life.	6(0)	9(9)	10(20)	25(75)	14	36	2.08(10)

Note: Almost Never (AN) = 0; Sometimes (S) = 1; Often (O) = 2; Almost Always (AA) = 3. The tally (# of clients responding) is entered in each column first followed by the product of the tally and the response value in parentheses—for example, item 1 under the AA(3) column reads 7(21), meaning that 7 clients responded Almost Always and this tally was multiplied by 3, resulting in a product of 21. The rank in the right-hand column indicates the order of greatest need, with the lower average scores indicating greater degrees of need.

    d. Is there a logical, efficient sequencing of questions (e.g., from general to specific questions; use of filter questions when appropriate)?

    e. Are closed- or open-ended questions appropriate? If closed, are the categories exhaustive and mutually exclusive? Do responses result in the desired scale of data for analysis (i.e., nominal, ordinal, interval)?

    f. Are the major issues covered thoroughly while minor issues are passed over quickly?

    g. Are questions with similar content grouped logically?

2. Wording questions

    a. Are questions stated precisely? (Who, what, when, where, why, how?)

    b. Does the questionnaire avoid assuming too much knowledge on the part of the respondent?

    c. Does each item ask only one question?

    d. Is the respondent in a position to answer the question, or must she make guesses? If so, are you interested in her guesses?

    e. Are definitions clear?

    f. Are emotionally tinged words avoided?

    g. Is the vocabulary at the reading level of the audience? If any technical terms, jargon or slang is used, are they the most appropriate way to communicate with this audience?

    h. Are the methods for responding appropriate? Clear? Consistent?

    i. Are the questions appropriately brief and simple?

3. Establishing and keeping rapport and eliciting cooperation

    a. Is the questionnaire easy to answer? (Questions are not overly long or cumbersome.)

b. Is the time required to respond reasonable?

c. Does the instrument look attractive (i.e., layout, quality of paper, etc.)?

d. Is there a "respondent orientation"?

e. Does the cover letter provide an explanation of the purpose, sponsorship, method of respondent selection, and anonymity?

f. Is appropriate incentive provided for the respondent's cooperation?

4. Giving instructions

a. Is the respondent clearly told how to record her responses?

b. Are instructions for return clear? Is a stamped return envelop provided? (pp. 355–356)

Group leaders conducting needs assessments must choose an appropriate response format: ordinarily, yes–no (or sometimes), multiscale formats (e.g., almost never, sometimes, frequently, almost always), Likert-type scales (e.g., very dissatisfied, dissatisfied, satisfied, very satisfied), true/false formats, or multiple-choice formats. Note the wording of items, the scaling method, and the single-page format of the needs assessment presented in Figure 16.2.

CONVERTING NEEDS TO PROGRAM GOALS AND OBJECTIVES   If the needs assessment is designed correctly, translating the results into goals and learning objectives is relatively easy. The first step is to prioritize the needs in order of importance and their relationship to the existing components of the program. Prioritization can be accomplished most easily by using the tallying, computing, and triangulation strategies mentioned above. Next, the needs must be matched with or translated into goals aligned with the program mission and standards. Finally, the goals are operationalized through the development of learning objectives. Erford (2007a, 2008b) provides an excellent nuts-and-bolts discussion of how to write learning objectives using the ABCD model: (A) Audience, (B) Behavior, (C) Conditions, and (D) Description of the expected performance criterion.

A reasonable goal stemming from the needs assessment shown in Figure 16.2 would be "To increase members' abilities to manage stress and anxiety." Notice how the wording of a goal is nebulous and not amenable to measurement as stated. In developing learning objectives related to goals, particular emphasis is given to specific actions that are measurable. For example, a possible objective stemming from this goal could be "After participating in a group counseling program and learning thought-stopping procedures, 80% of the members will experience a 50% reduction in obsessive thinking over a one-week period." Another possible objective might be "After participating in a six-week program on the importance of exercise with follow-up goal-setting monitoring, 80% of the members will engage in at least 20 minutes of aerobic exercise at least three times per week." Notice how the objectives designate the audience, the stated behavior, the means by which the behavior will be measured, and the level of expected performance. Several excellent resources exist for additional information on constructing needs assessments (e.g., Erford, 2007a, 2008a).

ACCOUNTABILITY: EVALUATING PROGRAMS AND ASSESSING OUTCOMES

In this age of accountability, program evaluation is more important than ever. Traditionally, however, professional school counselors have for many reasons failed to hold their programs and services accountable or to provide evidence that activities undertaken are achieving intended results. Some complained that the nature of what group leaders do is so abstract and complicated as to render the services and results unmeasurable. Others were so busy attempting to meet the needs of members that they shifted time that should be spent in evaluation to responsive interventions. Some lacked an understanding of how to implement the methods and procedures of accountability studies. Still others were unsure of the effectiveness of the services provided and shied away from accountability unless it was forced on them by supervisors.

Whatever the reason, the end result is a glaring lack of accountability that poses dangers for the future of the profession. Each contributes to a shirking of professional and ethical responsibility to ensure that the services provided to group members are of high quality and effective in meeting intended needs. Think about it from a business perspective. How long would a business last if it continued to engage in indiscernible or ineffective activities, the value of which was unknown to the business's consumers, managers, and employees? Such businesses are selected out for extinction. Now extend that thought to group work. Without accountability data to back them up, counseling services are often among the first services to go during budget cutbacks.

In the context of group work, leaders must be concerned with two areas of accountability: (1) process evaluation and (2) results or outcome evaluation. Both are important facets of the overall evaluation of a program, but are often addressed independently in group work accountability. Evaluation is the measurement of worth and indicates that a judgment will be made regarding the effectiveness of a program (Erford, 2008a). In an evaluation process, it is essential to be very specific about what you are measuring and how you are measuring it. This is made clear in the writing of specific learning objectives (see Erford, 2008b). Too often, leaders are not specific about what they are trying to accomplish and become frustrated when they fail to measure what they may or may not have achieved. If a leader doesn't know where she is heading, she must either get specific directions (write a specific, measurable objective) or be satisfied with wherever she ends up (perhaps being unable to demonstrate an effective group).

PROCESS EVALUATION

Process evaluation refers to the assessment of the group dynamics and interaction processes occurring within the group sessions, usually related to the leader, the members, and the interactions between the leader and the members. Understanding the group dynamics helps to improve the efficiency and effectiveness of the interactions. Several resources are available that provide ideas for conducting process evaluations. The *Handbook of Group Psychotherapy: An Empirical and Clinical Synthesis* (Fuhriman & Burlingame, 1994b) identifies numerous measures and methods for evaluating group processes and outcomes, as have works by DeLucia-Waack (1997, 1999) and Delucia-Waack, Gerrity, Kalodner, and Riva (2004).

Some interaction and process evaluation instruments used in the past include the Hill Interaction Matrix (Hill, 1966), Bales's (1950) Interaction Analysis Scale, and Simon and Agazarian's (1974) Sequential Analysis of Verbal Interaction (SAVI). Trotzer (1999) also developed structured leadership and member process instruments and, most recently, the Association for Specialists in Group Work has undertaken a project to develop a standardized and psychometrically robust process evaluation instrument.

In addition to standardized measures, process evaluation can be conducted through a variety of other methods, including peer/supervisor observation, informal member evaluation, and evaluation of videotapes. Colleagues with expertise in group work can observe sessions and provide feedback in an informal or formal supervisory relationship. While this is sometimes requested by the group leader when a group is at an impasse or not moving in an appropriate direction, observation by a colleague may provide helpful feedback at any point in a group counseling process.

Informal member evaluations should be conducted during each session to help the leader understand how group members are progressing and perceiving the group process. Members frequently give helpful feedback and make suggestions for improvement when presented with basic questions such as these:

- What did you like most (or least) about this session?
- What did and didn't work well or go well in this session?
- How could the session have been improved?
- What could the leader or members have done differently to make the session more successful?
- What was the most important gain or insight you realized in today's session?

Alternatively, members can journal about their session experiences and insights to communicate similar thoughts, feelings, and behaviors. Leaders should always keep in mind that some members may give inaccurate negative feedback, give inaccurate positive feedback, or say what they believe the leader wants to hear (i.e., they engage in social desirability responding by answering in a way that is socially acceptable).

Videotapes have the advantage of being an actual record of real-life events that can be reviewed at the leisure of the group leader, colleague, or supervisor. It is difficult to dispute the advantages of actually seeing and hearing oneself—repeatedly, if need be—engaging in the actual group process. Comments, sequences, and interchanges can be broken down and analyzed so that strengths can be identified and areas in need of improvement targeted. Videotaping is used extensively in training programs but unfortunately is infrequently used in clinical practice. Videotaped sessions are among the most effective process evaluation tools available.

RESULTS OR OUTCOME EVALUATION

Outcome evaluation (often called results evaluation) answers the question, how are members different because of the group work? Many leaders view outcome evaluation as a discrete component, but it is actually an integrated part of a continuous process for program improvement. All accountability procedures must have the institution's mission in mind because the institutional values and needs will determine the focus of study. Questions of worth and effectiveness are derived from a confluence of values, needs, goals, and mission, and these questions lead to the determination of what evidence must be collected. Evidence may exist in many places but typically is derived through the use of preplanned measures or from the performances or products students produce during program activities. Once information has been gathered, it must then be interpreted, and conclusions must be drawn from it regarding the program's or activity's worth, strengths, and weaknesses. Finally, the interpretations and conclusions must be used to change the program or parts of the program to improve it.

Goal setting for and the posing of new questions about the resulting revised program are used to prompt further programmatic changes. Many professional school counselors gather evidence and then stop, believing that the program has been evaluated and the job finished. Why spend valuable time collecting evidence and not use it to improve what you are doing?

Sources of Evidence

Both people and products merit discussion as potential sources of accountability evidence. Almost anyone—students, teachers, staff, administrators, parents, employers, graduates, community resource people, and so on—can serve as a helpful source of evidence. Numerous products can also be used. A short list includes portfolios, performances, ratings from external judges or examiners, observations, local tests, purchased tests, self-assessments, surveys, interviews, focus groups, and student work. Each of these sources or products can produce helpful evaluative data, but what is collected will be determined by the specific question to be answered.

Selecting Outcome and Process Measures

Perhaps the simplest of the individual (or ideographic) outcome assessment techniques is the behavioral contract. Behavioral contracts with criteria for success are negotiated during a group session, signed by the member making the contract, witnessed by the other group members, and distributed among the group members so all members know for what goals each member has contracted (Trotzer, 1999). Groups oriented toward the treatment of mental health concerns might use the Target Symptom Rating Form (Battle, Imber, Hoen-Saric, Nash, & Frank, 1965), which identifies symptom targets and provides a scale for rating severity. Target symptom rating could easily be adapted for use in other applications.

A more complex method for assessing individual outcomes is Kircsuk and Sherman's (1968) goal attainment scaling methodology, a criterion-referenced approach to describing changes in group members (Roach & Elliott, 2005). After stating a goal, the member determines descriptive criteria for five scale levels, ranging from +2 = "best possible outcome" through 0 = "no change in behavior or performance" to −2 = "worst possible outcome." Ratings for multiple goals can be combined through the application of Kiresuk's pseudo T score formula, yielding overall client growth values that can be averaged across group members to produce an overall evaluation of the group (Kiresuk, Smith, & Cardillo, 1994). Though originally developed for mental health applications, goal attainment scaling has been successfully used in schools to monitor academic growth and behavioral change with children and adolescents (Roach & Elliott, 2005).

A criticism frequently made of these ideographic methods is that goals or complaints are judged on a relative rather than an absolute basis and may ignore standard criteria for adjustment. When students set multiple goals, they are often not independent of one another and may even be stepped goals, with one goal being dependent on another for success.

The Progress Evaluation Scales (Ihilevich & Glesser, 1979), a set of seven empirically supported goals for individual and group counseling and psychotherapy, track progress toward goal attainment based on a continuum of objectively scaled outcomes using standardized definitions. The Progress Evaluation Scales map to the Kiresuk goal attainment scaling format and may be summarized by using Kiresuk's summary formula.

Beyond ideographic or individual outcome assessment measures, group leaders have a wealth of symptom, behavior, and attitude measures from which to choose. For example, a leader planning a group to alleviate test anxiety among high school students might choose a standardized measure of test anxiety, such as the State-Trait Anxiety Inventory, to assess group outcomes. Normed outcome assessment tools provide a way of putting individual group member scores into a broader context.

Descriptions of a multitude of outcome measures for individual and group applications have been provided in many published works (e.g., Antony & Barlow, 2002; Lyons, Howard, O'Mahoney, & Lish, 1997; Ogles, Lambert, & Fields, 2002; Ogles, Lambert, & Masters, 1996), and DeLucia-Waack (1977) has provided a description and discussion of outcome and process evaluation instruments popular among group workers. Table 16.4 lists group work measures related to screening/selection, leader behaviors/skills, group climate, therapeutic factors, and member behavior.

TABLE 16.4   Process and Outcome Measures Used in Group Work

Screening/Selection Measures
Elements (Schutz, 1992)
Group Psychotherapy Evaluation Scale (Van Dyck, 1980)
Group Therapy Survey (Slocum, 1987)
Hill Interaction Matrix (Hill, 1965, 1973)

Leader Behaviors/Skills Measures
Corrective Feedback Self-Efficacy Instrument (Page & Hulse-Killacky, 1999)
Group Counselor Behavior Rating Form (Corey & Corey, 1987)
Group Leader Self-Efficacy Instrument (Page, Pietrzak, & Lewis, 2001)
Leadership Characteristics Inventory (Makuch, 1997)
Skilled Group Counseling Scale (Smaby, Maddux, Torres-Rivera, & Zimmick, 1999)
Trainer Behavior Scale (Bolman, 1971)

Group Climate Measures
Group Climate Questionnaire—Short (MacKenzie, 1983, 1990)
Group Environment Scale (Moos, 1986)

Therapeutic Factors Measures
Critical Incidents Questionnaire (Kivlighan & Goldfine, 1991)
Curative Factors Scale—Revised (Stone, Lewis, & Beck, 1994)
Therapeutic Factors Inventory (Lese & McNair-Semands, 2000)
Therapeutic Factors Scale (Yalom, Tinklenberg, & Gilula, 1968)

Member Behavior Measures
Group Cohesiveness Scale (Budman & Gurman, 1988)
Group Observer Form (Romano & Sullivan, 2000)
Group Sessions Rating Scale (Cooney, Kadden, Litt, & Getter, 1991)
Hill Interaction Matrix (Hill, 1965, 1973)
Individual Group Member Interpersonal Process Scale (Soldz, Budman, Davis, & Demby, 1993)
Interaction Analysis Scale (Bales, 1950)
System for Multiple Level Observation of Groups (SYMLOG) (Bales, Cohen, & Williams, 1979)

Practical Program Evaluation Considerations

To be of practical value, assessment must be connected to real program concerns as well as the core values of the program. Avoid overwhelming the data collectors, focus on only one or several important questions at a time, and always select measures that will yield reliable and valid scores for the purposes under study. Oftentimes, ineffective program outcomes stem from poor or inappropriate measurement rather than faulty programming. Be sure to involve the relevant stakeholders and use a variety of approaches. Perhaps most important, do not reinvent the wheel. Use what you are already doing to generate useful data about program effectiveness. Also, don't be afraid to call on outside experts to consult on the development and evaluation of a program (Vacc, Rhyne-Winkler, & Poidevant, 1993).

It is good advice to start small and build on what is found to work; the methods and goals of individual programs are celebrated, and successes can be shared across programs. This often leads to a cross-pollination effect that yields both diversity of approach and homogeneity of results. In other words, over time, leaders will learn from each other what works and implement these strategies with their own populations after necessary refinements based on the needs of these differing client populations. Different can still be effective.

Aggregated Outcomes

The use of an aggregated hierarchical evaluation system is common in psychoeducational approaches in which there is a defined curriculum, goals, outcomes, and measurable objectives. Aggregation is the combining of results to provide a more global or generalized picture of group performance. While such a practice may deemphasize subgroup or individual performance, aggregation can be a valuable tool when it comes to evaluating how well counseling programs meet higher-level standards or goals. Due to their more abstract or generalized wording, goals (sometimes called standards) are difficult, if not impossible, to directly measure. This is why curriculum development begins with a statement of goals (standards), which are then further described through a series of outcomes (sometimes called competencies). While more specific and well defined, these outcomes are still ordinarily not amenable to direct measurement in the classic sense. Instead, we rely on specific objectives, such as those discussed in the earlier section on "Converting Needs to Program Goals and Objectives." Objectives are written in such specific, measurable terms that everyone (e.g., members, leaders, teachers, parents, administrators, significant others) can tell when an objective has been met. The use of objectives, outcomes, and goals can be conceptualized as an aggregated hierarchical model and is an important way that leaders can demonstrate the effectiveness of a counseling program. Figure 16.3 provides an example of this aggregated hierarchical model.

In Figure 16.3, note the alignment of objectives to outcomes to goals. Objective 1 measures Outcome 1, which is aligned with Goal 1. Likewise, Objective 13 measures Outcome 6, which is aligned with Goal 2. Such a hierarchical structure allows leaders to conclude that meeting the lower-order objectives provides evidence that the higher-order outcomes and goals have been successfully met. For example, assume the leader of a psychoeducational group provides evidence that Objectives 1–6 have been met. By extension, if Objectives 1 and 2 have been met, then Outcome 1 is met. If Objectives 3 and 4 have been met, then Outcome 2 is met. If Objectives 5 and 6 have been met, then Outcome 3 is met. Because Outcomes 1–3 are met, the professional school counselor has provided evidence that Goal 1 is met. Success! In addition, areas of programmatic strength have been identified.

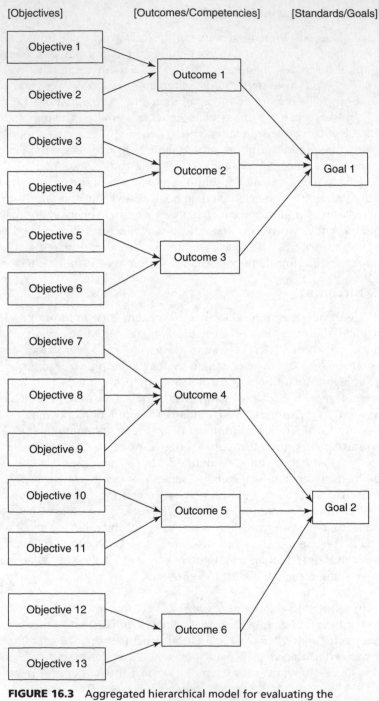

[Objectives]   [Outcomes/Competencies]   [Standards/Goals]

FIGURE 16.3 Aggregated hierarchical model for evaluating the effectiveness of a school counseling program.

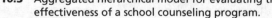

Again referring to Figure 16.3, now consider a second example in which the leader of a psychoeducational group provides evidence that Objectives 7 to 10 have been met but Objectives 11–13 have not been met. By extension, if Objectives 7 to 9 have been met, then Outcome 4 is met. If Objective 10 is met, but Objective 11 is not met, then Outcome 5 is either not met or, more accurately, is only partially met. If Objectives 12 and 13 have not been met, then Outcome 6 is not met. Now, because of some inconsistent results, interpretation is a bit cloudier. It is most appropriate to conclude that Goal 2 is only partially met because Outcome 4 is met, Outcome 5 is partially met, and Outcome 6 is not met. Given the inconsistency in meeting the outcomes, it is inappropriate to conclude that Goal 2 is met; it is equally inappropriate to conclude that Goal 2 is not met. A conclusion of "partially met" identifies the hierarchical set of goals, outcomes, and objectives as a programmatic area in need of improvement or of additional attention to, or revision of, the criteria for successful performance. From these examples, one can see that an aggregated hierarchical model can be a valuable curriculum evaluation method. It also underscores the importance of measurable objectives as the building blocks of an effective developmental curriculum.

Designing Outcome Studies

While any data collected on effectiveness can be helpful, in most instances professional counselors should measure outcome or results by designing a research-type study—not necessarily one that uses a true experimental design with participant randomization but one that yields verifiable, meaningful results through systematic data collection and analysis. The systematic collection of outcome data can yield some evidence that a leader's interventions have had some effect on members. Importantly, a bit of forethought and planning can lead to much more meaningful conclusions. Research studies are typically empirical in nature and involve some control over both how members are assigned to counseling interventions and when and under what circumstances data are collected. Erford (2008a) discussed helpful, easy-to-implement designs, and several of these designs that may be particularly useful to group leaders have been included in Table 16.5.

While a comprehensive treatise of outcome study design is beyond the scope of this book, what follows are some of the relevant points leaders should consider when designing outcome studies. Leaders generally receive an entire course in research that can be useful in this context. The interested reader should consult *Research and Evaluation in Counseling* (Erford, 2008a), a helpful source on research methodology and statistical analysis written specifically for professional counselors.

Answering these questions can help professional counselors determine which research design to use:

1. *Has the treatment already been implemented?* If it has, so much for planning ahead. If the intervention has not already occurred, the leader has many possible options. If the intervention has already occurred, the leader is relegated to a nonexperimental design, probably a case study or static-group comparison design. It is critical to think about outcome assessment in the early stages of planning for a group—and certainly before the group has begun.
2. *Can I randomly assign members to treatment conditions?* If the answer is yes, the leader is in an excellent position because randomly assigning members to the treatment group and to a wait list can lead to very meaningful designs. In fact, control over the random assignment of members is critical to implementing true experimental designs.

TABLE 16.5   Common Designs Used for Outcome Research

Nonexperimental Designs

1.	Pretest–posttest single-group design	O I O
2.	Case study	I O
3.	Static-group comparison	
	group 1	O
	group 2	I O

Quasi-experimental Designs

4.	Two-sample pretest–posttest design	R O
		R I O
5.	Nonequivalent control-group design	O I O
		O O
6.	Time series design	O O O I O O O

True Experimental Designs

7.	Randomized pretest–posttest control-group design	R O I O
		R O O
8.	Randomized posttest-only control-group design	R I O
		R O

Note: R = participants are randomly assigned to groups; I = intervention (implemented treatment or program); O = observation or other data collection method.

If the leader does not have control over the assignment of members, he or she must choose a quasi-experimental or nonexperimental design.

3. *Can I conduct (one or several) pretests, posttests, or both?* Usually, measuring the dependent variable both before (using pretests) and after (using posttests) is desirable, although not always essential.

The answers to these questions will help leaders choose the most useful and powerful design. For example, if the answers to the three questions are no, yes, and yes, respectively, the leader can opt for an experimental design (i.e., designs 7 or 8 in Table 16.5). If the answers are yes, no, and posttest only, the leader is relegated to a nonexperimental design (designs 2 or 3 in Table 16.5). As one can no doubt surmise, outcome studies require some level of planning early on in program development.

Most true experimental designs involve the randomization of participants, which also randomizes various sources of error, allowing for the control of numerous threats to validity. True experimental designs allow causative conclusions to be reached. This is a big advantage when leaders want to know conclusively if their interventions caused significant improvements in members. For example, if a leader wants to know if a group intervention designed to improve the symptoms of depression in members is effective, she could use the randomized pretest–posttest control-group design (design 7 in Table 16.5). She would begin by randomly assigning her members to two optimal-sized groups, designated control and treatment, and by determining a data collection method (e.g., test, observation) to measure an outcome of interest (e.g., anger management skills, social skills). She would then administer the "test" (called the *pretest*) to all participants in both the control and the treatment conditions. Next, she would implement the intervention (e.g., group counseling experience) to the treatment group but not to the control group. (*Note:* Those in the control group might experience nothing [e.g., they might be placed on a wait list], or they might undergo a "placebo" group counseling experience for some issue other than anger management skills or social skills). Upon conclusion of the treatment program or intervention, the group leader would again administer the test (this time called the *posttest*) to members in both groups. She would expect to see no change in the control group members' scores (i.e., she would expect to see no statistically significant difference between their pretest and posttest scores). However, if the group counseling experience is successful, she would expect to see a significant change in the treatment group members' scores (e.g., she would expect their posttest scores to show they had improved the relevant skills).

Of course, the other designs in Table 16.5 also could be used with this or other examples. However, quasi-experimental and nonexperimental designs do not allow group leaders to conclude that the treatment was the "cause" of the changes noted in the participants. Thus, in many ways, results or outcomes from studies with experimental designs are more valuable and powerful. Note that in this example, if randomization of participants is not possible, the same research design can be used, but it will now be considered quasi-experimental (see design 5 from Table 16.5).

Importantly, a lot of thought must be given to the design of the outcome measure used. Often, nonsignificant results are due not to the group work intervention but to the selection of an outcome measure that is not sensitive enough to demonstrate the effect of the treatment. Some outcome measures can be easily obtained because they are a matter of record (e.g., grade point average, number of homework assignments completed) or already exist in published form (e.g., Conners Parent Rating Scale—Revised [CPRS–R], Achenbach System of Empirically Based Assessment [ASEBA], Beck Depression Inventory [BDI–II], Children's Depression Inventory [CDI]).

The number of available outcome measures may be limitless. Still, sometimes group leaders need to design an outcome measure with sufficient sensitivity and direct applicability to the issue being studied (e.g., adjustment to a divorce, body image, social skills, peer self-efficacy). When leaders need to develop an outcome measure from scratch, the basics of scale development covered above in the discussion of needs assessments can be helpful. In addition, Weiss (1998) provided a dozen principles the assessor should consider:

1. Use simple language.
2. Ask only about things that the respondent can be expected to know.
3. Make the questions specific.
4. Define terms that are in any way unclear.
5. Avoid yes–no questions.
6. Avoid double negatives.
7. Don't ask double-barreled questions [e.g., two questions in one].
8. Use wording that has been adopted in the field.
9. Include enough information to jog people's memories or to make them aware of features of a phenomenon they might otherwise overlook.
10. Look for secondhand opinions or ratings only when firsthand information is unavailable.
11. Be sensitive to cultural differences.
12. Learn how to deal with difficult respondent groups. (pp. 140–142).

These principles apply to most types of data collection procedures.

Leaders can use a wide range of data collection procedures, each with advantages and disadvantages. Table 16.6 presents descriptions of several of the methods of data collection most commonly used by leaders.

TABLE 16.6   Common Data Collection Methods

1. *Interviews* of professional school counselors, key personnel, or members of stakeholder groups can provide valuable data. Interviews can be structured, semistructured, or unstructured. Structured interviews present a formal sequence of questions to interviewees with no variation in administration, thus generating clear evidence of strengths and weaknesses. Semistructured interviews combine facets of unstructured and structured approaches. Unstructured formats allow for follow-up and deeper exploration and are commonly used in qualitative studies. Usually, multiple respondents are required for patterns and conclusions to emerge. Face-to-face interviews are generally better than phone interviews, although usually more costly and inconvenient. Careful consideration must be given to question development, and interviewers must guard against introducing bias.

2. *Observations* can also be classified as informal or formal. Informal observations tend to yield anecdotal data through a "look-and-see" approach. Formal or structured observations usually involve a protocol and predetermined procedures for collecting specific types of data during a specified time period. Structured procedures tend to minimize bias. As an example of observation, professional school counselors can be observed implementing a group counseling session by a supervisor or peer.

3. *Written questionnaires, surveys, and rating scales* are usually paper-and-pencil instruments that ask a broad range of open- or closed-ended questions. Questionnaires and rating scales typically ask for factual responses, while surveys generally solicit participant perceptions. By far the greatest weakness of this data collection method is that many participants do not complete or return the instrument (i.e., it has a low return rate). It also requires a certain level of literacy. Few respondents take the time to write lengthy responses, so usually it is best to keep the questions simple and closed-ended, with the opportunity for participants to expand on a response if needed. Multiscaled response formats (e.g., Likert scales) often provide more helpful results than do yes—no questions. E-mailed or online versions of these instruments are becoming more commonly used.

4. *Program records and schedules* are a naturally occurring and helpful source of evaluation data. If stored on a computer in a database format, this kind of data is particularly accessible, and a professional school counselor is well advised to consider this ahead of time when determining how best to maintain electronic records and schedules. Archives should also be kept in good order to facilitate record searches. In particular, professional school counselors should keep previous program improvement documents and outcome study reports.

5. *Standardized and educator-made tests* provide objective measurements of student performance and progress in the academic, career, and personal-social domains. Individual, classroom, and schoolwide tests can be extremely helpful and powerful measures. Tests exist that measure academic achievement, depression, anxiety, substance use, distractibility, career indecision, and myriad other student behaviors. Likewise, professional school counselors can design and develop tests to measure student behaviors and characteristics, much like teachers design tests to measure academic achievement.

6. *Academic performance indicators* may include students' grade point averages or classroom grades, but they also include students' daily work behaviors/habits (e.g., attendance, homework completion, disruptions) and attitudes (e.g., academic self-efficacy, attitude toward school).

7. *Products and portfolios* are real-life examples of performance. A product is anything created by a client (or the professional school counselor) that stemmed from a program standard (e.g., artwork, composition, poster). A portfolio is a collection of exemplary products that can be evaluated to determine the quality of an individual's performance.

Single-Subject Research Design

Leaders do not always have access to members that can be randomly assigned to various experimental conditions. In fact, the majority of leaders need to document the effectiveness of services one group at a time and for widely varying presenting problems. An interesting experimental research design used by practicing group leaders is the single-subject research design (SSRD) (or the single-case research design). SSRD involves the intensive study of a single individual or a single group. This type of study examines member changes over a period of time both before and after exposure to some treatment or intervention. Importantly, the pressure for accountability within schools make SSRDs particularly helpful to leaders as they strive to document outcomes.

SSRDs start by measuring the state of the members before the intervention begins. This is called a baseline (no treatment) and is designated by A. The intervention is designated B. Ordinarily, the condition of each member is observed or measured several times during the baseline phase (A) and several times during the intervention phase (B). A line graph is usually used to display the member's behavioral changes over time. Line graphs are interpreted visually, rather than statistically. The behavior being observed or tracked (i.e., the dependent variable) is displayed on the vertical axis. Scores on a behavior rating scale, number of times a member gets out of his or her seat without permission, and scores on a depression scale, and number of negative self-talk statements are some examples of these observed or tracked behaviors that members may be trying to change. The horizontal axis usually indicates the observation session (i.e., passage of time). Member observations may occur each hour, day, or session, as determined by the leader. Data points indicate the member's score at each time of collection throughout the study, and the slope of the condition line indicates whether the member's condition has changed over time. Figure 16.4 provides a diagram of a commonly used SSRD, the A–B design.

There are numerous types of SSRDs, including the A–B design, A–B–A design, A–B–A–B design, B–A–B design, and multiple-baseline design. The two designs most commonly used by leaders (A–B and A–B–A–B) will be discussed here, but the interested reader should see *Research and Evaluation in Counseling* (Erford, 2008a) for an expanded discussion of SSRDs. The most common, the A–B design, introduces an intervention to the members after a baseline period during which the members act as their own control. In the A–B design, the member is observed or measured for several sessions (the pretreatment baseline phase, A), the intervention is implemented, and the member is observed or measured for several more sessions (the treatment phase, B). The general rule of thumb regarding the number of sessions to measure is this: Keep measuring until a stable pattern emerges, whether the pattern shows the treatment to be effective or not effective. A disadvantage of using the A–B design is that it does not control for extraneous or confounding variables.

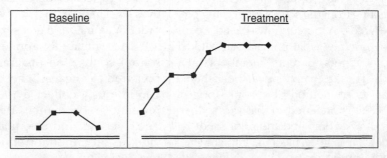

FIGURE 16.4   A–B design.

The A–B–A–B design may minimize the problem of extraneous variables because it includes two baseline periods interspersed with two intervention periods. Initially, the baseline (A) is established, and then treatment (B) is introduced. Once the treatment is shown to have the desired effect, the intervention is withdrawn to collect a second baseline (A). If the members' scores on the dependent variable return to a level of diminished effectiveness, the leader has provided evidence that the intervention was indeed responsible for the changes the members exhibited during the B phase. At that point, the treatment is reintroduced (B), and more observations are taken, the expectation being that a reintroduction of the previously effective treatment will return the members to a more effective condition. The A–B–A–B response pattern provides strong evidence that the intervention, not some extraneous or confounding variable, was responsible for changes in the condition of the members.

Putting It All Together: Working for the Future

The accountability movement in schools points to the need for leaders to focus on process and outcome evaluation. It is more essential than ever before that leaders-in-training, leaders, and researchers work together to establish effective group work practices. In the past, professional school counselors often viewed research as artificial or unnecessary. Such a view is counterproductive. Instead, students, leaders, and researchers must work together— quite literally—becoming collaborators in research and evaluation as well as consumers of research. Such collaboration will significantly improve our understanding of efficient and effective group practices and thereby improve personal practice and member outcomes.

Summary

Accountability involves the demonstration of responsibility for professional actions. Group leaders demonstrate accountability by providing evidence that answers several primary questions. First, what are the needs of the member and stakeholder populations? A needs assessment can be implemented using one of two primary methods. A data-driven needs assessment evaluates real needs demonstrated through derived information. Aggregated results are broken down (disaggregated) so they can be examined at the subgroup level. Such analysis is critical to demonstrate whether all members are benefiting from the school counseling program and services. A perceptions-based needs assessment determines what primary stakeholder groups (e.g., teachers, parents, members) perceive as needs. These perceptions can be gathered through a variety of methods, but some form of quantifiable result is preferred so that various perceived needs can be compared and prioritized.

Second, what is the result of the implemented services? Some argue that process evaluations and outcome studies are the most valuable facets of group work accountability. Data are collected to evaluate actions and interventions so that judgments can be made on the worth or value of services and programs. Often, traditional research designs can yield helpful and authoritative information about program or event quality. Because of the broad-ranging nature of goals and outcomes, leaders attempting to demonstrate the effectiveness of psychoeducational group work interventions may want to use an aggregated hierarchical model in which evidence is collected at the objectives level in order to demonstrate whether higher-order outcomes and goals have been met.

Accountability applies to every facet of a school counseling program. Leaders must be prepared to engage in accountability activities, continuously collect evidence, and report on program performance. Being responsible for one's actions and the quality of services provided is an important ethical and professional responsibility.

CHAPTER 17

Outcome Research in Group Work

BRADLEY T. ERFORD

PREVIEW

Leaders have an ethical responsibility to "use techniques/procedures/modalities that are grounded in theory and/or have an empirical or scientific foundation" (Herlihy & Corey, 2006, p. 39). Research has concluded that group work can affect members in powerful ways. This chapter reviews research on the effectiveness of group work with children and adolescents across a variety of settings, especially in schools.

OUTCOME RESEARCH IN GROUP WORK

Leaders have an ethical responsibility to use effective techniques and processes when working with students (American Counseling Association, 2005; Herlihy & Corey, 2006; Lambert, 1991; Lambert, Masters, & Ogles, 1991). Thus, group leaders must become familiar with current literature on group work effectiveness, commonly known as outcome research.

Ordinarily, outcome research in group work has involved three types of methodology: clinical trials, qualitative reviews, and meta-analytic reviews. Clinical trial studies are very common in the extant literature, typically consisting of a single study of a specific type of treatment or approach. Clinical trials are important and helpful because they use comparison groups (e.g., placebo, wait-list control, alternative treatment), outcome measures, and standardized treatment protocols (Sexton, Whiston, Bleuer & Walz, 1997). Use of such instruments and procedures enhances the replicability of results. However, clinical trials offer only a single result from a single study, and different studies using different methodologies frequently yield inconsistent or even contradictory results. One sees the problems with clinical trials frequently on television news programs. Nearly every day a new study is reported that contradicts previous studies on health, diet, or parenting. Inconsistency in the results of clinical trials can lead to great confusion among professionals and the public. Thus, group leaders are normally better off relying on accumulations and summarizations of numerous research results to inform practice, rather than on a couple of potentially unreliable studies. These accumulations of research can be conducted using either qualitative or quantitative research methodologies, each approach having strengths and weaknesses.

Qualitative analyses of accumulated research studies are probably more commonly employed than are quantitative summarization approaches. Ordinarily, a qualitative approach finds researchers examining and summarizing consistent and meaningful trends and findings across contexts, clients, and studies. Qualitative analyses conducted by content experts can yield reliable and meaningful results, but, due to their subjective nature, biased conclusions sometimes can result from qualitative reviews. Thus, procedural safeguards and criteria must be developed to ensure the robustness and replicability of results (Cooper, 1982; Ellis, 1991).

Meta-analysis is a specific quantitative technique that aggregates the results of numerous clinical trials using a meaningful quantitative index, commonly known as an effect size (ES). For experimental studies (e.g., clinical trials), an ES ordinarily is computed using the formula $[M_e - M_c]/SD_c$ (or some variation of this formula). Basically, this means that an ES is obtained by subtracting the mean of the control group (M_e) from the mean of the experimental group (M_c) and then dividing that difference score by the standard deviation of the control group (SD_c). Thus, an ES is an index score reported in standard deviation units of the control group sample. By extension, the ESs from various comparable studies can then be combined and averaged to yield a result across several or even hundreds of studies. Importantly, this index score is usually weighted according to the sample size, so that larger, more stable sample results are given greater weight than smaller, less stable sample results. To determine the strength of a given ES, it is compared to some criterion-referenced ES range, such as the popular ES range proposed by Cohen (1988). Cohen proposed that an ES of 0 indicates no effect of treatment, ES = .20 indicates a small effect of treatment, ES = .50 indicates a medium effect of treatment, and ES = .80+ indicates a large effect of treatment. Thus, an ES = .60 indicates a medium effect, while an ES of .15 indicates little to no effect.

Another way to interpret ESs is in terms of the number of standard deviations above or below the control group mean a given treatment score lies. For example, an ES of 0 means that the treatment and control group means were the same. Assuming that the variances of the treatment and control group samples are similar, one can conclude that the average client in the treatment group performed no better or no worse than the average participant in the control group. In other words, the treatment had no effect. On the other hand, if ES = .50, this means that the treatment mean was one-half a standard deviation above the mean of the control group. The "medium effect" associated with ES = .50 can also be expressed in terms of a percentile outcome, that is, ES = .50 means that the average client in the treatment group attained a better outcome than 69% of the control group participants (.50 standard deviations above the mean is a percentile rank of about 69). Likewise, ES = 2.00 not only is a large effect (i.e., >.80) but also indicates that the average participant in the treatment group performed better than 98% of the control group participants (2.0 standard deviations above the mean is a percentile rank of 98).

When an empirical study is correlational (usually involving the computation of a Pearson family r), Cohen (1988) suggested interpreting ESs according to the following criterion-referenced interpretive range: $r = .10$ (small), $r = .30$ (medium), $r = .50$ (large). There are many additional formulas for estimating the ES, but the reader of group outcome research will encounter these two indexes most frequently in the extant research.

At this point, it should be clear how meta-analysis can help compensate for methodological problems in some clinical studies by summarizing results across numerous similar studies. This helps to minimize study-specific error and generalize trends and significant results. While meta-analysis has been commonly used in counseling and psychological research, it has its critics (Ioaniddis, Cappelleri, & Lau, 1998; Shadish, 1996; Sharpe, 1997; Sohn, 1997), some of whom conclude that combining numerous studies into a single result simply spreads errors stemming from less well designed studies into better designed studies. At the very least, readers should consider meta-analysis to be a potentially helpful procedure for analyzing robust trends across studies, but they should view results with some caution, as is the case with any research study. With all of this information on clinical trials, qualitative reviews, and meta-analysis as context, we are now ready to explore the literature on research outcomes in group work.

HOW EFFECTIVE IS GROUP WORK?: AN INTRODUCTION TO GROUP OUTCOME RESEARCH

Hundreds of studies over the past half century have explored the effectiveness of group work, and the short answer to the question "How effective is group work?" is "very effective." This conclusion is consistently reached for both children and adults and regardless of whether the reviews of extant literature are qualitative/narrative (Abramowitz, 1976; Bednar & Kaul, 1994; Dagley, Gazda, Eppinger, & Stewart, 1994; Fuhriman & Burlingame, 1994a; Gazda, 1989; Kanas, 1986; Kaul & Bednar, 1986; MacKenzie, 1994, 1995; Orlinsky & Howard, 1986; Sternbarger & Budman, 1996; Toseland & Siporin, 1986; Zimpfer, 1990a) or empirical meta-analyses (Bednar & Kaul, 1994; Burlingame, Fuhriman, & Mosier, 2003; Fuhriman & Burlingame, 1994a, 1994b; Hoag, 1997; Hoag & Burlingame, 1997; Lambert & Bergin, 1994; McDermit, Miller, & Brown, 2001; McRoberts, Burlingame, & Hoag, 1998; Miller & Berman, 1983; Mitte, 2005; Robinson, Berman, & Neimeyer, 1990; Shapiro & Shapiro, 1982; Smith, Glass, & Miller, 1980; Tillitski, 1990; Whiston, Eder, Rahardja, & Tai, 2005).

Bachar (1998) reported that the results of meta-analytic reviews of group counseling outcome studies ordinarily yield ESs of about 0.70 or higher in comparison with control groups and of about 0.40 or higher in comparison with placebos (also see Table 17.1). As explained above, an ES of .70 means that the average member receiving counseling displayed a better outcome than 76% of control group participants (i.e., .70 standard deviations above the mean is a percentile rank of 76). In addition, most studies indicate little or no difference between individual and group counseling treatment effectiveness, although this generalization does not account for the fact that some specific conditions may be better addressed through individual counseling approaches (Hoag & Burlingame, 1997; McRoberts et al., 1998).

Group work has also been demonstrated to be effective with specific client groups experiencing internalizing disorders, such as clients with depression (Scott & Stradling, 1991; Vandervoort & Fuhriman, 1991), eating disorders (Zimpfer, 1990b), Obsessive-Compulsive Disorder (Krone, Himle, & Nesse, 1991), grief (Zimpfer, 1991), and sexual abuse trauma (Alexander, Neimeyer, Follette, Moore, & Harter, 1989; Cahill, Llewelyn, & Pearson, 1991; Winick & Levene, 1992), and there is general agreement that group treatment is both outcome-effective and cost-efficient (Scheidlinger, 1993; Yalom & Leszcz, 2005). In addition, groups have been shown to be effective in addressing externalizing disorders as well as a vast assortment of developmental and clinical issues. For example, Zimpfer offered meaningful reviews of clinical topics of importance to group leaders, including divorce and separation (1990a), bulimia (1990b), and bereavement (1991).

A frequently debated question over the years has been whether group or individual counseling is the more effective approach. In short, group treatment is as effective as individual treatment for most conditions as long as the group treatment is specific to the condition (Fuhriman & Burlingame, 1994a). And sometimes a simultaneous combination of individual and group approaches is most effective, as is likely the case with Borderline Personality Disorder (Slavinsky-Holey, 1983) and eating disorders (Bohanske & Lemberg, 1987; Franko, 1987). It is also essential to realize that some individuals benefit much more from group treatment than do others (Piper, 1994). McRoberts et al. (1998) indicated no significant differences between individual and group counseling interventions when counselor characteristics such as gender, training, and experience and the use of a co-leader/co-therapist were studied.

Table 17.1 provides a summary of some available meta-analyses that are referred to at times throughout this section. The remainder of this review of outcome research on group work effectiveness will focus on two primary areas: (1) process issues and (2) group research with children and adolescents.

TABLE 17.1   Selected Meta-analytic Studies from the Extant Literature on the Effectiveness of Group Work

Source	Outcome Explored	Population	ES
Burlingame, Fuhriman, & Mosier (2003)	Group counseling effectiveness	Heterogeneous*	0.58
Dush, Hirt, & Schroeder (1983)	Group counseling effectiveness	Heterogeneous	0.58
Faith, Wong, & Carpenter (1995)	Group sensitivity training	Heterogeneous	0.62
	Behavioral measures	Heterogeneous	1.03
	Self-report measures	Heterogeneous	0.44
Hoag (1997)	Group counseling effectiveness	Children	0.50
Hoag & Burlingame (1997)	Group treatment	School-aged	0.61
McDermit, Miller, & Brown (2001)	Group therapy for depression	Heterogeneous	1.03
Miller & Berman (1983)	Group counseling effectiveness	Heterogeneous	0.79
Robinson, Berman, & Neimeyer. (1990)	Group counseling effectiveness	Clients with depression	0.84
Shapiro & Shapiro (1982)	Group counseling effectiveness	Heterogeneous	0.89
Smith, Glass, & Miller (1980)	Group counseling effectiveness	Heterogeneous	0.83
Tillitski (1990)	Group counseling effectiveness	Heterogeneous	1.35
Whiston, Eder, Rahardja, & Tai (2005)	Group interventions	School-aged	0.36

* Sample includes children, adolescents, and adults.

PROCESS ISSUES IN GROUP OUTCOME RESEARCH

The process variables in group work can be complex and difficult to isolate and analyze because of the holistic nature of human interaction. Ordinarily, group process variables include facets such as (1) group planning characteristics, (2) group structure, (3) pregroup training, (4) therapeutic factors, (5) leader characteristics, (6) structured group regimens, and (7) outcomes based on different response sources.

Group Effectiveness Related to Group Planning Characteristics

In a fascinating, complex, and comprehensive meta-analysis, McRoberts et al. (1998) found no significant differences based on group size (less than nine or more than nine participants), group type (psychoeducational versus process), or group membership (open versus closed). In addition, McRoberts et al. (1998) reported that group work is more effective than individual counseling when 10 or fewer sessions are conducted, confirming the use of group work as a short-term treatment alternative (Budman, Simeone, Reilly, & Demby, 1994; Burlingame & Fuhriman, 1990). Faith, Wong, and Carpenter (1995) reported larger ESs for larger groups and for groups that meet for a greater number of sessions in their meta-analytic study of sensitivity training groups.

Group Structure and Effectiveness

Gazda (1989) identified a trend favoring the use of more-structured approaches to group work. Structured groups are more leader directed than are process-oriented groups, leading to greater standardization, efficiency, and replicability of the group experience. Rhode and Stockton (1994) reported that a lack of structure leads to client difficulties with interpersonal fears, cognitive distortion, subjective distress, and premature termination, resulting in their suggestion that structure be introduced early in the group process to help define boundaries and build trust.

The use of structured activities to build trust and cohesion has been well documented. Stockton, Rhode, and Haughey (1992) used structured group exercises to build group cohesion at the start of a group experience, while Caple and Cox (1989) found that early structured exercises help to enhance group cohesion at critical points later in the group's life. On the other hand, Lee and Bednar (1977) found that increased structure can lead to lower group cohesion, probably mediated by certain member personality characteristics. Therefore, structured group approaches should be used strategically and always matched with member personalities to enhance effectiveness. This is especially the case when counseling low risk takers because Evensen and Bednar (1978) found that low risk takers evaluate group experiences more negatively as group structure increases. Summing this complexity up quite nicely, Gazda, Ginter, and Horne (2008) concluded that "[t]he interaction between structure, group composition, leader characteristics, and group stage is always complex" (p.85) and deserves great attention in future research efforts.

The Effectiveness of Pregroup Training

Pregroup training involves personal, written, audiotaped, or videotaped procedures meant to prepare group members for entry into the group (Yalom & Leszcz, 2005). Pregroup training has been shown to boost treatment outcome (Hilkey, Wilhelm, & Horne, 1982), interpersonal interactions (Yalom, Houts, Zimberg, & Rand, 1967), and attendance (France & Dugo, 1985).

The Effectiveness of Therapeutic Factors

Therapeutic factors (e.g., cohesion, instillation of hope, altruism, universality) appear to differentially affect different populations and disorders (Kaul & Bednar, 1986) and even at different stages of group development. For example, Kivlighan and Mullison (1988) indicated that universality is very important early on in the group process but less so in later stages, while interpersonal learning is less important early on and gains importance in the later group stages. A study by Butler and Fuhriman (1983) indicated that group members perceive catharsis, interpersonal interaction, and self-understanding to be the most important therapeutic factors, providing evidence of the need for particular attention to these factors from group leaders. In contrast, Shaughnessy and Kivlighan (1995) criticized studies such as these for being too simplistic and, through a cluster analysis, showed that "self-reflective responders" value the triad of therapeutic factors mentioned above but that "broad spectrum responders" (the majority of group participants) actually endorse and benefit from all of Yalom's proposed curative factors.

Effective Leader Characteristics

Related to therapeutic factors, a great deal of the group work literature explores group leadership characteristics and their effect on outcome. Effective leaders have been shown to nurture a sense of hope in group members (Couch & Childers, 1987; Dykeman & Appleton, 1998) and display positive personal characteristics (e.g., positive attitudes, emotionally supportive behaviors) (Combs, Avila, & Purky, 1978; Stockton, Morran, & Velboff, 1987).

The Effectiveness of Structured Group Treatment Regimens

The 1990s produced a significant increase in group treatment protocols targeting specific diagnoses with standardized treatment regimens replicable across members, practitioners, and settings (Fettes & Peters, 1992; Hoag & Burlingame, 1997). For some, this represented a significant advance over the previous process-oriented and generic use of groups for heterogeneous members and presenting problems. In general, there seems to be an outcome advantage to groups using structured, treatment-manual-based approaches to group work. This has occurred concomitantly with the increased demand by health maintenance organizations for group treatment as a more time- and cost-effective delivery system for mental health services. Burlingame et al. (2003) indicated that these two factors, the maturation of the group counseling literature to provide diagnosis- and member-specific group treatments and the efficiency orientation of the current school reform and health-care reform movements, have coalesced to create the current demand for effective and efficient group work leaders.

Outcomes Based on Different Response Sources

Burlingame et al. (2003), in a very interesting meta-analysis of adult outcomes across 111 experimental and quasi-experimental studies, concluded that the source of the outcome report makes a difference in the overall ES. For example, objective sources of member progress yielded an ES of .31, leader report .35, self-report .56, independent rater .73, and significant other report .81. It can be surmised that the more objective the outcome source, the less effective the group treatment. Another way of framing this result could be that group members and those they associate with most frequently (i.e., significant others) may be expressing an element of satisfaction with the group treatment that empowers them to perceive the members as making more progress than do the more objective sources of outcome information.

GROUP OUTCOME RESEARCH WITH CHILDREN AND ADOLESCENTS

Numerous narrative reviews have been conducted on the effectiveness of group work with children and adolescents (e.g., Dagley et al., 1994; Dies & Riester, 1986; Sugar, 1993). Unfortunately, a general conclusion is that the sophistication of the research methodology is inferior to that in the extant literature available for adults. However, a number of meta-analytic studies have been conducted and, collectively, indicate that group work with children and adolescents is effective and as effective as individual counseling (Baer & Nietzel, 1991; Casey & Berman, 1985; Grossman & Hughes, 1992; Prout & DeMartino, 1986; Roberts & Camasso, 1991; Russell, Greenwald, & Shirk, 1991; Shirk & Russell, 1992; Weisz, Weiss, Alicke, & Klotz, 1987). Of course, some studies have pointed to interesting differential effects. For example, Tillitski (1990) indicated that adolescents report better outcomes when treated with group counseling than individual counseling but that children report the opposite effect (i.e., individual treatment is more effective than group work).

In general, group outcome research with the child and adolescent populations falls broadly into the following areas: (1) large-group psychoeducational approaches and (2) small-group approaches addressing developmental and clinical concerns.

The Effectiveness of Large-Group Psychoeducational Approaches With Children and Adolescents

Borders and Drury (1992), in a qualitative review of the literature, found support for classroom guidance activities—a staple of the comprehensive, developmental guidance movement so commonplace in school counseling programs today—but Whiston and Sexton (1998) and Wiggins and Wiggins (1992) found little empirical support for such activities in the experimental literature. In fairness, few high-quality experimental studies existed at the time, and in those that did, more-heartening evidence was available to support guidance activities at the elementary level (Hadley, 1988; Lee, 1993). Still, and to the contrary, several of the more rigorous studies have either found no improvement because of large-group intervention (Laconte, Shaw, & Dunn, 1993) or found less progress than when using individual interventions (Wiggins & Wiggins, 1992). Strein (1988) concluded that 103 of the 344 studies of large-group classroom guidance reviewed reach statistical significance and that the vast majority of the most rigorously controlled studies do not. And, finally, Gosette and O'Brien (1993) found that only 70 of 278 treatment comparisons reviewed support the use of large-group classroom guidance. These results are troubling, given the current emphasis on providing large-group guidance activities in schools, stemming from the comprehensive, developmental guidance movement championed by professional associations such as the American School Counselor Association. Certainly, more and better studies are needed to resolve this controversy.

Small-Group Approaches Addressing Developmental and Clinical Concerns With Children and Adolescents

Most of the counseling research studies involving school students explored the effectiveness of group counseling approaches (Prout & Prout, 1998), although the quality and sophistication of these studies were inferior to those of adult group outcome studies overall (Hoag & Burlingame, 1997). Still, Whiston and Sexton (1998) concluded that group approaches with school-age children are very effective in addressing social skills, discipline, and family adjustment problems. Hoag and Burlingame (1997) reported ESs of .72 for depression, .56 for behavioral disorders, .55 for learning disorders, .53 for children of divorce, and .32 for social problems.

Regarding depression in adolescents, Beeferman and Orvaschel (1994) reported that group counseling is a very effective treatment, with the best results coming from a combination of supportive group processes, cognitive-behavioral interventions, and some behavioral skills training and homework. Reynolds and Coats (1986) showed that relaxation training is just as effective as cognitive-behavioral interventions with adolescent group members. Among high school students, groups focusing on cognitive-behavioral approaches and relaxation appear particularly effective (Bauer, Sapp, & Johnson, 2000; Kiselica, Baker, Thomas, & Reddy, 1994).

Group approaches have been shown to produce positive outcomes for children of divorce in both the short term (Omizo & Omizo, 1988; Pedro-Carroll & Alpert-Gillis, 1997) and the long term (Pedro-Carroll, Sutton, & Wyman, 1999). Group counseling also has been used for many years to treat disruptive behavior disorders in children and adolescents. Braswell (1993) reported cognitive interventions to be especially effective, particularly her structured "think first—act later" procedure.

In general, Whiston (2007) suggested that group approaches with children have ample support in the outcome research literature, while further study of group work effectiveness with high school students is needed, primarily because of methodological issues. This is interesting in light of the general perception that adolescents learn and process best in peer-group interactions. Given that group work is effective with children and adults, it is reasonable to conclude that it is also likely to be effective with adolescents, but group leaders and researchers must collaborate to promote research with this population of students.

PREVENTING HARM IN GROUP WORK

The ethical imperative of nonmaleficence (i.e., do no harm) is a paramount consideration when engaging in group work. Unfortunately, as with any approach to helping, group leaders do acknowledge the possibility that some students may experience treatments that are not just ineffective but also potentially harmful. Kaplan (1982) reported that casualty rates for group interventions vary widely by approach but acknowledged that these rates are no higher than for other types of counseling. Group leaders can prevent harm to members primarily through efficient member screening and effective counselor behaviors.

Efficient Member Screening

Dykeman and Appleton (1998) listed a number of client contraindications for participating in group work: acute self-disclosure fears, Borderline Personality Disorder, extreme interpersonal sensitivity, low anxiety tolerance, low frustration tolerance, low motivation for change, marked emotional lability, paranoia, psychopathy, psychotic thinking, schizophrenia, severe depression, severe impulse control problems, and unstable medical condition. Students with any of these conditions will probably not benefit from group counseling and may lead to ineffective treatment for other group members. That said, a number of research studies have shown group work to be an acceptable and effective treatment for a number of these conditions, such as Borderline Personality Disorder and low motivation for change. Obviously, more research is needed before potential members can be summarily excluded from group counseling or psychotherapy experiences.

Effective Counselor Behaviors

Not surprisingly, Hadley and Strupp (1976) warned that poorly trained or skill-deficient group leaders can be harmful to group members. Obviously, leaders who permit clients with the contraindicated conditions listed in the preceding section to participate in group work risk client harm—and not just to the clients with the contraindicated conditions.

Likewise, Hadley and Strupp (1976) concluded that group leaders with certain personality traits—including absence of genuineness, coldness, excessive need to make people change, excessive unconscious hostility, greed, lack of interest or warmth, lack of self-awareness, narcissism, pessimism, obsessiveness, sadism, and seductiveness—could be harmful to clients. Lieberman, Yalom, and Miles (1973) reported that nearly 50% of all group work casualties are produced by the "aggressive stimulator" leadership style, which involves the leadership characteristics of high stimulus input, intrusiveness, confrontation, and challenge but demonstrating high positive caring. Obviously, group leaders who seek advanced group coursework and quality supervision are better able to increase skills and identify ineffective and harmful personal behavior.

IMPLICATIONS OF THE CURRENT STATE OF THE OUTCOME LITERATURE FOR GROUP WORKERS

While much helpful outcome research has accumulated over the years, much is still needed to help leaders skillfully implement group work. And this is where you, as a member of the next generation of group leaders, can build a better profession. There are three primary ways that group leaders can help: (1) collaborate with researchers, (2) advocate for outcome research funding, and (3) read the outcome literature and practice accordingly.

Collaborate With Researchers

Students and practitioners must collaborate with researchers whenever possible. Students interested in becoming group leaders should volunteer to help professors and other researchers. Research can be a long and intense process, often taking several years to complete a study and publish the results. However, students can provide valuable aid in conducting portions of studies, contributing to the final product. During this process, students will learn valuable practice, research, and evaluation skills. Likewise, practitioners can collaborate with researchers to conduct site-based action research and program evaluation with group members.

One practitioner's results with a handful of members, when combined with the handfuls of member results from other group leaders, can lead to meaningful results. Researchers frequently attempt to coordinate these field trials but struggle for lack of contacts in the field.

Consider making your work site available to researchers so that results can be aggregated across a number of sites. The large populations served by group leaders in schools and community agencies can be particularly useful for outcome research. Students who become active in research studies begin to understand the research process and are more likely to stay active in research after entering the field. Providing access to participants and helping to collect data are the two components of outcome research with which practitioners can be of greatest assistance.

Advocate for Outcome Research Funding

All group leaders must advocate for increased funding for outcome research. Ordinarily, funding for research comes from government agencies, private foundations, universities, and professional organizations (Erford, 2008b). This funding supports researchers in conducting the basic research meant to inform counseling practice and in communicating the resulting information to group leaders. Advocating for research funding by these sources is a professional responsibility that will generate new practice-improving findings—findings that will help group leaders understand how to better help group members meet their goals. This all starts with your advocacy efforts.

Read the Outcome Literature

Group leaders improve the effectiveness of their practice by reading and using the outcome research. In particular, group leaders should peruse the *Journal for Specialists in Group Work* (published by the Association for Specialists in Group Work), *Professional School Counseling* (published by the American School Counselor Association), *Group Dynamics: Theory, Research, and Practice* (published by the American Psychological Association), and the *International Journal of Group Psychotherapy* (published by the American Group Psychotherapy Association). Group leaders can perform an incredibly helpful service to colleagues by passing along helpful resources sifted from the literature.

Summary

Hundreds of studies have explored the effectiveness of various facets of group work. Still, much remains to be learned. This chapter briefly reviewed the extant research literature on group counseling outcomes as it relates to process issues and our work with adolescents and children. While much is already known about group work effectiveness, professional counselors should collaborate with researchers and conduct their own action research and evaluation studies to create new evidence of group counseling outcomes.

Professional counselors should advocate for increased funding for group work research and read and disseminate outcome research on effective group counseling practice to other practitioners.

Accountability applies to every facet of a counseling program. Leaders must be prepared to engage in accountability activities, continuously collect evidence, and report on program performance. Being responsible for one's actions and the quality of services provided is an important ethical and professional responsibility.

REFERENCES

Aasheim, L. L., & Niemann, S. H. (2006). Guidance/psychoeducational groups. In D. Capuzzi & D. Gross (Eds.), *Introduction to group work* (4th ed., pp. 269–294). Denver, CO: Love.

Abramowitz, C. V. (1976). The effectiveness of group psychotherapy with children. *Archives of General Psychiatry, 33,* 320–326.

Adams, K. (1994). *The way of the journal.* Lutherville, MD: Sidran Press.

Addison, J. T. (1992). Urie Bronfenbrenner. *Human Ecology, 20*(2), 16–20.

Agazarian, Y. M. (1997). *Systems-centered therapy for groups.* New York: Guilford Press.

Agazarian, Y. M., & Gantt, S. (2003). Phases of group development: Systems-centered hypotheses and their implications for research and practice. *Group Dynamics: Theory, Research, and Practice, 7,* 238–252.

Akos, P., Goodnough, G. E., & Milsom, A. S. (2004). Preparing school counselors for group work. *Journal for Specialists in Group Work, 29,* 127–136.

Alexander, P. C., Neimeyer, R. A., Follette, V. M., Moore, M. K., & Harter, S. (1989). A comparison of group treatments of women sexually abused as children. *Journal of Consulting and Clinical Psychology, 57,* 479–483.

American Counseling Association. (2005). *ACA code of ethics.* Alexandria, VA: Author.

American Counseling Association Professional Standards Committee. (1991). *Cross-cultural competencies and objectives.* Retrieved December 19, 2005, from www.counseling.org/Content/NavigationMenu/RESOURCES/MULTICULTURALANDDIVERSITYISSUES/Competencies/Competencies.htm

American School Counselor Association. (2004). *Ethical standards for school counselors.* Alexandria, VA: Author.

American School Counselor Association. (2005). *The ASCA national model: A framework for school counseling programs* (2nd ed.). Alexandria, VA: Author.

American School Counselor Association. (2007). *Position statement on group counseling* (Rev.). Alexandria, VA: Author.

Antony, M. M., & Barlow, D. H. (Eds.). (2002). *Handbook of assessment and treatment planning for psychological disorders.* New York: Guilford Press.

Arbuthnott, K. D., Arbuthnott, D. W., & Rossiter, L. (2001). Guided imagery and memory: Implications for psychotherapists. *Journal of Counseling Psychology, 48,* 123–132.

Arman, J. F. (2000). A small group model for working with elementary school children of alcoholics. *Professional School Counseling, 3,* 290–294.

Arman, J. F. (2002). A brief counseling model to increase resiliency of students with mild disabilities. *Journal of Humanistic Counseling, Education and Development, 41,* 120–128.

Asner-Self, K. K., & Feyissa, A. (2002). The use of poetry in psychoeducational groups with multicultural-multilingual clients. *Journal for Specialists in Group Work, 27,* 136–160.

Association for Specialists in Group Work. (1998). *ASGW principles for diversity-competent group workers.* Retrieved November 8, 2005, from www.asgw.org

Association for Specialists in Group Work. (2000). *ASGW professional standards for the training of group workers.* Retrieved February 23, 2006, from www.asgw.org

Association for Specialists in Group Work. (2006). *ASGW purpose.* Retrieved December 21, 2006, from www.asgw.org/purpose.asp

Association for Specialists in Group Work. (2007). *ASGW best practice guidelines.* Retrieved November 17, 2008, from www.asgw.org/best.htm

Axelson, J. A. (1999). *Counseling and development in a multicultural society* (3rd ed.). Pacific Grove, CA: Brooks/Cole.

Baca, L. M., & Koss-Chioino, J. D. (1997). Development of a culturally responsive group counseling model for Mexican American adolescents. *Journal of Multicultural Counseling and Development, 25,* 130–141.

Bachar, E. (1998). Psychotherapy—An active agent: Assessing the effectiveness of psychotherapy and its curative factors. *Israel Journal of Psychiatry and Related Sciences, 35,* 128–135.

Baer, R. A., & Nietzel, M. T. (1991). Cognitive and behavioral treatment of impulsivity in children: A meta-analytic review of the outcome literature. *Journal of Clinical Child Psychology, 20,* 400–412.

Bales, R. F. (1950). *Interaction process analysis: A method for the study of small groups.* Cambridge, MA: Addison-Wesley.

Bales, R. F., Cohen, S. P., & Williams, S. A. (1979). *SYMLOG: A system for the multiple level observation of groups.* New York: Free Press.

Bandura, A. (1989). Social cognitive theory. In R. Vasta (Ed.), *Annals of child development* (Vol. 6, pp. 1–60). Greenwich, CT: Jai Press.

Bandura, A. (1997). *Self-efficacy: The exercise of control.* New York: Freeman.

Barlow, C. A., Blythe, J. A., & Edmonds, M. (1999). *A handbook of interactive exercises for groups.* Needham Heights, MA: Allyn & Bacon.

Battle, C. C., Imber, S. D., Hoen-Saric, R., Nash, C., & Frank, J. D. (1965). Target complaints as criteria of improvement. *American Journal of Psychotherapy, 20,* 184–192.

Bauer, S. R., Sapp, M., & Johnson, D. (2000). Group counseling strategies for rural at-risk high school students. *High School Journal, 83,* 41–50.

Becvar, D. S., & Becvar, R. J. (1996). *Family therapy: A systemic integration* (3rd ed.). Needham Heights, MA: Allyn & Bacon.

Bednar, R. L., & Kaul, T. J. (1994). Experiential group research: Can the cannon fire? In A. E. Bergin & S. L. Garfield (Eds.), *Handbook of psychotherapy and behavior change: An empirical analysis* (4th ed., pp. 631–663). New York: Wiley.

Beeferman, D., & Orvaschel, H. (1994). Group psychotherapy for depressed adolescents: A critical review. *International Journal of Group Psychotherapy, 44,* 463–475.

Bemak, F., & Chung, R. (2004). Teaching multicultural group counseling: Perspectives for a new era. *Journal for Specialists in Group Work, 29,* 31–41.

Bemak, F., Chung, R., & Siroskey-Sabdo, L. A. (2005). Empowerment groups for academic success: An innovative approach to prevent high school failure for at-risk, urban African American girls. *Professional School Counseling, 8,* 377–390.

Berg, R. C., Landreth, G. L., & Fall, K. A. (2006). *Group counseling: Concepts and procedures* (4th ed.). New York: Routledge.

Bergin, J. J. (1993). Small-group counseling. In A. Vernon (Ed.), *Counseling children and adolescents* (pp. 299–332). Denver, CO: Love.

Bernardez, T. (1996). Women's therapy groups as the treatment of choice. In B. DeChant (Ed.), *Women and group psychotherapy: Theory and practice* (pp. 242–262). New York: Guilford Press.

Billow, R. M. (2003). Rebellion in group. *International Journal of Group Psychotherapy, 53,* 331–351.

Bireda, M. R. (2002). *Cultures in conflict: Eliminating racial profiling in school discipline.* Lanham, MD: Scarecrow Press.

Birnbaum, M., & Cicchetti, A. (2000). The power of purposeful sessional endings in each group encounter. *Social Work with Groups, 23,* 37–52.

Birnbaum, M. L., Mason, S. E., & Cicchetti, A. (2002). Impact of purposeful sessional endings on both the group and practitioner. *Social Work with Groups, 25,* 3–19.

Bohanske, J., & Lemberg, R. (1987). An intensive group process–retreat model for the treatment of bulimia. *Group, 11,* 228–237.

Bolman, L. (1971). Some effects of trainers on their T-groups. *Journal of Applied Behavioral Science, 7,* 309–325.

Borders, L. D., & Drury, S. M. (1992). Comprehensive school counseling programs: A review for policymakers and practitioners. *Journal of Counseling and Development, 70,* 487–498.

Bostwick, G. J., Jr. (1987). "Where's Mary?" A review of the group treatment dropout literature. *Social Work with Groups, 10,* 117–132.

Bowman, R. P. (1987a). Small group guidance and counseling in schools: A national survey of school counselors. *School Counselor, 34,* 256–262.

Bowman, R. P. (1987b). Approaches for counseling children through music. *Elementary School Guidance and Counseling, 21,* 284–291.

Bowman, R. P. (1995). Using metaphors as tools for counseling children. *Elementary School Guidance and Counseling, 29,* 206–216.

Bradley, C. (2001). A counseling group for African American adolescent males. *Professional School Counseling, 4,* 370–373.

Bradley, L. J., & Gould, L. J. (1999). Individual counseling: Creative interventions. In A. Vernon (Ed.) *Counseling children and adolescents* (2nd ed., pp. 65–95). Denver, CO: Love.

Brashares, A. (2003). *The sisterhood of the traveling pants.* New York: Delacorte Press.

Braswell, L. (1993). Cognitive-behavior groups for children manifesting ADHD and other disruptive behavior disorders. *Special Services in the Schools, 8,* 91–117.

Brigman, G., & Campbell, C. (2003). Helping students improve academic achievement and school success behavior. *Professional School Counseling, 7,* 91–98.

Brigman, G. A., Webb, L. D., & Campbell, C. (2007). Building skills for school success: Improving the academic and social competence of students. *Professional School Counseling, 10,* 279–288.

Brinson, J., & Lee, C. (1997). Culturally responsive group leadership. In H. Forester-Miller & J. A. Kottler (Eds.), *Issues and challenges for group practitioners* (pp. 43–56). Denver, CO: Love.

Brooke, S. L. (1995). Art therapy: An approach to working with sexual abuse survivors. *Arts in Psychotherapy, 22,* 447–466.

Brown, A., & Mistry, T. (1994). Group work with mixed membership groups: Issues of race and gender. *Social Work with Groups, 17,* 5–21.

Brown, D., & Trusty, J. (2005). School counselors, comprehensive school counseling programs, and academic achievement: Are school counselors promising more than they can deliver? *Professional School Counseling, 9,* 1–8.

Brown, N. W. (2004). *Psychoeducational groups: Process and practice* (2nd ed.). New York: Brunner Routledge.

Brown, N. W. (2006). A group image. In J. L. DeLucia-Waack, K. H. Bridbord, J. S. Kleiner, & A. Nitza (Eds.), *Group work experts share their favorite activities: A guide to choosing, planning, conducting, and processing* (Rev. ed., pp. 65–66). Alexandria, VA: Association for Specialists in Group Work.

Bryan, J. (2005). Fostering educational resilience and academic achievement in urban schools through school–family–community partnerships. *Professional School Counseling, 8,* 219–227.

Budman, S. H., & Gurman, A. S. (1988). *The theory and practice of brief therapy.* New York: Guilford Press.

Budman, S. H., Simeone, P. G., Reilly, R., & Demby, A. (1994). Progress in short-term and time-limited group psychotherapy: Evidence and implications. In A. Fuhriman & G. M. Burlingame (Eds.), *Handbook of group psychotherapy* (pp. 370–415). New York: Wiley.

Burlingame, G. M., & Fuhriman, A. (1990). Time-limited group therapy. *Counseling Psychologist, 18,* 93–118.

Burlingame, G. M., Fuhriman, A., & Mosier, J. (2003). The differential effectiveness of group psychotherapy: A meta-analytic perspective. *Group Dynamics: Theory, Research, and Practice, 7,* 3–12.

Butler, T., & Fuhriman, A. (1983). Curative factors in group therapy: A review of recent literature. *Small Group Behavior, 14,* 131–142.

Cahill, C., Llewelyn, S. P., & Pearson, C. (1991). Treatment of sexual abuse which occurred in childhood: A review. *British Journal of Clinical Psychology, 30,* 1–12.

Campbell, C. A., & Brigman, G. (2005). Closing the achievement gap: A structured approach to group counseling. *Journal for Specialists in Group Work, 30,* 67–82.

Campbell, C., & Dahir, C. A. (1997). *The national standards for school counseling programs.* Alexandria, VA: American School Counselor Association.

Campbell, L., & Page, R. (1993). The therapeutic effects of group process on the behavioral patterns of a drug-addicted group. *Journal of Addictions and Offender Counseling, 13*(2), 34–46.

Caple, R. B., & Cox, P. L. (1989). Relationships among group structure, member expectations, attraction to group and satisfaction with the group experience. *Journal for Specialists in Group Work, 14,* 16–24.

Capuzzi, D., & Gross, D. R. (2002). *Introduction to group counseling* (3rd ed.). Denver, CO: Love.

Carey, J., Dimmitt, C., Kosine, N., & Poynton, T. (2005). *An evidence-based practice approach to school counselor education.* Retrieved February 1, 2008, from www.umass.edu/schoolcounseling/CSCORPowerPoints.htm

Carlson, N. L. (1992). *What if it never stops raining?* New York: Viking Press.

Carrier, J. W., & Haley, M. (2006). Psychotherapy groups. In D. Capuzzi & D. Gross (Eds.), *Introduction to group work* (4th ed.). Denver, CO: Love.

Casey, R. J., & Berman, J. S. (1985). The outcome of psychotherapy with children. *Psychological Bulletin, 98,* 388–400.

Chandy, J. M., Harris, L., Blum, R. W., & Resnick, M. D. (1994). Female adolescents of alcohol misusers: Sexual behaviors. *Journal of Youth and Adolescence, 23,* 695–707.

Chaves, J. (1994). Recent advances in the application of hypnosis to pain management. *American Journal of Clinical Hypnosis, 37,* 117–129.

Chen, M., & Han, Y. S. (2001). Cross-cultural group counseling with Asians: A stage specific interactive approach. *Journal for Specialists in Group Work, 26,* 111–128.

Chen, M., & Rybak, C. J. (2004). *Group leadership skills: Interpersonal process in group counseling and therapy.* Belmont, CA: Brooks/Cole.

Chojnacki, J. T., & Gelberg, S. (1995). The facilitation of a gay/lesbian/bisexual support-therapy group by heterosexual counselors. *Journal of Counseling and Development, 73,* 352–354.

Chrispeels, J., & González, M. (2004). *Do educational programs increase parents' practices at home?: Factors influencing Latino parent involvement.* Cambridge, MA: Harvard Family Research Project.

Clark, A. J. (2002). Scapegoating: Dynamics and interventions in group counseling. *Journal of Counseling and Development, 80,* 271–276.

Cohen, J. (1988). *Statistical power analysis for the behavioral sciences* (2nd ed.). Hillsdale, NJ: Erlbaum.

Combs, A. W., Avila, D. L., & Purky, W. W. (1978). *Helping relationships: Basic concepts for the helping process.* Boston: Allyn & Bacon.

Connors, J. V., & Caple, R. B. (2005). A review of group systems theory. *Journal for Specialists in Group Work, 30,* 93–110.

Conroy, K. (2006). Getting to know you—Now and then. In J. L. DeLucia-Waack, K. H. Bridbord, J. S. Kleiner, & A. Nitza (Eds.), *Group work experts share their favorite activities: A guide to choosing, planning, conducting, and processing* (Rev. ed., pp. 33–36). Alexandria, VA: Association for Specialists in Group Work.

Conyne, R. K. (2006). Agenda setting for a team. In J. L. DeLucia-Waack, K. H. Bridbord, J. S. Kleiner, & A. Nitza (Eds.), *Group work experts share their favorite activities: A guide to choosing, planning, conducting, and processing* (Rev. ed., pp. 170–172). Alexandria, VA: Association for Specialists in Group Work.

Conyne, R. K., Rapin, L. S., & Rand, J. M. (1997). A model for leading task groups. In H. Forester-Miller & J. A. Kottler (Eds.), *Issues and challenges for group practitioners* (pp. 117–132). Denver: Love.

Conyne, R. K., Wilson, F. R., & Tang, M. (2000). Evolving lessons from group work for involvement in China. *Journal for Specialists in Group Work, 25,* 252–268.

Conyne, R. K., Wilson, F. R., & Ward, D. E. (1997). *Comprehensive group work: What it means and how to teach it.* Alexandria, VA: American Counseling Association.

Cook, E. P., Conyne, R. K., Savageau, C., & Tang, M. (2004). The process of ecological counseling. In R. K. Conyne & E. P. Cook (Eds.), *Ecological counseling: An innovative approach to conceptualizing person–environment interaction* (pp. 109–140). Alexandria, VA: American Counseling Association.

Cooney, N. L., Kadden, R. M., Litt, M. D., & Getter, H. (1991). Matching alcoholics to coping skills or interactional therapies: Two-year follow-up results. *Journal of Consulting and Clinical Psychology, 59,* 598–601.

Cooper, H. M. (1982). Scientific guidelines for conducting integrative research reviews. *Review of Educational Research, 52,* 291–302.

Corey, G. (1981). *Manual for theory and practice of group counseling.* Monterey, CA: Brooks/Cole.

Corey, G. (1995). *Group counseling.* Pacific Grove, CA: Brooks/Cole.

Corey, G. (2004). *Theory and practice of group counseling* (6th ed.). Belmont, CA: Thomson Brooks/Cole.

Corey, G. (2007). *Theory and practice of group counseling* (7th ed.). Belmont, CA: Thomson Brooks/Cole.

Corey, G., Corey, M. S., Callahan, P., & Russell, J. M. (2004). *Group techniques* (3rd ed.). Belmont, CA: Thomson Brooks/Cole.

Corey, G., Williams, G. T., & Moline, M. E. (1995). Ethical and legal issues in group counseling. *Ethics and Behavior, 5,* 161–183.

Corey, M. S., & Corey, G. (1987). *Group counseling: Process and practice* (3rd ed.). Monterey, CA: Brooks/Cole.

Corey, M. S., & Corey, G. (2006). *Groups: Process and practice* (7th ed.). Belmont, CA: Thomson Brooks/Cole.

Cottone, R. R., & Tarvydas, V. M. (2007). *Ethical and professional issues in counseling* (3rd ed.). Upper Saddle River, NJ: Pearson Merrill Prentice Hall.

Couch, R. D., & Childers, J. H. (1987). Leadership strategies for instilling and maintaining hope in group counseling. *Journal for Specialists in Group Work, 12,* 138–143.

Council for Accreditation of Counseling and Related Educational Programs. (2009). *2009 standards.* Retrieved February 23, 2007, from www.cacrep.org/2009Standards.html

Cuadraz, G. (1996). Experiences of multiple marginality: A case study of Chicana scholarship women. In

C. Turner, M. Garcia, A. Nora, & L. Rendon (Eds.), *Racial and ethnic diversity in higher education* (pp. 210–222). Needham Heights, MA: Simon & Schuster.

Cupal, D., & Brewer, B. (2001). Effects of relaxation and guided imagery on knee strength, re-injury anxiety, and pain following anterior cruciate ligament reconstruction. *Rehabilitation Psychology, 46,* 28–43.

Dagley, J.C., Gazda, G. M., Eppinger, S. J., & Stewart, F. A. (1994). Group psychotherapy research with children, preadolescents, and adolescents. In A. Fuhriman & G. M. Burlingame (Eds.), *Handbook of group psychotherapy* (pp. 340–369). New York: Wiley.

Darongkamas, J., Madden, S., Swarbrick, P., & Evans, B. (1995). The touchstone therapy group for women survivors of child sexual abuse. *Journal of Mental Health, 4*(1), 17–30.

Davis, L., Galinsky, M., & Schopler, J. (1995). RAP: A framework for leadership of multiracial groups. *Social Work, 40,* 155–165.

Day-Vines, N., Moore-Thomas, C., & Hines, E. (2005). Processing culturally relevant bibliotherapeutic selections with African American adolescents. *Counseling Interviewer, 38*(1), 13–18.

Day-Vines, N., Wood, S., Grothaus, T., Craigen, L., Holman, A., Dotson-Blake, K., et al. (2007). Broaching the subjects of race, ethnicity, and culture during the counseling process. *Journal of Counseling and Development, 85,* 401–409.

Dayton, T. (2005). The use of psychodrama in dealing with grief and addiction-related loss and trauma. *Journal of Group Psychotherapy, Psychodrama, and Sociometry, 39,* 15–34.

Deck, M., Scarborough. J., Sferrazza, M., & Estill, D. (1999). Serving students with disabilities: Perspectives of three school counselors. *Intervention in School and Clinic, 34,* 150–155.

DeLucia-Waack, J. L. (1977). Measuring the effectiveness of group work: A review and analysis of process and outcome measures. *Journal for Specialists in Group Work, 22,* 277–293.

DeLucia-Waack, J. L. (1996a). Multiculturalism is inherent in all group work. *Journal for Specialists in Group Work, 21,* 218–223.

DeLucia-Waack, J. L. (1996b). Multicultural group counseling: Addressing diversity to facilitate universality and self-understanding. In J. L. DeLucia-Waack (Ed.), *Multicultural counseling competencies: Implications for training and practice* (pp. 157–195). Alexandria, VA: American Counseling Association.

DeLucia-Waack, J. L. (1997). What do we need to know about group work: A call for future research and theory. *Journal for Specialists in Group Work, 22,* 146–148.

DeLucia-Waack, J. L. (1999, August). *Group psychotherapy and outcome measures.* Paper presented at the annual convention of the American Psychological Association, Boston.

DeLucia-Waack, J. L. (2000). Effective group work in the schools. *Journal for Specialists in Group Work, 25,* 131–132.

DeLucia-Waack, J. L. (2001). *Using music in children of divorce groups: A session-by-session manual for counselors.* Alexandria, VA: American Counseling Association.

DeLucia-Waack, J. L. (2006). *Leading psychoeducational groups for children and adolescents.* Thousand Oaks, CA: Sage.

DeLucia-Waack, J. L., Bridbord, K. H., Kleiner, J. S., & Nitza, A. (Eds.). (2006). *Group work experts share their favorite activities: A guide to choosing, planning, conducting, and processing* (Rev. ed.). Alexandria, VA: Association for Specialists in Group Work.

DeLucia-Waack, J. L., & Donigian, J. (2003). *The practice of multicultural group work: Visions and perspectives from the field.* Belmont, CA: Brooks/Cole.

DeLucia-Waack, J. L., Gerrity, D. A., Kalodner, C. R., & Riva, M. T. (Eds.). (2004). *Handbook of group counseling and psychotherapy.* Thousand Oaks, CA: Sage.

Denny, J. M. (1977). Techniques for individual and group art therapy. In E. Ulman & P. Dachninger (Eds.), *Art therapy: In theory and practice* (2nd ed., pp. 132–149). New York: Schocken Books.

DeRoma, V. M., Root, L. P., & Battle, J. V. (2003). Pretraining in group process skills: Impact on anger and anxiety in combat veterans. *Journal for Specialists in Group Work, 28,* 339–354.

deYoung, M., & Corbin, B. A. (1994). Helping early adolescents tell: A guided exercise for trauma-focused sexual abuse treatment groups. *Child Welfare, 73,* 144–154.

Dick, B., Lessler, K., & Whiteside, J. (1980). A developmental framework for co-therapy. *International Journal of Group Psychotherapy, 30,* 273–285.

Dies, R. R., & Riester, A. E. (1986). Research on child group psychotherapy: Present status and future directions. In A. E. Riester & I. A. Kraft (Eds.), *Child group psychotherapy: Future tense* (pp. 173–220). Madison, WI: International University Press.

Donigian, J., & Hulse-Killacky, D. (1999). *Critical incidents in group therapy* (2nd ed.). Boston: Brooks/Cole Wadsworth.

Donigian, J., & Malnati, R. (1997). *Systemic group therapy: A triadic model*. Pacific Grove, CA: Brooks/Cole.

Dossick, J., & Shea, E. (1988). *Creative therapy: 52 exercises for groups*. Sarasota, FL: Professional Resources Press.

Dossick, J., & Shea, E. (1990). *Creative therapy II: 52 more exercises for groups*. Sarasota, FL: Professional Resources Press.

Dossick, J., & Shea, E. (1995). *Creative therapy III: 52 exercises for groups*. Sarasota, FL: Professional Resources Press.

Downing, N. E., & Walker, M. E. (1987). A psycho-educational group for adult children of alcoholics. *Journal of Counseling and Development, 65,* 440–442.

Duch, B. J., Groh, S. E., & Allen, D. E. (Eds.). (2001). *The power of problem-based learning*. Sterling, VA: Stylus.

Dush, D. M., Hirt, M. L., & Schroeder, H. (1983). Self-statement modification with adults: A meta-analysis. *Psychological Bulletin, 94,* 408–422.

Dye, H. A. (1968). *Fundamental group procedures for school counselors*. Boston: Houghton Mifflin.

Dykeman, C., & Appleton, V. E. (1998). Group counseling: The efficacy of group work. In D. Capuzzi & D. R. Gross (Eds.), *Introduction to group counseling* (2nd ed., pp. 101–129). Denver, CO: Love.

Edelwich, J., & Brodsky, A. (1992). *Group counseling for the resistant client*. New York: Lexington Books.

Ellis, A. E. (1997). REBT and its application to group therapy. In J. Yankura & W. Dryden (Eds.), *special applications of REBT: A therapist's casebook* (pp. 131–161). New York: Springer.

Ellis, A. E. (2001a). *Feeling better, getting better, and staying better*. Atascadero, CA: Impact.

Ellis, A. E. (2001b). *Overcoming destructive beliefs, feelings, and behaviors*. Amherst, NY: Prometheus Books.

Ellis, M. V. (1991). Conducting and reporting integrative research reviews: Accumulating scientific knowledge. *Counselor Education and Supervision, 30,* 225–237.

Erford, B. T. (2000). *The mutual storytelling game CD*. Alexandria, VA: American Counseling Association Foundation.

Erford, B. T. (2001). *Stressbuster relaxation exercise* (Vol. 1). Alexandria, VA: American Counseling Association.

Erford, B. T. (2007a). Accountability. In B. T. Erford (Ed.), *Transforming the school counseling profession* (2nd ed., pp. 236–278). Columbus, OH: Pearson Merrill Prentice Hall.

Erford, B. T. (Ed.). (2007b). *Assessment for counselors*. Boston: Houghton Mifflin/Lahaska Press.

Erford, B. T. (Ed.). (2008a). *Research and evaluation in counseling*. Boston: Houghton Mifflin/Lahaska Press.

Erford, B. T. (Ed.). (2008b). *Professional school counseling: A handbook of theories, programs, and practices* (2nd ed.). Austin, TX: Pro-Ed.

Erford, B. T., Eaves, S. H., Bryant, E., & Young, K. (2010). *35 techniques every counselor should know*. Columbus, OH: Pearson Merrill Prentice Hall.

Erford, B. T., House, R., & Martin, P. (2007). Transforming the school counseling profession. In B. T. Erford (Ed.), *Transforming the school counseling profession* (2nd ed., pp. 1–15). Columbus, OH: Pearson Merrill Prentice Hall.

Erford, B. T., & McKechnie, J. A. (2002a). *Psychotherapeutic game: Self-concept*. Alexandria, VA: American Counseling Association.

Erford, B. T., & McKechnie, J. A. (2002b). *psychotherapeutic game: Perfectionism*. Alexandria, VA: American Counseling Association.

Erford, B. T., & McKechnie, J. A. (2002c). *Psychotherapeutic game: The AD/HD game*. Alexandria, VA: American Counseling Association.

Erford, B. T., Schlerf, L. L., & Carr, L. L. (2000a). *Psychotherapeutic game: Good grief*. Alexandria, VA: American Counseling Association.

Erford, B. T., Schlerf, L. L., & Carr, L. L. (2000b). *Psychotherapeutic game: Anger management*. Alexandria, VA: American Counseling Association.

Erford, B. T., Schlerf, L. L., & Carr, L. L. (2000c). *Psychotherapeutic game: Conflict resolution*. Alexandria, VA: American Counseling Association.

Erford, B. T., Schlerf, L. L., & Carr, L. L. (2000d). *Psychotherapeutic game: Changing families*. Alexandria, VA: American Counseling Association.

Erford, B. T., Schlerf, L. L., & Carr, L. L. (2001a). *Psychotherapeutic game: Studying skillfully*. Alexandria, VA: American Counseling Association.

Erford, B. T., Schlerf, L. L., & Carr, L. L. (2001b). *Psychotherapeutic game: Social skills*. Alexandria, VA: American Counseling Association.

Erford, B. T., Schlerf, L. L., & Carr, L. L. (2001c). *Psychotherapeutic game: Solving problems*. Alexandria, VA: American Counseling Association.

Evensen, E. P., & Bednar, R. L. (1978). Effects of specific cognitive and behavioral structure on early group behavior and atmosphere. *Journal of Counseling Psychology, 25*, 66–75.

Faith, M. S., Wong, F. Y., & Carpenter, K. M. (1995). Group sensitivity training: Update, meta-analysis, and recommendations. *Journal of Counseling Psychology, 42*, 390–399.

Fall, K. A., & Wejnert, T. J. (2005). Co-leader stages of development: An application of Tuckman and Jensen (1977). *Journal for Specialists in Group Work, 30*, 309–327.

Ferencik, B. M. (1992). The helping process in group therapy: A review and discussion. *Group, 16*, 113–124.

Fettes, P. A., & Peters, J. M. (1992). A meta-analysis of group treatments for bulimia nervosa. *International Journal of Eating Disorders, 11*(2), 97–110.

Flores, P. J. (1997). *Group psychotherapy with addicted populations: An integration of twelve-step and psychodynamic therapy* (2nd ed.). Binghamton, NY: Haworth Press.

Forester-Miller, H., & Davis, T. (2002). *A practitioner's guide to ethical decision-making* (2nd ed.). Alexandria, VA: American Counseling Association.

Foster, E. S. (1989). *Energizers and icebreakers for all ages and stages*. Minneapolis, MN: Educational Media.

France, D. L., & Dugo, J. M. (1985). Pretherapy orientation as preparation for psychotherapy groups. *Psychotherapy, 22*, 256–261.

Frank, J. D., & Frank, J. P. (1991). *Persuasion and healing: A comparative study of psychotherapy* (3rd ed.). Baltimore, MD: Johns Hopkins University Press.

Frankel, F., Myatt, R., Cantwell, D. P., & Feinberg, D. T. (1997). Parent-assisted transfer of children's social skills training: Effects on children with and without Attention-deficit Hyperactivity Disorder. *Journal of the Academy of Child and Adolescent Psychiatry, 36*, 1056–1064.

Franko, D. L. (1987). Anorexia nervosa and bulimia: A self-help group. *Small Group Behavior, 18*, 398–407.

Fuhriman, A., & Burlingame, G. M. (1990). Consistency of matter: A comparative analysis of individual and group process variables. *Counseling Psychologist, 18*, 6–63.

Fuhriman, A., & Burlingame, G. M. (1994a). Group psychotherapy: Research and practice. In A. Fuhriman & G. M. Burlingame (Eds.), *Handbook of group psychotherapy* (pp. 3–40). New York: Wiley.

Fuhriman, A., & Burlingame, G. M. (Eds.). (1994b). *Handbook of group psychotherapy*. New York: Wiley.

Furr, S. R. (2000). Structuring the group experience: A format for designing psychoeducational groups. *Journal for Specialists in Group Work, 25*, 29–49.

Gallogly, V., & Levine, B. (1979). Co-therapy. In B. Levine (Ed.), *Group psychotherapy: Practice and development* (pp. 296–305). Prospect Heights, IL: Waveland.

Gardner, R. A. (1971). *Therapeutic communication with children: The mutual storytelling technique*. New York: Jason Aronson.

Gardner, R. A. (1975). *Psychotherapeutic approaches to the resistant child*. New York: Jason Aronson.

Gazda, G. M. (1989). *Group counseling: A developmental approach* (4th ed.). Boston: Allyn & Bacon.

Gazda, G. M., Ginter, E. J., & Horne, A. M. (2008). *Group counseling and group psychotherapy: Theory and application* (2nd ed.). Boston: Allyn & Bacon.

George, R., & Dustin, D. (1988). *Group counseling: Theory and practice*. Englewood Cliffs, NJ: Prentice Hall.

Geroski, A. M., & Kraus, K. L. (2002). Process and content in school psychoeducational groups: Either, both, or none? *Journal for Specialists in Group Work, 27*, 233–245.

Gillam, L. (2006). What a character! In J. L. DeLucia-Waack, K. H. Bridbord, J. S. Kleiner, & A. Nitza (Eds.), *Group work experts share their favorite activities: A guide to choosing, planning, conducting, and processing* (Rev. ed., pp. 41–43). Alexandria, VA: Association for Specialists in Group Work.

Gladding, S. T. (1997). The creative arts in groups. In H. Forester-Miller & J. A. Kottler (Eds.), *Issues and challenges for group practitioners* (pp. 81–99). Denver, CO: Love.

Gladding, S. T. (1998). *Family therapy: History, theory, and practice* (2nd ed.). Upper Saddle River, NJ: Prentice-Hall.

Gladding, S. T. (2008). *Group work: A counseling specialty* (4th ed.). Upper Saddle River, NJ: Pearson Merrill Prentice Hall.

Glass, J. S., & Benshoff, J. M. (1999). PARS: A processing model for beginning group leaders. *Journal for Specialists in Group Work, 24,* 15–26.

Glasser, W. (1969). *Schools without failure.* New York: Harper & Row.

Glasser, W. (1986). *Control theory in the classroom.* New York: Harper & Row.

Glasser, W. (1999). *Choice theory: A new psychology of personal freedom.* New York: Harper Collins.

Gloria, A. M. (1999). Apoyando estudiantes Chicana: Therapeutic factors in Chicana college student support groups. *Journal for Specialists in Group Work, 24,* 246–259.

Glover, G. J. (1994). The hero child in the alcoholic home: Recommendations for counselors. *School Counselor, 41,* 185–190.

Gonsalkorale, W. (1996). The use of hypnosis in medicine: The possible pathways involved. *European Journal of Gastroenterology and Hepatology, 8,* 520–524.

Gosette, R. L., & O'Brien, R. M. (1993). Efficacy of rational-emotive therapy (RET) with children: A critical re-appraisal. *Journal of Behavioral Therapy and Experimental Psychiatry, 24,* 15–25.

Goulding, R. L., & Goulding, M. M. (1991). An intimate model for co-therapy. In B. Roller & V. Nelson (Eds.), *The art of co-therapy* (pp. 189–209). New York: Guilford Press.

Graham, K., Annis, H. M., & Brett, P. J. (1996). A controlled field trial of group versus individual cognitive-behavioral training for relapse prevention. *Addiction, 91,* 1127–1139.

Grayson, E. S. (1993). *Short-term group counseling.* Arlington, VA: American Correctional Association.

Greenberg, K. R. (2003). *Group counseling in K–12 schools.* Boston: Allyn & Bacon.

Grossman, P. B., & Hughes, J. N. (1992). Self-control interventions with internalizing disorders: A review and analysis. *School Psychology Review, 21,* 229–245.

Grothe, R. (2002). *More building assets together: 130 group activities for helping youth succeed.* Minneapolis, MN: Search Institute.

Guth, L. (2006). Getting to know each other. In J. L. DeLucia-Waack, K. H. Bridbord, J. S. Kleiner, & A. Nitza (Eds.), *Group work experts share their favorite activities: A guide to choosing, planning, conducting, and processing* (Rev. ed., pp. 44–46).

Alexandria, VA: Association for Specialists in Group Work.

Gutierrez, L. M. (1990). Working with women of color: An empowerment perspective. *Social Work, 3,* 150–153.

Hadley, H. R. (1988). Improving reading scores through a self-esteem intervention program. *Elementary School Guidance and Counseling, 22,* 248–252.

Hadley, S. W., & Strupp, H. H. (1976). Contemporary views of negative effects in psychotherapy. *Archives of General Psychiatry, 33,* 1291–1302.

Halbur, D. (2006). Ball in play. In J. L. DeLucia-Waack, K. H. Bridbord, J. S. Kleiner, & A. Nitza (Eds.), *Group work experts share their favorite activities: A guide to choosing, planning, conducting, and processing* (Rev. ed., pp. 47–48). Alexandria, VA: Association for Specialists in Group Work.

Haley, J. (1987). *Problem-solving therapy* (2nd ed.). San Francisco: Jossey-Bass.

Harman, M., & Armsworth, M. (1995). Personality adjustment in college students with a parent perceived as alcoholic or nonalcoholic. *Journal of Counseling and Development, 73,* 459–462.

Hawkins, D. (1993). Group psychotherapy with gay men and lesbians. In H. I. Kaplan & B. J. Sadock (Eds.), *Comprehensive group psychotherapy* (3rd ed., pp. 506–515). Baltimore, MD: Williams & Wilkins.

Hawkins, D. A., & Lautz, J. (2005). *State of college admission.* Retrieved December 12, 2007, from www.nacacnet.org/NR/rdonlyres/AF40D947-D5B0-4199-A032-5C7A3C5D0F49/0/SoCA_Web.pdf

Hayes, B. (2006). More or less. In J. L. DeLucia-Waack, K. H. Bridbord, J. S. Kleiner, & A. Nitza (Eds.), *Group work experts share their favorite activities: A guide to choosing, planning, conducting, and processing* (Rev. ed., pp. 49–50). Alexandria, VA: Association for Specialists in Group Work.

Hayes, R. (2006). Why are we meeting like this? In J. L. DeLucia-Waack, K. H. Bridbord, J. S. Kleiner, & A. Nitza (Eds.), *Group work experts share their favorite activities: A guide to choosing, planning, conducting, and processing* (Rev. ed., pp. 51–53). Alexandria, VA: Association for Specialists in Group Work.

Herder, D., & Redner, L. (1991). The treatment of childhood sexual trauma in chronically mentally ill adults. *Health and Social Work, 16,* 50–58.

Herlihy, B., & Corey, G. (2006). *Ethical standards casebook* (6th ed.). Alexandria, VA: American Counseling Association.

Herman, J. L., & Schatzow, E. (1984). Time-limited group therapy for women with a history of incest. *International Journal of Group Psychotherapy, 34,* 605–621.

Herr, E. L., & Erford, B. T. (2007). Historical roots and future issues. In B. T. Erford (Ed.), *Transforming the school counseling profession* (2nd ed., pp. 13–37). Columbus, OH: Pearson Merrill Prentice Hall.

Hilkey, J., Wilhelm, C., & Horne, A. (1982). Comparative effectiveness of videotape pretraining versus no pretraining on selected process and outcome variables in group therapy. *Psychological Reports, 50,* 1151–1159.

Hill, W. F. (1956). *HIM: Hill Interaction Matrix.* Los Angeles: University of Southern California, Youth Services Center.

Hill, W. F. (1965). *Hill Interaction Matrix.* Los Angeles: University of Southern California.

Hill, W. F. (1966). *Hill Interaction Matrix (HIM) monograph.* Los Angeles: University of Southern California, Youth Studies Center.

Hill, W. F. (1973). Hill Interaction Matrix (HIM) conceptual framework for understanding groups. In J. W. Pfeiffer & J. E. Jones (Eds.), *The 1973 annual handbook for group facilitators* (pp. 159–176). San Diego, CA: University Associates.

Hines, P. L., & Fields, T. H. (2002). Pregroup screening issues for school counselors. *Journal for Specialists in Group Work, 27,* 358–376.

Hoag, M. J. (1997). Evaluating the effectiveness of child and adolescent group psychotherapy: A meta-analytic review. *Dissertation Abstracts International, 57* (7-B), 4709.

Hoag, M. J., & Burlingame, G. M. (1997). Evaluating the effectiveness of child and adolescent group treatment: A meta-analytic review. *Journal of Clinical Child Psychology, 26,* 234–246.

Hobday, A., & Ollier, K. (1999). *Creative therapy with children and adolescents.* Atascadero, CA: Impact.

Hoff, B. (1982). *The Tao of Pooh.* London: Mandarin.

Holmes, S. E., & Kivlighan, D. M. (2000). Comparison of therapeutic factors in group and individual treatment processes. *Journal of Counseling Psychology, 47,* 478–484.

Horne, A., Nitza, A., Dobias, B., Jolliff, D., & Voors, W. (2008). *Connectedness is key: Using group process and peer influence to reduce relational aggression in high schools.* Manuscript in preparation.

Hoskins, M. (1985, April). *Therapeutic fairy tales.* Paper presented at the annual meeting of the National Association of Poetry Therapy, Chicago.

House, R. M., & Hayes, R. L. (2002). School counselors: Becoming key players in school reform. *Professional School Counseling, 5,* 249–256.

Hulse-Killacky, D. (2006). The names activity. In J. L. DeLucia-Waack, K. H. Bridbord, J. S. Kleiner, & A. Nitza (Eds.), *Group work experts share their favorite activities: A guide to choosing, planning, conducting, and processing* (Rev. ed., pp. 54–55). Alexandria, VA: Association for Specialists in Group Work.

Hulse-Killacky, D., Killacky, J., & Donigian, J. (2001). *Making task groups work in your world.* Upper Saddle River, NJ: Merrill Prentice Hall.

Hulse-Killacky, D., Kraus, K. L., & Schumacher, R. A. (1999). Visual conceptualizations of meetings: A group work design. *Journal for Specialists in Group Work, 24,* 113–124.

Hutchins, M. (2006). A what? In J. L. DeLucia-Waack, K. H. Bridbord, J. S. Kleiner, & A. Nitza (Eds.), *Group work experts share their favorite activities: A guide to choosing, planning, conducting, and processing* (Rev. ed., pp. 79–84). Alexandria, VA: Association for Specialists in Group Work.

Ihilevich, D., & Glesser, G. C. (1979). *A manual for the Progress Evaluation Scales.* Shiawasse, MI: Community Mental Health Services Board.

Ioaniddis, J. P. A., Cappelleri, J. C., & Lau, J. (1998). Issues in comparisons between meta-analysis and large trials. *Journal of the American Medical Association, 279,* 1089–1093.

Issacs, M. L. (2003). Data-driven decision making: The engine of accountability. *Professional School Counseling, 6,* 288–295.

Ivey, A. E., Pedersen, P. B., & Ivey, M. B. (2001). *Intentional group counseling: A microskills approach.* Belmont, CA: Wadsworth.

Jacobs, E. E., Masson, R. L., & Harvill, R. L. (2006). *Group counseling: Strategies and skills* (5th ed.). Belmont, CA: Thomson Brooks/Cole.

Johnson, D. W., & Johnson, F. P. (2006). *Joining together: Group theory and group skills* (9th ed.). Boston: Allyn & Bacon.

Johnson, I. H., Torres, J. S., Coleman, V. D., & Smith, M. C. (1995). Issues and strategies in leading culturally diverse counseling groups. *Journal for Specialists in Group Work, 20,* 143–150.

Kaduson, H., & Schaefer, C. (Eds.). (1997). *101 favorite play therapy techniques*. North Bergen, NJ: Jason Aronson.

Kahn, B. B. (1999). Art therapy with adolescents: Making it work for school counselors. *Professional School Counseling, 2*, 291–298.

Kanas, N. (1986). Group psychotherapy with schizophrenics: A review of controlled studies. *International Journal of Group Psychotherapy, 36*, 339–351.

Kaplan, R. E. (1982). The dynamics of injury in encounter groups: Power, splitting, and the mismanagement of resistance. *International Journal of Group Psychotherapy, 32*, 163–187.

Kaul, T. J., & Bednar, R. L. (1986). Experiential group research: Results, questions, and suggestions. In S. L. Garfield & A. E. Bergin (Eds.), *Handbook of psychotherapy and behavior change* (2nd ed., pp. 671–714). New York: Wiley.

Kaul, T. J., & Bednar, R. L. (1994). Experiential group research: Can the cannon fire? In S. Garfield & A. Bergin (Eds.), *Handbook for psychotherapy and behavioral change: An empirical analysis* (4th ed., pp. 201–203). New York: Wiley.

Keene, M., & Erford, B. T. (2007). *Group activities: Firing up for performance*. Columbus, OH: Pearson Merrill Prentice Hall.

Kim, B., Omizo, M., & D'Andrea, M. (1998). The effects of culturally consonant group counseling on the self-esteem and internal locus of control orientation among Native American adolescents. *Journal for Specialists in Group Work, 23*, 143–163.

Kiresuk, T. J., Smith, A., & Cardillo, J. (1994). *Goal attainment scaling: Applications, theory and measurement*. Hillsdale, NJ: Erlbaum.

Kiresuk, T. J., & Sherman, R. E. (1968). Goal attainment scaling: A general method for evaluating comprehensive mental health programs. *Community Mental Health Journal, 4*, 443–453.

Kiselica, M. S., Baker, S. B., Thomas, R. N., & Reddy, S. (1994). Effects of stress inoculation training on anxiety, stress, and academic performance among adolescents. *Journal of Counseling Psychology, 41*, 335–342.

Kivlighan, D. M., & Goldfine, D. C. (1991). Endorsement of therapeutic factors as a function of stage of group development and participant interpersonal attitudes. *Journal of Counseling Psychology, 38*, 150–158.

Kivlighan, D. M., & Mullison, D. (1988). Participants' perceptions of therapeutic factors in group counseling: The role of interpersonal style and stage of group development. *Small Group Behavior, 19*, 452–468.

Klein, T. J. B. (2001). Predicting team performance: Testing a model in a field setting. *Journal for Specialists in Group Work, 26*, 185–197.

Kline, W. B. (2003). *Interactive group counseling and therapy*. Upper Saddle River, NJ: Merrill Prentice Hall.

Kolko, D. J., Loar, L. L., & Sturnick, D. (1990). Inpatient social cognitive skills training groups with conduct disordered and attention deficit disordered children. *Journal of Child Psychology and Psychiatry and Allied Disciplines, 31*, 737–748.

Kottler, J. A. (2001). *Learning group leadership: An experiential approach*. Boston: Allyn & Bacon.

Kottman, T. (1995). *Partners in play: An Adlerian approach to play therapy*. Alexandria, VA: American Counseling Association.

Krone, K. R., Himle, J. A., & Neese, R. M. (1991). A standardized behavioral group treatment program for Obsessive-Compulsive Disorder: Preliminary outcomes. *Behavior Research and Therapy, 29*, 627–631.

Kupersmidt, J. B., & Coie, J. D. (1990). Preadolescent peer status, aggression, and school adjustment as predictors of externalizing problems in adolescence. *Child Development, 61*, 1350–1362.

L'Abate, L. (1999). Programmed distance writing in therapy with acting-out adolescents. In C. Schaefer (Ed.), *Innovative psychotherapy techniques in child and adolescent therapy* (2nd ed., pp. 108–157). New York: Wiley.

Laconte, M. A., Shaw, D., & Dunn, I. (1993). The effects of a rational-emotive affective education program for high-risk middle school students. *Psychology in the Schools, 30*, 274–281.

Lambert, M. J. (1991). Introduction to psychotherapy research. In L. E. Beutler & M. Crago (Eds.), *Psychotherapy research: An international review of programmatic studies* (pp. 1–23). Washington, DC: American Psychological Association.

Lambert, M. J., & Bergin, A. E. (1994). The effectiveness of psychotherapy. In A. E. Bergin & S. L. Garfield (Eds.), *Handbook of psychotherapy and behavior change* (3rd ed., pp. 143–189). New York: Wiley.

Lambert, M. J., Masters, K. S., & Ogles, B. M. (1991). Outcome research in counseling. In C. E. Watkins & L. J. Schneider (Eds.), *Research in counseling* (pp. 51–83). Hillsdale, NJ: Erlbaum.

Lazerson, J. S., & Zilbach, J. J. (1993). Gender issues in group psychotherapy. In H. I. Kaplan & B. J. Sadock (Eds.), *Comprehensive group psychotherapy* (3rd ed., pp. 682–693). Baltimore, MD: Williams & Wilkins.

Lee, C. C. (1995). Group work for a new millennium. *Together, 24,* 4.

Lee, F., & Bednar, R. L. (1977). Effects of group structure and risk taking disposition on group behavior, attitudes, and atmosphere. *Journal of Counseling Psychology, 24,* 191–199.

Lee, R. S. (1993). Effects of classroom guidance on student achievement. *Elementary School Guidance and Counseling, 27,* 163–171.

Leong, F. T. L. (1992). Guidelines for minimizing premature termination among Asian American clients in group counseling. *Journal for Specialists in Group Work, 17,* 218–228.

Lese, K. L., & McNair-Semands, R. R. (2000). The Therapeutic Factors Inventory: Development of the scale. *Group, 24,* 303–317.

Lieberman, M., Yalom, I., & Miles, M. (1973). *Encounter groups: First facts.* New York: Basic Books.

Linde, L. E. (2007). Ethical, legal, and professional issues in school counseling. In B. T. Erford (Ed.), *Transforming the school counseling profession* (2nd ed., pp. 51–73). Columbus, OH: Pearson Merrill Prentice Hall.

Line, B. Y., & Cooper, A. (2002). Group therapy: Essential component for success with sexually acting out problems among men. *Sexual Addiction and Compulsivity, 9,* 15–32.

Livneh, H., Wilson, L., & Pullo, R. (2004). Group counseling for people with physical disabilities. *Focus on Exceptional Children, 36*(6), 1–18.

Loesch, L. C., & Ritchie, M. H. (2004). *The accountable school counselor.* Austin, TX: Pro-Ed.

Lopez, J. (1991). Group work as a protective factor for immigrant youth. *Social Work with Groups, 14,* 29–42.

Lothstein, L. M. (1978). The group psychotherapy dropout phenomenon revisited. *American Journal of Psychiatry, 135,* 1492–1495.

Luft, J. (1984). *Group processes: An introduction to group dynamics* (3rd ed.). Palo Alto, CA: Mayfield.

Lyons, J. S., Howard, K. I., O'Mahoney, M. T., & Lish, J. D. (1997). *The measurement and management of clinical outcomes in mental health.* New York: Wiley.

MacKenzie, K. R. (1983). The clinical application of a group climate measure. In R. R. Dies & K. R. MacKenzie (Eds.), *Advances in group psychotherapy: Integrating research and practice* (pp. 159–170). New York: International Universities Press.

MacKenzie, K. R. (1990). *Introduction to time limited group psychotherapy.* Washington, DC: American Psychiatric Press.

MacKenzie, K. R. (1994). Where is here and when is now? The adaptational challenge of mental health reform for group psychotherapy. *International Journal of Group Psychotherapy, 44,* 407–428.

MacKenzie, K. R. (1995). Rationale for group psychotherapy in managed care. In K. R. MacKenzie (Ed.), *Effective use of group psychotherapy in managed care* (pp. 1–26). Washington, DC: American Psychiatric Press.

Makuch, L. (1997). *Measuring dimensions of counseling and therapeutic group leadership style: Development of a leadership characteristics inventory.* Unpublished doctoral dissertation, Indiana University.

Maples, M. F. (1992). STEAMWORK: An effective approach to team-building. *Journal for Specialists in Group Work, 17,* 144–150.

Marbley, A. F. (2004). His eye is on the sparrow: A counselor of color's perception of facilitating groups with predominately White members. *Journal for Specialists in Group Work, 29,* 247–258.

Marotta, S. A., & Asner, K. K. (1999). Group psychotherapy for women with a history of incest: The research base. *Journal of Counseling and Development, 77,* 315–323.

McClellan, R. (1994). *The healing forces of music: History, theory, and practice.* Rockport, MA: Element.

McClure, B. (1998). *Putting a new spin on groups: The science of chaos.* Mahwah, NJ: Erlbaum.

McCourt, F. (2005). *Teacher man.* New York: Scribner.

McDermit, W., Miller, I. W., & Brown, R. A. (2001). The efficacy of group psychotherapy for depression: A meta-analysis and review of the empirical research. *Clinical Psychology: Science and Practice, 8,* 98–116.

McLeod, P. L., & Kettner-Polley, R. B. (2004). Contributions of psychodynamic theories to understanding small groups. *Small Group Research, 35,* 333–361.

McRoberts, C., Burlingame, G. M., & Hoag, M. J. (1998). Comparative efficacy of individual and group psychotherapy: A meta-analytic perspective. *Group Dynamics: Theory, Research, and Practice, 2,* 101–117.

Merta, R. J. (1995). Group work: Multicultural perspectives. In J. G. Ponterotto, J. M. Casas, L. Suzuki, & C. M. Alexander (Eds.), *Handbook of multicultural counseling* (pp. 567–585). Thousand Oaks, CA: Sage.

Miller, R. C., & Berman, J. S. (1983). The efficacy of cognitive behavior therapies: A quantitative review of the research evidence. *Psychological Bulletin, 94,* 39–53.

Miller, W. R., & Rollnick, S. (2002). *Motivational interviewing: Preparing people for change* (2nd ed.). New York: Guilford Press.

Mills, J. C., & Crowley, R. J. (1986). *Therapeutic metaphors for children and the child within.* New York: Brunner/Mazel.

Mitchell, N. A., & Bryan, J. (2007). School–family–community partnerships: Strategies for school counselors working with Caribbean immigrant families. *Professional School Counseling, 10,* 399–409.

Mitte, K. (2005). Meta-analysis of cognitive-behavioral treatments for Generalized Anxiety Disorder: A comparison with pharmacotherapy. *Psychological Bulletin, 131,* 785–795.

Monfredo, M. G. (1992). *Seneca Falls inheritance.* New York: Penguin Group.

Moos, R. H. (1986). *Group Environment Scale manual.* Palo Alto, CA: Consulting Psychologists Press.

Moos, R., Finney, J. W., & Maude-Griffin, P. (1993). The social climate of self-help and mutual support groups: Assessing group implementation, process, and outcome. In B. S. McCrady & W. R. Miller (Eds.), *Research on Alcoholics Anonymous: Opportunities and alternatives* (pp. 251–274). Piscataway, NJ: Rutgers University, Center of Studies on Alcohol.

Morganett, R. (1990). *Skills for living: Group counseling activities for young adolescents.* Champaign, IL: Research Press.

Morganett, R. S. (1994). *Skills for living: Group counseling activities for children.* Champaign, IL: Research Press.

Morran, D. K., Stockton, R., Cline, R. J., & Teed, C. (1998). Facilitating feedback exchange in groups: Leader interventions. *Journal for Specialists in Group Work, 23,* 257–268.

Mosak, H. H. (2000). Adlerian psychotherapy. In R. J. Corsini & D. Wedding (Eds.), *Current psychotherapies* (6th ed., pp. 54–98). Itasca, IL: Peacock.

Mullen, B., Johnson, C., & Salas, E. (1991). Productivity loss in brainstorming groups: A meta-analytic review. *Basic and Applied Social Psychology, 12,* 3–23.

Muro, J. J., & Kottman, T. (1995). *Guidance and counseling in the elementary and middle schools.* Madison, WI: Brown & Benchmark.

Murphy, J. J. (1997). *Solution-focused counseling in middle and high schools.* Alexandria, VA: American Counseling Association.

Myrick, R. D. (2003). Accountability: Counselors count. *Professional School Counseling, 6,* 174–179.

Myrick, R. D., & Myrick, L. S. (1993). Guided imagery: From mystical to practical. *Elementary School Guidance and Counseling, 28,* 62–70.

National Board for Certified Counselors. (2005). *Code of ethics.* Retrieved December 19, 2007, from www.counselingexam.com/nce/resource/code.html

Nelson-Jones, R. (1992). *Group leadership: A training approach.* Pacific Grove, CA: Brooks/Cole.

Newbauer, J. F., & Hess, S. W. (1994). Treating sex offenders and survivors conjointly: Gender issues with adolescent boys. *Journal for Specialists in Group Work, 19,* 129–136.

Newcomb, N. S. (1994). Music: A powerful resource for the elementary school counselor. *Elementary School Guidance and Counseling, 29,* 150–155.

Newsome, D., & Gladding, S. (2007). Counseling individuals and groups in schools. In B. T. Erford (Ed.), *Transforming the school counseling profession* (2nd ed., pp. 209–230). Upper Saddle River, NJ: Merrill Prentice Hall.

Nichols, M. P., & Schwartz, R. C. (1998). *Family therapy: Concepts and methods* (4th ed.). Boston: Allyn & Bacon.

Nikitina, A. (2004). *Goal setting guide.* Retrieved January 16, 2006, from www.goal-setting-guide.com/smart-goals.html

Nitsun, M. (1996). *The anti-group: Destructive forces in the group and their creative potential.* New York: Routledge.

Oaklander, V. (1999). Group play therapy from a Gestalt perspective. In D. S. Sweeney & L. E.

Homeyer (Eds.), *The handbook of group play therapy: How to do it, how it works, whom its best for.* New York: Jossey-Bass.

Ogles, B. M., Lambert, M. J., & Fields, S. A. (2002). *Essentials of outcome assessment.* New York: Wiley.

Ogles, B. M., Lambert, M. J., & Masters, K. S. (1996). *Assessing outcome in clinical practice.* Boston: Allyn & Bacon.

Ohlsen, M. M. (1970). *Group counseling.* New York: Holt, Rinehart & Winston.

Ohlsen, M. M., Horne, A. M., & Lawe, C. F. (1988). *Group counseling* (3rd ed.). New York: Holt, Rinehart & Winston.

O'Leary, E. O., Sheedy, G., O'Sullivan, K., & Thoresen, C. (2001). Cork older adult intervention project: Outcomes of a Gestalt Therapy group with older adults. *Counseling Psychology Quarterly, 16,* 131–143.

Omizo, M. M., & Omizo, S. A. (1988). The effects of participation in group counseling on self-esteem and locus of control among adolescents from divorced families. *School Counselor, 16,* 54–60.

Orlinsky, D. E., & Howard, K. I. (1986). Process and outcome in psychotherapy. In S. L. Garfield & A. E. Bergin (Eds.), *Handbook of psychotherapy and behavior change* (2nd ed., pp. 361–381). New York: Wiley.

Ormont, L. R. (1984). The leader's role in dealing with aggression in groups. *International Journal of Group Psychotherapy, 34,* 553–572.

Ormont, L. R. (1988). The leader's role in resolving resistances to intimacy in the group setting. *International Journal of Group Psychotherapy, 38,* 29–45.

Orton, G. L. (1997). *Strategies for counseling with children and their parents.* Pacific Grove, CA: Brooks/Cole.

Pack-Brown, S. P., & Braun, C. (2003). *Ethics in a multicultural context.* Thousand Oaks, CA: Sage.

Page, B. J., & Hulse-Killacky, D. (1999). Development and validation of the Corrective Feedback Self-Efficacy Instrument. *Journal for Specialists in Group Work, 24,* 37–54.

Page, B. J., Pietrzak, D. R., & Lewis, T. F. (2001). Development of the group leader self-efficacy instrument. *Journal for Specialists in Group Work, 26,* 168–184.

Paisley, P. O., & McMahon, H. G. (2001). School counseling for the 21st century: Challenges and opportunities. *Professional School Counseling, 5,* 106–115.

Paivio, S. C., & Greenberg, L. S. (1995). Resolving "unfinished business": Efficacy of experiential therapy using empty-chair dialogue. *Journal of Consulting and Clinical Psychology, 63,* 419–425.

Parr, G., Haberstroh, S., & Kottler, J. (2000). Interactive journal writing as an adjunct in group work. *Journal for Specialists in Group Work, 25,* 229–241.

Pearson, V. (1991). Western theory, Eastern practice: Social group work in Hong Kong. *Social Work with Groups, 14,* 45–58.

Peck, H. L., Bray, M. A., & Kehle, T. J. (2003). Relaxation and guided imagery: A school-based intervention for children with asthma. *Psychology in the Schools, 40,* 657–675.

Pedro-Carroll, J. L., & Alpert-Gillis, L. J. (1997). Preventive interventions for children of divorce: A developmental model for 5 and 6 year old children. *Journal of Primary Prevention, 18,* 5–23.

Pedro-Carroll, J. L., Sutton, S. E., & Wyman, P. A. (1999). A two-year follow-up of a preventive intervention for young children of divorce. *School Psychology Review, 28,* 467–476.

Petrocelli, J. V. (2002). Effectiveness of group cognitive-behavioral therapy for general symptomology: A meta-analysis. *Journal for Specialists in Group Work, 27,* 95–115.

Piercy, F. P., & Sprenkle, D. H. (1986). Family therapy theory building: An integrative training approach. In F. P. Piercy (Ed.), *Family therapy education and supervision* (pp. 5–14). New York: Haworth.

Piper, W. E. (1994). Client variables. In A. Fuhriman & G. Burlingame (Eds.), *Handbook of group psychotherapy* (pp. 83–113). New York: Wiley.

Pollio, D. (2002). The evidenced based group worker. *Social Work with Groups, 25*(4), 57–70.

Posthuma, B. W. (2002). *Small groups in counseling and therapy: Process and leadership* (4th ed.). Boston: Allyn & Bacon.

Prochaska, J. O., & DiClemente, C. C. (1982). Transtheoretical therapy: Toward a more integrative model of change. *Psychotherapy: Theory, Research, and Practice, 19,* 276–288.

Prout, H. T., & DeMartino, R. A. (1986). A meta-analysis of school-based studies of psychotherapy. *Journal of School Psychology, 24,* 285–292.

Prout, S. M., & Prout, H. T. (1998). A meta-analysis of school-based studies of counseling and psychotherapy: An update. *Journal of School Psychology, 36,* 121–136.

Ragsdale, S., & Taylor, A. (2007). *Great group games: 175 boredom-busting, zero-prep team builders for all ages*. Minneapolis, MN: Search Institute.

Rapin, L. (2006). Your place in the group. In J. L. DeLucia-Waack, K. H. Bridbord, J. S. Kleiner, & A. Nitza (Eds.), *Group work experts share their favorite activities: A guide to choosing, planning, conducting, and processing* (Rev. ed., pp. 88–89). Alexandria, VA: Association for Specialists in Group Work.

Rapin, L. S., & Conyne, R. K. (1999). Best practices in group counseling. In J. P. Trotzer (Ed.), *The counselor and the group: Integrating theory, training, and practice* (pp. 253–276). Philadelphia: Accelerated Development.

Raskin, N. J., & Rogers, C. R. (1989). Person-centered therapy. In R. J. Corsini & D. Wedding (Eds.), *Current psychotherapies* (4th ed., pp. 155–194). Itasca, IL: Peacock.

Remley, T. P., & Herlihy, B. (2005). *Ethical, legal, and professional issues in counseling* (2nd ed.). Upper Saddle River, NJ: Prentice Hall.

Reynolds, W. M., & Coats, K. I. (1986). A comparison of cognitive-behavioral therapy and relaxation training for the treatment of depression in adolescents. *Journal of Counseling and Clinical Psychology, 54,* 653–660.

Rhode, R. I., & Stockton, R. (1994). Group structure: A review. *Journal of Group Psychotherapy, Psychodrama, and Sociometry, 46,* 151–158.

Riddle, J., & Bergin, J. J. (1997). Effects of group counseling on the self-concept of children of alcoholics. *Elementary School Guidance and Counseling, 31,* 192–201.

Riordan, R. J. (1996). Scriptotherapy: Therapeutic writing as a counseling adjunct. *Journal of Counseling and Development, 74,* 263–269.

Ripley, V. V., & Goodnough, G. E. (2001). Planning and implementing group counseling in a high school. *Professional School Counseling, 5,* 62–65.

Rittenhouse, J. (1997). Feminist principles in survivor's groups: Out-of-group contact. *Journal for Specialists in Group Work, 22,* 111–119.

Roach, A. T., & Elliott, S. N. (2005). Goal attainment scaling: An efficient and effective approach to monitoring student progress. *Teaching Exceptional Children, 37*(4), 8–17.

Roberts, A. R., & Camasso, M. J. (1991). The effects of juvenile offender treatment programs on recidivism: A meta-analysis of 46 studies. *Notre Dame Journal of Law, Ethics, and Public Policy, 5,* 421–441.

Robinson, K. E. (1994). Addressing the needs of gay and lesbian students: The school counselor's role. *School Counselor, 41,* 326–332.

Robinson, L. A., Berman, J. S., & Neimeyer, R. A. (1990). Psychotherapy for the treatment of depression: A comprehensive review of controlled outcome research. *Psychological Bulletin, 108,* 30–49.

Roller, B., & Nelson, V. (1991). *The art of co-therapy: How therapists work together*. New York: Guilford Press.

Romano, J. L., & Sullivan, B. A. (2000). Simulated group counseling for group work training: A four-year research study of group development. *Journal for Specialists in Group Work, 25,* 366–375.

Rosenbaum, M. (1983). Co-therapy. In H. I. Kaplan & B. J. Sadock (Eds.), *Comprehensive group psychotherapy* (2nd ed., pp. 167–173). Baltimore, MD: Williams & Wilkins.

Ross, M., & Berger, R. (1996). Effects of stress inoculation training on athletes' post-surgical pain and rehabilitation after orthopedic injury. *Journal of Consulting and Clinical Psychology, 64,* 406–410.

Rotheram-Borus, M. J., Bickford, B., & Milburn, N. G. (2001). Implementing a classroom-based social skills training program in middle childhood. *Journal of Educational and Psychological Consultation, 12*(2), 91–111.

Russell, L. (1992). Comparisons of cognitive, music, and imagery techniques on anxiety reduction with university students. *Journal of College Student Development, 33,* 516–523.

Russell, R. L., Greenwald, S., & Shirk, S. R. (1991). Language change in child psychotherapy: A meta-analytic review. *Journal of Consulting and Clinical Psychology, 59,* 916–919.

Rybak, C. J., & Brown, B. M. (1997). Group conflict: Communication patterns and group development. *Journal for Specialists in Group Work, 22,* 31–42.

Salazar, C. F. (2006). Conceptualizing multiple identities and multiple oppressions in clients' lives. *Counseling and Human Development, 39,* 1–18.

Scheidlinger, S. (1993). The small healing group—A historical overview. *Psychotherapy, 32,* 657–668.

Schein, E. H. (1969). *Process consultation: Its role in organization development*. Reading, MA: Addison-Wesley.

Schindler, V. P. (1999). Group effectiveness in improving social interaction skills. *Psychiatric Rehabilitation Journal, 22,* 349–354.

Schmidt, J. J. (2003). *Counseling in schools: Essential services and comprehensive programs* (4th ed.). Boston: Allyn & Bacon.

Schoenholtz-Read, J. (1996). Sex-role issues: Mixed gender therapy groups as the treatment of choice. In B. DeChant (Ed.), *Women and group psychotherapy: Theory and practice* (pp. 223–241). New York: Guilford Press

Schoettle, U. C. (1980). Guided imagery: A tool in child psychotherapy. *American Journal of Psychotherapy, 34,* 220–227.

Schreier, S., & Kalter, N. (1990). School-based developmental facilitation groups for children of divorce. *Social Work in Education, 90*(13), 58–67.

Schutz, W. (1966). *The interpersonal underworld.* Palo Alto, CA: Science & Behavior Books.

Schutz, W. (1992). Beyond FIRO–B—Three new theory derived measures—element b: behavior, element f: feelings, element s: self. *Psychological Reports, 70,* 915–937.

Scott, M. J., & Stradling, S. G. (1991). The cognitive-behavioral approach with depressed clients. *British Journal of Social Work, 21,* 533–544.

Search Institute. (2004). *Building assets is elementary: Group activities for helping kids ages 8–12 succeed.* Minneapolis, MN: Author.

Sears, J. T. (1991). Helping students understand and accept sexual diversity. *Educational Leadership, 49,* 54–56.

Seefeldt, R. W., & Lyon, M. A. (1992). Personality characteristics of adult children of alcoholics. *Journal of Counseling and Development, 70,* 588–594.

Seligman, L. (2001). *Systems, strategies, and skills of counseling and psychotherapy.* Upper Saddle River, NJ: Merrill Prentice Hall.

Sexton, T. L., Whiston, S. C., Bleuer, J. C., & Walz, G. R. (1997). *Integrating outcome research into counseling practice and training.* Alexandria, VA: American Counseling Association.

Shadish, W. R. (1996). Meta-analysis and the exploration of causal mediating processes: A primer of examples, methods, and issues. *Psychological Methods, 1,* 47–65.

Shapiro, D. A., & Shapiro, D. (1982). Meta-analysis of comparative therapy outcome studies: A replication and refinement. *Psychological Bulletin, 92,* 581–604.

Sharpe, D. (1997). Of apples and oranges, file drawers and garbage. Why validity issues in meta-analysis will not go away. *Clinical Psychology Review, 17,* 881–901.

Shaughnessy, P., & Kivlighan, D. M. (1995). Using group participants' perceptions of therapeutic factors to form client typologies. *Small Group Research, 26,* 250–268.

Shechtman, Z. (2004). Group counseling and psychotherapy with children and adolescents: Current practice and research. In J. L. DeLucia-Waack, D. A. Gerrity, C. R. Kalodner, & M. T. Riva (Eds.), *Handbook of group counseling and psychotherapy* (pp. 429–444). Thousand Oaks, CA: Sage

Shechtman, Z., & Pastor, R. (2005). Cognitive-behavioral and humanistic group treatment for children with learning disabilities: A comparison of outcomes and process. *Journal of Counseling Psychology, 52,* 322–336.

Shirk, S. R., & Russell, R. L. (1992). A reevaluation of child therapy effectiveness. *Journal of American Academy of Child and Adolescent Psychiatry, 31,* 703–709.

Shulman, L. (1992). *The skills of helping individuals, families and groups.* Itasca, IL: Peacock.

Sim, L., Whiteside, S. P., Dittner, C. A., & Mellon, M. (2006). Effectiveness of a social skills training program with school age children: Transition to the clinical setting. *Journal of Child and Family Studies, 15,* 408–417.

Simon, A., & Agazarian, Y. (1974). Sequential Analysis of Verbal Interaction (SAVI). In A. E. Simon & G. Boyer (Eds.), *Mirrors for behavior III: An anthology of observation instruments* (pp. 541–543). Philadelphia: Humanizing Learning Program, Research for Better Schools.

Sister Hazel. (2000). *Change your mind.* On *Fortress* [CD]. New York: Universal Records.

Slavinsky-Holey, N. (1983). Combining homogeneous group psychotherapies for borderline conditions. *International Journal of Group Psychotherapy, 33,* 297–312.

Slocum, Y. S. (1987). A survey of expectations about group therapy among clinical and non-clinical populations. *International Journal of Group Psychotherapy, 37,* 39–54.

Smaby, M. H., Maddux, C. D., Torres-Rivera, E., & Zimmick, R. (1999). A study of the effects of a skills-based versus a conventional group counseling training program. *Journal for Specialists in Group Work, 24,* 152–163.

Smead, R. (1995). *Skills and techniques for group work with children and adolescents.* Champaign, IL: Research Press.

Smead, R. (2000). *Skills and techniques for group work with young adolescents* (Vol. 2). Champaign, IL: Research Press.

Smith, M. L., Glass, G. V., & Miller, T. I. (1980). *The benefits of psychotherapy.* Baltimore, MD: Johns Hopkins University Press.

Sohn, D. (1997). Questions for meta-analysis. *Psychological Reports, 81,* 3–15.

Soldz, S., Budman, S., Davis, M., & Demby, A. (1993). Beyond the interpersonal circumplex in group psychotherapy: The structure and relationship to outcome of the individual group member interpersonal process scale. *Journal of Clinical Psychology, 49,* 551–563.

Sommers-Flanagan, J., & Sommers-Flanagan, R. (1997). *Tough kids, cool counseling.* Alexandria, VA: American Counseling Association.

Sonnenshein-Schneider, M., & Baird, K. L. (1980, October). Group counseling children of divorce in the elementary schools: Understanding process and technique. *Personnel and Guidance Journal, 50,* 88–91.

Sonstegard, M. A. (1998). The theory and practice of Adlerian group counseling and psychotherapy. *Journal of Individual Psychology, 54,* 217–250.

Sonstegard, M. A., & Bitter, J. R. (2004). *Adlerian group counseling and therapy.* New York: Brunner-Routledge.

Spitz, H. I., & Spitz, S. T. (1999). *A pragmatic approach to group psychotherapy.* Philadelphia: Brunner/Mazel.

Steen, S. (2007). *Linking social skills, learning behaviors, and social skills through group work: An exploratory study.* Unpublished manuscript.

Steen, S., & Bemak, F. (2007). *Group work with high school students at risk of school failure: A pilot study.* Manuscript submitted for publication.

Steen, S., & Kaffenberger, C. J. (2007). Integrating academic interventions into group counseling with elementary students. *Professional School Counseling, 10,* 516–519.

Sternbarger, B. N., & Budman, S. H. (1996). Group psychotherapy and managed behavioral care: Current trends and future challenges. *International Journal of Group Psychotherapy, 46,* 297–309.

Stockton, R., Morran, D. K., & Nitza, A. G. (2000). Processing group events: A conceptual map for leaders. *Journal for Specialists in Group Work, 25,* 343–355.

Stockton, R., Morran, D. K., & Velboff, P. (1987). Leadership of therapeutic small groups. *Journal of Group Psychotherapy, Psychodrama, and Sociometry, 39,* 157–165.

Stockton, R., Rhode, R. I., & Haughey, J. (1992). The effects of structured group exercises on cohesion, engagement, avoidance, and conflict. *Small Group Research, 23,* 155–168.

Stone, L. A., & Bradley, F. O. (1994). *Foundations of elementary and middle school counseling.* White Plains, NY: Longman.

Stone, M. H., Lewis, C. M., & Beck, A. P. (1994). The structure of Yalom's Curative Factors Scale. *International Journal of Group Psychotherapy, 44,* 239–245.

Strein, W. (1988). Classroom-based elementary school affective education programs: A critical review. *Psychology in the Schools, 25,* 288–296.

Stuart, O. (1992). Race and disability: Just a double oppression? *Disability, Handicap and Society, 7,* 177–188.

Sue, D. W., & Sue, D. (2003). *Counseling the culturally diverse: Theory and practice* (4th ed.). New York: Wiley.

Sugar, M. (1993). Research in child and adolescent group psychotherapy. *Journal of Child and Adolescent Psychotherapy, 3,* 207–226.

Tarver-Behring, S., & Spagna, M. (2004). Counseling with exceptional children. *Focus on Exceptional Children, 36*(8), 1–12.

Teague, J. B. (1992). Issues relating to the treatment of adolescent lesbians and homosexuals. *Journal of Mental Health Counseling, 14,* 422–239.

Thomas, C., & Nelson, C. (1994). From victims to victors: Group process as the path to recovery for males molested as children. *Journal for Specialists in Group Work, 19,* 102–112.

Thompson, C. L., & Henderson, D. A. (2007). *Counseling children* (7th ed.). Belmont, CA: Thomson.

Thompson, C. L., & Rudolph, L. B. (1996). *Counseling children* (4th ed.). Pacific Grove, CA: Brooks/Cole.

Thompson, L. (1990). Working with alcoholic families in a child welfare agency: The problem of underdiagnose. *Child Welfare, 69,* 464–471.

Tillitski, L. (1990). A meta-analysis of estimated effect sizes for group versus individual versus control treatments. *International Journal of Group Psychotherapy, 40,* 215–224.

Tobias, A. K., & Myrick, R. D. (1999). A peer facilitator–led intervention with middle school problem-behavior students. *Professional School Counseling, 3,* 27–33.

Tomori, M. (1994). Personality characteristics of adolescents with alcoholic parents. *Adolescence, 29,* 949–960.

Toseland, R. W., & Rivas, R. F. (2001). *An introduction to group work practice.* Needham Heights, MA: Allyn & Bacon.

Toseland, R., & Siporin, M. (1986). When to recommend group treatment. *International Journal of Group Psychotherapy, 36,* 171–201.

Trotzer, J. P. (1999). *The counselor and the group* (4th ed.). Philadelphia: Accelerated Development.

Trotzer, J. P. (2006). Boxed in: An activity for overcoming resistance and obstacles to problem-solving in groups. In J. L. DeLucia-Waack, K. H. Bridbord, J. S. Kleiner, & A. Nitza (Eds.), *Group work experts share their favorite activities: A guide to choosing, planning, conducting, and processing* (Rev. ed., pp. 96–100). Alexandria, VA: Association for Specialists in Group Work.

Trowbridge, M. M. (1995). Graphic indicators of sexual abuse in children's drawings: A review of the literature. *Arts in Psychotherapy, 22,* 485–494.

Tuckman, B., & Jensen, M. (1977). Stages of small group development revisited. *Group and Organizational Studies, 2,* 419–427.

Turner, S. (1993). Talking about sexual abuse: The value of short-term groups for women survivors. *Journal of Group Psychotherapy, Psychodrama and Sociometry, 46*(3), 110–122.

Ulik, B. J., & Cummings, A. L. (1997). Using members' artistic expressions as metaphor in counselling: A pilot study. *Canadian Journal of Counselling, 31,* 305–316.

Vacc, N. A., Rhyne-Winkler, M. C., & Poidevant, J. M. (1993). Evaluation and accountability of counseling services: Possible implications for a midsize district. *School Counselor, 40,* 260–266.

Van Dyck, B. J. (1980). An analysis of selection criteria for short-term group counseling clients. *Personnel and Guidance Journal, 59,* 226–230.

van Velsor, P. (2004). Training for successful group work with children: What and how to teach. *Journal for Specialists in Group Work, 29,* 137–146.

Vandervoort, D. J., & Fuhriman, A. (1991). The efficacy of group therapy for depression. *Small Group Research, 22,* 320–338.

Vella, N. (1999). Freud on groups. In C. Oakley (Ed.), *What is a group? A new look at theory in practice* (pp. 8–38). London: Rebus.

Vernelle, B. (1994). *Using and understanding groups.* London: Whiting & Birch.

Vernon, A. (1993). *Developmental assessment and intervention with children and adolescents.* Alexandria, VA: American Counseling Association.

Vernon, A. (1999). *Counseling children and adolescents* (2nd ed.). Denver: Love.

Vernon, A. (2002). *What works when with children and adolescents: A handbook of individual counseling techniques.* Champaign, IL: Research Press.

Vernon, A. (2004). *Counseling children and adolescents* (3rd ed.). Denver, CO: Love.

Vernon, A. (2007). Application of rational-emotive behavior therapy to groups within classrooms and educational settings. In R. W. Christner, J. L. Stewart, & A. Freeman (Eds.), *Handbook of cognitive-behavior group therapy with children and adolescents: Specific settings and presenting problems* (pp. 107–128). New York: Routledge.

von Bertalanffy, L. (1968). *General system theory: Foundations, development, applications.* New York: Braziller.

Waldron, H. B., & Kaminer, Y. (2004). On the learning curve: The emerging evidence supporting cognitive-behavioral therapies for adolescent substance abuse. *Addiction, 99,* 93–105.

Ward, D. E., & Litchy, M. (2004). The effective use of processing in groups. In J. L. DeLucia-Waack, D. A. Gerrity, C. R. Kalodner, & M. T. Riva (Eds.), *Handbook of group counseling and psychotherapy* (pp. 104–119). Thousand Oaks, CA: Sage.

Warm, S. (2006). Map of the world. In J. L. DeLucia-Waack, K. H. Bridbord, J. S. Kleiner, & A. Nitza (Eds.), *Group work experts share their favorite activities: A guide to choosing, planning, conducting, and processing* (Rev. ed., pp. 58–59). Alexandria, VA: Association for Specialists in Group Work.

Washington, O. G., & Moxley, D. P. (2003). Group interventions with low-income African American women recovering from chemical dependency. *Health and Social Work, 28,* 146–156.

Weiss, C. (1998). *Evaluation* (2nd ed.). Upper Saddle River, NJ: Prentice Hall.

Weiss, R. D., Jaffee, W. B., de Menil, V. P., & Cogley, C. B. (2004). Group therapy for substance use disorders: What do we know? *Harvard Review of Psychiatry, 12,* 339–350.

Weisz, J. R., Weiss, B., Alicke, M. D., & Klotz, M. L. (1987). Effectiveness of psychotherapy with children and adolescents: A meta-analysis for clinicians. *Journal of Consulting and Clinical Psychology, 55,* 542–549.

Wenz, K., & McWhirter, J. J. (1990). Enhancing the group experience: Creative writing exercises. *Journal for Specialists in Group Work, 15,* 37–42.

Whiston, S. C. (2007). Outcomes research on school counseling interventions and programs. In B. T.

Erford (Ed.), *Transforming the school counseling profession* (2nd ed., pp. 38–50). Columbus, OH: Pearson Merrill Prentice Hall.

Whiston, S. C., Eder, K., Rahardja, D., & Tai, W. L. (2005, June). *Research supporting school counseling: Comprehensive findings.* Paper presented at the annual meeting of the American School Counselor Association, Orlando, FL.

Whiston, S. C., & Sexton, T. L. (1998). A review of school counseling outcome research: Implications for practice. *Journal of Counseling and Development, 76,* 412–426.

Whitaker, D. S., & Lieberman, M. A. (1964). *Psychotherapy through the group process.* New York: Atherton Press.

White, A. (1998, November). *The volcano and you.* Paper presented at the North Carolina School Counseling Association Fall Conference, Winston-Salem, NC.

White, M., & Epston, D. (1990). *Narrative means to therapeutic ends.* New York: Norton.

Wiggins, J. D., & Wiggins, A. H. (1992). Elementary students' self-esteem and behavioral ratings related to counselor time-task emphases. *The School Counselor, 39,* 377–381.

Wilson, F. R. (1997). Group psychotherapy. In R. K. Conyne, F. R. Wilson, & D. Ward (Eds.), *Comprehensive group work: What it means and how to teach it* (pp. 169–197). Alexandria, VA: American Counseling Association.

Wilson, J., & Blocher, L. (1990). The counselor's role in assisting children of alcoholics. *Elementary School Guidance and Counseling, 25,* 98–107.

Winick, C., & Levene, A. (1992). Marathon therapy: Treating rape survivors in a therapeutic community. *Journal of Psychoactive Drugs, 24,* 49–56.

Winter, S. K. (1976). Developmental stages in the roles and concerns of group co-leaders. *Small Group Behavior, 7,* 349–362.

Worthen, B. R., Sanders, J. R., & Fitzpatrick, J. L. (1997). *Program evaluation: Alternative approaches and practical guidelines.* New York: Longman.

Wubbolding, R. E. (1991). *Understanding reality therapy.* New York: Harper & Row.

Wubbolding, R. E. (2000). *Reality therapy for the 21st century.* Philadelphia: Brunner-Routledge.

Yalom, I., Houts, P., Zimberg, S., & Rand, K. (1967). Predictions of improvement in group therapy. *Archives of General Psychiatry, 17,* 159–168.

Yalom, I. D., & Leszcz, M. (2005). *The theory and practice of group psychotherapy* (5th ed.). New York: Basic Books.

Yalom, I. D., Tinklenberg, J., & Gilula, M. (1968). *Curative factors in group psychotherapy.* Unpublished manuscript.

Yauman, B. E. (1991). School-based group counseling for children of divorce: A review of the literature. *Elementary School Guidance and Counseling, 26,* 130–139.

Zarle, T. H., & Willis, S. (1975). A pregroup training technique for encounter group stress. *Journal of Counseling Psychology, 22*(1), 49–53.

Zimpfer, D. G. (1990a). Groups for divorce/separation: A review. *Journal for Specialists in Group Work, 15,* 51–60.

Zimpfer, D. G. (1990b). Group work for bulimia: A review of outcomes. *Journal for Specialists in Group Work, 15,* 239–251.

Zimpfer, D. G. (1991). Groups for grief and survivorship after bereavement: A review. *Journal for Specialists in Group Work, 14,* 98–104.

Zutlevics, T. L. (2002). Towards a theory of oppression. *Ratio, 15,* 80–102.

INDEX

Survey, post group, 185
Survival, need for, 116
Suspension, from school, 254
Swarbrick, P., 249
"Swat the Balloon Relay" activity, 263
Systems theory, transition stage in,
    110–111

T

Talking stick, 52
Target audience, 291
Target Symptom Rating Form, 297
Task group(s), 4
    feedback sheet for problem-solving
        discussions, 197
    feedback sheet for topical
        discussions, 196
    high school mentoring program,
        202–206
    to identify issues for discussion, 195
    leader in, 5
    multiple, 6
    principles in leading, 191–200
    problem-solving discussions, 196
    in school setting, 6
    stages of, 5–6
    student support team, 200–202
    suggested readings, 201
    types of, 5
Tasks, group member
    feedback, 51–53, 296
    self-disclosure, 50–51
Tavistock Institute of Human
    Relations, 16
Teacher, as stakeholder, 284, 285
Teacher survey, 291
Teasing, therapeutic games for, 282
Termination, of group experience, 186
    follow-up, 32, 184–185, 304
    group leader's decision for, 32
    premature, 32, 166–167, 186
    techniques for, 182–184
Termination, of individual group
    session, 174–177
    techniques for, 177–181
Termination stage, 6
    awareness of others, 159
    challenges of, 160–161
    leader functions during, 162–165
    planning for future, 159–160
    in psychoeducational groups, 212
    self-awareness assessment and
        processing, 159
Testing. See also Outcome studies
    for anxiety, 297–298
    of boundaries, 118
    IQ test, 201
    math achievement test results, 287
    post group, 185
T-group. See Training group
Theater of Spontaneity, 15

Theoretically based group models
    Adlerian groups, 224–226
    behavioral groups, 226–228
    choice theory/reality therapy groups,
        233–236
    Gestalt groups, 228–230
    rational emotive behavior therapy
        groups, 230–233
Therapeutic factors measures, 298
Therapeutic games, 279–280, 282
    creative modifications in, 281–282
    flexibility and efficiency in, 282
"The Three Wishes" exercise, 271
Time series, outcome studies using, 302
Timing/timeliness
    of feedback, 52
    time effectiveness, 14
    during transition stage, 126–127
Topic-specific groups, 231
"Total Grade," 286, 287
Tough-aggressive response, 54
Training group (T-group), 16
Transference, of skills, 55, 227
    real world, 141–142
Transition stage
    anger management as issue in, 145
    common fears during, 116–117
    as critical group task, 110–113
    expression of issues during, 117–120
    leader's handling of, 120–122
    processing of process during, 124–125
"Trashing Problems" activity, 265
Trauma-focused sexual abuse
    treatment group, 250
Triangulation, 290, 294
Trotzer, J. P., 87, 120–121, 200,
    261, 295
Truancy, school, 254
True experimental designs, outcome
    studies using, 302
Trust level, 52–53, 93–94
    empathy and, 67, 70
    sexual abuse survivors', 248
Two-sample pretest-posttest design, 302

U

Unfinished business, termination stage,
    32, 165
"Unfreezing," 124
Universality, 19
Universities, psychoeducational group
    work in, 6

V

Values contracts, 172–173
Vella, N., 127
Vernon, A., 231, 232–233
Visual arts, interventions using.
    See also Expressive arts
    introductory rapport-building
        activities, 266–267

problem solving and goal-setting,
    270–271
reviewing past, present, and
    anticipating future, 268–269
Visual imagery, guided, 226,
    279, 280

W

Walker, M. E., 243
Warm, Susan B., 199
Warming-up period, 5
"We Are All Alike and Yet All
    Different" activity, 264
"We Are Siamese" activity, 262
Wechsler Adult Intelligence
    Scale, 288
Wender, Lewis, 15
Western Psychological Services, 282
A What? (Hutchins), 199
What a Character! (Gillam), 199
What if It Never Stops
    Raining?(Carlson), 232
What Is My Relationship to the Group?
    (Rapin), 200
White students, 289
Who Are You? game, 231–232
Why Are We Meeting Like This?
    (Hayes, R.), 199
Withdrawal response, 54,
    116, 119
Withdrawn group member, 119
Work style, content style v., 154
Working stage, 6
    attending to content v. process,
        137–138
    co-leadership during, 139–141
    elements of, 129–131
    goals of, 131–133
    group design, 147–150
    group foundation, 146–147
    group membership, 150–151
    leader's role in, 135–139
    members' role in, 133–135
    psychoeducational groups, 212
    real world, 141–142
Worthlessness, sense of, 248, 254
Writing, learning objectives, ABCD
    model, 232
Writing, therapeutic
    considerations for, 278–279
    of fairy tales, 275–276
    group exercises, 276–277
    journaling, 273–274
    letter writing, 275
    life-review exercises, 274–275
    scriptotherapy, 273

Y

Yalom, Irwin, 11, 18, 119,
    121, 124
Yalom's Therapeutic Factors, 11